State and Religion in the Arab World

This collection focuses on the controversial relationship between religion and the state within the Arab Spring context and the evolving debates on democratic transition. In this book, democracy is not questionable; it is hailed by all those vocal on the political scene. The array of opinions presented here varies from a call for a secular state based on Islamic philosophy to a call for setting democratic institutions before working on solving this religion-state dichotomy. Meanwhile some prefer to have an ambiguous stand on which side to back up, the liberals or the Islamists, despite a detailed criticism of the ossified ways of those calling for a religious state (Al-Majd). The book starts with an analysis and a detailed account of how the sensitive issue of the relationship between state and religion developed in Arab thought and society and it goes on to employ less the religious discourse in presenting their positions thus focusing on actual cases of this struggle for power in different Arab countries such as Tunisia and Egypt. The collection also provides insights and analysis of the ongoing debates and views on the role of religion in Libya and provides an analysis of the case of Morocco. In addition to this there is a special chapter that deals with how Muslim communities living in the West adapt to secular state politics. The collection ends with a thorough discussion by a number of Arab intellectuals and activists, Muslims and Christians alike, whereby core issues related to the debate on state and religion are presented. This discussion, in addition to reflecting the Islamist-secular dichotomy, demonstrates the richness of the ongoing debates that extend well beyond the discourse on this dichotomy.

This book is a compilation of articles published in *Contemporary Arab Affairs.*

Khair El-Din Haseeb is the founding Director of the Centre for Arab Unity Studies (CAUS) in Beirut and currently the Chairman of its Board of Directors and Executive Committee. He has played a highly active and influential role in Arab nationalist concerns and initiatives since the 1970's. From 1976 to 1984 he served as Chief of the Natural Resources Science and Technology Division of the United Nations Economic Commission of Western Asia. He is the author of numerous books and articles in both Arabic and English including: The Arab Spring: Critical Analysis (2013).

State and Religion in the Arab World

Edited by
Khair El-Din Haseeb

Routledge
Taylor & Francis Group
LONDON AND NEW YORK

مركز دراسات الوحدة العربية
CENTRE FOR ARAB UNITY STUDIES

First published 2015 by Routledge

2 Park Square, Milton Park, Abingdon, Oxfordshire OX14 4RN
711 Third Avenue, New York, NY 10017

Routledge is an imprint of the Taylor & Francis Group, an informa business

First issued in paperback 2018

British Library Cataloguing in Publication Data
A catalogue record for this book is available from the British Library

ISBN 13: 978-0-415-72118-9 (hbk)
ISBN 13: 978-1-138-38315-9 (pbk)

Typeset in Times New Roman
by Taylor & Francis Books

Publisher's Note
The publisher accepts responsibility for any inconsistencies that may have arisen during the conversion of this book from journal articles to book chapters, namely the possible inclusion of journal terminology.

Contents

Citation Information

The following chapters were originally published in various issues of *Contemporary Arab Affairs*. When citing this material, please use the original page numbering for each article, as follows:

Chapter 2
The state and religion in the fundamentals of Islam and contemporary interpretation
Rached Ghannouchi
Contemporary Arab Affairs, volume 6, issue 2 (May 2013) pp. 164–171

Chapter 3
State and religion in a revolutionary era: perspectives and demands of the Islamic awakening
Ridwan Al-Sayyid
Contemporary Arab Affairs, volume 6, issue 3 (August 2013) pp. 325–340

Chapter 4
Approaches to reforming contemporary religious discourse
Ahmad Kamal Abou Al-Majd
Contemporary Arab Affairs, volume 6, issue 2 (May 2013) pp. 172–188

Chapter 5
Religion and the state in contemporary Arab society: theoretically, practically and prospectively
Abdelilah Belkeziz
Contemporary Arab Affairs, volume 6, issue 4 (October 2013) pp. 505–523

Chapter 6
Problematics of political authority within Islam
Muhammad Mazouz
Contemporary Arab Affairs, volume 6, issue 3 (August 2013) pp. 341–357

Chapter 7
The state and identity: the relationship between religion and politics – Tunisia as an example
Salaheddine Jourchi
Contemporary Arab Affairs, volume 6, issue 3 (August 2013) pp. 358–375

Chapter 8
Relationship between state and religion: Egypt after the revolution
Tarek El-Beshry
Contemporary Arab Affairs, volume 6, issue 3 (August 2013) pp. 404–421

Chapter 9
Islamist political movements in Yemen
Abdulmalik Mohammad Abdullah Eissa
Contemporary Arab Affairs, volume 6, issue 1 (February 2013) pp. 41–70

Chapter 10
Relationship between state and religion in Saudi Arabia: the role of Wahabism in governance
Tawfiq Alsaif
Contemporary Arab Affairs, volume 6, issue 3 (August 2013) pp. 376–403

Chapter 11
Islamists in power: the case of the Muslim Brotherhood in Egypt
Hesham Al-Awadi
Contemporary Arab Affairs, volume 6, issue 4 (October 2013) pp. 539–551

Chapter 12
The relationship between religion and the state: the institution of 'Commandment of the Faithful' in Morocco
Ahmed Al Khamlichi
Contemporary Arab Affairs, volume 7, issue 1 (January 2014) pp. 54–81

Chapter 13
Representations of religion in secular states: the Muslim communities in Sweden
Rickard Lagervall
Contemporary Arab Affairs, volume 6, issue 4 (October 2013) pp. 524–538

Chapter 14
Religion and the State in Turkey and Iran: a comparative overview
Refat Sayed Ahmad
Contemporary Arab Affairs, volume 7, issue 1 (January 2014) pp. 36–53

Chapter 15
What changes have taken place in US foreign policy towards Islamists?
Fawaz A. Gerges
Contemporary Arab Affairs, volume 6, issue 2 (May 2013) pp. 189–197

Chapter 16
Towards an intellectual and political understanding of the question of religion and the state
Panel discussion
Contemporary Arab Affairs, volume 7, issue 1 (January 2014) pp. 82–114

Please direct any queries you may have about the citations to clsuk.permissions@cengage.com

Acknowledgements

The centre for Arab Unity Studies would like to express its appreciation to the Swedish Institute in Alexandria, Egypt, for its financial contribution towards the translation of these papers from its original language in Arabic to English.

Religion and the state in the Arab World: Introduction

Adbelilah Belkeziz

-1-

In our modern and contemporary history, there exists a relationship between politics and religion which is commendable and abounding with rewards and advantages for the nation and the rights of those it encompasses; a relationship that cannot be denied except by the ungrateful. Yet there exists another relationship between politics and religion that has emerged in recent times and that cannot be considered commendable – to say the least. This latter relationship has had very many negative effects on the unity of society, of people, and of the nation, as well as on social development. This apparent paradox should be no cause for surprise, given that all social and human phenomena – including the relationship between politics and religion – cannot maintain the same meaning under different circumstances. Consequently, the issue of advantage or disadvantage does not derive from either of the two extremes of the relationship between religion and the state; rather, it results from the relationship itself as the product of interaction between two basic elements. This relationship has different outcomes depending on the particular contextual circumstances within which it functions.

The commendable relationship between politics and religious symbolism was manifest during the battles for Arab national independence against colonial occupation. These took place in most Arab countries, though it has been more evident in the countries of the Arab Maghreb (western Arab countries) for several reasons which will not detain us here. The battles mostly took place between the 1920s and early 1960s; coinciding with the period of national independence movements worldwide. The commendable linkage between politics and religion was subsequently renewed during the period between the end of the 1980s and early this decade. This renewal was associated with the renewed challenge of occupation, the return of the nationalist issue to the forefront of the political project, and the emergence of resistance movements from the Islamic current, such as 'Hizbollah', 'Hamas', 'Al-Jihad Al-Islami', and some groups and battalions of the Iraqi resistance. The idea of *Jihad* (struggle) against the invading foreign enemy proved an effective force in mobilizing the public, garnering supporters, militarizing the youth, and rallying citizens and combatants on the two fronts of armed and popular political struggle. It also took the notion of national liberation to the level of sacred duty. No one can deny the decisive effect which that political mobilization for religion and religious symbols had on achieving many victories, and accomplishing a significant portion of the missions of national struggle.

Yet a different form of linkage between politics and religion, in evidence during the same time period, and the last 30 years especially, has produced very different results, not to say actual strife and significant wounds that have yet to come to a halt or be healed. Let us say simply that this different form of linkage has not been in any way commendable. How can it be commendable that domestic politics employs religion in confronting political rivals from the same religious sect and the same nation, and bring what is by nature uniting and unifying, into the field of disputation over political and worldly interests wherein divisiveness and conflict are natural?! The involvement of religion in political action, and in the internal struggle over power, has had a negative impact on contemporary Arab political life. It has also imposed unfamiliar rules upon political disputes, and infused into these a sectarianism that had previously been characteristic in the history of Islam and taken a toll on the unity of the *umma* (nation), and the unity of the state. This political investment in religion was not only negative in the case of groups advocating violence, as it may be believed, but was thus even in the case of moderate religious political groups. This is because this political investment did not stop at creating a state of political polarization, but added to that an indigenous and cultural polarization that has infused and pressured political life entirely, and generated the phenomenon of extreme and maximalist discourses, and values of mutual repudiation and exclusion...etc.!

What makes the link between religion and politics commendable in the case of national liberation, and negative in that of internal political strife?

In the first case, the advantage of the link is due to the fact that the struggle takes place between a whole nation and an occupier, where religion is a unifying and bonding factor. Thus the call for struggle will have its own nurturing environment, and religion will have a great effect in stimulating determination and in uniting through consensus. In the second case, however, the disadvantage is due to the fact that the struggle takes place within the nation itself – between its opposing forces contending for power and sovereignty. Certainly, invoking religion within this divided environment leads to its transformation from an inclusive and unifying force, into a mere political ideology with which one group confronts another.

When talking about the relationship between religion and the state, the discourse has to be very clear and this requires scrutinizing terminology, avoiding generalities and mediocre ‘postulates’, and thence identifying what is required with accurate expression, in order to avoid ambiguity, confusion, or error. The need for clarity acquires more importance with the gravity, sensitivity, and subtlety of the subject under discussion – as is the case with the one in which we are engaged here – the relationship between religion and the state. Any position in this regard has many significant consequences. Very often, these consequences surpass the realm of opposing opinions to what can be actually dangerous, when the discourse about the issue (religion and the state) becomes dominated by clannishness, extremes of opinion, claims of infallibility of views, and portraying opponents as plain wrong – perhaps even defaming and inciting against them – a situation not dissimilar to that which we have experienced for the past thirty years!

To be specific, when we ask ourselves about the role of religion in the state, and whether the effects are positive or negative – the answers will not be apparent unless we are clear about what we mean by religion. What is meant here is not **any religion**, but Islam exclusively is the subject of this discourse. Further, our concern is therefore with specific aspects of this religion. Firstly, religion in this case means the Quranic text;

second, it means the Prophet's *Sunna (the Prophet's way)* – thus religion basically means Muslims' thought, all of their generations, and all the institutions they have founded as religious institutions. Hence, if we mean by religion, the texts of the Holy Quran, we know – unquestionably – that there is no Quranic jurisprudence for the political issue, and that it embodies nothing that forces upon Muslims a specific system of governance. Instead, it has left it up to them to choose their own political system themselves. Alternatively, if by religion we mean the *Sunna* (way) of the Honorable Prophet, then the 'state' that he founded in Medina, he founded according to his own jurisprudence, and not according to a binding text; and, after him, he did not compel Muslims to follow a specific system of governance. Yet if by religion we mean, throughout our history, those amongst the jurisprudential and 'scientific' elites who debased themselves to the position of 'spokespersons of religion', then, those were not a unified body. They were dispersed into different sects and groups that beheld each other as erring, and did not share the same opinion on politics and the state.

Therefore, there is no sense in asking ourselves about the role of religion in the state if religion – Quranic text, *Hadith* (sayings of the Prophet), and *Sirah* (biography of the Prophet) – did not specify this role and show it to Muslims in the same way as it specified the duties related to belief and obligated their performance. As for what the role of religion is in the state according to the opinion of Muslim jurisprudents and theologians, this is a matter about which it can rightly be said that theirs is not a binding opinion because it originates from politics and the temporal, not from religion. This is also because such jurisprudence may be right or wrong, and because they are men and we are men who say what is reasonable and commendable, and because their jurisprudence had been associated with historical circumstances of their own and necessities of life suitable for them. This being the case, it is not prudent to view their sayings as applicable to Muslims at all times and places, unless we make a wrong assumption and deem them infallible; an assumption that cannot be held true by a sane mind!

However, asking the question about the role of religion in the state today, and connecting religion with Islamic movements, or considering them a representative of religion, is to commit a double mistake. It is to hand over to these movements a clerical role that they do not have; a role which is even alien to Islam and its teachings. In addition, it ignores that these movements are political ones with mundane demands even if they use religious terminology for this purpose by way of exploitation. And the problem is that most contemplation on the relationship of religion with the state immediately becomes engaged with the discourse on Islamic movements; this is an intellectual and methodological pitfall which has unfavourable consequences. Though the mere claim by Islamic movements to speak in the name of 'the Islamic reference' calls for reflecting on the problematics of the link of religion with the state – given the outcome of their intrusion in politics in the name of religion – because the issue of the link is nevertheless wider than just reflecting on 'partisan Islam', as limiting this issue to partisan Islam cannot but mean that we are reflecting on the relationship of politics with the state. Thus we notice the extent of confusion over 'the role of religion in the state'.

There exists an intermediary in the relationship between any religion and its adherents. I do not mean by intermediary the intermediation which has existed between them through the clerical institutions or the monastic bodies which debased themselves to the position of spokesperson of religion and its conveyer. But rather, I mean that the supposedly direct link – whether in Islam or Protestant Christianity – is not possible because it inevitably passes through an intermediate *knowledge network of interpretation* which itself determines the meaning of religion and religious teaching within the consciousness of all believers who receive the religious message discourse. This hypothesis is based on a contention (in hermeneutics) which says that the religious 'given' is not clear in itself, is not direct, and does not present itself in a clear way and with a sense of generality which produces in the minds of all adherents one definite meaning over which there is no discord. So the recipient – according to the teachings of contemporary hermeneutics – participates in constructing the meaning of the text he receives through the way he understands it, or the way he interprets it. Consequently, there exists no congruence in understanding texts amongst people; otherwise, there would have been no difference and variance among people within Islam or outside it.

Several factors control interpretation, that is, control this intermediary knowledge network between believers and the sacred text: the interpreter's knowledge, intellectual, or cognitive standards; conditions of time and space in which interpreting takes place; interests – explicit or implicit – behind the act of interpretation whether conscious or subconscious; the objective needs that lead into giving preponderance to one type of understanding relative to another possible type; and so on.

It may also be said that the ancients were alert to this fact at an early stage, and had realized that the religious text varies in the degree to which it reveals its meaning in different instances in the text. They made rules for classifying the Quranic texts – according to the degree of clarity or obscurity of signification. For example, they distinguished between those which had a definitive and those which had a hypothetical significance. No doubt, this is true; yet what jurisprudents have done in the past is a jurisprudence bounded by the conditions of their time. Definitely, they exerted an acknowledged scientific effort in confronting the intricacies of comprehension. Yet we should not insist on adhering to this jurisprudence as if it were a transcendental sacred. We are not, as well, at liberty to disregard the cultural and epistemological contexts within which this jurisprudence has been produced. Moreover, this does not prevent the contemporary Islamic mind from opening up to a new and different reading of the religious text which does not insist on the terms of classical jurisprudential interpretation, but instead it adds to it what is new in knowledge, concepts, and contemporary methodologies.

And perhaps the interpretation of our ancient jurisprudents was dedicated to enabling understanding through tools with which the cognizance of Muslims could differentiate that which is clear from the rest of the religious texts. This is similar to the differentiation of theologians – for the same reasons – between the verses of the Quran which are *muhkamaat* (precise) and the ones that are *mutashaabihaat* (open for interpretation). This means in the first place that they have confined the problem of understanding to the religious text itself: which varies between definite and hypothetical, and which is sometimes easy and often difficult. The state of affairs is that the problem does not lie in the Quranic text, nor does it lie in the discrepancy within it between the two levels of significance, but rather in the reading of its recipients; for those are the ones who vary in cognizance – like all other creatures.

In this respect, our aim is not to get into a theoretical discourse about the meaning of interpretation, or its terms and conditions, nor about jurisprudence and the evolution of the way in which it is perceived. What interests us is to accentuate the complexity of the relationship with the religious text, for Muslims, as well as for others who adhere to other monotheistic religions. Our interest is also to emphasize that it is inadmissible to pronounce in the name of Islam – be it now or in the past – especially when the discourse is about issues which are most controversial in the history of the community and the nation, and on which no religious ruling had been issued and as a result of which there are different interpretations, such as on the issues of the state, power, regime, and the relationships of the government with religion. So, as the religious text is void of teachings specific to this public domain, then viewing it as quite easy to talk about such teachings in the name of religion, or from a religious standpoint, is a form of fabrication and creation, whereby he who commits it and gets involved in it, is to be held accountable due to the serious consequences ensuing from such action and involvement.

Moreover, if it is true to say – and it is true – that many of the rulings on various dealings, which are still in practice today, were not derived from a religious text, but were inferred by the Islamic intellect through jurisprudence (comparative jurisprudence; and the jurisprudence of objectives), then these are viewed as rules not coming from heaven, but from the opinions of people on Earth. Consequently, these rules are not perceived to be sacred, as the sacred Quran, and it is possible – not to say essential – to amend them when needed and when the requirements of the development of Islamic integration calls for this. In the same vein, it is the general view that political jurisprudence is among those bodies of law requiring definitive amendment, and has to be considered a jurisprudence specific to the circumstances under which it has been issued.

He who talks about an Islamic state, or ‘a civil state whose reference is Islamic’, or about applying the rules of Shari’a (religious law) and so on, forgets that he does not talk about a topic which is a matter of consensus in vision and meaning for all Muslims. Here, we are not discussing whether it is possible or legitimate to base a state on religion, instead, we are trying to argue against a discourse – seriously rampant at the moment – which unjustly deems it easy to talk, as if about something intuitive, of issues which are neither intuitive nor axiomatic.

He who talks about an Islamic state, talks about a utopia; whether he imagines it similar to the ‘state’ of *Almedina*, or the *Caliphate*, or the *Sultanate* upon which the jurisprudents of legitimate politics had theorized and bestowed the cloak of the *Caliphate* in order to dress it up with religious legitimacy. It is no more possible to talk about a state of this type during the age of the modern state, for this is not the age of prophets, nor the Rightly Guided Caliphs, nor sultans of the type known by classical Islamic states. Indulging in a claim about the Islamic state is a kind of impossible nostalgia that deceives a schizoid consciousness separated from history and reality. Perhaps the only function of this indulgence is appealing to the emotions of believers through a heaven on Earth to gain their allegiance for a political project attired in religious symbolism.

He who talks about ‘a civil state whose reference is Islamic’, is the same as the one who talks about a religious state governed by secularism; he associates the non-associable in a mixed and hybrid way. This dexterity in hybrid naming thrives today, more than ever before, following a silent struggle over the meaning of the civil state: between those who meant by it the non-religious state and the ones who meant the state which is not controlled by military forces. Yet, distinguishing themselves from the military state was not sufficient for both the contenders in front of their public as they confront those who argue for the civil state – that has only one meaning in modern history. Therefore, they sought supplements for the verification of identity, to generate by this the claim of 'the civil state whose reference is Islamic'. This claim resembles many others such as 'The Islamic Economy' and 'The Islamic Nuclear Bomb'... etc!

As for the call for the implementation of the provisions of the Islamic Shari'a, this ignores two interrelated issues. First, the provisions of Shari'a are open to interpretation and Muslims have interpreted them since the time of the companions of the Prophet – and their opinions differed on their implementation (note the position of Omar Ibn El Khattab regarding the prescribed penalties in the year of Alramadh, [and] his position regarding the division of the booty in Surat Al-Anfal, i.e. not to divide the two lands among the combatants). Interpretation is jurisprudence and could be proved right or wrong. Thus, the implementation of the jurisprudence, in fact, becomes an implementation of one interpretation of the Sharia's multiple interpretations; that is to say, it finally becomes a human jurisprudence that is not infallible and cannot conform with the text. Second, Muslims follow different doctrines in politics and general jurisdiction. Muslim Sunna differ from Muslim Shiites in their conception of the ruling system, in deciding to whom the rule will be handed, and what the origin of legitimacy in this rule is, what and who is the source of power, and what the type of the relationship between the religious and the temporal in this rule is. There are other sects that have different stances on the issue of the ruling system such as Zaydism, Ibadism, and the branches of Ismailism. Therefore, it is impossible for anyone to talk about the implementation of the Shari'a provisions with utmost confidence as if it were something that necessarily conforms to the text and gives the same meaning for all Muslim groups.

Anyone who talks, today, about the relationship between religion and the state in an attempt to insist on the 'Islamism of the state' or its Islamization, or basing its workings on the provisions of religion, is claiming for himself a prophetic role that he does not have, the heavens have not entrusted to him, and he has not inherited from the Prophet. Thus, this talk is merely an opinion of his own, and a political view which he has assumed for himself and decided to confer with the apparel of transcendental legitimacy by weaving the sacred and religious into the construction of political discourse. And if the one who talks about the issue has the right, in politics, to be inspired by the history of Islam – as no one is entitled to deny him this right – he does not have the right to present it to people *as* religion or the position of religion (i.e. Islam) on politics, authority, and the state, as many claim. Instead, it should be presented as an attempt to draw inspiration by borrowing and making use of the experience of Arabs and Muslims throughout history. Moreover, it is not binding for anyone except those who are convinced by it, as it is neither a Qoranic revelation, nor one of the religious obligations. Persisting with the identification between religion and the political project will only lead to antagonism between Muslims who follow different doctrines, and transform the lives of citizens into a testing ground for new political utopias!

-2-

We are confident that the best relationships between religion and the state are those that maintain their distinctness from each other. Thus it leaves no chance for an intertwinement between the temporal and the religious whereby either one of them may impose tutelage on the other. This idea that we are trying to defend here is the quintessence of a prolonged humanistic and intellectual observation of the exorbitant prices paid by both the state and religion for instituting interpenetration and identification between them during certain well known moments of political history. The intervention of clerics in politics and the state, or the intervention of politicians therein in the name of religion, have brought disasters for the societies concerned, their stability, and civil peace amongst societal members and communities. Similarly, the intervention of the state in religion has brought about the same catastrophes: be it in the name of controlling it or in the name of casting it away or eliminating it. Our Arab societies today do not need to live through such catastrophes and suffer their destructive effects within both religion and the state.

It is true what Sheikh Rashed El-Ghannouchi says: that the realm of the state is what is public, and the realm of religion is what is private. The realm of the state is that of public interests which are worldly and variable, and which are subject to deliberation and agreement after a series of struggles over them, and mutual concessions and compromises. Whereas the realm of religion is belief which does not change under the effect of interests because it is related to the world of what is absolute – not to the world of what is relative. In the public realm (i.e. politics, the state), the principle of accountability is general, and goes back to the people and their representatives. Whereas in the private realm of belief, God alone is the one who may hold us responsible or answerable, because the relationship of the believers with Him is direct wherein no monastic mediation intervenes. He who mixes up between the two realms treats unjustly both religion and the state – the particularity of each of them – thereby, elevating what is relative to the rank of the absolute, and lowering what is absolute to the level of the relative! It is only the distinction between the two realms that preserves for each its stature in the life of the individual and the community. It preserves for belief its spiritual purity, and its function in relation to ethics and creed. It even makes possible founding politics as a public realm, and a space for competition over programmes of social change.

When identification and exact matching between the religious sphere and the political and state spheres happened during the Middle Ages, with grievous costs ensuing, this was before the establishment of the modern state. By modern state, is meant the national state wherein authority abides by a social contract and a main statute for the state (constitution), which checks the power of the ruler and subjects him to the rule of law. The constitution as well distributes power among institutions which have separate authority, subjects executive power to legislative control and legal accountability, consolidates the autonomy of the judiciary system and its authority, and expresses the general will of the people as the source of sovereignty and power. Historically, this form of (modern) state was established during the period when interpenetration existed between religion and the state: totally in the case of a theocratic state, and partially in a Sultanate. It is believed that the modern state is no more a European or Western particularity, but rather, it has become a universal fact. And we are a part of modern humanity, and of modern nations from which we do not differ except by the stage of development. And we have realized, two centuries ago, that our only way to develop is through founding this modern state. This has requirements from which no one turns away except the doomed, or the one caught in a schism, whose body lives in one age, while his brain exists in a different age!

Perhaps the Islamic movements exaggerated, some fifty or so years ago, when they identified religion with politics (the state) throughout their political discourse, and in the writings of their sheikhs and advocates, for historical or political reasons which imposed on them such excess in tightening the relationship between religion and politics. And perhaps among these reasons was the ongoing presence of colonial authorities ruling in some states where these movements originated, or the rise of ruling regimes fanatically against religious thought and religious groups, and strongly biased toward secularism of the Jacobin and Kemalist types. Yet such excessiveness is no longer justified today, given the retreat of the negative attitude towards religious culture amongst modern political and cultural elites, and at a time when all or most of these elites, have acknowledged the right of these Islamic movements to legal political activity in their capacity as political parties. The right policy today vis á vis this 'calamity' of excessiveness or in extreme differentiation, is to adopt a middle course. Adoption of the extremes will breed nothing but a slide of Arab political life into the unknown, wherein the relationship between the different forces is based on mutual estrangement and exclusion.

In Arab societies today, the argument about the question of religion and the state takes two deviant forms. The first is raising the political and the state realm to the status of the transcendental, and perceiving them through religious standards – this is the position of fundamentalist Islamism. The second is transforming secularism from political neutrality towards religion into a position hostile to religion, that is, to a new doctrine! This is the position of the (Arab) Jacobin fundamentalist Secularists. These two deviations, intellectual ones, establish grounds for a prolonged political dispute with unknown consequences.

Let us consider the first intellectual deviation. Bringing politics and the state out from the civil realm into the religious realm represents a new basis for the meaning of the state that has no basis in Islam, even if it takes place in the name of Islam! This transforms the state into some new creature which owns a guidance message on Earth. It becomes a watchman of people's beliefs, taking charge of performing the role of 'Promotion of Virtue and the Prevention of Vice', and directing people's lives according to a religious standard which only rulers and those who serve as their spokesmen have the right to define and impose on society as God's law, or as the only correct interpretation of God's law. In this case, the state is no more a tool commissioned by society to manage public affairs; instead, it is rendered one of the tools of religion, which assumes performing the job of advocacy!

There is no need for us to emphasize two issues in the history of Islam which are known to those who are familiar with this history, they are even known to the majority of Muslims – at least those who are in the circle of the Sunnah (orthodox sect of Islam). The first is that prophecy was sealed by the prophecy of Muhammad bin Abd Allah (peace be upon him), and that after him no one has the right to resume advocacy, otherwise, he will be claiming for himself a role too big and noble for him. The second issue is that politics and the state are not part of the fundamentals (i.e. dogma), but they belong to the branches of endeavour that fall within the realm of jurisprudence; the faith of the believer and his being a Muslim does not depend on his position on these branches, or on their position vis á vis him.

Within the first issue, we are faced by extremely serious problems, because those who hold the message of religion as if it were politics, in the name of a religious duty which they claim for themselves, commit two mistakes that reinforce one another. They claim for themselves roles that were not allotted by the divine messages except to prophets and messengers, which are advocacy, proclamation, and urging people to be guided by the teachings of religion. The only explanation for assuming these roles is that there exist those who assign themselves as delegates to reopen what falls exclusively within the prerogatives of Prophethood! Then they call upon non-religious tools (i.e. the party, the state…) to perform what they consider religious advocacy, thus they stain religion with the transgressions of politics and the evils of its contentions and disputes, and they design their understanding of religion to fit their political interests! And while committing each of these two mistakes, they bring about damage for religion, the biggest – and worst –of which is producing a church which allots to itself roles that the Christian church used to allot to itself during the Middle Ages. This was rejected by the scholars of Islam who were steadfast to the independence of theology from politics from the time of Imam Malek until that of Sheikh Muhammad Abduh. That is, throughout the history of Islam, it has been decided that the function of scholars – scholars of religion and not the partisan Islamists – is good advice; this does not fall under the rubric of 'advocacy' and forcing people to adopt a certain opinion under the pretext of being the opinion of Shar' (religious law). Hence, in his refutation to the claim of religious power, the reputable scholar, Muhammad Abduh, went to the extent that he considered the jobs of the Mufti and Sheikh in Islam as civil jobs.

The problems with which we are confronted in the second issue are no less significant than those confronted in the first one. Digression in [or conflation between] power, the state and the scope of belief is a serious matter in Islam (at least with respect to the Sunnite sect, as long as the Imamate is a cornerstone of Islam according to the Imami Shi'a, except for the Zaidis) and an evident borrowing of the example of the theocratic state in the name of Islam – which denounces monasticism, and demolishes religious authority, as written by Mohammad Abduh. Islam left the issues of Muslims a matter of consultation among them and did not require the establishment of a state as conditional for their faith, nor considered their Imam the Caliph of Allah on Earth: as the Caliphs and their scholars wrongly claimed since the Abbasids rose to power! Exaggerated ideas of foreign (from Kharijites) or clerical European origins have infiltrated our field of discussion for more than half a century, and the 'Indian Islam' was its 'gateway', exemplified in the idea of 'governorship'. These ideas presented themselves, and still do, as the vision of Islam towards the state and the system of governance, and this has nothing to do with Islam. In fact, these ideas have deemed Muslim societies faithless, and Jahilia (pertaining to the pre-Islamic era), and accordingly, it is legitimate to force them into Islam by brutal force! Muslim blood was shed and is still being shed due to the idea of *takfir* (deeming others as infidels) and the 'Rules of Apostasy' applied to enemies who do not share these exaggerated views. Even the political Islamic forces which joined the 'faithless' democratic game were also subject to being viewed as infidel, such as the 'Muslim Brotherhood'. Therefore, the extremist fundamentalism has thrown our societies and nations into a dark tunnel due to this serious deviation in understanding the relationship between religion and state.

In our contemporary political culture and Arab political communities there exists a form of secularism that is no less dangerous than the *takfiri* fundamentalists in terms of the results it brings, even if it is presented differently. This form of exaggerated secularism could be described as the French concept of secularism ('*Laïcisme*').which is tantamount to anti-religious. Mohammed Arkoun has described it as akin to the French Jacobin model. This type of secularism has a philosophic positivist or atheist content; thus it seems to be a new philosophy or a new doctrine, similar to religious doctrines, even if it is antagonistic to religion, instead of a political philosophy which insists on the independence of its realm from that of religion and the state. In its exact theoretical conception, as in its historical reality, secularism has meant the neutrality of the state towards religion and non-interference in it, on the basis of the independence of the field of politics and the state (public) on the one hand and the field of religion (private) on the other. By contrast, the extremist version of 'Laïcisme' – means hostility towards religion and beyond that, seeking to exclude and marginalize it, restrict religious freedom, and restrain the practice of faith! If it was crystal clear, for any knowledgeable person, that this meaning disagrees with the original meaning of secularism, as well as contradicts and denounces it, then this person takes the concept of secularism beyond its original significance and renders it similar in its meaning to that of atheism!

Secularism is not a philosophy on religion, doctrine and faith that takes a cognitive position regarding religion: whether positively or negatively, but it is the outcome of the contemporary political philosophy which produced the field of independent politics and equipped it with the modern rules which make it a field of civilized civic competition and – before that – a field of loyal representation, and free expression of demands and objectives. Therefore, secularism does not fight religion nor support it, but takes a neutral position towards it when it is attributed to public affairs. Nonetheless, in the scope of private and personal issues in religion, which is its natural scope, there is no contradiction between being secular and religious at the same time, as both descriptions include two different areas of life: the public area, and private area, so that confusing between them is impermissible in the perspective of secularism. In this connection, those who assume secularism and religion are at odds are puzzled when they hear the term 'Christian secular forces', for example, deducing that it must be some kind of – a hybrid incoherent structure between two inconsistent extremes!

Indeed, the alteration of the original meaning of secularism and its replacement with another meaning that implies hostility towards religion or at a minimum leads to a collision with religion, is an inheritance from the French Revolution and its Jacobin extremist era which witnessed the emergence of both tendencies of positivism and Laïcisme in the nineteenth century and their negative stance towards religion. The Bolshevik revolution inherited this oppositionist tendency, among other things, from Jacobin political values, such as violence. Moreover, an atheist philosophical tendency in nineteenth century historical materialism, influenced by the Feuerbach perspective on religion and Christianity, compounded this trend. Yet, secularism in the rest of Europe (outside France and Soviet Russia) and in the American continent was understood differently. Unfortunately, most of the Arab secularists – who are liberals or leftists – have been influenced either by the French Jacobin secularism or the Soviet socialist secularism. (Few of them were influenced by the Turkish Kemalist secularism; which is not that different from these two in its opposition to religion.) Yet, other Arab secularists, significant in number and influence, did not fall into the trap of the Jacobin and Bolshevik theories regarding religion, and continued to understand its meaning from its theoretical and philosophical basis (as prevailed in the English and German traditions) or from the political history of its implementation in the Protestant communities, mainly in Britain, United States, Germany, and Holland, and this kept them away from falling into an extremist view of the relation between religion and state.

The paradox in the Jacobin and atheist versions of secularism has drawn even non-secularists from the Islamic forces into it; thus, they continue to view it with great apprehension, as an atheistic tendency or idea so that the secularist and atheist became synonymous! The idea that settled in their minds is that secularism is an 'Atheist

Philosophy' hostile towards religious faith and that its exclusion of religion from political life means excluding it from society and the nation… etc. These erroneous certainties have prevented them from seeing the substantial system of guarantees granted by secularism to freedom of belief and the practice of religious rites, as well as protecting religion from state interference in its affairs and civil institutions. No doubt, the leakage of this Jacobin perspective of secularism into the ranks of Muslims is part of a general Arab culture that has been indoctrinated by political modernity from its French centre and received from it – though to different extents – its intellectual orientation. However, there is no doubt, as well, that the anti-religious secularism in the Islamic conscience was formed as a result of two factors: the position of extremist Arab secularism in the form of Jacobism and Bolshevism and the position of the Catholic Christian environment in France that opposes the secularism of its state. In this way, the tree of secularism in France has overshadowed the other secularisms in the European forest which did not witness this severe clash between religion and state.

Is Arab 'Partisan Islam', today, capable of pursuing the method followed by Christian democratic parties in contemporary European societies, and thus of reconciling with secularism and accepting it as a rule for the state and system of governance and – thus - discontinue the illegitimate confusion between the state and religion?

Needless to say, we do not mean by this question all Islamic political movements, but only the moderate ones among them, which have renounced violence, 'reconciled with the democratic choice' and refrained from considering democracy as 'infidelity' under the pretext of consecrating the 'governorship of people' instead of the 'governorship of Allah', etc. These include parties and forces which came to power recently, or are still partners in governance, such as the 'Muslim Brotherhood' in Egypt, 'Nahda' movement in Tunisia and the 'Justice and Development Party' in Morocco, which have in common their gradual adoption of the principles of a contemporary political system – though in different ways and to different degrees.

We may bring the question closer to our cultural and civilizational environment by re-asking it in the following way: Are the Arab Islamic movements capable of pursuing the method of the Turkish 'Justice and Development Party' in its reconciliatory position towards secularism whose governorship of the state and political system in Turkey is indisputable? We pose the question in the Turkish-Islamic context so that there will be no claim that the model of Christian democratic parties cannot be adopted because it reflects a different social and cultural experience, especially in western communities. Nonetheless, we can say that the Christian democratic model which the Justice and Development Party in Turkey is trying to apply, is based on a generalizable equation which is the same equation that the Turkish Islamists are trying to apply. This equation underlies acquiring inspiration from religious values in political action and the political project, and respecting the secularity of the state, and not compromising it in the name of religion. Neither Western Christians nor Muslim Turks find anything wrong in preserving for this equation the equilibrium upon which it is based. They define themselves as politicians who interconnect with the value system of their religion, yet, for them, it is indisputable that they are secularists who believe that the state should not interfere in religion, and that religion should not interfere in the state. Moreover they find no contradiction in being believers and secularists simultaneously. The Islamists, in Egypt and other Arab countries, were shocked when they heard Recep Tayyip Erdogan say that he is a Muslim and secularist at the same time, because their dormant consciousness could not be receptive to such ideas!

In the approach to this issue, we tend to believe that the Islamic movements in the Arab world are not ready to go through the same path of development that the Turkish Justice and Development Party pursued, for many reasons, objective and subjective. These reasons are related to the difference in development of the political, economic, and cultural structures in Turkey and in Arab societies. They are related, as well, to disparities in the levels of intellectual and cultural preparedness, and the levels of development of political culture, between the Turkish Islamic movement and Arab Islamic movements.

The values of the modern civil state in Turkey took root, during the last eighty years, and transformed into a kind of general political culture in society. Whatever may be said in relation to the violence of the Kemalist secularism against religious institutions, which undoubtedly existed, its traditions have become familiar in public life, and respected by public opinion, and even by the Islamic movement. That was not the case in the Arab countries where the relationship between the state and religion has continued to be troubled, ranging between identifying them with each other and ideological exploitation, whether by the ruling elites or 'Partisan Islam'. Furthermore, the successive Turkish Islamic parties ('Welfare Party', 'Virtue Party', 'Justice and Development Party') are in fact descendants of a secular state and a modern civil political culture. Therefore, they do not contradict secularism, as stated by their leaders and successive presidents of these parties – Necmettin Erbakan and Recep Tayyip Erdogan. The same does not apply to the Arab Islamic movements which developed in political environments unlike the Turkish one, and which have traditional ideas on the relationship between religion and politics, and religion and the state. This is the case, for example, with the Muslim Brotherhood in Egypt. Perhaps the chances of the transformation of moderate 'partisan Islam' in the direction of the Turkish example will become even less likely with the rise of hard-line 'Salafist Islam', and the 'Jihadi' Islam, whereby moderate 'partisan Islam' will be afraid to lose ground to the more extremist competition of they give up on talking in the name of religion.

We might need a long time before the Islamic movements re-consider their position regarding secularism, and adopt the same path of Western democratic Christianity, and Turkish political Islam. The passage of time required may be similar to the decades it took Islamic movements to reconcile with partisanship, on which Hassan Al-Banna expressed utter disapproval; and to reconcile with democracy and the authority of the people, which Sayed Qutb considered as an aggression against the Dominion of God. However, the evolution of the Islamic Movement in this direction is also subject to the development of the political culture in society, and the reinforcement of the values of political modernity within the state.

-3-

The plan of this book is to capture all the issues and problematics raised above, as well as others that could not be accommodated within this introduction. The aim of the Centre for Arab Unity Studies is that this book provides a special opportunity for collective reflection, and incorporating various voices, on one of the most complex contemporary Arab socio-political issues and a relationship that will determine the shape of Arab life and socio-political experience hereafter.. For this reason, the studies included here dela with a complex mix of contemporary and historical political and intellectual currents. The contributors are all specialized researchers and academicians, and because the issue is one of controversy between two weighty intellectual and political currents, it was imperative that this book include the contributions of iconic representatives of both currents, thus securing a diversity of opinions which can be beneficial to understanding. The themes explored in this introduction are reflected in the arrangement of the material into sections and chapters in the book, and in the approaches of the scholars included.

While preparing the detailed scheme of the book, the Centre was keen to take into consideration several facts related to the subject of religion and the state and incorporate them in its design:

The first consideration is that thinking about this subject is not new in the Arab intellectual heritage, and the human intellectual heritage in general. There is a wealth of knowledge in this respect which the researcher cannot disregard. It was essential therefore to enable the contributors to have space to explore and explain the intellectual and theoretical heritage upon which they chose to develop their ideas. In addition, there is not only one approach to the issue, but many and diverse ones, in line with the points of view and their diversity (philosophical, historical, socio-political, socio-cultural, and so on). Thus it was required that the participant researchers would belong to these different schools, specialties, and methodologies so that the treatment of the issue be as rich and diverse as possible.

The second fact is that there exists a history of links between religion and the state, in Islamic Arab sociology, and human sociology in general (in the Middle Ages and the modern age), and it is not possible, nowadays, to talk about such relationships in ignorance of the relevant history. It would simply not be productive. So space has also been made to explore the history of how links between the state and religion have evolved, including in societies of Islam in the past, and more recently (especially the Arab ones), and in the societies of the Christian West, and then the secular West. The objective has been to know how these links were lived, and how their negative engagements were undone; that is, for the sake of using the lessons of historical experience as a base for resolving the difficult contemporary ones.

The third fact is that the problematic link between religion and the state imposes itself today in Arab political life like never before, especially after the Arab revolutions have created a new political scene whereby the Islamic political movements have become a major force. In this political scene, the political programme of the Islamic political movements imposes an acute form of association between religion and the state – between religious law and life. Therein, the secular and civil powers display palpable fear of the devolution of power to those haunted by the referential position of religion; they also display different ways of confronting political investment in religion and sacredness, the aim of which is the acquisition and monopoly! Meanwhile, it was necessary while structuring the book, to consider the current relationship between religion and the state in the societies of the Arab (Islamic?) Spring (Tunisia, Egypt, Libya, Yemen), and in societies where political regimes arrogate to themselves religious legitimacy (Saudi Arabia, Morocco); this, in order to analyze the contexts of association and connectedness – the actual – between the two extremes.

The fourth consideration is that the relationship of the political and religious has been experienced since early Islam - the same as it is being lived today within the Arab world. Thus we have witnessed, since the end of the 1970s, the ways through which Islamic parties and forces, have gained power within the 'Islamic world': through a military coup (Pakistan, Sudan), or a coup d'état followed by elections (Pakistan,

Indonesia), or a revolution (Iran), or by national liberalization and alliance with the United States of America and the West (Afghanistan), or by a 'revolution' and American Creative Chaos (Tunisia, Egypt, Yemen, and especially Libya), or by elections (Turkey, Morocco). Thus, the precedent of the 'Islamic World', merited a space in this book whereby it may be included in thinking about the issue, within the Arab sphere, due to the remarkable overlapping between the two spheres. It was therefore considered necessary to include research and analysis on the experience of the relationship between religion and the state in Turkey and Iran, in the hope that this might open up a possibility for the Arabs of 'making use' from two contradictory experiences.

The fifth reality is that the relationships between religion and the state are lived by Muslims even outside their land, in diasporas where they constitute religious communities different from their original ones, especially in countries based on secularism. This experience deserves to be studied from several aspects, perhaps the most important of which are to explore: how Islam can coexist with secularism; are Muslims in diasporas affected by values inherent to a secular society; how does their citizenship intersect with their religious affiliation or become estranged from it; how do they put their religious differences into practice; and how do they understand these in societies whose systems adopt neutrality towards religions?

The studies in this book have covered most of these issues and dimensions. The reader will notice that the material has been presented in a scientific and analytical spirit, and that the language of advocacy and ideology is not favoured; the preference, rather, has been to hold to the traditions of composed, democratic, and rational dialogue, without descending into a tone of hectoring that the subject of discussion may tempt. No doubt the caliber of the contributors to this book and their awareness of the tradition of academic standards at the Center, have insured a democratic scientific standard of contributions, with a sedate vocabulary. Consequently, these have provided the reader with a sophisticated collective volume on questions of religion and the state in the Arab World, which will serve as a valuable reference source – similar to other scientific texts that have been published by the Centre for Arab Unity Studies throughout the past thirty five years.

The state and religion in the fundamentals of Islam and contemporary interpretation

Rached Ghannouchi

President of the Tunisian Ennahdha Movement

From a historical perspective, there has always existed a distinction between the state and religion in Islam, yet no separation. Moreover, there are many types of secularism and many interpretations in Islam. The elite in Tunisia adopts the French type of secularism whereby a most complete separation between the state and religion exists. The case advanced here is that a large part of the unfolding discussions and debates in the context of the ongoing struggle is based on an ambiguous understanding of secularism and Islam. Secularism is not an atheist philosophy, but a series of arrangements and measures designed to ensure freedom of thought and belief. The way of arriving at an equation that guarantees people's rights and freedoms is by delineating religion's constants and variables. Modern democratic mechanisms are the best manifestation of *shura* in Islam, whereby interpretation is no longer an individual act but a collective one performed by the people's representatives.

The relationship between state and religion is one of the most important issues facing us in Tunisia today, especially since we are in the process of drafting a new constitution and building a new system which we hope will be democratic and respects human rights. What follows is an explication of how Islam makes a distinction but not a separation between the state and religion, and how the mechanisms of modern democracy are the best way to protect the value of freedom, that is enshrined in Islam, from hegemony by the state.

(Mis)perceptions of secularism

This is a complex issue that imposes on us the need to address the relationship between Islam and secularism; but is it a contradictory and mutually exclusive relationship or an intertwined relationship? At the heart of this question is the relationship between Islam and governance and Islam and the law, and these are problematic issues. When we speak about secularism and Islam, it seems as if we are speaking about clear and evident concepts when in fact a considerable amount of ambiguity and multiple meanings are involved, because there is not one but many forms of secularism. This is also the case with Islam, given all that exists on the scene; what we actually have is more than one Islam, in the sense that we have more than one understanding of it.

Secularism appears as a philosophy, the fruit of deep philosophical contemplations that came to disprove and combat idealistic and religious philosophies; but this is not the case. Rather than a philosophy or existential theory, secularism appeared and developed in the West as a set of procedural solutions aimed at solving a series of problems that plagued Europe at the time. The most important among these were the repercussions of the Protestant Reformation that caused a schism in Western Christianity, tore apart the consensus within the Catholic Church, and ignited the religious wars of the sixteenth and seventeenth centuries. This is how secularism appeared on the scene.[1]

Secularism, therefore, was actually a series of procedural measures aimed at re-establishing the consensus torn apart by religious conflicts. Here, the question imposes itself as to whether we need secularism, given that it is a set of procedural measures? The most important of these measures is perhaps the neutrality of the state, in other words, the state as a neutral actor that does not favour one religion over another, or interfere in people's conscience. The state pertains to the 'public' sphere and religion to the 'private' sphere. This is what these measures have ultimately led to, despite certain differences regarding the relationship with religion. In the United States, religion flagrantly encroaches onto the public sphere, and despite certain differences, it still wields considerable influence. The leaders' speeches are full of religious references, and religion is present as an issue in election campaigns as well as school prayers, not to mention issues such as abortion and its religious significance. The reason is that America was established by Evangelical immigrants fleeing religious persecution in Europe, which is why it is seen as the 'Promised Land', i.e. the land where the dreams of the Torah and the New Testament will be fulfilled.

The French philosopher Alexis de Tocqueville said that in America there is 'a new route to political power, a route based on the church rather than on inherited land'. This reflects how the Church is, in a sense, the strongest party in America in light of the considerable influence it wields in American society – which is not the case in Europe. For while over 50% of the population attend church in America, in Europe that number does not exceed 5%. In Europe, the difference between the French and Anglo-Saxon concepts of the relationship between state and religion is also apparent. In Great Britain both temporal and religious authority is vested in the Queen, while the most complete separation is found in the French model, due to the clashes throughout French history between the revolutionary state and the heritage of the Catholic Church. However, though a single model of secularism does not exist even in Europe, our Tunisian elite is influenced by a very particular brand, even from the Western perspective, namely the French model of secularism. It is a brand in which religion is barred entirely from the public sphere, and the state sees itself as guardian of the nation's identity, which explains why religion and all its symbolisms are not allowed to trespass onto the public sphere. This is what made France, for instance, the only country to ban the *hijab* (head cover) worn by some Muslim women, since to my knowledge no similar national legislation involving the *hijab* has occurred anywhere else in Europe, meaning that it all goes back to the particular French perspective of the relationship between state and religion.

The most important measure that secularism has invented at this level is perhaps state neutrality, meaning that the state is the guarantor of religious and political freedoms and should not intervene in favour of one side or the other. We therefore ask whether Islam needs to follow suit, i.e. enforce state neutrality vis-à-vis different religions.

Islam and the state

The foundation of Islam has embodied both state and religion since its inception; the Prophet (pbuh) is the founder of both the religion and the state at the same time. The first *bay'a* (acclamation) was by the group that came from Yathreb to Mecca, and was a religious *bay'a* involving the belief in God and His Prophet (pbuh). The second *bay'a* by a group of Medina companions was political, and vowed to protect the Prophet (pbuh) and his companions when he was among them, even with their swords, if the city were attacked. The name of this city is very important here, since the city that was once called Yathreb had its name changed to 'Al-Madina' (the city), a clear indication that Islam is not only a religion but also has civil and urban connotations. It transports people from the level of life in the desert to the level of urban life, which is why returning to live in the desert after living in the city is considered a major sin. It is no wonder then that the birthplace of Islam is "the mother of all cities", since wherever Islam goes cities rise. The city that the Prophet (pbuh) founded therefore indicates that Islam is an urban rather than a desert religion, which is why this first city was called Al-Madina, a name fully deserved since it involves moving the warring tribes from the tribal level of life in the desert to the urban level, i.e. the state level.

The Prophet (pbuh) led the faithful in the *masjid*; He was at the same time a religious *imam* and a political *imam* who ruled and adjudicated among the people, led the army, concluded agreements, and undertook all necessary measures. The first and most important among these, and the main subject of interest here, is that after arriving in Madina the first thing he did was to build a *masjid*, and the second was to draft a constitution by the name of 'Al-Sahifa'. This constitution, perhaps one of the oldest in the world, comprises a collection of agreements between the *Muhajireen* and *Ansar* (immigrants and loyalists) and their respective tribes, which the Prophet (pbuh) considered an *ummah* (a nation/community) together with the Jewish tribes who lived in Madina who the Prophet (pbuh) considered an *ummah* exclusive of all others. The reference here being to the political rather than the religious *ummah*. Here, we will stop at the most important terminology modern Islamic thought has produced, thanks to Mohammad Salim al 'Awwa and Mohammad 'Amara, namely drawing a 'distinction between the religious and the political', as opposed to the concept of separating the religious from the political, in the Western context.

In Al-Sahifa, the distinction between the religious and the political is clear; the Muslims are an *ummah* with a doctrine, as are the Jews, and together with other inhabitants of the city they form a separate *ummah*, an *ummah* open to all who wish to join it, including future generations and those who 'came after them'. It is the concept of the political *ummah*. This distinction has been clear in the behaviour of the Prophet (pbuh) even though people sometimes confused what qualifies as religious, and requires observance and commitment, and what qualifies as political, and is open to interpretation. This distinction sometimes confused the companions, who asked the Prophet (pbuh): is this part of the revelations and we have to commit to it, or is it opinion and advice? If it were revelation, he would say so, and if it were political, he would say it is opinion and advice, and they were then free to disagree with him. On more than one occasion the companions contradicted the Prophet (pbuh) in his capacity as head of state. Sheikh Taher Bin 'Ashour explained what he called the Prophet's (pbuh) statuses (*maqamat*) very well, for he had different ones; when he had the status of Prophet, people owed him total receptivity and obedience, and when he had the status of army and political leader, he could decide on a position for the army yet a companion could come and tell him, by God, the other position is better, and he would actually change his mind and agree with that companion.

One day, the Prophet (pbuh) encountered a group of people in Madina threshing (*yuabbirouna*) the palm trees, and said to them (in his capacity as a citizen of Mecca rather than an expert on agriculture), I do not think what you are doing is useful. Upon hearing that, the Madina people, or some of them, thought that what he said was part of the revelations and did not thresh the palm trees that year, with the result that the harvest was bitter. So they asked him: why did you order us to do that? He replied: you should know better about your own livelihood. It is therefore not religion's role to dictate agricultural, industrial or even governance mechanisms, or the manner of managing state affairs; these involve particular technologies and people's minds are well equipped to learn from experience what best to do. Religion's role is to provide us with answers on major existential issues: our origin, fate and the reason we were born; it provides us with a value system and a set of principles to steer our thinking, behaviour and governance system in the right direction, i.e. a set of guiding values.

Guiding principles and values

Neither since its inception nor throughout its history did Islam experience separation between state and religion, in the sense of removing religion from everyday life. Ever since the Prophet's (pbuh) time until today, Muslims never ceased to be affected, to a larger or lesser extent, by their view of themselves as Muslims who should turn to Islam and its teachings for inspiration and guidance in their civil life, while drawing a clear distinction between the two. This distinction between what is religious and what is political is clear even to the scholars who differentiated between the way people interact with each other (*mu`amalat*) and the way they express their faith (*`ibadat*), the latter being considered the domain of observance (prayer, fasting, and the reason why we pray five times a day and genuflect sometimes three and sometimes four times). This is the domain of observance and consistency, for which the mind is not equipped; for in the domain of doctrines and tenets, where problems are scarce, the mind is not equipped to ascertain the truth. On the other hand, the domain of public interaction is where people seek their personal interests, because Islam came down to help the faithful achieve their aspirations. Major scholars, from Al-Shatbi to Ibn 'Ashour, have recognized that different faiths have come down mainly to bring justice and achieve people's interests, through mental efforts under religious guidance, intentions, principles and values. This is why the domain of public interactions has continued to evolve, including the state system, and represents variability, while all that relates to doctrine, ritual and moral values represents consistency.

Throughout the history of Islam, the state's behaviour has in one way or another been affected by Islam, and laws based on Islamic values were enacted by people as they understood them. Despite that fact, countries have remained Islamic not because their laws, behaviour and measures are based on the revelations, but thanks to human interpretations that are either supported or contradicted by other interpretations. For example, when the Abbasid State wanted to intervene and impose a certain interpretation of Islam on the *ummah*, it is said that Imam Malek was summoned by Al-Mansour who told him that there are so many differences and interpretations in the one religion that there was fear the *ummah* might be dispersed, and asked him to collect all the tenets and interpretations in a single vision. When Imam Malek did just that in a book entitled *Al-Mowatta'*, Al-Mansour was so impressed that he wanted to make it the binding law of the entire Muslim *ummah*. Imam Malek was very frightened by the idea and said: 'No, don't do that O Prince of the Faithful! The Prophet's companions are spread throughout the land bearing with them a lot of knowledge, and this is what has reached me of it; so let people choose what they want.' This is how it happened that North Africa follows one school of jurisprudence, the people of Egypt follow another and the people of Syria yet another; in the absence of a Muslim church what remains is the freedom of interpretation. This naturally means that there will be several interpretations for the same source, and nothing is wrong with that if it lays the ground for freedom of thought, interpretation, and political and sectarian diversity.

Modern mechanisms of democracy

However, if we want to enact laws in such a diverse environment, we need a mechanism to help us do that, and the best that man has produced so far in this domain are perhaps the mechanisms of democracy and elections. The fact that these generate representatives for the *ummah* renders today's interpretation a collective rather than an individual act that the nation's representatives perform in the absence of a church that represents the sacred on earth, and of someone who speaks in the name of the Koran and the divine will. The only manifestation of the divine will is inherent in the nation itself, which it expresses through advocacy rather than by the monopolizing of a certain *imam*, political party or state. This is why Imam Ahmad launched his well-known revolution. The story goes that during his reign, when he noticed how dispersed the Muslims were, Al-Ma'moun, who was a highly intellectual man, contemplated forging consensus among the *ummah* round a single opinion, having been influenced by the Mu'tazila School which, despite its fame, was an intellectual school, though many intellectuals were misled by their intellect into trying to impose the fruit of their thoughts on the people. Al-Ma'moun did indeed decide to impose on the people a certain interpretation of the Quran, and a certain understanding of the Islamic doctrine. The revolution that Imam Ahmad led was manifested in his rejection of the state's hegemony over religion, as a result of which he was persecuted and tortured, though in the end he succeeded in turning public opinion against the state, until Al-Ma'moun relented and changed his mind. Today, the Islamic world is still free of any church's influence, and individual countries continue to follow this or that denomination, without allowing the state any domination over religion.

Thus, while the problem in the West centred round the means of liberating the state from religion, and mounted many revolutions to achieve that, a major aspect of our problem is how to liberate religion from the state, and prevent it from imposing its hegemony on it, so it would remain a societal issue that allows all Muslims to read the Quran and understand it in their own way. There is nothing wrong with a diversity that involves a wide margin of tolerance. In the case where Muslims need a new law, modern democratic mechanisms are the best manifestation of *shura* in Islam, whereby interpretation is no longer an individual act but a collective one performed by the people's representatives.

The absence of a church is very important to our traditions. Our Shia brethren are perhaps the only ones to have the idea of a religious establishment; however, though no such establishment exists in the Sunni world, there is an institution of *ulema* (religious scholars) whose members are by nature different from one another, and hold different opinions. This is why we will continue to need a mechanism to enact laws, and will need not one but a collection of *ulema* and intellectuals who confer with each other in a free atmosphere; ultimately, the legislature is the only institution legally mandated to enact laws, because it is elected.

The debate in Tunisia today

An intense process of give and take is today unfolding on the Tunisian political scene between secular currents, which we could describe as hardline, and Islamist currents, to which the same description also applies, of which the latter wants to impose a top-down interpretation of Islam and use the state to do so, while the former wants to void the state of all traces of Islam, and void the laws, academic curricula and culture from any religious influences on society. What is worth noting, however, is that rather than waning, religion is actually witnessing a revival in our society, as is the case in other regions of the world. The role that the Catholic Church has played in the development of Eastern Europe is not that different from what is taking place in our country, starting with the Polish Pope John Paul II, and the support of the Russian Orthodox Church's Archbishop for Vladimir Putin, which helped him reach the presidency. Thus, at a time when the world is witnessing a religious revival – especially in the Islamic world – some oppose the slightest religious influence on the state's educational and cultural policies. In fact, we do not need the state and its apparatus to impose Islam; people's spirits usually reject all that is imposed on them. Islam is the religion of an entire people rather than an elite and the main factor that has allowed it to survive is not state power, since the state was often a burden on Islam, but its receptivity among the faithful. Despite that, many members of the Islamist currents and others fear the liberation of religion from the state, and allowing it to become a public matter. The latter are actually extremely worried, even obsessed with fear of Islam's freedom, which is very unfortunate indeed.

Islam guides from within

The issue of state neutrality is not entirely risk-free if the aim is to separate religions from the state, given that the state is a human product while religion is divine revelation. Though the distinction between what is divine revelation and what is political was very clear to the early Muslims, any attempt to separate between the two, as the French see it or based on the Marxist experience, might lead us into an adventure that might end up hurting both. The liberation of politics from religion is to turn the state into a mafia, the economy into a free for all, and politics into a form of deception and charlatanism, which is what is actually happening in the West, despite some positive aspects. World politics are today governed by a group of financial middlemen who have a lot of money, and by extension the media, and thus have ultimate control over the politicians.

People deeply need religion because humans need spiritual and value-driven guidance; when confusion becomes overwhelming, they need the concept of right and wrong, and the ability to distinguish between them. Thus, in the absence of a church that acts as the only arbiter between right and wrong, there is room for debate between the people and the elite, via the intellectuals and the media.

The liberation of religion from both politics and the state could be fraught with danger, as well; the situation could get out of hand and matters could depart from their proper context. Therefore, the way of arriving at an equation that guarantees people's rights and freedoms, since religion came to ensure that this actually happens, is to go back to the issue of distinguishing between religion and politics, and delineate religion's constants and variables.

Our legislators should be imbibed with the values of their religion even when they are in the process of enacting laws; at this point, they should need neither the guidance of the Ministry of Religious Affairs nor of the Sharia scholars because these values are already embedded in them. The same goes for the political leaders; they should not perform their responsibilities because of pressure from outside, but because they are fully convinced of what they are doing. Forced religious observance is of no value at all. There is no value whatsoever in using the state's power to turn people from rebels into hypocrites; God Almighty created them free. Moreover, the fact is one can control people's outward behaviour but not what lies deep within them.[2]

Freedom of the people and responsibilities of the state religion's main orbit is not the state's apparatus but people's personal convictions. On the other hand, the state's responsibility is above all to serve the people as citizens, including the provision of employment, health and good-quality education; their hearts and their religion should be left to God, because freedom is the principle that has the greatest value in Islam.[3] Therefore, a country is Muslim to the extent that it identifies with Islamic values, without the intervention of a religious institution, because there is no such institution in Islam anyway. What there are, however, are a people and an *ummah* free to decide for themselves, through institutions, what religion means to them.

This is why, when the people of Mecca turned their backs on religion, the Prophet (pbuh) gave them an alternative, saying, 'Do not stand between me and the people', which, had they done so, would have spared him the need to emigrate and leave his homeland. Thus, because his call had the power of so much conviction and the strength to attract, they were able to respond to it through a different proposition, which is why Muslims believe that Islam is so powerful in itself that there is no need for compulsion at all. When the voice of Islam says, 'Give me your evidence if you are sincere,' the challenge it raises is not a voice in the wilderness; this Muslim's challenge goes to the very core of the intellectual and political struggle.

A big part of the unfolding discussions and debates in the context of the ongoing struggle is based on an ambiguous understanding of secularism and Islam. A big part of the reason why such a misunderstanding exists is due to the fact that while some adopt secularism as an atheist philosophy, others see it as a series of arrangements and measures designed to ensure freedom of thought and belief. This is why Abdul Wahhab Al-Massiri distinguished in his writings between partial and total secularism, the latter being modelled after the Jacobin movement in French history that waged war on the priests, and raised the slogan 'When the last king is hanged with the entrails of the last celibate priest, mankind may hope to be happy'. The latter is the expression of a specifically French concept of secularism, and not of secularism as a set of procedural arrangements to ensure freedom in society.

The same ambiguity applies to Islam since some believe that Islam wins when it denies people's freedoms and imposes prayer, fasting and the *hijab* by force, at a time when such behaviour would be considered a failure rather than a success. As a matter of fact compulsion in religion produces only hypocrites, and God Almighty considered hypocrisy as the biggest sin, and relegated hypocrites to the lowest level of Hell fire, since they are the lowest of the low.

What we ought to do, therefore, is accept the principle of citizenship and the premise that the country does not belong to Zeid, `Amr or this or that party, but to all its citizens equally. All citizens, regardless of their beliefs and backgrounds, whether they are male or female, were endowed by Islam with the right to be citizens with equal rights: the right to believe in whomever they want within the framework of respect for one another, and to behave according to the law that they themselves have enacted through their representatives in parliament.

Notes

1. There is no agreement on the pronunciation of the word 'secularism' in Arabic; there are two different ways of pronouncing it: the first, *'Ilmaniya*, derived from *'ilm*, or science; the second, *`Alamaniya*, derives from `Alam, or this world, and refers to all that is profane, and therefore is the more appropriate term.
2. This is why there are two examples of the *hijab* issue: one where the state mandates it and the other where it bans it. Once, when I was travelling from a Muslim country's airport, all the women on the flight were wearing the *hijab*; however, once the aeroplane was airborne, the *hijab*s quickly disappeared. This is the result of a failure of proper education because the educational tools in this particular country could not ensure the citizen's piety except through force. In another country, with conditions similar to what we had in Tunisia under the dictator Ben Ali, women were prevented by the state from wearing the dress that best reflects their true identity, which is yet another form of failure.
3. This is why I opposed all means that force people to do anything, and addressed an issue that some consider thorny, namely 'riddah' - apostacy, which touches on the state's responsibility to limit people's freedom of belief. If there is agreement on the principle that there is no compulsion in religion, then I defended the principle of freedom in both directions: the freedom to join a religion and the freedom to leave it, because religiosity has no meaning when it is forced, and the Muslim *ummah* is better off without the hypocrites that hide apostasy deep within them yet pretend on the surface to be true believers and Muslims, because Islam will not be strengthened with this sort of behaviour. Freedom is the basic value that anyone who wants to join Islam should arm himself with, since professing one's Islam should be the expression of the individual's free will, based on awareness and evidence.

State and religion in a revolutionary era: perspectives and demands of the Islamic awakening[†]

Ridwan Al-Sayyid

Islamic Studies, Lebanese University, Beirut, Lebanon

This paper tackles the relationship between Islam and the state in light of the ongoing revolutions. It focuses on two perspectives: the Islamists' claim that the Shari'a and not the *umma* (community) are the source of legitimacy in the evolving regimes; and that it is the duty of the state to protect religion and apply the Shari'a. The main disadvantage of these propositions is that they preclude the Umma both from political power and Shari'a, thus pitting it against these two assets which become manipulated to its disadvantage by those holding power. On the other hand, an open-minded and reformist Islamic perspective believes in people regaining the prerogative to rule themselves, guided by their intellect and the public good. The main call for the Arab uprisings is to quit political Islam, which seems to be the major threat to religion, and dangerously divisive for societies.

Islam and the state: background to the current debate

Islamic thought on religion and the state went through four different stages, from the 19th century to the onset of the Arab revolutions, and today it is in the midst of a fifth stage. The first stage stretches from Al-Tahtawi (1834) to Khair Eddin El-Tunisi (1867/1972), and although both men had a strong awareness of the West and Western awakening, they came from entirely different cultural backgrounds. Al-Tahtawi was an Al-Azhar man who went by chance to Paris, spent five years in the city and wrote a book about it entitled *Takhlis al Ibirz fi Talkhis Paris.*[1] He worked for 50 years as a public employee in different government departments in Egypt, during which time he wrote and translated several books. He was well versed in the French culture of his time, and tried to reconcile in his writings and translations the concepts and institutions he learned about in France and Islam's religious and cultural heritage. He was a strong believer in Mohammad Ali's development project, and was very impressed by the idea of public utilities which he thought were the secret behind France's reawakening, with his main advocacy revolving round the need to root this notion in Islamic societies. Although Al-Tahtawi saw nothing wrong in or with Islam, he thought that there was a need to select and adapt those Islamic values that lead to awakening and reform, and were forgotten by Mohammad Ali's project and

---

[†]This paper was originally presented at the Symposium on Religion and the State in the Arab World, convened by the Centre for Arab Unity Studies (CAUS) and the Swedish Institute of Alexandria in Al-Hammamaat, Tunisia, October 2012.

the Ottoman state, especially since he thought they were in line with all that he saw and read in France about that country's revolutionary experience.[2]

Khair Eddin El-Tunisi, by contrast, was a statesman from his early years and occupied several high positions in Tunis and Istanbul. In his book entitled *Aqwam al-Masalik fi Ma'rifat Ahwal al-Mamalik* (The Best Path towards Learning the Kingdoms' Conditions) (El-Tunisi 1867/1972), he recounts how the awakening unfolded in several European countries, and he wrote a piece at the beginning of the book similar to Ibn Khaldun's Introduction, in which he called for the establishment of institutions that promote public utilities, since they were so instrumental in Europe's successful reawakening. What is noteworthy here is the role he foresaw for Islam in convincing the pious public that religion accepts and even encourages taking utilities into account when building new institutions. However, because he was not aware of the sources of jurisprudence and Islam's fundamentals, it is very probable that the scholar Mohammad Bayram helped him in this regard.[3]

The second stage of Islamic thought on state and religion in recent times had Al-Azhar as its symbol, then Sheikh Mohammad Abdo (1905), Mufti of Egypt, and after him, at the zenith, Abdo's student, Sheikh Ali Abdel-Razek. It is well known that Mohammad Abdo saw many reversals of fortune after the failure of the Urabi Revolution and the British occupation of Egypt; yet he became convinced of two ideas that stayed with him throughout his professional life, and during his time in exile, namely reform of the education sector and reform of religious thought and institutions, which is why he became active on several fronts, all of which were aimed at improving the religious domain. One of the facets of enlightened religious thought is to contribute to a social, political and cultural reawakening, which is why Abdo worked at reforming Al-Azhar's curricula and interpreted, or began to interpret, the Koran. He did that for two main reasons. The first was to affirm rules as a key element in both the prosperity and disintegration of nations, and in the appearance and disappearance of civilisations. The second was to refute the need for imitation and insistence on preserving old ways, and instead open the door to independent interpretation and reveal Islam's authentic values, including the concepts of the civil state and civilian rule in Islam. Based on what he said in the context of his debate with Farah Antoun, he believed that there was an overlap between state and religion throughout history, as well as at the current time, although Islam does not advocate theocracy like the Catholic experience in Central Europe. The reason is that, in Islam, politics is a civilian matter that rests on the two key principles of justice and freedom.[4] However, although Al-Tunisi died at quite a young age, in 1905, he managed to inspire and encourage dozens of Egyptians and Arabs to establish modern educational institutions, and take part in a European-style awakening culture, since working for progress is one of the tenets of Shari'a. This line of thinking reached its apogee in one of his students' – Ali Abdel-Razek's – books entitled *Islam wa Usool al-Hukm* (Islam and the Fundamentals of Governance) (Abdel-Razek 1925a), in which he said that the Prophet (ﷺ) came to establish neither a state nor a religious political system because his appeal was purely religious in nature.[5]

The third stage, stretching from the 1920s to the 1950s, witnessed an Islamic religious revival and was dominated by the issue of identity. One of this rich stage's first manifestations was the response of Muhammad Rashid Rida (1865–1935), one of the closest students to Mohammad Abdo and publisher of the famous *Al-Manar Magazine*, to Mustafa Kamal, who had separated the Caliphate from the Sultanate (1922). Rida wrote a famous series of articles – first published in *Al-Manar*, then collected in a book entitled *Al-Khilafa aw al-Imama al-Ozma* (The Caliphate or Grand Imamate) – in which he said that the Islamic Caliphate was a religious state (Rida 1922). When Mustafa Kamal annulled the caliphate in Turkey in 1924 and founded a secular state, the strange thing was that the first reactions to that act came from India and Egypt, two countries that were not under Ottoman rule. This shows that the issue was not a matter of dealing a blow to a certain religion or destroying a particular political–religious institution, but was rather motivated by a fear among the ascending elite for the identity of the community and the state after the rise of the nation-state, in the period between the two world wars. The problem was no longer what we do in order to advance but how do we safeguard our religion, including the caliphate, one of its symbols (Kawtharani 1996, Balqaziz 2004).

The second phenomenon to appear during this period was the foundation of religious and cultural identity movements such as, among others, the Muslim Brotherhood in Egypt in 1928, the Muslim Youth Association in 1927, the Islamic Youth Movement in the Greater Syria region in 1933, the Ansar al-Sunna, The Shari'a Association, etc. All these movements, groups and associations, whose appeal was originally religious and educational in nature, eventually turned to politics, including in Egypt, Syria, India, Java, Sumatra and Central Asia, in the decades that followed. Besides educating the youth about Islam, these groups had two main objectives in mind: combating Westernization in public and private life, and combating colonization and political and military invasion (Al-Sayed 1977; see also Umleil 1985). This stage also witnessed a gradual separation between the nationalist and Islamist currents, with the exception of the Maghreb countries, where the division of the elite between nationalists and Islamists was delayed to the 1960s and 1970s.

The fourth and most defining stage of Islamic thought on the relationship between state and religion stretches from the early 1950s to the onset of the Arab Revolutions in 2010. During its first three decades, i.e. from the 1950s to the 1970s, what became known later as 'the Islamist awakening' made its appearance on the scene and rose to dominance, as did the notion of the comprehensive Islamic regime, accompanied by an over-abundant amount of literature on the subject. Also during these three decades, many of these Islamist movements and societies became strong political parties with lofty titles. According to the Islamist concept, Islam is a comprehensive life system for both society and state, covering all doctrinal, social and economic aspects. It is based on three interconnected notions: (1) that Shari'a rather than the *umma* – the wider Muslim community – is the basis of all legitimacy in the state and society, and/or it must be in order for the state and society to remain Islamic; (2) the importance of the state and the political regime for religion's survival; and, therefore, (3) that the state is mandated with the key responsibility of ensuring that the two above notions are implemented, namely the application of Shari'a or God's rule on earth.[6] According to Hassan Al-Banna's early writings, Islam is a religion and a world, a *Mushaf* (Islamic holy book) and a sword (Abu Fares 1999; Zakariya 2013; see also Abdel-Fattah Nabil 1984); according to Abdel-Kader Odeh, the state is religion and religion is the state;[7] and according to Al-Mawdudi and Sayed Qutob, religion's predominance in the state is God's rule on earth, which is why God chose humankind and the faithful in particular to be His caliphs (successors) (Al-Mawdudi 1960, 1968, 2000, n.d.; also cf. Qutob 1993, 1995, 2008). This is what the inevitable Islamic solution that Sheikh Yousef Al Qaradawi coined in the 1970s actually means (Al-Sayyid 1997).

Why this enmeshment between state and religion, or why did they become necessary for one another in the Islamist perspective? Divisions appeared between the nationalist and Islamist elites in the 1930 and 1940s, and became an open conflict in the 1950s and 1960s, when the military ('the officers') came to power in the Arab and Islamic world. The impact of the Cold War that began in the late 1940s and dominated the world on the military, political, economic and cultural levels, was instrumental across the Arab and Islamic world. There were also the problems that occurred and grew at the very heart of Islam's cultural and political hub, such as the occupation of Palestine by the Zionists that was aided and abetted by the West, and with no opposition from the Soviet Union. There were the measures and massacres that accompanied the secession of India's Muslim territories and the establishment of Pakistan in 1947, and all the adversarial or anti-secular and leftist literature promoted by many Arab and Muslim intellectuals in league with the officers' governments, or with this or that side in the Cold War. There were the cultural wars raging at the margins of the Cold War, during which both the Islamists and the nationalists and communists were used to this or that side's advantage. There were the repeated military failures and autocratic policies of the governments in power that ended up sidelining large segments of the population from the cycles of production, and alienating them from the country's diminishing political life. There were the acts of repression that directly targeted young Islamist sympathisers whom the state lumped with the wider group of Islamists, i.e. the main body of opposition to the military regimes (Al-Sayyid 2007). Last but not least, there was the weakness, failure and subservience of Sunni institutions that cost them both their attraction and strength of cause, and left tens of thousands of Islamist-leaning individuals wavering between trusting these institutions, turning to the jihadists or joining the relatively less radical Muslim Brotherhood or one of its offshoots (Chamseddin 1992).

The 1980s witnessed a number of important developments as well, the first of which was the Islamic Revolution in Iran that succeeded in establishing a theocracy, whose ideas were similar to the Brotherhood's regarding the comprehensive Islamic system, except that the Iranian version had the particular distinction of emanating from the Jaafari Shia sect. This distinction centres round the concept of '*wilayet al-faqeeh*' (governance of the jurists) that manifested itself at the time in the difference between the Shia theocracy and the Sunni nomocracy, among partisan and non-partisan Islamists. The second important development was the split within the ranks of the Islamists between the jihadists, waging a war on both the domestic and foreign fronts, and those who, having adapted to the status quo, rejected violence despite their insistence on Islamizing the state and society by taking part in the country's political life, to the fullest extent possible, under the ruling government's shadow. The third development involves the new interpretations launched by the Muslim Brotherhood, and some intellectuals close to them, that promote reconciliation between the Islamists and the regimes in power, in a flagrant abandonment of the issues of governance and openness towards democracy. However, although this openness did not produce any clear intellectual results, but rather practical ones, it brought to the fore Sheikh Mahdi Shamseddin and his ideas on the *umma*'s self-guardianship, and Rached Al-Ghannouchi (Al-Ghannouchi 1993) and his efforts to crystallize the tenets and rules of an Islamic democracy, or a democracy that does not conflict with Islam.

However, the end of the Cold War did not help develop or promote such an openness; a global war was launched on Iraq after it invaded Kuwait, and the Americans announced the dawn of a new hegemonic era, the era of their own hegemony on the post-Cold War world, in tandem with the military regimes tightening the noose around the Arab people's necks, with American support. Throughout those 20 years of invasion and occupation neither the Islamist jihadists nor those who adapted to life under those regimes were able to rest and reap the fruits of their growing popularity; the domestic war against the Islamists had turned into a global War on Terror. This compelled the late Egyptian researcher Nazih Al-Ayoubi to say in his book, *Overstating of the Arab State* (1994),[8] that the obstruction in the Arab governance system and the Arab state will continue, and will be intercepted by armed Islamist rebellions that will quickly subside amid the repression, the failure of the state's functions, and America's support for these subservient regimes against the Islamists and other opposition groups.

The Arab Revolutions

The new movements calling for change and the outbreak of the Arab Revolutions ushered in an entirely new era. However, although I will not delve into this point at this moment, it is necessary here to draw attention to three important points: the first is the predominance of slogans calling for freedom, dignity, justice and democracy. These slogans became so predominant that Al-Azhar's leading clerics, having issued a statement on the future of governance in Egypt, followed up immediately by stating that the main reference of the new system should be Islam and that the new governance system should be constitutional, modern, democratic, pluralistic and based on citizenship (*Wathikat al-Azhar Hawla Mustaqbal Misr* 2011). The text's authors – a group of Muslim clerics and Muslim and Christian intellectuals, including members of the Brotherhood and Salafist movements – were prepared to mention in the text that, among other features, the new regime should have a civil character, had the Brotherhood and Salafists not objected to the inclusion on the grounds that civilian means secular in people's minds. I will return to this point below.

The second point is that although the tone of these slogans became gradually more subdued, their frequency did not wane – and I am still talking about Egypt here – during the referendum on the constitution and still focused on matters related to Egypt's threatened Islamic identity, despite the fact that Article Two of the 1971 Constitution, which states that Islam is the state religion and Islamic Shari'a is the main source of legislation, was not open to debate or subject to a referendum. The same happened during the campaigns for the People's Assembly and Shura Council elections, during which the slogan 'Islam is the Solution' and calls for the application of Shari'a law began to escalate this time on the part of the Muslim Brotherhood and the Salafists. The same is happening again in the lead up to the referendum on the new constitution and the new round of elections to the People's Assembly and Shura Council, nullified by the High Constitutional Court. The third point is that the revolutions have included partisan Islamists who have adopted the slogans of these revolutions. This has pushed – until the time being – the Islamist intellectuals who are a major party in rebuilding the new regimes to undertake a critical review of the doctrinal tenets coined when they were still sidelined and persecuted. This revision excludes some general statements which make these arguments go in line with – or against – the Turkish, or Iranian, models.

Based on the above, we have the following two intellectual propositions to ponder: the first proposition concerns the Islamists' founding principle and its three pillars: the Shari'a (rather than the *umma*) as the basis of legitimacy in the state and society, the state as necessary for safeguarding religion, and its fundamental religious duty to implement Shari'a. The second proposition, which appears in this paper's title, concerns the state and religion in the era of revolutions: the awakening and its demands.

What is noteworthy in the Islamists' arguments on the relationship between the state and religion, which took place in the 1930s and 1940s, whether or not the latter were affiliated to a party, are that they were dogmatic in nature and the outcome of identity-based thinking. Ali Abdel-Razek was the last to rely on the sciences of jurisprudence and theological debates (*Ilm al-Kalām*),[9] and the lessons that the *umma* learned from history when pursuing the rise of the Caliphate and its trajectory throughout the ages. However, subsequently the Islamists, including scholars, theologians even, historians and constitutional experts, based their entire doctrine on the Koran and their own personal and dogmatic interpretation of *aya*s (verses) related to the issues of governance, orders, authority, succession rules and caliphate. Judge Abdel Kader Odeh, for example, a notable scholar on account of his book about criminal legislation in Islam, did not behave like a scholar or a historian in his strong statement in favour of the Islamic state, or in his book entitled *Al-Islam wa Awda'una al-Siyasiya* (Islam and Our Political Condition) (Odeh, n.d.). The same could be said about other Islamist authors, up until the 1980s. I remember that in 1967, when our professor Mohammad Dia'eddin Al-Rayyes was teaching us his book *Al-Nathariyat al-Siyasiya al-Islamiya* (Islamic Political Theories) (1979), one of our Egyptian colleagues objected to what he was saying and told him that he suspected him of being secular, or else 'Why would you not follow Sheikh Mohammad al-Ghazali's reasoning regarding the state and religion, and be done with it.' Dr Al-Rayyes, who was not bothered by that at all, smiled and said to the student, 'I will answer you like Professor Mahmoud Shaker answers those who do not understand him: Here the crux of the matter is different!' The student said, 'You made the matter more confusing!' The Professor answered, 'Yes I did; after Sayed Qutob's '*Maalem fil-Tareeq*' (Landmarks on the Road), nothing more can be said!' Al-Rayyes, like other traditionalist students of Islamic thought, understood the statement of Al-Mawardi (450 A.H., i.e. after Hegira) that the imamate was set for the succession of Prophethood in guarding religion and administering worldly life and that 'set' implies being agreed upon amongst the first Muslim generation, and not a religious matter or a matter of revelation. The main function of the imamate is worldly politics or the management of public affairs. As for the term 'guarding religion', Al-Mawardi explained it as: preserving it according to its classic customs and basic rules, and, as also elucidated by Al-Rayyes, that religious freedoms should be maintained in matters of doctrine and faith, meaning that the state has no role to play in religion, and religious scholars have no role in the management of public affairs.

The two spheres have been coexistent since the issue of the Koran's creation was put to rest in the third century *hijri*. As for the source of legitimacy, given that the imamate is based on a selection process, legitimacy is vested in the *community* whose decision-makers nominate those who are fit to rule, based on conditions and criteria delineated by Mawardi. In *Ghiath al-Umam* (The Relief of Nations)[10] Imam Al-Joueini (478–*hijri*), a contemporary of Mawardi, criticized his visions and decisions on several issues, including the statement that the source of authority or of the imamate's legitimacy is vested in the power of the mind and *tradition*, and said that shura and consensus are the sources of legitimacy since it is based on a selection from among the *umma* (Al-Joueini, 1400 hijri [2 December 1978 – 21 November 1979]). Al-Joueini believed that Mawardi's misconception on this matter is due to the influence of the orators' tenets, and their argument with the Shias who believe that the imamate is one of the fundamentals of religion. This is not so, however, neither in the case of the imamate's fundamentals nor in its functions. Those who talk about it ought to leave the imamate alone because it is rooted in the *umma* and consensus, and because its functions are procedural and administrative rather than religious and doctrinal.

What is strange is that the orators referred to by Al-Joueini kept insisting on including a chapter on the imamate at the end of their books, at the beginning of which they state that the imamate is not a matter of belief, but an administrative and procedural matter where independent interpretation, personal opinion and interests are common, and therefore has room for right and wrong, which is not the case with doctrinal decision. For a long time doubts have revolved around whether the imamate was a sacred matter or not, for reasons that will now be explored.

Examining the Islamists' contentions

In Islam, the state was established during the Prophet's time and the Rashideen Caliphs, and their poets and scholars have throughout the ages endowed authority, all kinds of authority, with a sacred aura (did the Umayyad since Abdel Malek bin Marwan and the Abbasids not call themselves God's successors?) on the premise that since the imamate is the implementation of God's law, it acquires sanctity from the nature of its function on earth. However, the Prophet (ﷺ) did not intervene in worldly matters as he did in matters of faith; for while he used to say that all matters of faith are divine and binding, he consulted others on worldly matters, including his companions and the experts. In times of war and peace, as in matters of property and financial management, he applied different criteria on different occasions, and there was no legal code of conduct for imams and caliphs even during the Rashideen period, since each, in the effort to secure and safeguard the public interest, followed his own path based on the requirements of his time and reign. Al-Joueini and his student Al-Ghazali had something to say adopting the Shari'a as a reference and applying its laws. In Islam, the state did not have the right to legislate either in the name of God or in that of this or that caliph, and from the fourth century *hijri* until the end of the Classical period, religious scholars complained about the interference of politics in the Shari'a, and of transgressions in matters related to punishment and reprimand, and to public and private funds.[11] It is known today that Sultan Sulaiman (called al-Qanooni, 'the lawgiver') used to issue orders of a religious nature which elicited a lot of complaints because of their impact on people's rights, or the rights of certain sectors of the population, forcing him to ask Sheikh Al-Islam Abu al-Saoud to study these orders, and then agree or disagree with them. Political authority, whether in the hands of a caliph, a sultan or both, has no legitimate reason to interfere in religion, and when it happened, it neither had an impact nor constituted a legal precedent. In the span of one-and-a-half centuries, several debates took place on the issue, and many Ottoman sultans issued a series of orders on 'dedication or consecration of money' – a purely procedural matter even if it had religious and financial incentives; the orders that were ultimately deemed legitimate and approved were the object of consensus among the Jurists.[12]

We are still in the Classical period and the issue still revolves around authority, the basis of its legitimacy and its responsibilities. The matter would not have merited so much debate had it not been for the difficulties and trouble that our people, religion and the management of our public affairs have encountered in the past century. These matters were clear to a large extent when Sheikh Mohammad Abdo decided, in the context of his debate with Farah Antoun, that authority in Islam – in the *umma*'s historical vision and experience – was civil. Sheikh Mohammad Abu Zahra told us in the late 1960s, during one of his lessons at Al-Azhar, that although Sheikh Mohammad Abdo's opinion was correct, the reasoning behind the view that authority in Islam is civil, i.e. that Islam never had a clerical authority, was weak because clerical authority or the authority of religious figures is not the religious state's only formula. Considering religion or the infallible Shari'a as the root of authority, or the source of its legitimacy, or basing legitimacy on that assumption rather than on the *umma*'s will, was tantamount to endorsing the religious state! And when a student asked him why Abdo did not pay attention to that, the sheikh answered with irony: because the Imam did know then what Al-Banna and Sheikh Hassan Ma'moun came to know later on! The Islamists succumbed to the fundamentalist view of legitimacy and admissibility, which caused an ominous deviation in the way they thought and viewed the *umma* and its authority, beginning in the 1940s. Among the reasons for that is the fear of falling victim to what the Europeans fell victim to at two different points in their history: during the Middle Ages when they based authority on the divine right of the pope or king, and in modern times, i.e. in the national state era, when they eternalized the state by separating it from religion and granting it absolute powers, including the power to legislate, enact and implement laws.

In the 1930s, 1940s and beyond, the Europeans witnessed the bane of fascist and communist populism and, in both these cases, though the masses appeared as mighty creatures with legendary power, their fate rested ultimately in the hands of powerful despots – as the Koran sees them – who wielded the power of absolute compulsion. This power was vested in them by the authority of the people or by popular authority, and by the laws in effect, laws that could have been written for them or for those like them who came before them, by people just like them who allowed them to wield the power of life and death over country and subjects. It should not be forgotten that, starting in the theoretical and ideological formation period, in the 1940s, to the onset of the Arab revolutions in 2010, the Islamists were neither outside the power structure nor part of the opposition as much as they were subconsciously outside the public mainstream, and in the constitutional and totalitarian period. For all these reasons, they subconsciously saw the Classical experience as an antithesis, or that it ought to be an antithesis, to the Western experience, given the way it deals with religion, political affairs and state-building.

Seen from this perspective, we can understand why they fear democracy and the *umma*'s authority as much as they do repression and autocracy. For their part, because the Muslim promoters of the awakening went through a different experience, their fear progressed beyond autocratic repression, and they attempted – following the Western experience based on the constitution and separation of powers – to restrict the ruler's powers, and they reinterpreted the *shura* in view of reintroducing political connotations left behind centuries ago, specifically those that refer to the separation of powers and restriction of the ruler's powers through the constitution, the government, and elected *shura* councils that more or less resemble Western parliaments.[13] This is how it happened that in the span of half a century history produced two different if not contradictory explanations for the same texts. In fact, through study trips and direct contact with the colonial administrations, the Arab promoters of the awakening were witness to different aspects of European military, political, legal and cultural experiences, and the positive aspects encouraged them to be inspired and imitate them. They were helped in that by two factors: (1) the fact that they did not consider the European experience relative to the relationship between state and religion worthy of imitation, whether in the Middle Ages or the modern period; and (2) that they did not have their own Islamic political project, which meant that they were not part of the struggle for power but rather supported – or some of them supported – existing political and cultural currents and sometimes even helped launch and develop them. However, in the era of identity and its thought and dogma, the Islamists began working on a political project directly opposed to Western thought and experience after trying and failing to be part of the political experience unfolding at the time.

In some of my books (Al-Sayyid 1977, 1997), I predicted that we would have witnessed a different modern Islamic experience in thinking about the nature of authority and the state, and about the relationship between the public and religion, and Shari'a and the law, had the early Islamists who lived through electoral or ministerial experiences, or collaborated later with the officers' populist governments, achieved a certain level of success. Yet, it was a period of dogmatic and totalitarian beliefs even on the part of those who considered themselves liberals and secularists in the 1950s and 1960s, let alone those harbouring religious tendencies. Moreover, if all Arab officers can become autocrats, immortal leaders and objects of the crowds' adoration, whereby the dead among them is an example and the living a hope; if history, both before and after that, was rife with inevitabilities that the people will ultimately triumph through their own power, why is truth then not a third or a fourth option besides capitalism and socialism, and why are the great historical right and truth not vested in a divine contradictory inevitability, namely the Islamist inevitability, or the Islamist solution according to Sheikh Yousef Al-Qaradawi?[14]

The Islamist ideologues, whether affiliated with a party or not, decided ultimately to replace the *umma* with Shari'a[15] as the main reference point and the source of legitimacy and power, given its divine origin and based on the notion that people are a source of threat to religion, rather than the despots and their Westernized supporters! However, because they advocated the implementation of Shari'a as the Islamic solution, they gave it the status of a binding law, and how could Shari'a not be binding when it has a divine source? And since there is need for an implementation tool, nothing is more appropriate in this respect than the state itself, which should be tasked with safeguarding religion and applying its Shari'a. This is a vision of disparate elements stitched together from the Middle Ages and modern European experience, and from what they saw as the right image of the governance system in Islam, based on the Koran and the experience of the Prophet and Rashideen caliphs.

The two worst aspects of this vision or dogmatic model lie in the fact that Shari'a and authority are taken away from the *umma* and placed in confrontation with it, and that religion and its Shari'a are placed in the political authority's hands. The harm in the first case, i.e. making the Shari'a rather than the *umma* the source of authority, is that it places Shari'a outside the *umma* instead of being its protector, and turns Shari'a into a repressive authority in the name of God, which is harmful to religion and its moral values. The harm in the second case is that it places religion in the political authority's hands under the pretext of implementing it, which is then used as a whip in the name of God. In this context, given that we were incapable of ridding ourselves of Gaddafi for 40 long years, although he had nothing but his Green Book and revolutionary committees, how would it be if the Koran became a tool in the political authority's hands? However, the Islamists' image of the interim Islamic experience with the relationship between state and religion is false, since even the religious scholars say that neither during the caliphate nor the sultanate was the state based on Shari'a, or enjoyed legislative powers. Shari'a, which is made of doctrines, tenets, morals and procedures, was the domain of preachers and experts on the fundamentals of religion, while legislation was in hands of scholars – and the difference between Shari'a and jurisprudence is vast and well known, especially since consensus is one of the sources of jurisprudential legislation, and the best way to draft laws is through *ijtihad* (independent religious interpretation). In any case, we now live in different times and have different experiences, meaning that there is no need to imitate or go the fundamentalist route, as the Islamists did, or make a total break, as our illustrious intellectuals did in the last phase. 'This is a people that have passed away; they shall have what they earned and you shall have what you earn, and you shall not be called upon to answer for what they did' (Sourat Al-Bakarah (The Cow), verse 134).

Retrieving clarity of vision

What interests us is the vision that best fits our nation's historical experience, which includes the Koran, the Prophet, the caliphate, the good, the wicked, the despots and the pious, and its own internal and general logic. It is a vision that says that the *umma* is the source of administrative, procedural and conventional power, and embraces the Koran, religion, Shari'a and their moral codes. Its relationship with the religious domain is different from its relationship with the political domain; for while religion is a free individual choice and no one has power in or on it, the religious ritualistic and moral public domain is rooted in moral guidance, *fatwas* (religious edicts) and education, the responsibility for which was historically and in modern time in the hands of religious institutions which, although not divine, were sometimes quite skilful. However, it was often in the hands of politicians, which is why the Islamists were able recently, and on several occasions, to challenge and transcend thanks to their popularity, new mass appeal, the poor relations between the people and the authorities, and the good standing that religious officials enjoy with these authorities, or their subservience to them.

The open and reformative Islamic vision of this new era in which the people have once again the right to manage their own affairs does not pass judgement on people except for what concerns their rights, interests and managerial acumen in safeguarding and improving the public utilities, and establishing institutions capable of protecting, managing and owning the administration. This is why it is natural for them to opt for modernity, constitutionalism, pluralism and democracy based on the principle of citizenship, which is what the revolutions' slogans have told us, and we read in the Al-Azhar document. As for the public administration of the religious domain, we should think about it differently in this age of freedom, and not be hasty in deeming an institution useless or a failure. What is required here is neither to sanctify nor to render infallible as the Catholics and Shia do, nor add cosmetics similar to the Protestants. What is required from and for the public administration of religious domain is freedom, renewal and the strength necessary in order to perform its four remaining responsibilities: leading prayers, issuing *fatwas*, religious education and general guidance, lest this drags us into a bigger problem, namely the fear that people in authority will regain control of religion and allow it to fall prey to the dogma, faith, *fatwas* and education of the partisan Islamists or religious hardliners who, for the past two years and well before, have challenged our beliefs, faith and customs, and disrespected people's rights and dignity.

Let us therefore think well about religion in the era of freedom, as Marcel Gauchet (2007) has said. Religion embraces and is embraced by the Muslim community, and the authorities, whether elected or unelected, have no right to interfere for or against it, because it is a matter of faith and as well as set of morals and values left to the individual's discretion. Religion is where these two options meet at public level, and the authorities' role is to safeguard and protect it, as Al-Mawardy said, as one of the people's basic rights and freedoms, and no more.

Conclusion

As explicated above, the wider perspective on our historic experience considers the *umma* as the main source of authority, or the source of the regime's legitimacy, as a whole. As long as the basis is clear, there is no need for fabrication or for reconciling between the visions of the Middle Ages and the modern era, like most theoreticians of the Islamic state have done in recent times. The most salient proof of that are the slogans raised by the revolutions' youths in favour of a modern political society and a civil state, which made the people go down with them to the streets. It was the period that followed the 'eternal' republican regimes, rather than the post-revolutionary period, that pushed political Islam to the fore and forced it to bring the issues of the previous stage out of its secret and open recesses, including alienation, ostracism, revivalism and tension, in order to reach and maintain power without reconsidering the theories of the pre-revolutionary period. This forced everyone, including friend and foe and those who are neither, to discuss these issues, issues that are in fact deep wounds in our identity, consciousness and reality. However, because public affairs and their management are of interest to the public, and it is an alert public, there is no fear for the state and the new political society in the middle term,[16] although – contrary to what most people think – there is fear for religion itself.

On the one hand, we have the bountiful populism of the Muslim Brotherhood and the thundering explosions of the Salafists, both of whom heavily and assiduously use religion to insert themselves into the state and the struggle over power, sometimes under the pretext of Islamizing the state and, at others, of amending people's religious beliefs and practices! Religion is at the heart of society, of its values and of its social, cultural and human fabric. On the other hand, the state's gut is hard and destructive and capable of dismembering religion, which divides and disperses our human society, not to mention the reaction it produces in the middle term against religiosity and the religious, and against other social and political groups.

During this historical period, therefore, the threat to religion comes from three different directions: first, from the claim that religion has a comprehensive political and economic system of its own; and second from the contention that Shari'a law should be implemented in order to correct or complete the doctrinal and legislative system, and implement its political and economic theories. The third direction is the appropriation of religion in the struggle over power, whereby a certain party asks citizens to vote for it because its religion is better and more correct, while another asks people to vote for it and adopt its programme because it is better from the religious point of view. Saying that Islam has its own governance system and own economy places too heavy a burden on the religion's shoulders. This fact became clear when, soon after Dr Mursi's election, the Brotherhood quickly called for a civil state, when they had spent an eternity disparaging the concept on the premise that people were confused between the terms 'civil' and 'secular'. The failure in the economic field also became apparent when they quickly abandoned the concept of Islamic economics and turned to the International Monetary Fund (IMF) for a loan. In the eyes of friends and allies, these two cases reveal a quick and positive ability to adapt, though the question remains as to what impact this will have on the partisan and religious public's consciousness.

The fear here does not come from the Brotherhood or the Salafists' doctrine (the latter having quickly formed political parties when they were once firmly against parties and elections) but from their astounding pragmatism, to say the least. It is a pragmatism that began with the comprehensive system theory that is directly linked to the vision of the state and the management of public affairs. Nevertheless, the thesis of 'implementing the Shari'a' is the most dangerous threat to religion. Ever since Hassan Al-Banna, the Islamists have sought to sidestep the secular process of separating between state and religion, a process that Sayed Qutob (2008) called 'peevish schizophrenia', although the 'implementation of Shari'a' does exactly the opposite since it separates Shari'a and religion from society, then re-imposes them using the state and its authority. This turns Shari'a into a despotic ideology, endows political power with a religious dimension and religious responsibilities, and claims that the faith and religion in today's state and society are wanting due to inadvertence, ignorance or apostasy, and should be reinstated. This unfolds at a time when God Almighty has said in *Surat* Al-Ma'eda: 3: 'This day have I perfected your religion for you, completed My favour upon you, and have chosen for you Islam as your religion [...].'

The question here is why did these revolutions break out? Did they break out in order to complete or implement the religion, or to reform and improve the management of public affairs? Neither Islam nor its Shari'a were as prevalent in old Muslim societies as they are in today's society; then why this persistent *prattle or idle talk* in visions and concepts? This prattle is a threat to religion and its Shari'a, to our societies, and to their religious and human well-being and their moral values. Is it a cultural revolution like Mao Zedong and Kim Il Song's Revolutions, with their inhumane absolutist claim? As to the overuse of religion in the religious and political struggle, or in the competition over power in the state and society, it managed in this short span of time to divide homes, families and groups in Tunisia, Libya, Egypt, Yemen and, perhaps, elsewhere to such an extent that we risk no longer praying together, believing in the same faiths or performing the same rites.

The above justifies neither the despotism of the past era nor the West's campaigns against Islam. There is also an overwhelming fear for the Islamic identity among large swathes of the population, as there is fear of Islam among many Arab and Muslim intellectuals, not to mention the societies that surround us and beyond. Professor Taha Abdel-Rahman (2011) published an important book on the philosophy of religion, entitled *Ruh al-Din* (The Spirit of Religion), in which he expresses the fear that secularism would, among other things, remove religion, its morality and impact not only from the state, but also from society as a whole. I do not know how this could happen as long as religion and its moral code remain deeply embedded in individuals, groups and societies, and maintain a direct or indirect influence, as has always been the case, on the state and society. Religion will also not be threatened by secularism or any other movement as long as we stay away from the Islamists' policies towards religion and society. Let us therefore leave political Islam behind so that our religion can maintain its serenity, unity, rituals and values, and remain the religion of the vast majority, as Imam Abu Hanifa said. As for our Islam-fearing intellectuals, although they have spent the last five decades trying to liberate us from Islam, and trying to liberate Islam from us, the recent revolutions have finally put these illusions to rest.

We have to admit, however, that we are in the middle of a stage in which concepts regarding our relationship with our religious and cultural heritage overlap and intertwine. We need a big step forward and work on raising public and cultural awareness about religion and its symbolism, which often takes on a ritualistic form. Under conditions of anxiety, the symbolic is mistaken for liturgical. The ritualistic, as well, masquerades as belief and, in times of great change, belief takes on the form of an absolute concept. The fact that the dark decades of the 20th century have divided the Islam of the majority, i.e. the Sunnis and ahlul Jamaa, into three warring groups: the Salafists, the Brotherhood and the Sufis, risks turning our one religion, under the authority's hegemony, into a multiplicity of religions and seeing its different currents engage in a violent internal conflict, just like the three hundred-year war between the Catholics and Protestants.

The saying goes that you should not count your eggs before they hatch; the reality is, however, that the eggs have already hatched, yet the people are divided round the issue into three groups: those who accept that the hatching did take place, but the eggs are still there; those who believe that the hatching has not yet taken place; and those who believe that there were no eggs to begin with.

Notes

1. Editor's Note: Upon his return from France, Al-Tahtawi published a book in which he reflected upon the issues facing Muslims by referring to France and what may be learned from it. The title of the book, *Takhlis al Ibirz fi Talkhis Paris*, is a reflection of the style and language of those days, but might best be translated as 'Refinement of Gold through Recapitulating Paris'.
2. For Al-Tahtawi's political ideas, see Al-Tahtawi (1834, 1872, 1847); these books have been published several times and readers are referred to Amara (1973–1977). Cf. Jad'an (1981) with al-Sayyid (1977) and Balqaziz (2004).
3. Cf. El-Tunisi (1867/1972) with al-Sayyid (1977) and Balqaziz (2004).
4. Cf. Amara (1972–1973), and work on intellectual and educational reform in his Part 3, with Abdo (2002) and Al-Haddad (2003), which was consulted for the author's general assessment; also cf. Balqaziz (2004, 48–52).
5. Cf. Abel-Razek (1925b, 82) with Kawtharani (1996) and Jad'an (1989); see also Al-Sayyid and Balqaziz (2001).
6. Cf. Moussa (1964) with al-Mubarak (1981); also cf. Al-Sayyid (2007) with Al-Sayyid and Balqaziz (2001).
7. Cf. Odeh (n.d.) with Al-Ayoubi (1992); see also Al-Qaradawi (2001).
8. Cf. Al-Sayyid (1977) with Balqaziz's (2004).
9. *Ilm al-Kalām* (Arabic: علم الكلام), literally the study of 'speech' or 'words', is the Islamic philosophical discipline of seeking theological principles through debates.
10. Cf. Yaseen (2008, pt 1).
11. Cf. Al-Sayyid (2011).
12. Cf. Repp (1989) and Al-Sayyid (1989); see also 'Waqf al-Nuqood' and discussions round the issue and its institutions in Arnaout (2011), the notion being in contrast to usury in Ottoman society; and on the role of Sheikh al-Islam Abi Saoud, see Zubaida (2007, 188–201).
13. Cf. from Shura and the developments in the manner of viewing it in Al-Sayyid (1994); and Ghanem (1993); and cf. Al-Sayyid (2006); see also Zubaida (2007).
14. Cf. Al-Qaradawi (1971) with Al-Qaradawi (2001), and (1988).
15. Cf. Al-Sayyid (2006); my opinion in somewhat different in that text. See also Ghalioun (1991).
16. Some researchers believe that 'the presence of religion everywhere' does not prevent the transition to democracy due to the people's new and keen awareness of their rights; cf. Roy (2012).

References

Abdel-Fattah, Nabil. 1984. *Al Mushaf wal Saif, Sira' al-Deen wal Dawla fi Misr* [The Holy Book and the Sword, The Struggle between Religion and the State in Egypt]. Cairo: Madbouli Bookshop.

Abdel-Rahman, Taha. 2011. *Ruh al-Deen, min Deeq al-Ilmaniya ila Si'at al-I'timaniya* [The Spirit of Religion from the Narrow Confines of Secularism to the Wide Spaces of Affiliation]. Beirut: Arab Cultural Centre.

Abel-Razek, Ali. 1925a. *Islam wa Usool al-Hukm* [Islam and the Fundamentals of Governance]. Al-Mansoura.

Abdel-Razek, Ali. 1925b. *Risala la Hukm. Wa Deen la Dawla* [A Message Not a Rule, and a Religion Not a State]. Cairo: Matba'at Misr.

Abdo, Mohammad. 2002. *Al-Islam baynal 'Ilm wal Madaniya* [Islam Amidst Science and Civilization]. Damascus: Dar al-Mada.

Abu Fares, and Mohammad Abdel-Kader. 1999. *Al-Fiqh al-Siyasi 'indal Imam al-Shaheed Hassan al-Banna* [The Political Jurisprudence of the Martyr Imam Hassan Al-Banna]. Amman: Dar Ammar.

Al-Ayoubi, Nazih. 1992. *Al-Arab wa Mushkilat al-Dawla* [The Arabs and the Issue of Statehood]. Beirut: Al-Saqi.

Amara, Mohammad, ed. 1972–1973. *Al-A'mal al-Kamila li-Mohammad Abdo* [The Complete Works of Mohammad Abdo, 5 pts]. Beirut: Arab Institute for Studies and Publication.

Amara, Mohammad. 1973–1977. *Al-A'mal al-Kamila lil-Tahtawi* [The Complete Works of Tahtawi]. Beirut: Arab Institute for Studies and Publication.

Arnaout, Mohammad, 2011. *Dirasat fi Waqf al-Nuqood* [Studies on the Consecration of Funds]. Beirut: Dar Jadawel, 2011.

Al-Ayoubi, Nazih. 1994. *Overstating of the Arab State*. Beirut: Saqi Books/Dar al-Saqi.

Balqaziz, Abdel-ilah. 2004. *Al-Dawla fil-Fikr al-Islami al-Mu'aser* [The State in Modern Islamic Thought]. 2nd ed. Beirut: Centre for Arab Unity Studies (CAUS).

Chamseddin, Mohammad Mahdi. 1992. *Fil-Ijtima' al-Siyasi al-Islami: al-Mujtama' al-Siyasi al-Islami, Muhawalat Ta'seel Fiqhi* [Islamic Political Thought: Islamic Political Society: An Attempt at Entrenching Jurisprudence]. Beirut: Al-Moassasat al-Duwaliyya lil-Dirasaat wal-Nashr.

Gauchet, Marcel. 2007. *Religion in Democracy*. Translated into Arabic by Shafiq Muhsen. Beirut: Al-Munazzama al-Arabiya lil-Tarjama.

Ghalioun, Burhan. 1991. *Naqd al-Siyasa, al-Dawla wal Deen* [Critiquing Politics, the State and Religion]. Beirut: Arab Institute for Studies and Publication.

Ghanem, Ibrahim B. 1993. "Review of Tawfic al-Chawi's *Jurisprudence of Shura and Consultation*." *Ijtihad Magazine*, 6 (25): 267–278.

Al-Ghannouchi, Rached. 1993. Al-Hurriyat al-Aamah fil Dawla al-Islamiya [Public Freedoms in the Islamic State]. Beirut: Centre for Arab Unity Studies (CAUS).

Al-Haddad, Mohammad. 2003. *Kira'a Jadida fi Islah al-Khitab al-Dini [A New Perspective in Reforming Religious Discourse]*. Beirut: Dar al-Tali'a lil Tiba'a wal Nashr.

Jad'an, Fahmi. 1981. *Usul al-Taqaddum 'inda Mufakiri al-Islam fil-Asr al-Hadith* [The Bases of Progress of Islam's Modern Day Intellectuals]. Beirut: Al-Mu'assasa Al-Arabiyyah lil-Dirassaat wal-Nashr.

Jad'an, Fahmi. 1989. "Nathariyat al-Dawla fil Fikr al-Islami al-Mu'aser" [State Theories in Contemporary Islamic Thought]. In *The Politics of Arab Integration*, vol. 1, 107–138, edited by Ghassan Salameh and Giacomo Luciani. Beirut: Centre for Arab Unity Studies (CAUS).

Al-Joueini, Abu-l-Ma'ali. 1400 *hijri* [2 December 1978 – 21 November 1979]. *Ghiath al-Umam fi Iltiath al-Thulam* [The Relief of Nations through Eradicating Injustice], edited by Abdel-'Atheem Al-Deeb. Qatar: Qatar University.

Kawtharani, Wajih. 1996. *Al-Dawla wal Khilafa fil Khitab al-Arabi Iban al-Thawra al-Kamaliya* [State and Khilafa in Arab Thought at the Time of the Kamalist Revolution]. Beirut: Dar al-Tali'a.

Al-Mawdudi, Abu El-A'la. 1960. *Nahnu wal Hadara al-Garbiya* [US and Western Civilisation]. Beirut: Dar al-Fikr.

Al-Mawdudi, Abu El-A'la. 1968. *Nathariyat al-Islam fil Siyasa wal Qanoon wal Dustour* [Islam's Theory in a Political, Legal and Constitutional Sphere]. Beirut: Dar al-Fikr.

Al-Mawdudi, Abu El-A'la. 2000. *Al-Islam wal Jahiliya* [Islam and the Jahilya Period]. Beirut: Dar al-Fikr.

Al-Mawdudi, Abu El-A'la. n.d. *Al-Khilafa wal Mulk* [Khilafa and Kingship]. Kuwait: Dar el-Kalam.

Al-Mubarak, Mohammad. 1981. *Nitham al-Islam, al-Hukm wal Dawla* [The Islamic System, Governance and the State]. 4th ed. Beirut: Dar al-Fikr.

Moussa, Youssef. 1964. *Nitham al-Huokm fil Islam* [The Governance System in Islam]. Cairo: Dar el-Ma'rifa.

Odeh, Abdel-Kader. n.d. *Al-Islam wa Awda'una al-Siyasiya* [Islam and Our Political Condition]. 7th ed. Beirut: Al-Risala Institute.

Al-Qaradawi, Yousef. 1971. *Al-Hulul al-Mustawrada wa Kayfa Janat ala Ummatina* [Imported Solutions and How They Hurt Our Ummah]. Beirut: Al-Risala Institute.

Al-Qaradawi, Yousef. 1988. *Al-Siyassa al-Shar'iyyah fi Daou' Noussus al-Shari'a wa Makacidiha* [Shari'a Politics in Light of Shari'a Texts and their Objectives]. Cairo: Maktabat Wehbeh.

Al-Qaradawi, Yousef. 2001. *Min Fiqh al-Dawla fil-Islam* [State Jurisprudence in Islam]. Cairo: Dar al-Shorouq.

Qutob, Sayed. 2008. *Al-Mustaqbal li hathal Deen* [This Religion's Future], 18th printing. Cairo: Dar al-Shurouk.

Qutob, Sayed. 1993. *Muqawemat al-Tasawor al-Islami* [Constituent Elements of the Islamic Vision]. 4th ed. Cairo: Dar Al-Shorouk.

Qutob, Sayed. 1995. *Maalem fil Tareeq* [Landmarks on the Road]. Cairo: Dar al-Shorouq.

Al-Rayyes, Mohammad Dia'eddin. 1979. *Al-Nathariyat al-Siyasiya al-Islamiya* [Islamic Political Theories]. 7th ed. Cairo: Dar el-Tourath.

Repp, Richard. 1989. "Qanoon and Sharia in the Ottoman context–Translated by Ridwan Al-Sayyid. *Ijtihad Magazine*, 2: 153–173.

Rida, Muhammad Rashid. 1922. *Al-Khilafa aw al-Imama al-Ozma* [The Caliphate or Grand Imamate].

Roy, Olivier. 2012. "The transformation of the Arab world." *Journal of Democracy*, 23 (3): 1–20.

Al-Sayyid, Ridwan. 1977. *Siyasat al-Islam al-Mu'asir* [Politics of Contemporary Islam]. Beirut: Dar al-Kitab al-Arabi.

Al-Sayyid, Ridwan. 1989. "Mufti Istanbul - Dirasat fi Thuhoor Mansab Sheikh el-Islam fi al-Dawla al-Uthmaniyya [Mufti of Istanbul – a Study of the Emergence of the Position of a Mufti for the State]". Review of the *Mufti of Istanbul*, by Richard C. Repp. *Ijtihad* 1(3): 239–245.

Al-Sayyid, Ridwan. 1994. "Mas'alat al-Shura wal Nuzoo' al-Imbaratory fi Daou' al-Tajriba al-Tarikhiya lil-Ummah." [The Shura Question and the Emperor Trend in Light of the Ummah's Historic Experience]. *Ijtihad Magazine*, 6 (25): 29–44.

Al-Sayyid, Ridwan. 1997. *Al-Sira' alal Islam* [The Struggle Over Islam]. Beirut: Dar al-Kitab al-Arabi.

Al-Sayyid, Ridwan. 2006. "The Islamic political thought crisis." In *Azmat al-Fikr al-Siyasi al-Arabi* [The Arab Political Thought Crisis], edited by Ridwan Al-Sayyid and Abdel-Ilah Balqaziz's. 2nd ed., 19–21. Damascus: Dar al-Fikr.

Al-Sayyid, Ridwan. 2007a. "Al-Deen wal Dunya, wal Deen wal Dawla fil Islam al-Mu'aser" [Religion and the world and religion and the state in contemporary Islam]." *Omani Tasamoh Magazine,* 19: 12–22.

Al-Sayyid, Ridwan. 2007b. ""Al-Mu'assassa al-Deiniya baynal Ihya'iyat was Sulutat" [The religious institution between the revivalist movements and the authorities]." *Omani Tasamoh Magazine* 20: 128–156.

Al-Sayyid, Ridwan. 2011. "Politics and *Sharia*, politics and legitimacy and *Sharia* and the law." In *Al-Jawhar al-Nafees fi Siyasat al-Ra'ees* [The Valuable Jewel in the President's Policies], edited by Ibn Al-Haddad, 51–61. Beirut: Ibn Al-Azraq Centre.

Al-Sayyid, Ridwan, and Balqaziz Abdel-Ilah. 2001. *Azmat al-Fikr al-Siyasi al-Arabi* [The Arab Political Thought Crisis]. Damascus, Dar al-Fikr.

Al-Tahtawi, Rifa'a. 1834. *Takhlis Al-Ibriz* ....

Al-Tahtawi, Rifa'a. 1847. *Manahij al-Albab al-Misriya fi Mabahij al-Adab al-Asriya* [Egyptian Core Curricula in the Best of Modern Literature].

Al-Tahtawi, Rifa'a. 1872. *Al-Murshid al-Amin lil-Banat wal Banin* [The Faithful Guide for Boys and Girls].

El-Tunisi, Eddin Khair. 1867/1972. *Aqwam al-Masalik fi Ma'rifat Ahwal al-Mamalik* [A Straightforward Methodology to Learn about Kingdoms], edited by Al-Munsef al-Chnoufi. Tunis: Al-Dar al-Tunisiya.

El-Tunisi, Eddin Khair. 1867/1972. "Introduction." In *Aqwam al-Masalik fi Ma'rifat Ahwal al-Mamalik* [A Straightforward Methodology to Learn about Kingdoms], edited by Al-Munsef al-Chnoufi, 49–53. Tunis: Al-Dar al-Tunisiya.

Umleil, A. 1985. *Al-Islahiya Al-Arabiya wal Dawla al-Wataniya* [Arab Reform and the National State]. Beirut: Dar a-Tanweer.

Wathikat al-Azhar Hawla Mustaqbal Misr [Azhar Document on the Future of Egypt]. 19 June 2011. Accessed April 3, 2013. http://onazhar.com/page2home2.php?page=3&page1=5&page2=39/.

Yaseen, Abdel-Jawad. 2008. *Al-Sulta fil Islam* [Authority in Islam]. Beirut: Arab Cultural Centre.

Zakariya, Barraq. 2012. *Al Dawla wal-Shari'a fi-l-Fikr-il-Arabi-l-Islami-l-Mu'asser* [State and Shari'a in Modern Arab and Islamic Thought]. Beirut: Markaz-il-Hadara li-Tanmiyat-il Fikr il-Islami.

Zubaida, Sami. 2007. *Law and Power in the Islamic World*. Translated by Abbas Abbas. Beirut: Dar Al-Madar al-Islami.

Approaches to reforming contemporary religious discourse[†]

Ahmad Kamal Abou Al-Majd

Professor of Law and Member of The Islamic Research Board at Al-Azhar

This article attempts to attenuate the exaggerated polarization in contemporary religious discourse in Egyptian society emanating from two flawed positions: a wrong conception of 'applying Shari'a'; and a wrong intention whereby deliberate cultural exclusion is practised to eradicate any religious orientation. The main subject of this article are manifestations of deviation of this discourse from the orientation of the original frame of reference of religion: (1) The call for Islam through scaring and intimidation; (2) the tendency to be tough on people, thus increasing obligatory duties and decreasing what is permissible; (3) inattention to the objectives of Shari'a and focusing on its literal aspect; (4) inattention to priorities; (5) belittling the role of the mind in Islamic conceptualization; (6) immersion in the past; and (7) Muslims' relationship with others. Nevertheless, rationalizing 'religious discourse' and working out a kind of consensus seems to be of utmost importance.

Introduction

The subject of this paper is the contemporary religious discourse currently widespread in Egypt, as well as more generally in Arab and Muslim countries. The discourse has flourished amidst expressions of anxiety emanating from different circles about the phenomenon of the ascent of representatives of the Islamic movement to positions of political power. The concern here is that this ascent may affect political and social life in many Arab and Islamic countries, including the future of non-Muslim minorities therein. The phenomenon is perceived as a serious danger to the future of national consensus and stability. The potential danger ought not be underestimated, especially if it portends confrontations which consume time and energy, and opens the door for foreign plans intended to weaken, or even abort, the role of Egypt and of many Arab and Islamic countries in a way that could ultimately endanger the independence of these countries.

Before sending this study to the Symposium on Religion and the State in the Arab World, I wondered about the appropriateness of the choice of the subject of research, namely: contemporary religious discourse, during a critical stage in the history of the Arab world. Yet this hesitance dissipated as I noticed, together with many researchers,

---

[†]This paper was presented at the Symposium on Religion and the State in the Arab World, convened by the Center for Arab Unity Studies (CAUS) and the Swedish Institute of Alexandria in Al-Hammamaat, Tunisia, October 2012.

the renewed escalation of the effect of the religious discourse within the general political and cultural context that prevails in Egypt and the Arab and Islamic worlds. Nevertheless, I feared that the timing of my address might give rise to suspicions about the motives behind it. Some may deem it an impermissible acceptance of blatant foreign intervention in our most particular cultural and religious matters. They may see it also as a tacit acceptance of the cultural hegemony on the part of one or more big powers trying to extend their influence on others, thus claiming legitimacy in determining the 'terminology' and the objective constituents of the cultures of others.

I would like to remind the reader that, together with many writers, and those who have preceded us, I have been critiquing, for more than 20 years, some representations of the prevailing religious discourse. Those of us interested in culture, and religious discourse in particular, have been continuously critiquing the content of the prevailing discourse and the approach of those in charge of it; perceiving a genuine need for this critique and review. For example, on my part, over the years I have published, in Egyptian and Arab newspapers, around 20 articles that focus on religious debate and its properties. They also focus on elements of stagnation or excess in some representations of the prevalent religious discourse in our homeland. In addition, they highlight the necessity of revising this discourse, and in the process correcting the understanding of many of those in charge of it, to relate to Islam itself – dogma, morality, Shari'a – and clarifying for them the relevance of this revision to Islam. These writings concomitantly call for renovating Islamic thought, in general, and *Al-Fiqh* or Islamic jurisprudence in particular. Here, I am keen to emphasize that mine is one amongst many opinions on this current discourse.

Before specifying the approaches to reforming contemporary religious discourse, this study will proceed by specifying what is meant by religious discourse and by observing the main deficiencies or distortions in contemporary discourse.

This is not meant to be in connection with the religious 'text', be it the Qu'ran or the *Sunnah*. The Book of God is the word of God Almighty; it is all truth, all wisdom and all light. It is saved and remembered by the will of God Almighty. This is called to attention in the honoured verse from Sourat Al-Hajar interpreted as (*We have, without doubt, sent down the Message; and We will assuredly guard it (from corruption)*).[1] The *Hadith* of the Messenger of God (ﷺ) is as well a revelation where the meaning comes from God Almighty and the expression from the Messenger of God (ﷺ) who is bestowed with the gift of speech. Yet all texts need *tafseer* (explanation) ruled by methodological controls that have to be undertaken to avoid subjectivity and lack of insight. A vast discourse on *tafseer* had taken place during the age of Sadr Al Islam, and a good part has been going on during the past few years. It all revolves around 'the text' and the attempt to constrain it with the historical context within which it had been revealed to the Prophet (ﷺ). Through *tafseer*, the specialists and scholars explore the 'objectives' of the texts, which enables fitting the ruling mentioned in the texts to the contemporary or renewing facts. This grants texts permanent validity and eternal meanings through the 'renovation' that the *Hadith* or sayings of the Prophet (ﷺ) had pointed to. In his collection of the *Sunnah*, Abu Dahoud narrated that 'God sends to this *umma* at the beginning of every hundred years, one who renews the matters of its religion'. Upon enquiry, this does not necessitate that the one who renews is one person showing up once every hundred years; it can well be that renovation is the work of a group, or a scholarly or religious school; meanwhile the work need not be limited to one year every hundred years.

The religious discourse upon which I focus here is that of advocates, preachers, orators, muftis and researchers, when presented to the public as rectifying the sound description and the right understanding of Islam including its dogma, moral system, literature and its Shari'a or laws. Defined thus, this religious discourse has a major role in the formation of the 'Muslim mind' and conscience wherein the public gets its perception of Islam, and the world in its light. The importance of rationalizing this discourse increases when two things, which are common for almost all Islamic countries, are taken into consideration. The first is widespread illiteracy, and religious illiteracy in particular. This hinders connection with the sources of proper religious knowledge, and the approved references of *Tafseer* (interpretation of the Qu'ran), the sciences of *Hadith* (explaining the sayings of the Prophet; ﷺ), *Syrah* (knowledge about the life of the Prophet; ﷺ), and *Fiqh* (jurisdiction). This illiteracy makes religious discourse, the way we have defined it, the major, if not the only, source of religious knowledge, and mainly responsible for mapping 'religiosity' and shaping the 'pious' for individuals, community and the other. The second commonality is the ever-growing wave of religiosity, in protest against contemporary materialism and the accompanying deterioration in the 'type' of prevailing human relations, together with corruption within intra-group relations and the international community. This deterioration is one of the causes of phenomenal egoism and individual and collective violence which take various forms in accordance with the variations of its domains; from individual and governmental violence, to terrorism – national and international – to civil, regional and international wars.

In addition to protest, this wave of religiosity expresses a renewed keenness on connecting to the roots and basic rules of belief, culture and conduct. These latter are seen to determine 'identity', emphasize the meaning of cultural 'specificity', and facilitate a distinct sense of belongingness to a certain culture and specific *umma* (nation). Moreover, religiosity, when associated with its basic rules of belief and conduct, and when it understands these rules well, and employs them right, is a phenomenon worth observance and encouragement. It is a source of guidance for the individual, and discipline for the group. It encourages goodness and reform, and guards against committing corruption and corrupting others. Eventually, it leads to an enhancement of humaneness within a community, and between different communities within the international system. This ascension of humaneness, facilitates cooperation, invests in human diversity, helps respect the rights of individuals and groups, and opens the door to social and world peace. But, when religiosity deviates from its basic rules, and when it detaches from its frame of reference, even if by good intentions it becomes a flawed religiosity. This leads the individual and community into mental and emotional states far removed from the conception that 'religion' intends to nurture. Besides, religion is an appeal, a call and a discourse whose aims come into effect in the people to the extent that they respond rightly to this call and appeal: (*but if they had done what they were (actually) told, it would have been best for them, and would have gone farthest to strengthen their (faith)*).[2]

By reviewing the current religious discourse which determines the image of the modern devout, it becomes evident that there are seven manifestations of deviation of this discourse from the orientation of the fixed frame of reference of religion. The religion I am referring to in this study is 'Islam' that has been known through its main sources: the Holy Qu'ran, the *Sunnah* and *Syrah* of the Prophet (ﷺ). The *Syrah* is an embodiment of the Revelation as exemplified in the life and the human conduct of the Prophet (ﷺ); this being to make it easy for people, during His life, and after Him, to realize the guidance in the Book and *Sunnah* – within the creed and through following the Shari'a.

The seven manifestations of this deviation are the main subject of this presentation. I believe that the best way to reform contemporary religious discourse is to go through each of these manifestations; meanwhile showing, as much as possible, the extent of their deviation from the sound approach to understanding Islam, figuring out its dogma and establishing its order in society.

Before discussing the manifestations of deviation, it goes without saying that it is a mistake to generalize when making a judgment, and that the 'discourse' of some preachers, writers and muftis is free from such deviation. These have provided Islam – and its practice – with a bright image linked to the basic rules, responsive to people's needs, and aware of the changes that took place in the world around them; changes that have been imposed by an intertwined human development in multiple fields. Nevertheless, I as well as many others think that the predominant image of contemporary religious discourse needs criticism and a calm revision, free from exaggeration and dramatization.

The first element: scaring and intimidation

The first element of contemporary religious discourse, the most widespread and the one most in need of revision is the call for Islam through scaring and intimidation. Among the repercussions of this defect is the driving of many religious people to embark on religiosity 'scared' and frightened, pursued by cries of stern warning of painful and humiliating agony awaiting them on Doomsday. This resort to scare tactics fills souls with anxiety, and denies them tranquillity and contentment. It may equally hinder them from good constructive work, which is the Muslims' message in this world and their way to happiness in afterlife; the reason being that the panicky and fearful are not fit to build up great civilizations and assume responsibility for this construction. Violating this approach to a rightful Islam cannot be a matter of controversy, as the Prophet (ﷺ) – like other Prophets and messengers – have been sent by God as witness, preacher and harbinger, who calls for God – by His permission – and is a guiding light. He (ﷺ) is a witness that the words of God had reached people, that He had reminded them of His blessings and verses, and that He promises them success in life and the good reward in the Hereafter. Beyond that, he is as well a harbinger reminding them of the consequences of arrogance and ingratitude despite warning, proof of argument, and clarification of the truth (*And they rejected those Signs in iniquity and arrogance, though their souls were convinced thereof*);[3] (*that mankind, after (the coming) of the Messengers, should have no plea against Allah*).[4]

Thus, Islam has always combined reward and intimidation to urge souls and minds to adopt rightness, establish justice, and seek goodness for people. So it is no longer the right of anyone to make intimidation the only tool of this urging, and the sole approach in calling for belief and setting up Islam. Moreover, overlooking the approach of reward means overlooking God's compassion and forgiveness; for He the Almighty, is the Merciful, the Loving and Loved, the Forgiving, the Relenting … And He is the one who tells his worshipers: (*Say: 'O my Servants who have transgressed against their souls! despair not of the Mercy of Allah: for Allah forgives all sins: for He is Oft-Forgiving, Most Merciful*);[5] and He, the Almighty, says: (*but My Mercy extendeth to all things*).[6] And our Prophet (ﷺ) has told us about the Glorious God Almighty saying in a *Hadith* Kudsi: '*O son of Adam, if you bring me all the flasks in the world full of sins, I shall bring you its flasks full of forgiveness*'. Given all this, no one has the right – despite his goodwill – to adopt the Book partially, and spread amongst the believers an atmosphere of fear, intimidation and panic. This diminishes the meaning of 'being close to God', 'cheering up through knowing him' and 'heading towards his love'; all emanating from His grace Almighty – as the *Hadith* says. Calling people to God through intimidation only is not a rightful approach to Islam. Its consequences may not be evident to the preacher, mufti or adviser; yet the result is having panic replace reassurance, and fear block the sense of security and satisfaction which are states of true belief and its effect on the soul: (*O assured self. Return satisfied and satisfying to your Lord*);[7] and (*God blessed them and they were satisfied by Him*).[8]

Temptation, together with preaching, remains the main way to attract souls to righteousness. In most people they are effective like magic, and spread within souls an atmosphere of peace of mind, tranquillity and contentment. They make the rivers of goodness flow towards Him, based on a main reality and belief that God has created his worshipers 'good' according to *Hadith* Kudsi. And when the rivers of goodness flow, the energy for work, creativity and construction flows; these are major aims of human existence on this planet (*It is He Who hath produced you from the earth and settled you therein*).[9] It is only fear that brings in deterioration and contraction, whereas tranquillity and assuredness bring in motion, progress and boom.

The second element: the tendency to be tough on people

The essence of being tough is: increasing obligatory duties and decreasing what is permissible; in addition to choosing the toughest matters, most arduous and most likely to invite embarrassment, when there exists an alternative that can avoid embarrassment and bring in ease. The hardliners – at all times – have a misperception of their mission and its limits; they imagine themselves guardians of religion and of people; this is why they are in a continuous anxiety that easing up on God's worshipers may lead into a departure from the boundaries of God and the rules of Shari'a. They also forget that they are advocates and messengers, not guardians of anyone. Obedience and disobedience remain vested in individuals and the assignees who will be asked about it while within the hands of their Creator who taught them that (*Let there be no compulsion in religion: Truth stands out clear from Error*).[10] His Prophet (ﷺ) had taught them as well that what they encounter on the Day of Judgment is no more than the fruit of their deeds 'being returned to them'.

Hardliners imagine that their strictness may push away evil and deviousness, and close the door to excuses for evading the rules of Shari'a. They even forget that locking out excuses is a secondary (stand by) source for jurisprudence and *fatwa*; and that as it locks out evil, it opens up the doors of goodness. They forget as well that the reference for allowing or prohibiting actions and behaviours is the Creator Almighty; and that being austere to the extent of getting close to 'prohibiting what is *Halal*' (allowed by God) is not less sinful than 'allowing the prohibited'. This is evident in His saying Almighty: (*But say not – for any false thing that your tongues may put forth – 'This is lawful, and this is forbidden'*).[11]

Austerity, above all, may bring people under the impression that obedience to God is arduous, and that religiosity is tough and laborious, which may tempt many to 'give up totally on Shari'a' as Ibn Qayyem Al Jawziyyah says. Strictness, in reality, is the easier jurisprudence and not the best one. The fact of the matter is as the reputable jurist Sufiyaan Al Thaouri (God bless his soul) said: 'knowledge is not in austerity – this, everyone is good at. Knowledge is the easy and confident.' The *Hadith* of the Prophet (ﷺ) mentions that people have to do easy as well as tough things that God Almighty may bring about.

The advocates, mosque preachers, speakers and muftis need to know without any doubt, obstinacy or controversy that the rules of Islam have been built on facilitation, relief and eliminating hardship; not on making things arduous, embarrassing and toilsome. This comes from the fundamentals of Islam that are deemed unquestionable through many texts in the Qu'ran and *Hadith*. God Almighty says justice: (*Allah intends every facility for you; He does not want to put you to difficulties*);[12] and He says: (*He has chosen you, and has imposed no difficulties on you in religion*).[13] He also says: (*For the present, Allah hath lightened your (task), for He knoweth that there is a weak spot in you*).[14] In description of the mission of our Prophet (ﷺ) He says: (*he releases them from their heavy burdens and from the yokes that are upon them*);[15] He also teaches Muslims that the approach of Islam for determining the permissible and the prohibited is an approach of making life easier for people, alleviation of their burdens, and pardoning many deeds and behaviours.

The Almighty says: (*O ye who believe! ask not questions about things which, if made plain to you, may cause you trouble. But if ye ask about things when the Quran is being revealed, they will be made plain to you, Allah will forgive those: for Allah is Oft-Forgiving, Most Forbearing*).[16] In indication to the meaning of this verse the Prophet (ﷺ) says in a *Hadith* told by Al Hakem citing Abi Al Darda': 'What God made permissible in His Book, is permissible, and what He had made prohibited is sinful, and what He has been silent about meant pardon, so accept from God His perfection, as God is not to forget anything.' Then he recited His saying Almighty: (*And never is your Lord forgetful*).[17] Aisha (God bless her) describes the approach of the Prophet (ﷺ) in jurisprudence in her saying: 'Whenever the Prophet (ﷺ) had been given the choice between two things, He had chosen the easier provided it was not a sin', as He was the most distant from it.

In comparing which is better – being strict on people or easing matters for them – two things have to be taken into consideration. The first is the content of the message of Islam, and the second is the main rules of advocating Islam and the approach to this advocacy.

The content of the message of Islam relates to determining the position of the Muslim individual and the Muslim community on life. In some samples of contemporary Arab discourse, there exists a peculiar call for being at odds with life, an incitement to asceticism, turning away from life and describing it as a rotten dead body, labelling those who seek it as despicable. This advocacy may distract the Muslim public from engagement with life, the pursuit of building the world, and competing for pioneering and leadership positions. It is a call contradictory to the clear advocacy of Islam for useful work and toiling in search of a livelihood and achieving the balance referred to by the two verses in His saying Almighty: (*But seek, with the (wealth) which Allah has bestowed on thee, the Home of the Hereafter, nor forget thy portion in this World*),[18] and His saying on behalf of the good believers: (*And there are men who say: 'Our Lord! Give us good in this world and good in the Hereafter, and defend us from the torment of the Fire!'*).[19]

Commendable asceticism is the one associated with power, not with helplessness; and the true believer is the one who works for his life as if he will live forever, and for his afterlife as if he will die tomorrow. The right Islamic approach is the one full of hope, optimism, looking forward to the future, and preparing for it. This is the meaning expressed in *Hadith*, yet few are the times that its reader notices its considerable connotation of the positive position of Islam on life. The Prophet (ﷺ) says: '*If one of you has to leave this life while he is holding a palm shoot in his hand, and could manage to plant it, then he will be rewarded*' (*Hadith*).

Islam, here, does not set Muslims in conflict with life, and the right Muslim does not detest people and this world, nor does he spend his life in a fictitious battle against its powers and rules. This cannot be the case when they are made by God who had created everything well, then He gave guidance. Besides, how can this be the case when, unlike afterlife, this is the place for work and the land of trial! Moreover, how can this be the position of a Muslim on life where God bestowed on him His blessings – be they visible or not – and created for him everything that exists in life, then called upon him to build it using the power of the mind and work; and loved to see from him, among other things, the effect of His blessing on him.

The position of a Muslim on life is an extremely important issue that has to be noticed by those working on religious discourse; a defect in this regard opens a main door to perversion amongst some young groups that embark upon religiosity by withdrawing from society. In isolation, they are instructed to hate life and hate people, and they set up a psychological cold war in which they put on trial those who differ from them. And away from the light of knowledge and tolerance, there comes into being disengagement from society, accusation of contemporary people with infidelity, and characterization of this age as akin to pre-Islamic paganism. These are serious scourges that celebrated scientists have warned against; in this Ibn El Kayyem says:

> This is why accusing the Moslem of infidelity and sins should be avoided, as this is the first heresy that had appeared in Islam. Thus those who had accused Muslims of infidelity have absolved themselves from laying their hands on the blood and money of Muslims; they called their homeland the homeland of Hijrat, and rendered the homeland of Muslims a homeland of disbelief and war.

As for the approach to the advocacy, it is necessary to take into account the conditions of those being addressed; otherwise the message of the advocate will not reach them especially that it does not touch upon their reality or relate to their concerns and preoccupations. This is what we call 'individualization of *fatwa*' and 'individualization of jurisdiction'; that is, the ruling should respond to the state of the inquirer, his capabilities and his circumstances. This has been the Prophet's approach (ﷺ) in *fatwa* and jurisdiction. One good example is permitting the Ethiopians to dance and sing at the house of prophecy, or close to His mosque. When Omar contested that, He did not accept his contention but He (ﷺ) referred to him saying: 'Let them Omar.' He (ﷺ) also permitted his wife Aisha to look at them until she felt sufficed. She (may God be pleased with her) noticed that He (ﷺ) had done that out of consideration to her young age then; so she said, according to Bukhari and Moussallem, 'Take into account the young girl keen on amusement.' I wonder whether the hardliners notice these sublime humane meanings; can they facilitate as much as their prophet (ﷺ) has therein? He (ﷺ) even said to Aisha, after she had been to a wedding of a girl to a man from the Ansar clan: '*Aisha, amongst them, was it amusing? The Ansar are a folk who like fun*' (*Hadith*).

Tailoring a *fatwa* according to the circumstances of the inquirer is a fundamentalist or proper approach attributed by some scholars to custom – as a complementary source for Shari'a rulings. In this respect, the famous Hanafi jurist Ibn Aabdeen says:

> Many rulings vary with time due to change in custom, development of new needs, or corruption. Thus, if jurisdiction remains unchanged, it will lead into trouble and harm for people, and will violate the rules of Shari'a which is based on alleviation, facilitation, and avoiding harm and corruption.

This rule of facilitation has been expressed by a reliable contemporary jurist as follows: 'Nowadays, he chooses the most facilitating not the most prudent.'[20]

The third element noticed in the prevailing religious discourse is inattention to the objectives of Shari'a and being content with the surface aspect of texts and letters

This pure textual approach, which pays no attention to the objectives, is called by some 'excess' or an error of 'Salafism' – a word we tend not to use within this context because it has several connotations. It was used by Ibn Taymiyyah and others, in the realm of dogmas and theology, in reference to the approach of commitment to the Qu'ranic texts involving the issue of doctrine. These are texts that repudiate any similarity between the Creator Almighty and His creatures. Here the authors do not emulate philosophers, some of whom express ideas about analogy, embodiment or pantheism – which is the unity of existence whereby the creator and created merge. As for the area of Shari'a and the ensuing jurisprudence, Ibn Taymiyyah had liberated himself from the literal approach. He had reached wonderful interpretations through his vision of the objectives which underpinned texts. The historians of *Fiqh* – jurisprudence – considered him amongst the modernizers; they even considered him the leader of modernizers. As for those with a narrow literal view of Qu'ranic and prophetic texts, they mistrust every faith or jurisprudence calling for modernization and employing reason in understanding texts, explaining them, and applying their ruling to the continuously renewed facts. Their justification is that this opens the door to whimsical jurisdiction, and that a good Muslim is a follower rather than an innovator. This is not a tenable argument; 'following' – to which we were commanded – means following the clear sighted wise people, not the driven imitators. Moreover, the innovation from which we have been banned, is introducing into religion what is alien to it as a supplement or omission, or unknowingly attributing a saying to God.

As for commendable innovation, it is the product of jurisprudence employing inductive methodology and using several texts. This has to be in light of an awareness of their overall objectives, and an understanding of the public interests which are expressed in writing or kept unfettered whereby the jurists take pride in interpreting. The nation, based on the work of these jurists, aims to achieve these interests without departure from a definitive text, meanwhile dropping those interests that are not valued by the public.

The issue of objectives is rightly expressed by Imam Al Shatibi in his endorsements (Endorsements in the Rules of Jurisdiction): 'all the obligations of Shari'a go back to achieving its objectives in the created …'. He – God bless his soul – also details these objectives in respect to guardianship of religion, oneself, offspring, honour and money. Concomitantly, he establishes the interests related to these objectives, in a descending order going from necessities, to needs, to improvements (luxuries).

Knowing the jurisprudents' decision on how to guard these interests is indispensible for those working in religious discourse. These interests have varying statuses – and hence a method is needed to reconcile them in case of conflict; thus helping the jurist, mufti or judge provide priorities in case they compete. So, jurisprudents have set up various rules in this regard, the most prominent of which is the well known rule which prioritizes 'avoiding harm' over 'gaining an advantage' in any matter. Some examples of this rule are as follows:

- The confirmed interest is given priority to the unconfirmed one.
- The interest of the community is given priority over that of the individual.
- The interest of the majority is prioritized over that of the minority.
- The long-run interest has priority over that of a transient or temporary one.

It is surprising how some dismiss these principles which are dictated by logic, prudence and intuition, especially when the Holy Qu'ran guides us to this approach. This approach includes rules of worshipping, though absolute obedience is the main rule, in compliance with His, the Almighty, saying: (*It is not fitting for a Believer, man or woman, when a matter has been decided by Allah and His Messenger, to have any option about their decision*).[21] He, the Almighty, shows the intention behind the duty of prayer by saying: (*for Prayer restrains from shameful and unjust deeds*),[22] and He points to the wisdom behind the duty of fasting by saying: (*that ye may (learn) self-restraint*).[23] He as well points to the purpose of the duty of *Zakaat* (alms) by saying: (*that so thou mightiest purify and sanctify them*).[24] He points to the wisdom behind the duty of *Hajj* (pilgrimage) by saying: (*That they may witness the benefits (provided) for them, and celebrate the name of Allah*).[25]

Moreover, the True *Hadith* discloses the annulment of acceptance and reward for the act of worship when it is void of its real objectives. The Prophet (ﷺ) says that: *he who has not given up on saying falsehoods and wrongdoing, then God do not need their abandonment of food and drink.* And He says that: *many of those fasting earn nothing from their fast except hunger and thirst.* The most prominent Egyptian jurist El Izz Bin Abd El Salam sums up these meanings in his well-known saying 'everything that abstains from getting its objective, is useless'.

Realizing the aims and objectives of Shari'a jurisdictions would make the application of it of utmost benefit to the individual and community. But when jurisdictions are detached from their purposes and the link between Shari'a commands and their objectives no more exists, then, utility would be lost, and people get trapped in hardship, intransigence and embarrassment. In this respect, Ibn El Kayyem has a precise and wise saying:

> Mind that Shari'a is all fair, all justice, and all mercy; so every issue that has moved from fairness into tyranny, from justice into cruelty, and from mercy into its opposite, does not pertain to Shari'a, even if it had been included in it through interpretation.

The fourth element: inattention to setting priorities and ranking religious obligations

In fact, amongst the most complicated problems faced by movements of ideological and social change, are fixing the starting point of this change, and ranking priorities in reform programmes. This becomes more complex when it comes to religious discourse within the context of Islamic action. Here, ranking underlies tensions emanating from different considerations and various criteria, because ranking is not only based on an assessment of 'which is more important' regarding the social good, but rather, it is based on two more intertwining elements:

- Ranking values within the context of the overall belief system based on Islam. This ranking may not necessarily coincide with that based on the social good – the way it is seen by people or by the majority.
- The degree of evidence, and the reliability of the source on which the discussed ruling is based. So, what is evident with an absolute certainty usually has a better chance to be included in the reform programmes, than what is based on demand and urgency. Expressed differently, topics that are less evident may rank lower on the list even when compared to topics seen as less important but enjoying more evidence.

Nevertheless, we think that the degree of evidence of a partial proof should not be the only key element in determining the ranking of actions. A partial proof may be totally evident, yet this may not affect the ruling; something which calls for adopting an unbiased criterion derived from several texts – not from one only. We do not want to elaborate more on this technical issue which may require expertise to be understood. Yet, we would like to establish that those who practice religious discourse and address it to people, cannot disregard the social context in which they work, or determine their own personal priorities which are isolated from people's needs in different times and places. They cannot count on their assumption that Islam is 'ruling not ruled', and that people have to reorder their lives based on these priorities setup for them by those reformists and advocates. Jurisdiction, jurisprudence and rulings have to guard people's interests; this guardianship is the essence of the 'Shari'a policy'. Ibn El Kayyem says that the policy of Shari'a is part of Shari'a, and not a partner or substitute. As defined by Ibn Akeel, it is: 'doing what people usually do, yet closer to goodness and further from corruption'.

Now we move away from this scientific analysis to the issue of setting priorities, and we take a closer look at where many of the devout have come to. Their distorted religiosity was shaped within the context of the religious discourse which determined their vision of Islam and their duties in its light. They, for example, do not distinguish between the basics of the dogma, without which the meaning of faith in God, credence in His Prophet, and belief in the Day of Judgment remain deficient and subsidiary maters – distantly related to the basics – such as visiting tombs, building shrines and swearing to other than God! Some incessantly insist on these subsidiary things; they draw people to them, thus preoccupying the public with them to the extent that pointless and useless argument prevails. Among these subsidiaries – and perhaps this is a clear example that we repeatedly encounter – is their non-differentiation between ordinances, that is, the things that the Jurist Almighty had made a duty, and the things he ordered such as wailing and '*istihbab*' (doing certain things that may please God). So some neglect obligations, and stress that they and others should abide by matters that do not transcend the scope of wailing and '*istihbab*'. Meanwhile, most of them cannot differentiate between individual duty – which is the duty of every assigned individual whereby the observance of others to this duty does not absolve him from doing it – and collective duties which are a must for the *umma* as a whole, whereby if an individual or a sufficient number of individuals do it, all the rest are purged. In addition, the common devout – under the effect of what they receive from religious discourse – do not differentiate between issues on which jurists have consensus, and those on which there are different opinions between different schools of jurisdiction or within the same school.

Practically, the outcome of this defect in understanding the order of religious rules and obligations is that many people – men, women and youngsters – busy themselves doing things that do not rank high amongst priorities, and neglect things that are much more valuable. This becomes evident upon exploring the questions and requests of *fatawa* or jurisdictions posed by most young men and women to scholars, muftis and those who talk about Islam. For example, they ask about trivialities of worship and about matters related to forms and appearances, in addition to details whereby jurists have had different opinions yet adopting one instead of the other does not lead into sinning or missing an interest in life or a reward in the afterlife. Suffice it to point here to a great defect or deviation along the path upon which many religious youngsters find themselves: When someone gets to know his religion anew and has the intention to abide by its obligations and prohibitions, he proceeds by determining to abide by specific formats of supplication, invocation and praise, intent upon performing certain methods and supererogatory acts, and manifesting a strong disapproval of those who are lenient in performing them. He expresses this by releasing his beard, shortening his garment, wearing the loose gown, (with a look that has no roots in religion and no weight in Islamic Jurisdiction). This, in turn, is a matter of private formality not related to religion. Actually, it is one of the customs, and people's fashion is not fixed according to our teacher Sheikh Abd El Wahab Khlaf – God bless his soul. Then he (the newly religious) proceeds to give advice to his mother, father, brothers and sisters in a non-tactful, smug and arrogant manner. Thus, he neglects a main principle of Islam, namely, the honouring and reverence of parents and treating them well – a duty that God Almighty has set immediately after the ordinance of believing in Him, which is the most basic dogma for Muslims. This command is echoed in the saying of the Almighty: (*Thy Lord hath decreed that ye worship none but Him, and that ye be kind to parents*),[26] as well as His saying which determines for the Muslim the ranking of kindness to parents: (*But if they strive to make thee join in worship with Me things of which thou hast no knowledge, obey them not; yet bear them company in this life with justice (And consideration)*).[27]

The fifth element: inattention to the role of the mind and the importance of science in building Islamic conceptualization

This inattention exists in two fields. First, the general field which attributes to the human mind a main role, in addition to the role of transcription, that is, the texts of the Qu'ran and *Hadith*. This is the realm of understanding the nature that surrounds us, and the generalities of life which Muslims share with all God's creation. The second field is that of jurisdiction and knowledge of the Shari'a rules related to the actions of people – individuals and groups.

In fact, the issue of the role of the mind in the presence of transcription, that is, the texts whose origin is the divine revelation sent down to the prophets and messengers, is an ancient one in human thought and in the history of monotheistic religions. Discussing it would take us astray from this attempt to monitor the 'loopholes' that exist in the prevailing religious discourse that we encounter. Yet, we are keen on stating precisely and in full clarity in front of our Muslim nation, and in front of young generations and Muslim Youth, that it is high time to put a limit and an end to this erroneous opposition between the mind and revelation. We have to know that the Grantor of 'knowledge and mind' is the Owner of 'Shari'a' that we are ordered to follow, that is, the Grantor of the mind is the Revealer of the 'transcriptions'; and that recounting in religious matters is not sufficient and is never an alternative for learning, jurisdiction or awareness. The wise pious Muslim has to read with awe the Book of God that was revealed to our Prophet (ﷺ). Contemporary Muslims have to give up for good the approach of superstition in understanding religion and its texts, and the approach of disabling the minds without which the texts cannot be comprehended. They also have to know for sure that the rules of Shari'a are not punishments imposed by God on assignees as He Almighty is needless of people, and the texts are not but evidence and signs for the fulfilment of Shari'a. Finally, they have to realize that the *umma* should be relieved from the disaster of giving up on jurisprudence and vision in order to be able to do something – anything to end the mortal stagnation and emerge from its prolonged cultural dormancy.

Those who are scared of the mind and its power, and are concerned that the minds may tread over the realm of texts, should be reminded that God Almighty guarantees the safekeeping of these texts, and that jurisprudents and scientists had been – and still are – the heirs of prophets in guarding these texts. Yet the real crisis of our prevailing culture and contemporary religious discourse lies in dethroning the mind, and the retreat of the status of science in the minds of many devout. Moreover, if the problem of the world around us is that some people imagine that the mind can – without transcription and the guidance of revelation – lead us into right guidance, then our problem – we, most Arabs and Muslims – is that we have incapacitated the mind, and that both the populace and elite have resorted to transcription. Hence, many stopped the minds from working, and some stopped their pursuit and good work. Thus reliance on God (normally associated with perseverance) has been mixed up with dependence, contentment has become blended with laziness, and chastity mixed up with disability. So, while people overall advanced we went back, and as the world moved on we froze. There is no good in a religious discourse which does not confront this loophole and tackle this disorder.

The sixth element: deep immersion in the past, distraction from the present, and fear of the future

A quick exploration of the prevailing religious discourse reveals a highly idiosyncratic phenomenon whereby most of this discourse – sometimes all – relates to the past. It almost stops at the age of prophecy, Al Sahaba, and some of the predecessors, to the extent that public perception of Islam has become limited to the history of this epoch plus the biography of the four orthodox caliphs – with the just Omayyad caliph Omar Bin Abd El Aziz sometimes being added. This is a disease that poses a serious danger to our generation. This generation suffers from twisted necks due to incessant backward traction; it retreats to the past, and is preoccupied with the self. Its futile – yet ever ready – argument is that: he who gets detached from his past cannot expect much from his future. This is a refuted argument, or this is a right recourse with bad intentions. None of the rational pious believers advocate detachment from the past, disregarding the entire heritage, belittling the sanctity of texts revealed to the Messenger of God (ﷺ), or belittling the credit of the companions of the Messenger of God (ﷺ) who lived with him, received wisdom from him, followed the example of his life, and were the link between his time and their successors.

Yet, two more things need to be highlighted. First, the past, upon consideration, is not of our making; we take pride in its glories, but without contributing to it. Moreover, the past with its many years, is a vast field which brought together right and wrong, guidance and aberrance; therein justice and cruelty wrestled and Islam fought with infidelity and hypocrisy. After all, not everything old is useful, and not all that has passed is good in the sense that it has to be regurgitated and abided by in delusion. Second, indulging with the past detracts from dealing with the present, looking ahead to the future, getting prepared for it, and celebrating it. I wonder how some preachers, speakers and muftis could have missed noticing the tremendous speed at which human sciences and knowledge move with forms and manifestations unimagined by the ancients. How could they have isolated their minds and conscience, together with the minds of their audience and listeners, from the quick pace of life around them!

The time has come when the predominant tune of contemporary religious discourse should be a call for the whole generation whereby it unplugs its ears, and moves blurring monotony and stagnation away from its eyes. Thus, this generation may yet prepare for considerable work and a quick paced long struggle, looking far into the future, and move somewhat away from the past with which it has limited itself and become trapped, believing that this draws it closer to God Almighty.

The seventh element: the Muslims' relationship with others

This issue is of extreme importance; and upon a good understanding of it, the future of social relations within Muslim society, and the relations between Muslims and other people of the world depends. Regrettably, some versions of contemporary religious discourse make huge mistakes as they describe this relationship to 'the Muslim public'. The main mistake is building up a psychological and social barrier separating Muslims from the rest of people, added to another barrier separating Muslims within the same society. The consequence is 'besieging' Muslims within closed circles that obstruct their communication with others, and leave them in isolation, which is damaging for them and others. Moreover, this wrongly legitimizes the too many claims stating that Islam poses its followers against non-Muslims and those with a different vision, in a continuous state of 'sacred religious struggle (*jihad*)' with continuous loops. Accordingly, it is claimed that they will remain strangers in the contemporary human procession, and that the gap between them and other peoples will remain wide because of their adoption of the concept of '*jihad*' and continuously enlarging its connotations. It is also claimed that this gap will enlarge because of their insistence on their being totally different from other peoples, that their dogma and culture provide no space for difference, and that they are not keen on coexistence with 'others' in equality, mutual recognition, and dialogue which is not hindered by difference.

In fact, the 'relationship with the other' falls into two different spheres. First, the internal sphere, that is, the disagreement among Muslims. Second, the relationship of Muslims with non-Muslims who belong to other doctrines and cultures.

When discussing the first sphere, it should be noted that a Muslim individual is not a guardian of another Muslim individual, and that difference in ideas and positions between Muslim individuals, under the banner of the same religion, is very possible. Actually, it has to be noted that this is useful for the *umma*; it should not be a source of intolerance or division, rupture of relations and exchange of accusations. Difference, in no way requires that one of the parties has to be a believer with the other being an evil-doer and rogue, because right and wrong in jurisdiction is not the same as orthodoxy and sin. The Qu'ran reminds us – and we rarely remember – that the unity of the *umma* does not prevent disagreement amongst its members; but rather, the believers – despite their disagreement – remain 'like a structure that pulls itself together'. Even if disagreement worsens and gets to the brink of fighting, which is forbidden, the two parties remain 'brothers' and 'believers'; (*If two parties among the Believers fall into a quarrel, make ye peace between them: but if one of them transgresses beyond bounds against the other, then fight ye (all) against the one that transgresses until it complies with the Command of Allah*).[28] This is why we urge those who work in Islamic discourse to reconsider their position, and re-contemplate the verses of the Holy Book and the Prophet's (ﷺ) *Sunna*, so that they may know – anew – how Islam has considered diversity, multiplicity of opinions, and difference of cultures a blessing requiring thankfulness 'through recognition' which is pointed to in the Almighty's saying: (*and made you into nations and tribes, that ye may know each other (not that ye may despise each other)*).[29] They are also urged to go back centuries in time to hear Imam Abi Hanifa saying, 'This knowledge of ours is an opinion, and it is the best we could do, so if someone presents a better one, we will accept it.' They are also advised to hear Imam Al Shafi'i saying, 'our opinion is true with the possibility of being wrong, and the opinion of others is wrong with the possibility of being right'. Subsequently, they may remember that the *Sahaba*, the interlocutors of the Prophet (ﷺ) who stayed close to Him and learned from Him religion, knowledge and action, had disagreed on many things, and that those who followed had disagreements in opinion more than the *Sahaba* had. Moreover, the Imams who are the founders of the main schools of Islamic Jurisdiction, had their own rules of jurisdiction, and their own jurisdictions in the branches of jurisdiction, added to the positions that they have worked out together. None had spoken improperly of another, not to mention accusation with lack of morality or faith. This honourable record is one of the imprints of the precise vision in the main rules of belief in Islam, and one of the fruits of the belief that wisdom is not limited to anyone, but distributed instead amongst individuals – spread amongst them all – and that he who seeks it has to look for it in others, even if those others were not part of the geographic or historic boundaries of Islam.

As for the relationship with non-Muslims – this is the second sphere – the Holy Qu'ran has taught us to use the best argument: (*Repel (Evil) with what is better: then will he between whom and thee was hatred become as it were thy friend and intimate!*).[30] The Holy Qu'ran has also shown us that being fair to them and charitable (charity offers more than what fairness does) is the straighter way: (*Allah forbids you not, with regard to those who fight you not for (your) Faith nor drive you out of your homes, from dealing kindly and justly with them: for Allah loveth those who are just*).[31]

When it comes to difference in religious doctrines, the great golden rule – which is impossible to repeal or change – is His the Almighty's saying: (*Let there be no compulsion in religion*),[32] the Qu'ran has shown the practicability of this rule in His saying on behalf of the believers (*Say: 'Ye shall not be questioned as to our sins, nor shall we be questioned as to what ye do'*).[33] This has been echoed in many other verses: God Almighty says to His prophet: (*Wilt thou then compel mankind, against their will, to believe!*);[34] and says to him (*Therefore do thou give admonition, for thou art one to admonish. Thou art not one to manage (men's) affairs*).[35]

Apparently, the bitter feeling due to political, economic and military retreat of the contemporary Islamic peoples has pushed many advocates into being involved in instigating Muslims into pitting themselves against the whole world, and getting into a battle of confrontation with the 'other' – with a tendency for exclusion. I still remember, with surprise and deep sorrow, a preacher who had been leading the Friday prayer that I had been performing twenty years ago. He concluded the Friday sermon with a prayer against the 'infidel': that God may enumerate and decimate them, thus getting rid of them all; moreover, rendering them – together with their money – spoils to the Muslims. Then, he had an idea – to detail the curse which he had pounded at them, meanwhile displaying his knowledge of the names of some countries. Thus, he went on mentioning their nationalities and countries to the point where he left no European country excluded in his general 'curse' that concluded his sermon.

This is all a flagrant deviation from the right path of Islam, and a clear violation to the orthodox rules – *Sunnah* – of the Prophet (ﷺ) of God, and His *Sirah* and manner of advocacy to God. In testimony stands the incident whereby his companions asked him to curse the polytheists; he rejected saying: 'I have not been sent as an execrator, but rather in mercy'. After all, times have changed, the world has changed, and Muslims are no more aligned alone in one country, while the non Muslims are aligned in countries wherein Muslims do not enter or reside. With this major development, many arrangements that were formulated by ancient jurisprudents have become obsolete. This implies that dividing the world into a land of war and a land of Islam no more has the same connotation. Moreover, we – Muslims – are not, and have never been, in an incessant state of war with non Muslims; instead, all of us together with them have become partners in the same procession, exchanging the fruits of experience and expertise, and employing our diversity of doctrines and cultures for the good of humanity. We cooperate in what we have agreed upon, and excuse each other for what we disagree upon, meanwhile – each among his own group – committed to what he believes in. It would be a good idea if our jurisprudents provide the *umma* with new formulations explaining the new relationships between Muslims and non-Muslims, in what deserves to be called 'jurisprudence of coexistence and interconnection' instead of jurisprudence of 'isolation and separation'.

Finally, though it seems extended, this is a quick stance on contemporary religious discourse, whereby it is reaffirmed that we are not oblivious to some sincere efforts for rationalizing this discourse. Here, there is a fact that we hope will not be refuted based on search for self defence, apology for default or flattery to those in power. The fact is: this religious discourse needs to undergo a true revolution, the main pillars of which are more knowledge and jurisdiction, more critical thinking related to jurisdiction, and more knowledge of the complex reality. Without a sincere scientific effort exerted along the path of this revolution, any discourse about an Islamic awakening, or an Islamic project for renaissance, will be but verbal crackle, unrhymed speech no chanting in it, flowing talk to no avail, and a chitchat which is neither good for religion nor makes a good life.

Conclusion

Thence, this study on 'contemporary religious discourse' has been framed in a way I have not personally determined. It has been determined by the acute polarization that has been existent for many years between: the 'Islamic current' including its diverse subsidiaries with varying conceptualizations of the 'centrality of applying Shari'a'; the currents that coexist with it within the current 'social context' of Arab and Islamic peoples; and all intellectual currents and political orientations of other forces – be it liberal, secular or calling persistently for a civil state. My opinion has been – and still is – that there exists a huge exaggeration in conceptualizing this 'polarization' and in posing the issue as if it were irresolvable. I also think that an enquiry should be made regarding the incentives of those who unexpectedly have shown keenness on posing this polarization as if it were a most urgent challenge that Egypt and the Arab and Islamic worlds face after the success of the so-called 'Arab Spring'. This success has led to the arrival of some currents with an Islamic orientation, which is described by its owners and their opponents as aiming at founding regimes with an Islamic reference. They both suppose that this Islamic reference is expected to limit rights and freedoms of non Muslim minorities in the Arab and Islamic worlds. This issue, in my own opinion, had been set years ago; the general cultural and juridical state of affairs in Egypt confirms this fact. Many rules had been adjusted to become compatible with the Islamic Shari'a. Article 2 of the 1971 constitution confirms the ideological, cultural and political affiliation of Egypt to the so-called Islamic orientation; nevertheless, there remained considerable remnants which violate equality between the Muslims of Egypt and its religious minorities. This is why, on my part, I could not have disregarded these facts; and together with the millions of Egyptians, I am keen on the launch of the Revolution after its realization and its passing its preliminary stages.

My own assessment is that this exaggeration in portraying 'the issue of Islamic Shari'a' emanates from one of two positions – both of which I perceive as flawed. The first is produced by a wrong conception of the process of 'applying Shari'a'. The second comes from a wrong intention whereby deliberate cultural exclusion is practised to eradicate any religious orientation. This is being done through raising slogans which disregard the real issues facing our society during these decisive moments in our history. In conclusion, and due to the utmost importance of rationalizing 'religious discourse', it is perceived as perfectly appropriate not to disregard this discourse, but instead, work out a kind of consensus on it.

Notes

1. Interpretation of the Koran, Sourat Al-Hajar, verse 9.
2. Interpretation of the Koran, Sourat An-Nysaa, verse 66.
3. Interpretation of the Quran, Surat Al-Naml, verse 14.
4. Interpretation of the Quran, Surat Al-Nisaa, verse 165.
5. Interpretation of the Quran, Sourat Az Zoumar, verse 53.
6. Interpretation of the Quran, Sourat Al-A'araf, verse 156.
7. Interpretation of the Koran, Sourat Al-Fajr, verses 27–28.
8. Interpretation of the Koran, Sourat Al-Ma'edah, verse 119.
9. Interpretation of the Koran, Sourat Hood, verse 61.
10. Interpretation of the Koran, Sourat Al Bakarah, verse 256
11. Interpretation of the Koran, Sourat Al Nahl, verse 116.
12. Interpretation of the Koran, Sourat Al Bakarah, verse 185.
13. Interpretation of the Quran, Sourat El Hajj, verse 78.
14. Interpretation of the Quran, Sourat Al Anfal, verse 66.
15. Interpretation of the Quran, Sourat Al A'araf, verse 157.
16. Interpretation of the Quran, Sourat Al Ma'idah, verse 101.
17. Interpretation of the Quran, Sourat Mariyam, verse 64.
18. Interpretation of the Quran, Sourat Al Quasas, verse 77.
19. Interpretation of the Quran, Sourat Al Bakarah, verse 201.
20. He is Dr Youssef Al Karadawi, cited in Al Karadawi (2004), 26.
21. Interpretation of the Holy Qu'ran, Sourat Al Ahzab, verse 36.
22. Interpretation of the Holy Qu'ran, Sourat Al Ankabout, verse, 45.
23. Interpretation of the Holy Qu'ran, Sourat Al Bakarah, verse, 183.
24. Interpretation of the Holy Qu'ran, Sourat Al Taoubah, verse, 103.

25. Interpretation of the Holy Qu'ran, Sourat Al Hajj, verse, 28.
26. Interpretation of the Koran, Sourat Al Issra', verse 23.
27. Interpretation of the Koran, Sourat Lukman, verse 15.
28. Interpretation of the Koran, Sourat Al-Hajaraat, verse 9.
29. Ibid., verse 13.
30. Interpretation of the Qu'ran, Sourat Fussilat, verse 34.
31. Interpretation of the Qu'ran, Sourat Al Mumtahana, verse 8.
32. Interpretation of the Qu'ran, Sourat Al-Bakara, verse 256.
33. Interpretation of the Qu'ran, Sourat Saba', verse 25.
34. Interpretation of the Qu'ran, Sourat Younes, verse 99.
35. Interpretation of the Qu'ran, Sourat Al Gashyia, verses 21–22.

Reference

Al Karadawi, Youssef. 2004. *Easing the Fiqh for the Modern Moslem in the Light of the Qur'an and the Sunnah: Towards an Easing and Modern Fiqh; in For the Main Rules of Requiescence; Fiqh el Ilm*. Cairo: Wehbeh Library.

Religion and the state in contemporary Arab society: theoretically, practically and prospectively[†]

Abdelilah Belkeziz

Faculty of Arts and Humanities, Hassan II University, Casablanca, Morocco

Through an examination of the different types of relationships between religion and the state, this article argues that the two extremes of this relationship – namely, the case whereby the state exploits religion and the one where it tries to banish it – ultimately lead to the emergence of political Islam as a reaction. Political Islam can be seen as employing religion to gain political power, hence reinforcing the worldly aspects and self-interest of a certain group at the expense of intellectual, ethical and doctrinal considerations. Practically speaking, political Islam has pushed the idea of an Islamic state to suicidal theocratic ends. The main factor behind the ascent of Islamists to political power is the political vacuum resulting from the retreat of the left, added to absolute obstructionism in the political domain. In an attempt to redeem religion and the state in contemporary Arab society and end the struggle between Islamists and secularists, four suggestions are presented: (1) recognition of the right of any political movement to derive its basic ethos from religion, or religious heritage, on condition that this is considered a personal endeavour rather than a religious issue; (2) stressing the civil nature of all parties, whether secular or religious; (3) respecting the civil nature of the state; and (4) abiding by the democratic circulation of power. In sum, a revitalization of the modern state system is inevitable.

Relationships between the state and religion: three models

A study of the various types of relationships that existed between state and religion in recorded political history reveals three major and distinct models of the state. First is the state whose identity is based on religion and claims to apply the rules of religion. Second is the state whose source of legitimacy – sometimes along with other sources – is religion, wherein the state invokes religion as one of the tools justifying its rule and its policies. The third model is that of the state that has a neutral relationship with religion or religions, where legitimacy is derived from secular, human sources and where there is no room for any form of exploitation of religion in politics. The first model is that of the 'theocratic (religious) state', the second is that of the 'sultanate' (the caliphate and the smaller states that succeeded it, in Islamic history) and the ancient Asian 'empire state' (ancient China, Japan and Iran), and the third is 'the modern secular state'. According to this classification, there are three different models, each

[†]This paper was originally presented in the Joint Symposium on 'Religion and State in the Arab World' convened by the Center for Arab Unity Studies and the Swedish Institute – Alexandria in Hamamat, Tunisia, 15–17 October 2012.

with its own fundamental nature: a religious state, a state that purports to be religious and a non-religious state. Nevertheless, the differences between the three models are not sharply defined. As will be explained below, some traits of a given model may infiltrate into another model.

These three models may not represent the entire range of possible relationships among the religious, the social and the political realms in every state in history. They may not be the only models depicting the relationship between religious absolutism and state relativism (other national experiences that we know nothing of or that we have not yet studied may exist). Yet they certainly represent the most evident categorization of the relationship between religion and political society in human history. More importantly, having existed through many centuries across extensive geographical locations and in various societies, these three models are unaffected by position in time and place; hence, their representativeness and their suitability as models for study.

The theocratic state model was prevalent in Europe in the late Middle Ages, following the fall of the ancient empires and the spread of the Church's power from the spiritual realm to the worldly, political realm. With the passage of the reins of command to the class of ecclesiasts (men of religion) in this state model, the religious and the political became identical; the state and the Church (in this case Catholicism) were the same. For a long period of history, the effective rulers of some parts of Europe were popes. They appointed and dethroned kings, and they alone had the authority to punish, to forgive and to define truth, in both religious and temporal matters. Legitimacy in the theocratic state was based on the claim to the divine right to rule, and the state waged wars based on this right. To disobey the state was to deviate from religion; it was an act of heresy and a menace to God's kingdom on Earth, just as free thought and scientific discovery were defamations of religious tenets, acts of apostasy that led to the guillotine and to the gallows.

The era of the religious state was a dark period in the history of Christian Europe, and the struggle against it, at the start of the Modern Era, was a tragic period. To comprehend the exaggerated secular extremism of the past two centuries (the most glaring example of which was French secular extremism), it must be seen as a reaction to the religious extremism practised by the Church in its seizure of political and state power and its attempt to eradicate the civil character of the state.

As will be shown, this type of state did not come into being in the history of Islam. However, the model did pass into the thinking of a number of modern and contemporary Muslims, as a result of an exaggerated understanding of the connection between state and religion in Islam, involving some (conscious or unconscious) revival of Khawarij and imamist ideas. Among these ideas is the concept of governorship (jurisdiction of a governor) espoused by some contemporary Sunni Muslim thinkers, such as Abul-A'la Al-Mawdoudi. Drawn from both the Khawarij context and medieval Christian theocracy, this idea was later theorized and explained by Sayed Qutb. Also in this category is the 'Providence of the Jurist' concept in contemporary Shia Islam, which has its historic origins in imamist political jurisprudence and which Muntaziri and Khomeini borrowed from the thinking of Imam Al Nouraqi (18th century). These two concepts[1] are innovations in contemporary Islamic awareness and have no basis in Islamic political theory. The resultant controversy over the relationship between the state (and politics) and religion led to a serious turn of events whose dramatic consequences we continue to live with today. That, however, is another matter.

The second model (a state that invokes religion as a foundation for its legitimacy) was prevalent in the ancient Islamic and Asian worlds and continued to exist up until two centuries ago. In Islam, this model was represented by the caliphate and its successor sultanate states; in Asia, it was represented by the empire states that arose in China, Japan and pre-Islamic Iran. The state, in these examples from history, was not a religious state of the medieval Christian model; unlike the European ecclesiastics, its rulers did not claim the divine right to rule. Nevertheless, this state model was based – largely – on religious legitimacy. Although the relationship between matters political and matters religious was an open one, religion and the state (particularly in the Islamic states) were not identical, contrary to the beliefs of many Muslim and Orientalist scholars (e.g. Lewis 1988) who made erroneous judgments and reached incorrect conclusions based on those mistaken beliefs (Lewis 1988, 52).

In the history of Islam, political power was not religious power. At no time were rulers men of religion. However, as Muslim imams, the succession of ruling caliphs did need religious legitimacy. This religious legitimacy came, first, from the caliph's selection by those who had the right to solve problems or make decisions according to the conditions set out in the books on political legitimacy concerning imams (Ben Al Hussein Abu Ya'la Al Farra' 2000; Ben Taymia Al Harani 2000; Al-Joueini 1996; El Mawardi 1982). The caliph also derived religious legitimacy from the performance of religious duties, such as leading prayers and fighting to defend the existence of the 'Abode of Islam' and to protect the unity of the nation. Yet the caliph also derived legitimacy from his alliance with the official jurisprudential institutions and from their reinforcement of his legitimacy.

It is important to note the difference between a religious authority and one that uses religion to legitimize itself – especially when the sources of legitimacy of this authority decline (as in the case of the Islamic sultanate state following the end of the caliphate in the second half of the fourth century of the Hegira). The only other similar example of this type of relationship between state and religion is that of the ancient Asian empire state in the Far East and in the Middle East. To varying degrees, these states derived their authority from religious legitimacy. Men of religion (Buddhists, Zoroastrians, followers of Mazdakism, etc.) played great roles in the daily lives of these empires and in the policies of their emperors (Weber 2006). For the most part, however, religious institutions in these countries did not directly engage in political rule. Instead, they remained, like their Islamic counterparts, either semi-independent or completely devoted to the religious realm. The involvement of the emperor or the king in religion had become a ritualistic one and he was only the nominal representative of religion (just as the caliphs and sultans were nominal representatives of Islam).

Humanity came to know the secular state model (the non-religious state or the state that is impartial to the religion of society and the people) approximately two centuries ago when it first spread across Europe (its birthplace) before spreading across the world (either implanted by foreigners or established by locals inspired by the European model). This state does not derive its authority from any higher or extra-state ideal; it derives it from the sovereign source of authority: the people. The state legitimizes itself through the accomplishment of purely civil functions (ensuring the security, well-being and freedom of its citizens, and upholding laws that all its citizens agree upon, promulgated by the people's representatives in elected institutions). The secular state's credo is politics, meaning the public good. It is based on the strict separation of religion from the public sphere in legislation, administration, education and citizenship rights as defined by secular law, a separation that delineates strict boundaries and leaves no room for doubt.

Contemporary history has seen two varieties of this secular state: a secular state that does not oppose religion and does not impose restrictive legislation on the religious realm;

and the extremist secular state, violently opposed to religion under the pretext of upholding its secularity. The first secular state model was established in most West European societies and in North America (the only deviation, and that only relatively, is the French secular state). Spreading out from this geopolitical location, this state model was adopted by many societies in Asia and in South and Central America. This variety of secular state is based on the principles of state respect for religion and of non-interference in the religious beliefs and religious freedom of citizens. There are no state restrictions on the spread of religious ideas in society through publications issued by privately owned publishing houses. There is a tolerance for religion in schools and public life, and political parties whose principles are inspired by the Christian faith, such as the Christian Democrat parties in Europe, are allowed to form. The second secular state model is an extremist one that tends to base its secular political position vis-à-vis religion on philosophical principles: positivism (in the French case) or materialism (Soviet and Communist models). Mustapha Kemal Ataturk's secular state in Turkey was inspired by this anti-religion model. Consequently, in the Kemalist model, the separation between state and religion turned into an eradication of religion! From the second half of the 19th century and up to the present, the thinking of Arab secular elites has been influenced, to varying degrees, by European secular ideas – particularly by French Positivism, Soviet Communism and the Kemalist exclusionary model (because of the shallowness of its ideas, political rulers were more tempted by the latter, however, than were the elites).

The three models representing the relationship between state and religion are not strictly differentiated or mutually exclusive. Some features of one model may cross into another (a state that invokes religion as a basis of legitimacy may borrow certain theocratic and secular traits, or a contemporary modern secular state may, for example, borrow some of the characteristics of a theocratic state). In the French positivist model, for instance, secularism was transformed into the sacred (and inviolable) religious faith of the state!

Applications and variances in the Arab context over time

Though it seems more intense in the past three decades, the present-day tension between religion, on the one hand, and the state and politics, on the other, is not new to Arab history. It has persisted throughout the history of the Arabs and Muslims, ever since the rise of religion and the emergence of the state. Because of the complementarity that arose between state and religion and persisted for some time, this quarrel had no obvious effect at the time when the two (state and religion) were being established simultaneously. With the passage of time, however, the quarrel became more evident and the antagonism between those speaking in the name of the ruler (sultan) and those speaking 'in the name of the Koran' was quite serious in certain instances, and at times even violent. This conflict was, in reality and at all stages, a conflict between politics and politics rather than between religion and politics. Nevertheless, the fact that once a party based its policy on religion, made use of religious terms and used religion to justify its ends, it created the impression that this historical conflict was between religion and politics. This is the exact state of affairs that is being reproduced today in discussions of the political and the religious in contemporary societies – whether the rhetoric adopted is theoretical (which is rare) or ideological–political (which is much more prevalent)!

The preoccupation, both in the past and today, with the nature of the relationship between the state, politics and religion does not arise from naught; it is justified by realities on the ground and is the result of the link between religion and the state since the beginning of history. The fact that the rise and spread of religion led to the creation of the state, that the religious message resulted in the Prophet's political project in Medina, that the state of the Rightly Guided Caliphate drew legitimacy from following the ways of the Prophet in governing the state of Medina, that the Umayyad[2] and Abbasid caliphs, the sultans and emirs needed to exhort religious legitimacy to buttress their political legitimacy, were not mere details. Nor is it insignificant that modern Arab and Islamic states feel compelled (even after the end of the caliphate and the emergence of the contemporary state) to set up *fatwa* and Islamic jurisprudence and study councils, and that the demand for jobs in these councils is growing, as are the calls for expanding their role of providing religious justification to official policies. All these precedents and developments show that preoccupation with this relationship is not contrived. Nor is it introduced into our politics expressly to cause trouble or to divert politics from their natural path. This preoccupation raises historical, objective questions that cannot be ignored. At the same time, the fact that the nature of the relationship between the state and religion continues to be questioned shows that societies, states and political experience have not yet managed to provide the appropriate answer, thereby freeing our lives of the problems resulting from past and present conflicts regarding this relationship. That, however, is not the main object of concern here.

Needless to say, the place occupied by religion in the state, and the relationship between the two, has changed from one period to another in the history of Islam, depending on the level of development in the Islamic political realm, the nature of those wielding state power at any given historical moment, or the extent of control over religious authority. In the state of Medina (from its foundation and up to the Prophet's death) religion occupied a greater and more influential position, because at that time the state was a stage in the spreading of religion and one of its tools, headed by a leader whose religious legitimacy and authority were undisputed. The privileged position of religion in the state remained unchanged under the rule of the Rightly Guided Caliphate. However, although religion continued to be the main source of legitimacy, its position in the state certainly diminished compared with what it had been during the Prophet's lifetime. There were many reasons for this, among them the expanding space occupied by politics in the state, along with the extension of the state's objective and imperial boundaries and the consolidation of the worldly juridical character of caliphs' actions, combined with the fact that the caliphs' actions were not infallible, etc. Certainly, the end of the Rightly Guided Caliphate saw a further diminishment of the position of religion in the state of Islam, accompanied by an enlargement of the political role. With time, the imbalance between the positions of religion and politics in the state increased, particularly after the caliphate had become no more than a symbolic authority, and the bases for political decisions ceased to be founded on religion, but were shaped instead by such factors as predominance, power, might and partisanship (Ibn Khaldoun 1973).

Yet, regardless of the final balance of power arrived at in the course of Islamic experience (in which the geographical area of religion diminished), politics and political power continued to seek a measure of timeless legitimacy; a legitimacy imposed by a higher power,[3] represented by religion. Thus, any rule based on predominance and conquest (Conquered Emirates), for example, was forced to seek a symbolic religious legitimacy for itself in the caliphate, even though this symbol no longer represented anything. When it became impossible to appeal to this kind of legitimacy, religious scholars attempted to fill part of the void. Of course, this was not the case everywhere;

differences concerning the legitimate sources of power existed among religious communities belonging to different sects. Such differences cannot be overlooked, especially those that arose between Shia and Sunni Muslims. Both groups agree on the necessity of setting up the imam's position, given that both religion and the state require this – but they disagree on the rationalization behind it and have different views of the imam's judgment in religious doctrine and its usefulness.

The study of Sunni and Shia imamist theories and the differences in the political doctrine of the two communities do not fall within the subject of this paper. What is of concern here is that, despite these differences, both Sunni and Shia Muslims believe in a durable relationship between religion and state. While both communities view the position of imam as a necessity for the nation and a prerequisite for religious and worldly matters, to the Sunni community the position of imam is not a basic tenet of religious doctrine, but a complementary one that does not affect faith. This is contrary to the Shia imamist doctrine that considers the position of imam to be an article of faith, not part of Islamic jurisprudence. This difference is not a minor one. Historically, one of its main results was that although Sunnis allocated considerable space to religion in the state, the Sunni state was never a religious one. Conversely, the concept of the state among imamists is very close to that of a theocratic state ruled by men of religion (i.e. jurisprudent religious scholars, representatives of the Absent Imam), a state that cannot be held accountable due to the infallibility of whomever occupies the position of imam. However, beyond the two communities' disparate views concerning the closeness of the relationship between the religious and the political realms, between the state and religion, there lies a common denominator; the centrality of the religious factor to the state and to political power, where religion constitutes the foundations of lawfulness and legitimacy. Until the emergence of the modern state in Arab and Islamic societies, the state evolved upon this basis in the history of Islam.

The contemporary context

The phenomenon of associating religion with the state did not end in modern contemporary Arab political history, although it did lessen in degree after the establishment of the 'modern' state in the Arab world. It is well known that the traditional sultanate state model, inherited from the Middle Ages of Islamic history, continued to exist into modern history, even after the advent (with the European technological conquest and the imperialist occupation of Arab countries) of the modern state, two centuries ago. In some Arab countries, the sultanate state persisted, in terms of the state's absolute power, or of the relationship between state and religion and the traditional religious and legal foundations of legitimacy – in the Weberian sense. However, the interaction between this state model and modern state models in other Arab countries generated a timid, hybrid political chemistry in the heart of the sultanate state when it first encountered political modernity in the 19th century.

This hybrid formation of the 'modern' state in contemporary Arab countries is due to the arduous and deformed nature of the birth of this state, and thence the shock of confronting modernity and the need to adapt, to a degree, to the basic principles of the modern political system. The extent of this adaptation varied in accordance with the degree of acceptance of modernization and the level of political and social development in a given Arab or Islamic country, in addition to the measure (imposed directly or by way of external pressure) of colonial modernization introduced into the country from the 19th century. The Ottoman political reform movement (Ottoman Tanzimat) is probably the most obvious example of the attempts, begun in the mid-19th century, to introduce reforms in Arab and Islamic countries. Although the political modernization contained in the Ottoman reforms surpassed that of Egyptian, Tunisian and Moroccan reform movements, the relationship between state and religion remained similar to that which existed in the traditional, inherited sultanate state where the system of rule was based on religious legitimacy (also the case in the Moroccan example). In Egypt, under the rule of Mohammed Ali and his family, the importance of religious legitimacy as a source of legitimate rule was largely reduced, although Al-Azhar (like Al Zeitouna in Tunisia and Al-Qarawiyyin in Morocco) continued to provide the state and society with this legitimacy. While Mustapha Kemal Ataturk's abolition of the caliph position ended the relationship between state and religion in modern Turkey, the continuance of the Emaret Al Mu'mineen (the institution of the Commander of the Faithful) in Morocco maintained it, without, however, founding the state on religion, as in the case of modern Saudi Arabia. In modern Iran, placing the ruling family on an equal level with religious scholars meant that men of religion played a role in assessing the religious legitimacy of public policy, although this role was reduced after Shah Mohamed Reza Pahlavi's 'White Revolution'.

The nature of the relationship between state and religion in Egypt and Tunisia was being adjusted slightly at the time of their occupation in the early 1880s (which was followed by the occupation of other Arab countries in the 20th century), but the essence of the relationship remained unaltered. Religion had stopped being one of the prerequisite foundations of the state, although Islam continued to be cited in some constitutions, where it is described as the religion of the state. In other constitutions, Islamic Sharia is cited as a source of legislation (to what degree depends on individual constitutions; it may be 'a source', a 'principal source' or 'the principal source'). The state is no longer obliged to justify its existence by protecting or defending the 'Abode of Islam', implementing Sharia law, reinforcing the sacred duty of defending the land of Muslims, upholding the word of God on Earth, or any of the things that constituted the legitimacy base of the traditional state. State legitimacy is based on other, civil, not religious, functions in accordance with purely social objectives, such as national unity, socialism, development, democracy, freedom, etc. Systems of law and legislation are entirely man-made, enacted by parliaments, governments, kings, presidents and emirs for the public good, for the good of the people and in the best interest of the state and the nation; and not in the name of God, in whose name most states (with rare exceptions) have ceased to claim to speak. It is only natural that this transformation affects the sources of legitimacy of the 'modern' state in the Arab world. Not only because this state is the successor of the colonial state (a state implanted into Arab society during the colonial era), but also because its system of laws and legislation are derived from civil philosophy, which is the foundation of state legitimacy and includes all the ruling – and alleged – principles that entails (unity, development, democracy, etc.).

Nevertheless, the temporal nature of the 'modern' Arab state did not transform it into a purely secular state comparable with the secular states in Western societies, because the separation between the religious and the temporal was not quite complete and because various forms of relationship between the state and religion continued to develop in the working system of the state. The overlap between religion and state is greater in some countries (such as Saudi Arabia, Morocco, Sudan and to some extent Jordan), where the legitimacy of power, of the elite or of the ruling family is still purportedly based on religion; it is less in countries where the ruling elite does not claim religious legitimacy. However, all these states experience a degree of overlap between religion and state, and this relationship is continuously being revised, in varying degrees and at different rates. In all Arab countries (with the exception of parts of Lebanon), the state still controls the religious realm. It establishes religious advisory institutions (Dar Al Efta') and appoints the office of '*mufti*', or an association of religious scholars empowered to do so. It supports the role of this institution and finances all its associations, and also oversees and funds Islamic endowments and places of worship and finances the employees who work in them. The state also supports religious education (known in Morocco as 'authentic education') and incorporates religious teaching into official education programmes. Moreover, in these countries the civil status system and its laws are based on Islamic law, not on secular, man-made laws, etc. In short, while the state's relationship to religion has not been severed, it has been regulated, both in theory and in practice, to comply with the principles of secularism.

Thus, the limits to the alleged 'modernity' and 'secularism' of this state are perceived, as well as its opportunistic relationship with religion. This section has shown this state to be a hybrid one, composed of a peculiar combination of two state models: the sultanate state and the modern secular state.[4] In truth, this structural hybridization is the mediocre modernization pattern[5] upon which contemporary Arab policies, economies and social systems were, and continue to be, constructed.

Crisis in contemporary state–religion relations

Since the emergence of the modern state in Arab and Islamic countries, two forms of state intervention in religion and religious affairs have taken place. Although the motivation, means and objectives were different for each form, the results and effects were identical; to varying degrees, the relationship between the religious and the political in contemporary societies entered a state of sharp and prolonged crisis. The first form of intervention (the most prevalent in state policies) is the exploitation of religion towards political ends. The second is the marginalization and exclusion of religion, more often than not through violent means.

Exploitation of religion for political ends

The first form of state intervention in the religious realm is prevalent in Arab countries, such as Saudi Arabia, Morocco, Sudan and, to some degree, Egypt. Pretexts and justifications vary from pretending to political legitimacy founded on a religion, supervising and completely controlling the religious realm, and exploiting social religious sentiment and traditional religious forces in the battle against liberal, leftist or national opposition groups. State appropriation and monopolization of religion was not identical in the examples mentioned above; it differed from one country to another depending on the degree of historical development, on the one hand, and on that of political development, on the other. Moreover, the strength of a state's grasp on religion and the degree of control it exercises over it are not always linked to the degree of 'religiosity' of the state, or to the religious nature it tries to lend to its policies.

The complementarity between the religious and the political in Morocco, for example, is the result of a long historical experience, and goes back to establishment of the Idrisid dynasty over 1200 years ago, where the person of the sultan was both imam and emir, holding both religious and temporal authority. The sultan's religious legitimacy was not – as it was in the Idrisid and Alaouite dynasties – always derived from his noble lineage as a descendant of the Prophet; it was based on the position of imam that he continued to occupy – even in dynasties headed by rulers of Berber (Amazigh) descent, such as the Almoravid and Almohad dynasties. The identification of the religious with the temporal in the state did not change much, even after its political institutions were modernized in the second half of the 19th century, under the reigns of Sultan Mohamed IV and Sultan Al-Hassan I, nor after Morocco became a French 'protectorate' (in 1912), and not even after its independence in the mid-1950s. The king continues to be the Commander of the Faithful; he is in charge of the religious realm and empowered to establish its scholarly institutions and other religious bodies. Nevertheless, throughout the different stages of its history (and in spite of the above), the Moroccan state was never a religious state. It has never claimed to rule by Sharia law, the 'religious institution' has never played a role in political life, and has never attempted to shape public policies or to confer Islamic characteristics on these policies.

The case in Saudi Arabia is very different. The king is not an imam with religious legitimacy; the Saudi state was first established on the basis of on an alliance between emir and sheikh, between the sword and religion, between the Al Saud family and the Wahhabi movement. The family and the movement rationalized and enabled one another; the Wahhabi movement enabled the Saudi project of unifying the peninsula by providing it with religious legitimacy, and the state enabled the Wahhabi institution to become an official institution with authority in public affairs. The state had to nurture this alliance, which is the base of its foundation, by adjusting its policies to the demands and standards of those religious institutions. This did not change when the state entered the economic and social modernization stage in the mid-20th century, and especially under the reign of King Faisal. The partnership between the Al Saud family and the Wahhabi institution has continued to reproduce itself, each partner needing the other equally. This has remained so, even in instances when the alliance came under some pressure, as in the aftermath of the 11 September 2001 twin attacks on New York and Washington, DC. Although (unlike Morocco) the religious and the temporal did not come together in the person of the king in Saudi Arabia, the degree of state intervention in the religious realm is much higher in Saudi Arabia than it is in Morocco. Additionally, the political, temporal and civil realms are immeasurably greater in the Moroccan state compared with the Saudi state, due to the difference in the level of political development.

State intervention in the religious realm in Sudan has taken a different shape. Ga'far Al-Numayri's regime laid no claim to legitimacy based on religion. However, the regime's alliance with the Muslim Brotherhood, on the one hand, and its desire to compete with the religious legitimacy of the Al-Ansar and Khatmeya groups, on the other, impelled it to don a religious garb. This was rapidly followed by the imposition of Sharia law in a country of multiple religions, laying the foundation for the South (predominantly non-Muslim) Sudan problem; and the armed insurgence led by John Garang. This adventure undermined the state, society and national unity, finally resulting in the wretched division of the country, called for by the National Salvation Revolution for 20 years, and finally realized! Renewed state intervention in the religious sphere occurred in Sudan, to a measure unprecedented since the military coup staged by Lieutenant General Omar Hassan Al Bashir in 1989 toppled Al Sadiq Al-Mahdi's civilian government, after Al-Numayri had been deposed. Al Bashir's alliance with Hassan Al-Turabi and their complete control over the political realm (prior to their separation) was an example of an attempt to transform the state completely by basing its political system on the application of Sharia law. The destruction of the Sudanese entity that came with the secession of the South, the violent civil wars that preceded it, as well as the regime's bloody and tyrannical rule, were the bitter fruits reaped from the foolish exploitation of religion for political and state purposes!

As for Egypt, the state continued to impose control over the religious sphere and to exploit religion in its battles with opposition groups, taking advantage of Al-Azhar's standing as the source of religious reference in the Islamic world. For 40 years the state used Al-Azhar's institutions and its sheikhs to service its internal policies (the 'Open Door' policy, suppression of liberal opposition groups, 'Jurisdictive defamation' of Islamist movements, unconditional and unlimited prolongation of the presidential term, and providing legal coverage for sectarian strife policies). The state also used Al-Azhar to support its external policies (opening up to the West and the United states, the Camp David Treaty and reconciliation with the enemy, spreading the policy of normalization with Israel throughout the Arab world, blockading resistance movements in Palestine and Gaza, conspiring against Iraqi and the Lebanese resistance, etc.). The state interfered in Al-Azhar's internal affairs, imposing chosen officials and at the same time enabling them to interfere in the details of private and public life (political, social, cultural, literary and artistic affairs). This reached the extent of banning books and movies, forcing couples to divorce and issuing decisions reminiscent of those issued by the Church in the Middle Ages! The official orchestration of religious tensions between Muslims and Copts (partly revealed in the wake of the 25 January 2011 revolution) and the references to a possible eruption of sectarian strife were only a few of the tragic results of the relationship established between state and religion in Egypt wherein the former used the latter to promote its political ends.

Marginalization and exclusion of religion

Besides the first form of relationship between state and religion (the interventionist, annexing, exploitative form), another form of relationship developed in some Arab and Islamic countries, one that has different foundations, but identical results: the marginalization and exclusion of religion. The principal characteristic of this form of relationship is the state's tendency to exclude religion from public affairs, by force of law, or by an exaggerated supervision and constriction of the religious realm. This relationship exists in varying models and degrees in Arab and Islamic countries, depending on the boundaries and foundations of a country's political framework, on its political history, and on its level of modernization. To describe this model briefly, the example of three countries will be used: Turkey, Iran and Tunisia.

Modern, Kemalist Turkey is the most glaring example of the exclusionary form of relationship between state and religion. Mustapha Kemal Ataturk imposed a very harsh and radical form of secularism on a country where political and religious authority had been united in the institution of the caliphate. The harshness of this model did not lie in the separation of state and religion, which was a necessity for the establishment of the modern secular state that Ataturk hoped to build after he had abolished the caliphate. It lay in his insistent antagonism towards all religious manifestations in Turkey, not only at the state level, but also at the social level! This included the steps he took to change the time and calendar systems, to change the Turkish script (from the Arabic to the Latin alphabet), to impose restrictions on religious institutions, to remove religion from education programmes, to attempt to wipe out Turkey's Islamic history, to sever the country from its historical and cultural roots, and to separate it from its Arab and Islamic surroundings. As a state, Kemalist Turkey opted for westernization; a forced westernization that it believed could only be attained through complete obliteration; more precisely, by attempting to destroy Turkish society's cultural and religious identity. The rationale behind this violent antagonism to religion was the belief that Islam stood in the way of Turkey's modernization – a belief that was dispelled three generations after the Kemalist Cesarean surgery took place in Turkey.

Iran's policy vis-à-vis religion during the reign of the last shah, Mohamed Reza Pahlavi, was not as radical or as violent as that of Kemalist Turkey. The shah continued, in the midst of the White Revolution to display ostensible respect for religion, the religious institution and the men of religion in Qum. However, his far-reaching modernization aspirations led him to impose restrictions on all religious activity, particularly activity that touched upon public life. Iran continued to separate state from religion. It secularized education and restricted religious teaching, striving rapidly to strip society of all its religious manifestations in an attempt to westernize it and wipe out its Islamic identity. All these factors together constitute grounds for asserting that the Iranian state adopted a systematic exclusionary policy towards religion and the religious realm, a policy that the westernized Iranian ruling elite of the time assumed was best suited to accomplishing political modernization. However, unlike Kemalist secularism, which strove to pave the way towards a democratic system of government in Turkey, the shah's secularism only laid the foundations for an autocratic, dictatorial political system!

The example of Bourguiba's Tunisia also represents the exclusionary relationship between state and religion. Since attaining independence in the mid-1950s, Tunisia lived under a liberal political system that strove to build a modern state based on the Western state model (the French model in particular). By following the French example, Tunisia experienced some of that model's secular violence toward religion. While the Bourguiba state continued to declare its respect for the standing of Al Zeitouna and religious institutions and to oversee Islamic endowments and religious affairs, it also marginalized them considerably, imposing restrictions on institutions and religious education. The state reacted violently to the creation of the Islamic Tendency Movement (*harakat al itigah al islami*), and the Tunisian president often behaved in ways that aroused and provoked religious sentiment among large sections of the population. Provocative state policies toward religion and the religious sphere reached their zenith in the post-Bourguiba era, turning into a raging exclusionary war on religion under the rule of deposed dictator Zine El Abidine Ben Ali. The Islamic movement (Al Nahda) was not the only victim of this exclusionary policy; the entire religious realm in Tunisia suffered from it.

Consequences – political Islam

The relationship between state and religion is different in each of the two models for which some examples in the Arab nation and the Islamic world have been rapidly reviewed. Extensive interference aimed at the monopolization and subjugation of the religious sphere, taking over religious institutions, and exploiting religion to legitimize state power and the ruling regime is not the same as excluding religion, pushing it out of public affairs, marginalizing religious institutions, and stripping society and the state of their Islamic character. There is a definite difference between the views adopted by each model of the position of religion in society and the relationship between state and religion in that society. This difference puts the two models at opposing ends of the spectrum. Nevertheless, the results produced by both models are very similar, if not identical. The most apparent common result of both models (countries where religion is excluded and those where it is subjugated) is the creation of a political problem for ruling regimes: the rise of Islamic political movements (Islamist movements), known as 'Political Islam'.

These Islamist movements seemed an objective wave of protest resulting from state policies in the two models described above (the exclusionary and the subjugatory), and led these states down a final, inevitable route. Where the relationship between state and religion was one of subjugation and monopolization, the rise of Islamist movements threatened the state's monopoly of religion and its domination over the religious realm, undermining its ability to control both single-handedly. Political Islamist movements contested the state's right to speak on behalf of religion and to represent it before public opinion and the people, particularly in light of the diminished stature, resulting from their adoption of positions in the service of state authority, of official religious institutions (scholarly and doctrinal). In many cases, the state was forced to play down its religious image in order to force the opposition to minimize its religious nature. By doing so, the state aimed either to 'expose' the opposition before the public as a movement exploiting religion, or to deprive it of the religious energy used to fuel its political agenda. In both cases, the state discovered that its exploitation of religion had been a serious mistake, with extremely grave and dangerous consequences. Matters were no different in states where the relationship with religion was exclusionary. Islamist political movements flourished in the vacuum created by the state's retreat from the religious realm and the atmosphere of open animosity created by its antagonistic policies toward religion and religious sentiment. Turkey may be the most obvious example of this model (the Al Refah, the Al Fadila and the Justice and Development Islamist parties rose from the ruins of its extremist secularism). However, Khomeini's Iran also avenged itself of the shah's secularism, sweeping it away completely, just as the Al Nahda Party and the Salafists in Tunisia avenged the implementation of a Tunisian form of French secularism in a country where religion is still part of the national culture and public life.

Implications of the rise of Islamist political movements

Islamist political movements are accused of thrusting religion into the arena of political manipulation and of subjecting Islam to a process of over-politicization. They are accused of emphasizing Islam's temporal aspect at the expense of tenets of faith, ethics and intellect, thereby transforming it from a universal faith (for the entire nation) into the political ideology[6] of a party competing for power against other parties harbouring identical aspirations. Not only is this accusation true, but also it is closer to being a *depiction* of the facts than an accusation. Arabs and Muslims are today witnessing a phenomenon of the politicization of religion that is both glaringly obvious and unprecedented. To be precise, they have been witnessing this phenomenon for a little over 80 years, ever since Sheikh Hassan Al Banna founded the Muslim Brotherhood organization and introduced the concept of an Islamic state into the modern and contemporary Arab political awareness. Over the past 50 years this concept has been interpreted in exaggerated terms in the declarations of Islamist movements that have transformed the idea from its original constructive meaning into terrifying and suicidal theocratic interpretations.

Islamist political movements did not invent the politicization of religion. As explained above, this had already been done by the ruling political elites in Arab and Islamic countries. In fact, Islamist political movements took note of this politicization, realized its usefulness, and adopted it as a sure means of attracting and mobilizing public support. It is important, when attempting to interpret this 'disastrous state of affairs', to have the necessary amount of objective sensitivity and comprehension to understand that Islamist political movements were literally forced to follow this route. When ruling elites use religion to justify their adoption of policies that are contrary to the state's interest, enlisting a large army of hired 'religious scholars' to help them do so, it is only to be expected that someone will use identical tools to counter these abortive and foolish policies. The author does not mean to make excuses for these movements, or to imply that their politico-religious protests are legitimate reactions. The concern here is to explain the historical background of this phenomenon, the consequences of which we are living with today, and to point out that the ruling elites, through their foolish actions and disgraceful manipulation of religion and the fates of societies, are responsible for flinging open the doors to the unknown.

The birth of the first Islamist political movement in the Arab world in the late 1920s (Mitchell 1977) – the Muslim Brotherhood – signalled, for the first time in modern history, a change in the strategy of basing a political agenda on a religious foundation. From an official state strategy, first used by the state, it was transformed into a popular, non-governmental strategy adopted by political groups. 'Partisan Islam' or 'militant Islam' was born of the strategy of manipulating the sacred that had been adopted by the 'modern' state, galvanizing the exact same elements and claiming the same source of legitimacy to counter this strategy, but aiming at different political ends. Partisan Islam may not be the first example of the association between religion and a popular political agenda in modern history; the Sufi faith had made this association at the end of the 18th century. Nevertheless, it is certainly the clearest example of this association, one that has taken Islam deeper than ever into the political arena and the struggle for power, favouring the political elements in Islam's cultural and belief tradition over the elements of faith, ethics and education.

'Partisan Islam' rapidly succeeded in its competition with the state over the exploitation of religion in political life. Of course, a main source of its success is that it protests against ruinous and ever-deteriorating social and political conditions. Another is its masterful, idealistic discourse, replete with promise and hope that heals daily wounds using wisely chosen politico-ideological terms, as well as the serious failures accumulated by previous political (nationalist, Marxist and liberal) protest movements that were unable to break through the solid wall of deterrence. Partisan Islam also owes its success to the abject failure of state attempts to make use of religion in the political sphere and the noticeable deterioration of official religious institutions. This is demonstrated by the fact that state-directed scholarly and legal Sunni Islam (its discourse, institutions and men) no longer has sufficient persuasive power to enable it (as in the past) to mobilize the public into its ranks. The increasing tendency of official religious institutions to justify state policies enraged great portions of the public who suffered from the catastrophic material, social and economic effects of these policies (tyranny, corruption, the misdistribution of resources, brazen submission and the humiliating preferential treatment of foreigners). The partisan Islamist protest movement had to appear to be rebelling against the savage, tyrannical state and its adulterated political Islam (or its hired religious ecclesiastics), positioning itself as a worthy successor entitled to inherit both political and religious power.

In its constant protests over the past 90-some years, partisan Islamism never protested against the association of political and religious power, an association that is reproduced in its own Islamist project. Instead, it protested against a specific facet of this association that it found hateful and abhorrent: the use of 'religious teaching' to service political power, without referring to its legitimate interests.

Religious teachings were used in the interest of state politics, and more specifically to promote the welfare of ruling elites. For many years, competition from partisan Islamism made it impossible for official Islamic scholarly institutions to wield influence of any significance in Arab societies. Because of their bias for the ruling authority and their rationalization of ruling policies, the standing and credibility of these institutions diminished in the eyes of the public. Parallel to the continuing rise of Islamist partisanship and popular Sufi Islam, official scholarly Islamic institutions experienced a period of decline and decay. The damage sustained to the image and stature of Al-Azhar over the past decades (in Egypt and in other Arab countries) and the erosion of respect for its learned sheikhs (so revered in the past) is a prime example of this phenomenon. It is common today to hear daily insinuations against official Islamic institutions, their leaders, their sheikhs and their representatives, as well as criticism of the *fatwa*s, decisions and positions adopted by these institutions – pronounced by spiteful Islamists rather than by secularists, as in the recent past.

Islamist political movements were born of the crisis in the relationship between the state and the religious realm (both in its subjugation/interference and marginalization/exclusionary forms). They were also the result of the catastrophic failure of the ecclesiastic function of official religious institutions. Born of these propitious conditions, they fed upon elements of two phenomena that have controlled Arab political life for decades, opening the way (since the early 1970s in particular) for the spread of partisan Islamist political, religious and organizational activities. The two phenomena are the political failure of leftist democratic, nationalist and socialist movements; and the strangling political deadlock created by mounting Arab tyranny. There is no reason to view the two phenomena as separate or coincidentally simultaneous. The two are deeply and tightly bound, making it impossible for the researcher to comprehend the implications of one phenomenon separately from the other.

There is no doubt that the emergence of the Islamist political movement precedes its crisis with political leftism by at least 40 years. For 40 years the movement struggled to survive in a cultural and ideological environment that resisted it – especially in the 1950s, 1960s and part of the 1970s. However, it soon found itself facing a suitable political moment: the defeat of the leftist nationalist lawmaker after the 1967 war, and later in the wake of the counter-revolution against leftist expansionism. Those moments marked the beginning of the return of partisan Islam to the scene. Partisan Islam benefitted from the overthrow of the Nasserist heritage in Sadat's Egypt and the huge amounts of Arab political funds provided by opponents of the nationalist/leftist project. However, the true turning point in the progress of partisan Islam was the success of the Islamic Revolution in Iran (1979), followed by the beginning of the battle of Jihadist Islam against the Soviet occupation of Afghanistan. With the defeat of the democratic project in the Lebanese civil war (1975–1977) and that of the Palestinian revolution in the 1982 war, Arab (national socialist) leftism's lost its last remaining support base in Lebanon, and was forced to retreat into exile. The late 1980s and early 1990s saw the final dramatic defeat of Arab leftism and its political project, following the collapse of the Socialist Bloc and the dismemberment of the Soviet Union and the destruction of Iraq after the Second Gulf War (February 1991).

The political vacuum created by the defeat of Arab liberal movements in the mid-20th century (which had been largely occupied by Arab Marxist nationalist leftism in the early 1950s and the first half of the 1970s) is the same political vacuum left by the leftist retreat in the early 1970s, and occupied by the forces of partisan Islam ever since. To borrow the phrase of Aristotle: politics – like nature – fears a vacuum. Based on relations of conflict, it needs a minimum degree of equilibrium, imposed (by law and objectively) by its own special dialectic. Despite the differences and contradictions between the foundations, visions and programmes of Arab leftist and Islamist movements (political, economic, social, educational and cultural), the two agendas share a certain idealism. This made it possible to exchange political idealism with another form of idealism that differs only in terms of justification and basic principles of thought. Nevertheless, the forces of partisan Islam were most successful in exploiting the resource of religion, neglected by the (nationalist Marxist) secular Left, and which the ruling regime and the Islamist movement continuously competed to control. This resource proved to be extremely valuable to the Islamists, when it became apparent that society (burdened by tyranny, exploitation, poverty and marginalization) was in dire need of a protest discourse of a soothing quality that offers new outlets for alleviating the pains of tyranny and oppression.

Regardless of the many other different factors that facilitated the rise and growth of partisan Islam, the political vacuum that resulted from the retreat and decline of leftist movements was, in general, the factor that created the conditions necessary for the emergence of Islamists and their rise to the pinnacle of politics. In countries where this vacuum appeared early, such as Egypt, Sudan, Syria and Iraq, Islamist movements were able to spread across, and permeate through, society from the second half of the 1970s. In other countries, such as Tunisia, Kuwait, Lebanon, Bahrain, Jordan, Algeria and Palestine, where it appeared relatively late, the growth of Islamist movements began in the 1980s, mostly in the second half of that decade. In Morocco, the Islamist movement dates back to the early 1970s. However, because leftism remained strong until the end of the 20th century, political Islamism was only able to make a real political breakthrough in that country after the creation of a great political vacuum, when the Left formed a 'coalition' government, headed by the great socialist leader, Abdel Rahman Al Yussufi, in 1988. It must be stated at this point that the term 'political vacuum' is not meant to be insulting to Islamist movements nor is it used in an attempt to belittle their present leading political position by claiming that they thrive on the political misfortunes of other political forces. This does not diminish from the principles and values of these movements; it is a natural historical phenomenon of human society. Conflict between generations, ideas and movements is part of the logic of politics and history. That a given movement takes over the stature, influence and role of another is only natural.

The political vacuum factor is related to another factor, one that is probably at the base of all factors and causes and that accounts for the surfacing of religion in contemporary Islamism's discourse of dissent. The fact is that the oppressive ruling elite's monopolization of politics and authority completely closed access to the political arena, to the extent of eradicating the very existence of this arena, thereby forcing social and political struggles to express themselves in non-political language and terms; ethnic[7] (tribal, clan, etc.), functional and religious language! That Islamist movements use the absolute language of religion to speak of the relative problems of this world has not always been a voluntary choice; in many cases (when they were not allowed to act as political movements with social agendas), the adoption of this language was the only option open to them. Established political regimes compounded the problem by refusing to recognize this movement as a political movement with a social agenda and its insistence on labelling it as a form of religious extremism, exploiting the 'moderate' Islam of the majority and its aversion to extremism. The most obvious proof that large sectors of the Islamist opposition were forced to use religious language in their political discourse is that, after they were allowed access into the political arena in the 1980s, they began to play down their aloofness towards politics (in Egypt, Tunisia, Jordan, Yemen, Kuwait, Morocco, Algeria, Sudan, etc.). The Islamist opposition started using the same political language and logic as other political parties, and reshaped its agenda to fit the demands of political activity – to such an extent that partisan Islam's political pragmatism often surpassed that of secular politicians.[8]

While the exploitation of the sacred in politics may have resulted from the absence of a political arena, where politics is practised according to its natural rules, using political terms, or even from the total inexistence of this arena;[9] the degree and extremity of political exploitation of religion was not equal among all parties. In addition to the 'moderate' political Islamist forces (and sometimes born from within them), emerged extremist forces that introduced the non-political into politics, transforming political conflict into an unbearable hell, for the state and for society both.

Some precepts for addressing the crisis

Can the turbulent relationship between politics, state and religion come to a healthy end that safeguards religion and society in contemporary Arab society, and close the chapters of offensive, useless and unproductive conflict between Islamists and secularists?

It is too early to claim that this will be possible in the near future, because there are no signs on the horizon of the preconditions to this happy conclusion. One of these preconditions is that the state be an independent entity that is separate from and above cultural conflicts. Attaining this distant objective would not mean depriving politics, as an objective social contender, of the ideal political conditions it needs. Nor would it prevent society from coming to an agreement on the transitional precepts required for further action until the conditions for the separation of politics from religion develop naturally, and a modern political sphere, free of all overlap and confusion, is born. Of course, this modern political sphere will not be born magically, without explanation, reason or introductions; it will grow out of a process of historical accumulation. Common accord on a set of transitional precepts constitutes part of the accumulation of circumstances required for the emergence of this modern political sphere. If accord cannot be reached, it may be necessary to go down an obligatory historical route to complete the creation of the desired entity. Anyone who imagines that creating politics and state as an independent entity can be achieved through strict laws and legislation aimed at preventing the introduction of the religious and the cultural into politics (in other words, by forcibly freeing politics of all that is not political), would be mistaken. Numerous ruling elites have tried this illusory option, only to fail miserably. The complete independence of the political sphere will only occur when society, or the majority of society, agrees to it of its own free will. This common accord will be difficult to reach before the political culture promoting this modern concept of state comes to prevail in a society. To this moment, this culture is not prevalent in Arab societies, or, at least, it has become the culture of political minorities. This reinforces the belief in the need for agreement on a set of transitional precepts for the development of the political sphere and implanting in it the basic values of a modern secular system (transparency, dialogue, disagreement, compromise and agreement).

What is meant by transitional precepts to regulate the relationship between the religious and the political in ways other than those that exist today in most Arab countries (subjugation/interference and marginalization/exclusion)? Naturally, since they are described as transitional, these basic precepts are exceptional (although necessary) and not natural. That is, they are not founded on the recognized precepts regulating the relationship between the religious and the political in the modern secular state. Although exceptional, they were used in other societies where secular elites conceded the existence of some sort of relationship between politics and religion, and recognized the right to draw inspiration from religious principles in politics and political action (Turkey being the latest example). Obviously, the Christian Democratic political parties in Germany, Italy and other European countries, and the Islamist parties in Turkey (Al Refah, Al Fadila and Justice and Development) constitute examples that are far more developed than partisan Islamism existing in Arab countries today.[10] Given the disparity of circumstances and levels of development, the two examples cannot be compared. Nevertheless, the smooth, balanced relationship between religion and politics in these countries can be used as an ideal to aim for here – on condition that the Arab political elite (religious and secularist) recognizes the need to reach an accord on establishing suitable foundations for working toward this end.

In this context, four fundamental precepts are presented:

- First Precept: Conceding the right of any political movement to draw inspiration from religion and religious heritage in forming the founding principles of its political agenda, on condition that this inspiration is regarded as an expression of the political and philosophical thought of the inspired movement, to be criticized and contradicted as a body of thought; not as religious doctrine. It will be up to the people, as the final source of authority, to judge whether to adopt this line of thinking or not. Secularists must understand that no one may prohibit a group of people from founding politics based on religion. Ruling elites have previously tried to do so, through legal, legislative and violent means; yet three-quarters of the Islamist movements in the Arab nation (if not more) emerged and grew under this prohibition. Rather than follow this path, which has brought devastating results to societies, it would be better to concede this right and to regulate it through peaceful dialogue between both parties, indeed, among everyone in society.
- Second Precept: Underlining the non-religious nature of all political parties (Islamist and secular) to safeguard the difference in nature between politics and religion, between the absolute and the relative, between the realm of interests and the realm of faith; while this presupposes that secularists concede that Islamist movements are political movements, it presupposes, too, that Islamist parties accommodate their principles and programmes to the logic and basic precepts of partisan activity, following the successful example of the Al Nahda movement in Tunisia, a quarter of a century ago. A part of this accommodation process is to work on politicizing party discourse, to stop resorting to religious mobilization, manipulating the sacred and embroiling religion in political conflicts.
- Third Precept: Respecting the secular nature of the state and not exploiting election results to alter its identity, whether in an anti- or pro-religion direction, or to make religion the ruling authority in the state. The state is an abstract social entity

that surpasses its individual social components. There is no such thing as a religious or an atheist state, a state whose citizens are believers or non-believers. It is not the state, but Heaven, that judges people's religious faith. To perceive the state as such is to raise it above the relative, temporal condition that necessitated its creation, to embody and manage the public good, and it constitutes a search for an end that is beyond it (Laroui 2001).

- Fourth Precept: Respecting the democratic process of power succession and not tampering with the foundations on which it is built or with the political calendar regulating power succession. This includes the respect of the basic state regulations (the constitution) and abstaining from introducing constitutional amendments aimed at the restriction of civil liberties, or from tailoring the constitution to the benefit of a particular group, or amending it to increase presidential powers and similar politically corrupt ends. It also includes not restricting access to the political arena through constitutional means and in the name of popular democratic legitimacy.[11]

Finally, to establish this kind of modern secular state, a period of training is needed. This may take a decade, a generation or longer, but there is no escaping it if a modern political sphere is to be built in contemporary society, where the relationship between state and religion is rectified, so that politics and society never have to deal with its problems again.

Notes

1. For a critical interpretation of the concepts of 'governorship' and 'Wilayat al-Faqih' (rule of the jurist cleric), see Belkeziz (2009).
2. Ignatius Goldziher does not share this point of view. In his opinion, little attention was given to religion and religious legitimacy during the period of Umayyad rule (Goldziher 1984, 67).
3. For more on this concept and its importance to the system of politics, state and legitimacy, see Arkoun (1984).
4. For more on this dual combination, see Laroui (2009).
5. To read about this mediocre pattern, see Ghalioun (1991).
6. For a more detailed account of this, see Belkeziz (2008a)
7. For a detailed explanation, see Belkeziz (2008b).
8. This is said although it is conceded that pragmatism may also be a characteristic of what is called the 'law of necessity'!
9. For a more detailed view, see Belkeziz (2007).
10. The Al Nahda movement in Tunisia may be the most successful example of secular political Islam, in other words, a political Islam that believes – along Turkish lines – that no contradiction is involved if citizens are members of an Islamist party and believe in the secularism of the state. However, this is only an assumption that Al Nahda will have to prove, now that it is in power.
11. This was the path followed by the regimes of Ben Ali, Mubarak and Ali Saleh, where the constitution was amended to allow for successive presidential terms!

References

Arkoun, Mohammed. 1984. *Pour une Critique de la Raison Islamique, Islam d'hier et d'aujourd'hui*. Paris: Maisonneuve et Larose.

Ben Al Hussein Abu Ya'la Al Farra', Mohammed. 2000. *Al Ahkam al Sultaneya* [Sultanate Rulings] [corrected and commented on by Mohammed Hamed Al Feqy]. Beirut: Dar Al Kuttub Al Ilmiyyah.

Belkeziz, Abdelilah. 2007. *Al Sulta wa al Mo'arada: al Majal al Seyassi al Arabi al-Mu'asser (Halat al Maghreb)* [Power and Opposition: Contemporary Arab Political Domain (The Case of Morocco)]. Casablanca: Al Markaz al Thaqafi al Arabi.

Belkeziz, Abdelilah. 2008a. *Al Islam wa al Siyassa: Dawr al Haraka al Islamiya fe Sawgh al Majaal al Siyassi* [Islam and Politics: The Role of the Islamic Movement in Shaping the Political Sphere]. 2nd ed. Beirut and Casablanca: Al Markaz al Thaqafi al Arabi.

Belkeziz, Abdelilah. 2008b. *Al Dawla wa al Mujtama': Jadaliyyaat al Tawhid wa Alinqissam fi al Ijtima' al Arabi al Mu'asser* [State and Society: Dialectics of Unity and Division in Contemporary Arab Society]. Beirut: Al shabaka al Arabiyya lil Abhath wa al Nashr.

Belkeziz, Abdelilah. 2009. *The State in Contemporary Islamic Thought*. London: I. B. Tauris; and Beirut: Centre for Arab Unity Studies (CAUS).

Ben Taymia Al Harani, Abu El Abbas Ahmed Ben Abdel Halim. 2000. *Al Seyassa al Shar'iyyah fi Islah al Ra'i wal Ra'iyyah* [Legitimate Politics for Reforming Leader and People]. Beirut: Dar Al Kuttub Al Ilmiyyah.

Ghalioun, Burhan. 1991. *Le Malaise Arabe: L'Etat Contre la Nation* (Cahiers Libres). Paris: La Découverte.

Goldziher, Ignatius. 1984. *Etudes sur la Tradition Islamique* [Studies on Islamic Tradition]. Vol. 2 [Translated by Léon Bercher]. Paris: Librairie d'Amérique et d'Orient, Adrien Maisonneuve.

Ibn Khaldoun, Abū Zayd 'Abdu r-Raḥmān bin Muḥammad. 1973. *Al-Mukaddimah*. Beirut: Dar Al-Kitab Al-Arabi.

Al-Joueini, Abu Al Ma'ali Abd el-Malek Ben Abdallah (Imam of the Holy Sites). 1996. *Ghiyath al-Umam fi Iltiath al Tholm* [Saving Nations by Avoiding Injustice] [Marginal notes by Khalil Mansour]. Beirut: Dar Al Kutub Al Ilmiyyah.

Laroui, Abdallah. 2001. *Mafhoum al Dawla* [The Concept of a State]. 7th ed. Casablanca and Beirut: Al Markaz al Thaqafi al Arabi.

Laroui, Abdallah. 2009. *Min Diwan al Seyassa* [On Politics]. Beirut and Casablanca: Al Markaz Al Thaqafi Al Arabi.

Lewis, Bernard. 1988. *Le Langage Politique de l'Islam*. Paris: Gallimard.

El Mawardi, Abul Hassan Ali Ben Mohamed. 1982. *Al Ahkam al Sultaneya wal Welayat al Diniya* [Sultanate Rule and Religious States]. Beirut: Dar Al Kuttub Al Ilmiyyah.

Mitchell, Richard B. 1977. *Al Ikhwan al Muslimoon* [The Society of the Muslim Brothers] [Translated by Abdel Salam Radwan and Mona Anis]. Cairo: Maktabet Madbouli.

Weber, Max. 2006. *Sociologie de la Religion* [Translated and presented by Eleanor Kalinowski]. Paris: Flammarion.

Problematics of political authority within Islam

Muhammad Mazouz

Mohammad V University, Philosophy Department, Rabat, Morocco

This paper sets out to disentangle what is discernible from the historical record and the evidence from legendary accounts of the spread of Islam by conquest. It argues that rather than by the sword, Islam came to Spain through the development and succession of ideas. The paper further deconstructs the theory of Islamic governance, attributing forms of rule not to Islamic teachings but to prevailing power structures and struggles. It is contended that what is known of specific incidents reaches us through the narration of the incident, rather than by its physical existence. If a serious event takes place, it reaches us through a serious Hadith (like the Prophet's Hadith), but if the incident is not very significant or did not take place at all – but an authority wants it to have happened – it reaches us as a legend. The legend starts where history ends, and takes its place to complete the story's events. History depicts and legend narrates.

First: the spread (or diffusion)

Political Islam emerged early on and almost inadvertently at a moment in the history of humanity. It grew at such a surprisingly fast pace that its adversaries hardly paid attention to the Muslims' *intentions* in the early years of activism (the attacks and conquests). Even the Prophet's (ﷺ) message was not taken seriously by the notables of Quraish, but was mostly the object of ridicule. However, this message addressed and threatened not only lowly polytheists, but also kings and emperors who were asked to join the Muslim call and adhere to its principles. This historian is surprised at the Prophet's courage when He sent messages to Heraclius of Byzantium, the Shah of Persia, Negus of Ethiopia, Macocas of Alexandria, etc. supported by a small group of companions, both Muhajireen and Ansar (immigrants and loyalists) while his addressees were the potentates of states and empires! It almost turns the historian's head when he studies in detail the early Muslim conquests of half the old world, or three-quarters of it later on, in a record amount of time.[1]

The historian is also astounded at the sight of all those tumbling empires, states, cities and fortresses, strewn around like autumn leaves! How could the historian's imagination review these events and link them to the real causes behind them? In these events, the religious, political and social are rolled into one, whereby one factor takes no precedence over the other, turning the outcome into a cause, and the cause into an outcome. Often, the astounding success of the new religion, or the conquests that followed it, is attributed to the strength of the religious doctrine in total disregard of the ethnic, tribal and economic reasons involved. Religion does not explain history; it is history that explains religion.[2]

Andalusia was conquered in a strange sort of way, akin to a series of events behind which stands a mythical hero.[3] Here we have Tariq bin Ziad crossing the (Gibraltar) Strait with a few thousand warriors on four ships borrowed from the City of Cadiz, thanks to the good auspices of Ceuta's governor, Julian the Visigoth. As Tariq stepped down on the Green Island, he ordered that the ships be burned and delivered his famous speech, in literal Arabic, to fighters, the majority of whom hailed from Amazigh stock! Here is a man escaping defeat in the Mashreq, travelling thousands of kilometres in order to establish an Idrissian State in the farthest corner of the Maghreb! And here we have another escapee from defeat in the Mashreq rebuilding the Umayyad State in Andalusia! Conquests no longer needed formidable armies, but just one 'escapee' capable of building states and kingdoms at the far end of the world!

Although the Spanish historian Ignacio Olague, writing in the 1970s, cast doubt on the scenario outlined above, no one paid attention to his explanation of the way the conquest of Andalusia unfolded. Olague expressed his doubts initially with some general critical remarks in which he says:

> When the Caliphs sent their armies to conquer the world, their aim was to spread the new faith rather than for the sake of the conquest itself; to do that, the Caliph had to occupy and control in order to impose change on the non-Muslim communities. Since such a project requires a mighty state and a strong government, and since a social infrastructure such as this logically requires a rich inhabited land, it presupposes that in the Seventh Century the Arabian Peninsula was entirely different from the way it is today. However, we have unequivocal proof now that the Peninsula's inner desert is an ancient one. It looks today as it did during the Muslim call, i.e., its people were – almost exclusively – nomadic Bedouin tribes. So where did the Caliphs find their reservoir of men and money, a reservoir necessary to achieve their plans and aspirations?
>
> (Olague 1991, 23)

If the conquests encountered such obstacles upon setting out from the Arabian Peninsula to Greater Syria and Iraq, one can only imagine the obstacles they would have encountered when they crossed into Egypt and North Africa, not to mention the fact that Greater Syria was under Byzantine rule and Iraq under Persian rule! The Arab armies would have had to cross some 3000 kilometres along the southern shores of the Mediterranean, an arid desert tract that suddenly changes into rough mountainous terrain (Aures, Rif and Atlas Mountains), to reach the Sea of Darkness where another 2000 kilometres of hardship awaited them. Olague remarks to Lévy-Provençal that, 'One of the basic conditions is a good harvest so that the army could supply itself well before setting out [...] in the years of drought it is impossible to contemplate going to war.' He then asks (Olague 1991, 26) 'How could an army of forty thousand men cross the most deprived region on the face of the earth, at the end of the Seventh Century?' He concludes with the following assumption: 'Even if this did actually happen, this army would have reached North Africa completely exhausted, to a place where well-trained Berbers waited to destroy it as soon as possible' (27). 'How could the Arabs think of invading the Iberian Peninsula when they had just arrived from the Arabian Peninsula exhausted from war?' Over and above that, Olague adds that there are geographic obstacles and logistical challenges that make it difficult to cross the southern shores of the Mediterranean, with the knowledge that the Berbers did not have naval vessels:

> Even if the Arabs had small boats they would have had to find skilled captains, especially since the Straits of Gibraltar, that link the ebb and flow of the Mediterranean to the Atlantic Ocean, are beset by strong currents that flow in both directions, and are constantly battered by strong winds. It is a dangerous passage known as the ships' cemetery.
>
> (28)

Where did the Arabs get ships with which to cross the Strait? Did they carry them on horseback when they reached North Africa?[4]

About this matter, Olague says:

> Essentially, only a seafaring people like the population of Qadiz could achieve such a feat, especially since the people of this city have been travelling to England since the Third Millennium BC, in search of tin. Moreover, this city's sailors were able to sail along the West African coast of Africa and had even perhaps circumnavigated the Horn of Africa. It was probably these sailors who also helped the Vandals/Germanics to sail in the opposite direction. Even after the age of decline – in the early Eighth Century – Qadiz's sailors still owned transport vessels capable of ferrying troops. The question is however: why did the people of Andalusia provide such a service to those who came to subjugate them? And if we assume that Tariq had managed to double-cross the Iberians and hide his intentions from them, then why did these sailors help Mousa bin Nuseir ferry supplies to Tariq, a few months after that?
>
> (29)

If the men did indeed cross the Strait, how did they obtain horses after landing in the Green Island? Did a battle take place on the island? Where are the invaders' tombs? Do historical documents and archaeological excavations indicate the presence of an Islamic cemetery from that era?

The oldest text that speaks about the invasion and conquest of Andalusia dates from the latter half of the ninth century, i.e. around half a century after the crossing took place. Subsequent historical texts, by both Muslim and Christian historians, gave the event a legendry dimension: it is a legend of invasion for one side and of conquest for the other. These texts blame the event on a divine miracle: a divine victory for one side, and divine punishment for the other.[5] According to the conquest legend, Tariq bin Ziad crossed the Strait with 7000 men then burned all the ships (a foolish step in terms of military strategy because he cut his own supply lines!), followed a few months later by Mousa bin Nuseir with 18,000 men. Where did this invader/conqueror obtain double that number of ships again? Did he burn them like Tariq did after landing? Did the fighters ever return to the southern shores to see their sons and wives? Did the army commanders not think of these issues? Were they as confident as that? What was the fate of Tariq whose name disappeared immediately after the conquest? What fate awaited the few conquerors when they stood face to face with a Germanic Visigoth population estimated at around 10 million people (knowing the latter's prowess on the battlefield!)? Was there any resistance? How did it all unfold?

There are two possible answers to the above questions: either a miracle of sorts took place during the conquest, or these events never took place at all.

Whether a miracle took place or these events never happened, the process of describing, analysing, building a scenario and other theoretical processes that the historian undertakes fall apart, opening the way to counter stories, narratives and tales. As Umberto Eco has put it, 'Those things about which we cannot theorize, we must narrate.' Here below is the story of the conquest as the narrators recounted it and the historians transmitted it.

> Witiza, the last Visigoth King of Andalusia, died leaving three sons: Olmund, the eldest, Romulus and Ardabast; since the latter were still young their mother assumed guardianship of their father's royal dominion in Toledo. Roderick, who was a leader in their father's dominion, deviated from the path with some of his combat companions and occupied Toledo. When Tariq bin Ziad conquered Andalusia – during the reign of Al-Walid bin Abdul-Malek – Roderick wrote to King Witiza's sons, who had grown and were now riding horses, asking them to pledge their loyalty to him and join him against the common enemy. He then set out to meet Tariq. When the two parties met, Olmund and his brothers decided to double-cross Roderick. That night, they sent a message to Tariq informing him that Roderick was once one of their father's dogs, and asking him for safe passage in order to meet him in the morning, and for help in regaining their father's lost dominion in Andalusia. This included three thousand villages, called from then on the '*Kings' Share.*' In the morning, they and their companions joined Tariq and thus became the reason for the conquest"
>
> (Abu Bakr Mohammad bin Omar bin al-Qoutiya in Al Abyari 1989, 29–30)

We conclude from the above tenth-century text that the issue involved a civil war among the Western Visigoth kings, who sought help from the rulers of provinces under their control in northern Morocco at the time. Had it not been so, how can we explain the cooperation between the sailors of Qadiz and the governor of Ceuta, and later on that of Tangiers, when they got involved in this civil war?[6] The issue was therefore regaining the throne that Roderick had usurped from the sons of Witiza, the lawful king; it is a Visigoth versus Visigoth war! If this were the case, what did the Arabs and Muslims have to do in the matter? How did Islam infiltrate Andalusia? How were Islamic states and kingdoms established and made to last for eight centuries?

The Muslims successfully crossed into Spain and scored a victory for the same reason that allowed them to prevail in the Arab Mashreq. According to Olague (1991), this reason is the supremacy of Arianism in Byzantium's eastern provinces and the Visigoth territories in the West. The fact that Arianism was a Unitarian Christian sect that denied Christianity's divine nature and rejected the trinity principle explains the speed of the conquest and lack of resistance by the inhabitants of these territories. The 'Orthodox' religion was able to triumph only when it married religion with power, i.e. when it became an official state religion (of the Roman Empire in particular). In the Iberian Peninsula, however, the conflict between the two religions ended with the defeat of Orthodoxy and its retreat to the poor north at the time (the Asturias Mountains and Basque country), while Arianism triumphed in the rich south (Andalusia).

Witiza belonged to Arianism and Roderick to the Orthodox religion; thus, when the civil war ended with an Arian victory, the Iberian Peninsula was cleansed with blinding speed because the local inhabitants adhered to this Unitarian religion. This coincided with the advent of new ideas from the Arabian Peninsula, similar to those of the Visigoths in North Africa and the Iberian Peninsula. This allowed the Muslim culture to spread in Andalusia not as an alien or distant culture, but as a process of renewing and rejuvenating the prevailing religious and spiritual atmosphere at the time. The state that controlled Andalusia in the eighth and ninth centuries was not Islamic but Arian.[7] The culture that prevailed in that state gradually developed and acquired Islamic characteristics, thanks to an Arabization process and the activities of a group of preachers who diligently imparted the principles of the new culture. They used the allure of the Arabic language to impart principles similar to those of the local inhabitants, at a time when the principles and symbols of the Arian doctrine were part of the state system, and of all commercial and monetary affairs.[8] This is why Olague arrives at the conclusion that there was no invasion of Andalusia, but the development and succession of ideas. This means that in Andalusia neither was Islam spread by the sword nor was the Islamic state founded on dead bodies; it spread through a process that he called '*la idea/fuerza*'. He says in this context:

> We conclude from similar movements that the spread of Islam was the result of *idea/fuerza* rather than the ability to launch armed military attacks. Just like Hellenism was able to prevail in the past and the West today, Islam's hegemony cannot but be the outcome of *idea/fuerza*. To continue believing that populations in whose countries impressive civilisations prosper are ready to abandon their beliefs and change their customs just because a band of horsemen has defeated them militarily, is a childish way of looking at social life. The issue has to be understood from the intellectual and cultural perspective: There was no military invasion but a revolutionary crisis and a call borne by scholars, not generals. Only scientists can understand and lead the movements of populations; military supremacy cannot prevail for eight centuries in Andalusia, and forever in vast areas of the world.
>
> (Olague 1991, 66)

Islam did not prevail by the sword but through *idea/fuerza*, and Spain was not occupied by the Arabs as the legend of the conquest claims. There was no invasion; or else, where did the original inhabitants go? How could they evaporate from the pages of history books?

Today, Spain is having difficulty reconciling itself with its history, and is trying very hard to hide eight centuries of Islamic rule in an effort to link its present directly to its Roman and Visigoth past. This difficulty is the outcome of efforts by traditional historians to obliterate some 10 million Iberians from the pages of history, and claim that they had sought refuge in the Valleys of Asturias in the north, to organize a resistance (for eight centuries) and launch a war to regain the country usurped by the Muslims! The Restoration Wars waged by the Catholic kings were not wars of liberation as much as they were wars of invasion and occupation, concludes Olague, because they invaded from the south rather than the north!

Second: the conduct of governance

Islam was not spread by the sword and no great army was mobilized for the task, as traditional history claims. What actually took place was a series of local rebellions and revolutions by the original inhabitants of the land, and the entrenchment of prevailing (Arian) beliefs in the eastern Byzantine and Western Visigoth provinces. The Persian provinces in turn witnessed the entrenchment of their own religions, including, among other, the Manichean and Zoroastrian sects. Who believed, for example, that the Umayyad state was an Islamic state at heart? The history books are full of examples of Umayyad rulers deviating from the tenets of religion, whether at the Sharia or doctrinal level. Did Mu'awiya not give a speech to 'the general populous' of Quraish men telling them: 'If you think me not the best among you, I am the best for you!'[9] Did Abu Sufyan, prior to that, not face Abu Bakr (may God's blessings be upon him), reject his nomination as caliph and address his people saying, 'Do you accept your sons of Abed Munaf to have someone from the Bani Tamim clan as your ruler?[10] By God, I shall fill the valley with horses and men.'

When the caliphate moved to Baghdad, the Muslim state was Islamic in form but Persian at the core. Once the Persian hegemony had waned, governance fell into the hands of the Turks[11] and, after the Ottoman Caliphate, it was the turn of Western colonialism. In the wake of colonialism's retreat, the fact that the political situation reverted back to different national groups and tribes means only one thing: lack of a purely Islamic governance theory. If the Arabs had a known political system they would have taken it along with them to the newly conquered lands, and if they had an organized army they would have been able to impose their own administration system. It was rather the contrary: it was the Arabs who copied other people's political, administrative and economic systems. Did Omar bin Al-Khattab (may God's blessings be upon him) not establish the 'Donations Office' to organize booty and taxes? Who staffed these offices at different periods of the Islamic Caliphate State? And, prior to all that, what was the Rashideen Caliph's vision of governance? Did they resolve the affairs of state based on a clear theory that relied on laws (like the Roman laws) or on constitutional provisions (like the Greek constitutions) that everyone was subject to, or did they resolve them by the sword? Al-Shahristani (1980, 22) says, 'The greatest discord among the *ummah* was over the imamate; at no time was a sword drawn for a religious purpose like it was against the imamate.' It is square zero in politics when the sword speaks in lieu of the tongue.[12] For although the Ansars' position, embodied by the slogan 'one prince from us and one from you', dissolved in the face of the Muhajireen's position, embodied by the slogan 'the imamate in Quraish', this did not resolve the conflict but simply concealed it for a while: three caliphs were assassinated despite the imamate remaining in the hands of Quraish.[13] The Umayyad era arrives and the caliphate is still in the hands of Quraish, though this time in the shape of a 'formidable royal authority'. This change from the caliphate to the formidable royal authority also took place by the sword; did Mu'awiya not address Quraish when he arrived in Madina the year he assumed power, saying, 'By God, I did not become ruler because of your love for me or your pleasure in my appointment, but I had to fight you with my sword!'? A single tribe, Bani Umayya, seizes power by the sword, and the tribe's rule is brought down only by another tribe, when it became strong enough, as Ibn Khaldoun has said. Bani Abbas brought down Bani Umayya's rule thanks, this time round, to a grudge born and bred in Khurasan, in the name of avenging the Bani Hashem tribe. With this, Islam's political history appears as a struggle between two tribes, Bani Umayya versus Bani Hashem; the conflict between the tribes produces only one form of governance based on grudges and partisanship, 'the more ruthless the ruler, the more deference he is owed!'

When contemporary Islamic thought, including the Salafist and fundamentalist currents, returns to the era of the Rashideen Caliphs in the belief that it was the golden age of Islam, they are motivated by the desire to avoid any fallout from the 'redoubtable royal authority's' experience, i.e. the hereditary governance model that the Umayyads had established by the sword. However, any return to the Rashideen caliphs necessarily collides with another obstacle, namely the infighting among the Prophet's companions. How could anyone sidestep these historical events? Or, at least, how could they be justified? Denying that there was infighting among the companions is a useless exercise, and justifying it is hard to accept.[14] This is sedition and sedition is worse than murder! What remains then from the Rashideen caliphs' experience? What good would it do to repeat the same experience as it happened? Does the contentious and bloody relationship among the Companions – in which the Prophet's widow got involved – serve as an example for future generations or as a model for the present one? This is a historical not a doctrinal experience, which is why the imamate experience was not accepted as one of religion's fundamentals, except unwillingly,[15] and why it was the last issue to be addressed by this science's final compilations. The scholars of religion's fundamentals considered the imamate a subsidiary rather than a core issue, and therefore placed it under jurisprudence rather than the spoken word. It is a Sharia rather than a doctrinal issue and, as such, it involves matters such as inheritance, marriage, etc., however based on its own particular rules. This means that any talk about the imamate should be confined to the search for the right conditions regarding the appointment of the imam from a legal perspective, without getting involved in issues such as who is more deserving of the succession, the favoured imam versus the availability of a better option, or challenging the legitimacy of a certain imam, etc. or in any other issues that divided the imamate into parties and groups. This is how the issue of the imamate was lost between jurisprudence and the spoken word! The issue of the imamate was lost because the Muslims wanted to resolve it in advance, but like all other resolved issues, this would have subjected it to the rules of the Sharia and fitted into a jurisprudential mould. However, things do not always go according to one's hopes and intentions because historical events were not the object of consensus, the sword, bloodletting and mutual calls for revenge took over; in other words, they entered into an endless vicious circle of revenge.

Ahlul Sunna (the Sunni Community) believe that the caliphate issue would have been resolved for good had it not been for the appearance of new phenomena, especially in conjunction with Othman and Ali's (may God's blessings be upon them) caliphate. Thus, although the early Muslims disagreed over the imamate and the Ansar accepted the acclamation of Saad Ubada Al-Khazraji, Quraish said that:

> the imamate should be from Quraish. The Ansara then gave in to Quraish when Abu Bakr told them that the Prophet (pbuh) said that the Imamate should be in Quraish. This disagreement still goes on today because Dirar and the Khawarej said that the imamate could go to someone from outside Quraish.
>
> (Al-Baghdadi 1982, 13)

Therefore, after the consensus came the disagreement; what is to be done, then?

Regardless whether the above Hadith is true or not, whether it came after or during the fact or directly from the Prophet himself (ﷺ), history has voided it of its effectiveness and significance because the issue has been resolved by the sword, rather than the Hadith, and because there are other rival Hadiths that say the exact opposite.[16] This means, among other things, that every incident has its own Hadith: every (historical) event has its own Prophet's Hadith to support it, whether this Hadith was written before, during or after the event took place. The Hadith aims to cut the event down to size and void it of its historical significance in order to bend it in a manner that fits the idea. Integrating the event into the Hadith aims to create an example and a model; what exemplary model remains from the Islamic experience?

What is certain, for reasons mentioned above and others not mentioned, is that this model will be drawn neither from the Umayyad nor from the Abbasid experience, which leaves us with the experience of the Rashideen caliphs, the Prophet's friends. Sometimes, this experience is represented by the event itself and, at others, by the Hadith (whether it is the Prophet's or not). When it is represented by the event, all the bloodletting that has taken place obliterates the example, since no bloody experience could serve as a golden rule except if the colour of blood becomes the event's symbol! Where does the example of the experience come from, then? It comes from the principle: the principle of *shura*. It is the manner in which the imamate was decided, based on acclamation. What is the nature of this principle? And what is the truth about *shura*?

Shura relies on choice rather than appointment, which indicates a lack of consensus among the *ummah* on one system, as long as the Shia adhere strictly to the text and in appointments. Over and above that, *Shura* does not require consensus, per se. Imam Al-Juweini says:

> Know that a decision on the imamate does not require consensus; the imam is appointed even if there is no consensus among the *ummah*. The proof is that when Abu Bakr was appointed imam, he immediately *began* to address the Muslims' affairs and did not wait for the companions to spread news of his appointment to all the countries. No one denied him his actions or asked him to wait; when consensus is not a condition for deciding the imamate, numbers and limits become unnecessary.
>
> (Al-Juweini 1950)

The acclamation of an imam does not require specific numbers or limits: a single person from among the decision-makers is enough to decide the fate of the imamate,[17] for an unlimited period of time! If the imam's tenure is not limited by a specific time period, and if the decision could be taken by a single individual, what remains of good governance, then? What remains of the Shura principle? Who will consult with whom?

Third: the making of a legend

Ibn Khaldoun believes that:

> Royal authority is a natural quest of partisanship rather than a choice; it is part of life and its organisation. Wherever there are laws, religions or any other matter that concerns the public, partisanship is an integral part; it is necessary for making any claim […] partisanship is necessary for the community and only in its presence could God's will be implemented. Al-Sahih says: 'God has never sent a prophet except with protection from his people'
>
> (Ibn Khaldoun 1981, 202)

Therefore, only in the presence of partisanship would God's will be implemented, and would not be otherwise. Once it is implemented through partisanship, it is the community's turn to make it acceptable to everyone. This is exactly what transpired at the Saqifa meeting, and during the ensuing acclamation and *Shura*. Even the caliphate's transformation into a formidable royal authority found cover in the community; and if the tribe offers protection to its prophet it is not a free gesture. It has to do with providing a doctrinal cover that bestows legality on 'the matter', before distancing any adversaries asking for a share of power, or to be part of it. Did the Ansar not ask to share power with Quraish and brandished the slogan 'One prince from us and one from you,' only to see their attempts quashed by the call for 'the imamate in Quraish'? However, the conduct of the political struggle does not stop at slogans (be they religious or temporal); it transcends them to the hidden reasons that these slogans epitomize. If the Ansar themselves coined their slogan (a temporal slogan), who coined the Muhajireens' slogan (a religious slogan);[18] was it the tribe or its dead prophet? And who coined the Hadith that says 'the caliphate will last thirty years after me then will turn into a formidable royal authority'? Was it the Bani Umayya tribe or the prophet of the larger tribe that encompasses the smaller tribe?

If the formidable royal authority ended up in the hands of the Bani Umayya tribe, and if we concede that the above is correct, we cannot but be surprised by this turn of events; for it would have been more fitting, likely and suitable for this authority to end up in the hands of Bani Hashem (the Prophet's tribe). So what was the secret behind Bani Umayya's seizure of power? If the Hadith was right (i.e. if it was not written during the Umayyad period), and if the Prophet knew that the formidable royal authority will fall into the hands of Bani Umayya, it means, among other things, the alienation of his own tribe from power. Did the Prophet acquiesce to this turn of events? The fact that the formidable royal authority passed into the hands of the Bani Umayya means that the tribe that was His main enemy during the spread of His call would reap the fruits of His efforts in building a state, and uniting the tribes under the *ummah*'s banner. To say, however, that the Hadith's contents is in the realm of 'miracles', i.e. it reports on the unknown in a neutral manner, means that events unfold based on the balances of power, thus making 'royal authority a natural quest of partisanship rather than a matter of choice', as Ibn Khaldoun says.

Al-Maqrizi had already expressed his discontent and surprise at Bani Umayya's illegal seizure of power, and turning it into a formidable royal authority; he says:

> I was often surprised at Bani Umayya's seizure of the caliphate – given their distance from the Prophet's origin compared to the Bani Hashem's proximity to it – and wondered, how could they have allowed this to happen? And how do Bani Umayya and Bani Marwan Bin Al-Hakam, the man expelled and cursed by the Prophet (pbuh), relate to this Hadith given the enmity between Bani Umayya and Bani Hashem in the Jahiliya days? There is also Bani Umayya's enmity towards the Prophet (pbuh), the extreme harm they caused him and their attempts to prove him a liar in all that he said since God sent him the revelations and rightful religion, until he conquered Mecca, the city graced by God Almighty, when some of them joined Islam, as is well known.
>
> (Mou'nes 1998, 25)

No reason was found for the enmity between the Bani Umayya and Bani Hashem tribes, except in the legend,[19] meaning that the enmity between them was eternally fated and inescapable, which is why it continued after Islam and did not remain confined to the Jahiliya period. To illustrate that, Al-Maqrizi (Mou'nes 1998, 71–74) enumerates the members of the Bani Umayya tribe who fought the Prophet (ﷺ), showed enmity towards him and mistreated the Muslims when they became governors of provinces in the Peninsula, Yemen, Greater Syria, Iraq, etc. He then wonders about why events unfolded as they did, and why the situation deviated from its path in a manner that allowed Bani Umayya to take a firm grip:

> I still wonder, after all these many years about the matter, and others like it, for too long a period to mention, and continued to ask all the scholars, historians and news carriers I encountered [...] until it became clear to me, God be thanked, why Bani Umayya seized the caliphate and deprived Bani Hashem of it.
>
> (71–74)

What is this reason? Al-Maqrizi realised that the real power rested in the hands of Bani Umayya during the Prophet's life,[20] and it was only natural for it to remain in their hands after his death. Could Abu Bakr (the Prophet's successor) have changed the situation, he who belonged to a tribe that bears no grudge and displayed no partisanship towards anyone? Did Abu Bakr's policy differ from that of the governors that the Prophet appointed to the provinces? Did Omar's policy differ as well? When Othman became caliph, he 'added insult to injury' by bringing his tribal kinsmen closer to him, and lavishing the Muslims' money on them. When protests and revolutions erupted in reaction to that, he refused to relinquish power and uttered his famous statement, 'I will never remove a shirt God has sewn [...] or trousers that God has woven.' There was no choice then but to remove him by the sword, which brought about the great sedition.

First the event takes place then the Hadith narrates it; however, moving from the event to the narrative is replete with ambitions, intentions, wishes, objectives and aspirations. And because the matter has to do with the people's fate and future of the *ummah*, the narrated tale becomes the actual incident (the incidents of the invasion, acclamation, conquest, crossing, imamate and emirate, etc.). However, each incident has its particular significance (the battles of the camel, Siffin, Yarmouk and Qadisiya, al-'Iqab, al-Zallaqa, etc.), and because the incident itself does not reach us, since it is impossible for it to do so, what does reach us is the narration of the incident, which explains the need to integrate the incident into the narrative and the event into the Hadith, replete with the hopes and aspirations that express the *ummah*'s soul, rather than its physical existence.

If a serious event takes place, it reaches us through a serious Hadith (like the Prophet's Hadith), but if the incident is not very significant or did not take place at all – but I want it to have happened – it reaches us as a legend. The legend starts where history ends, and takes its place to complete the story's events. History depicts and legend narrates. History tells us exactly what happens, calls things by their name, verifies numbers, articulates suppositions and list all the reasons to ensure accuracy. The legend, on the other hand, humanizes the event, inflates numbers and quantities, inflates the dimensions of creatures, exaggerates the results, confuses time and space, does not respect the logical sequence of events, does not search for reasons and does not care about the relationship between cause and effect.

When historians wrote about the era of conquests, they found no incidents during the crossing of the Strait to depict. However, since an Islamic state was already established there, they concluded that the Muslim army had come to North Africa all the way from the Arabian Peninsula then crossed the Strait to the northern shore. But how did the crossing take place, and who crossed over? From all the tales that reached them, historians found only legends, since this period's contemporaries saw neither large armies nor formidable massacres. There was no invasion and no resistance. Thus, when these historians could not make a logical analysis and had no mental vision of the events – since there is nothing but a historical white-out – they reached out to the legend as a lifesaver.[21] This legend claims that the reason for the conquest was Roderick's enmity towards Witiza's sons, with the Muslims coming to the latter's rescue! As for their victory over the enemy (whose enemy?), it was a done deal and an eternally fated event.[22] The legend speaks about the global code that does not change, while history speaks about victories and defeats that took place as a result of mistakes committed in battle, or a strategic genius. The historian speaks about actual events that could have happened in a different way, and about unexpected events due to changing convictions, betrayal or another catalyst: everything is relative.

Conclusion

Here we are face to face with (our) history, and with events that reached us through narratives. This is why every time a Muslim historian recounts an event or an incident he appends to it the phrase 'God only knows'. This means that Islam's history is fraught with legends, and therefore needs long and diligent efforts to demythologize it, as Paul

Ricœur calls the process. Demythologizing occurred in the West after long efforts and a considerable amount of sacrifice that eventually culminated in the religious Reformation, followed by a series of political and cultural revolutions that allowed many layers of legend to be peeled off, to reveal the human beings concealed underneath a mass of interpretations and explanations, emanating from a variety of conflicting backgrounds and currents. This is why we cannot talk about democracy before we 'delegendify' names, titles, persons, families, clans and tribes, etc. because before being a system, democracy is a relationship. Therefore, in order for this relationship to exist, we should first see one another as we truly are: we look but do not see! This explains why we resort to threats and promises of impending doom whenever serious disagreements arise between us, and the powerful among us move to action and 'fill the valley with horses and men'.

Notes

1. The conquest sequence unfolded as follows: Syria (636 AD), Palestine (638), Mesopotamia (639), Egypt (642), Persia (643), Libya and Tunisia (747), Cyprus (649), Punjab (664), North Africa (701) and the Iberian Peninsula (711–713). In the west, the conquest stopped on the doorstep of the French city of Poitier in 732, while in the east, it stopped at the gates of Constantinople in 717.
2. How does the historian explain – with calm objectivity – the Battle of Yarmouk that took place in 636 in Syria, and culminated in Byzantium's defeat, followed three years later by the Battle of Qadisiya that culminated in Persia's defeat?
3. Let us ponder the following historical events: North Africa was conquered between 701 and 710 by Mousa bin Nuseir; one year later, around 7000 men crossed the Strait to the Green Island upon a request from Julian (Ceuta's governor) who wanted to avenge the rape of his daughter by Roderick, who also usurped the throne from Witiza, the Visigoth king. Roderick's 100,000 man army was defeated by Tariq's 7000 fighters, then in turn Mousa bin Nuseir crossed the Strait to take part in the conquest; this is how Andalusia was conquered by the Muslims in the span of three years!
4. The writer of *Akhbar Majmou'a fi Fateh al-Andalus wa Thikr Oumara'iha- Rahimuhom Allah- wa-Alhuroob el-Waki'ah Biha Baynahom* (Reports on the Conquest of Andalusia, Naming its Princes – May God Rest Their Souls – and Mentioning the Wars Between them Therein), says that the man called Julian invited the Arabs to invade Andalusia to avenge his daughter's honour, for 'when Roderick became King, he desired the daughter of Julian and he raped her, and people wrote to her father saying that Roderick had raped her. The latter became very angry and said, "By the Faith in Christ I will obliterate his reign. I will make a trap for him ('dig under his feet')." He then sent a message to Mousa declaring his allegiance and inviting him to come to visit his cities, once Julian had made a deal satisfactory to him and his companions. He described Andalusia to him and invited him to come, after the year 90. Mousa bin Nuseir sent one of his loyal men [...] by the name of Abi Zar'a with 400 men and one hundred horses, in four ships' (al-Abyari 1989, 16–17). Also according to this source, Tariq bin Ziad then crossed in these same boats into Andalusia with his men, 'with no other means'; see *Akhbar Majmou'a fi Fateh al-Andalus* (16–17). Olague (1991, 28) casts doubt on the incident saying, 'Julian lent the Arabs four boats each accommodating no more than 50 men in addition to the crew. If this was the case Tariq would have needed to make thirty-five trips to ferry his army across, i.e., seventy days, because this kind of boat requires at least one whole day to cross the distance. If we take into account the weeks of bad weather during which no trips can take place, then the crossing would have required three months. This is only feasible if those who made it ashore were able to escape a massacre in order to welcome those who will follow them.'
5. The Muslims base themselves on the notion of the 'small group' that manages to defeat the big group thanks to God's support, who gave them victory over the non-believers, a notion that prevailed before that among Christians and Jews. The Muslims explain their conquest of Andalusia as God standing with them, while they explain their expulsion from it as

punishment for straying away from the true faith's principles. In turn, the Christians explain the invasion of Andalusia as a divine punishment for the sins they committed, while they saw the Restoration Wars led by the Catholic kings as a divine victory due to their return to the righteous path.

6. Julian was Governor of Ceuta and Tariq was Governor of Tangiers. Olague (1991) believes that the 'ic' in Taric's name goes back to the old Germanic language, which means 'son of'. Many original Visigoth/Germanic names had the same ending: Roderic, Ervic, Viteric, Almaric, Gessalic, Alaric and Ilderic. In Arabic, the name Tariq comes from the subject of the word '*taraqa*' (advance on a path, to strike with a hammer), which makes it possible that the name could be the nickname Muslim chroniclers gave to the victorious leader, which eventually replaced the original one. It is also possible that they Arabized his Germanic name Taric to Tariq, which made sense to them (Olague 1991, 198, n. 14). The inhabitants of Tangiers still call Gibraltar 'Jabal Tor or Tar' (the mountain of Tor or Tar); did the public's memory preserve the original name and pass it orally down the generations?
7. Olague (1991, 249–250) says, 'In the first half of the Ninth Century, Cordoba's writers did not know of Mohammad's existence; in 849 AD, one of this school's authors learned some information about the Prophet Mohammad, though this information concerned events that took place abroad and not in his country, which traditional historians claim was Islamised a century and the half later. [...] We have precise and conclusive documents regarding this discovery and we can specify the year in which Cordoba's School learned about Mohammad's existence, and about some of his beliefs. There is no doubt that prior to 849 AD the learned among this Christian minority who lived in the state capital – considered by traditional history as an Islamic State – had never heard anything about Mohammad and had no idea what his beliefs consisted of.'
8. In the Archaeological Museum of Madrid and the Public Library in Paris are gold coins from the early eighth century; they are the Byzantine Piaster 'Solidus' and bear Byzantine inscriptions and Latin etchings; coins with Arabic script do not appear before the ninth century. Coins from the late eight century were in both Arabic and Latin. Until very late in the eighth century, Iberian coins did not resemble the Arab dinar at all; on one side of them was written 'Solidus Feritus in Spania', and the other side bore a Visigoth symbol, specifically an eight-sided star. The Unitarian phrase is unequivocal: In the name of God, there is no God but the just God, He has no equal. Olague (1991, 158–159) comments saying, 'Despite its appearance, this is not an Islamic term. The term reflects the core of Arian conciliatory beliefs. In this case like in others, the myth of the conquest has led to faulty rulings. In these etchings, as in others that belong to other religious sects of the early middle ages, we need to envisage the development of unitarian notions in the days that immediately preceded Islam. What confirms this precedence and the style of these expressions is their high complexity compared to the simpler short Islamic expression: "There is no God but God", meaning that there is no need to confirm to the believers that God is One and has no equal. With Islam unitarian monotheism reached its simplest and clearest form. On the other hand, Islam is a divinely revealed religion: God revealed it to the Prophet to preach the new religion. The term that epitomizes His principles – the testament of faith – indicates that the Prophet who spread the religious call: "There is no God but God, Mohammad is the Prophet of God", means that one cannot envisage Islam without the Prophet. As to the writings on the Eighth Century Iberian coins, they do not refer to Mohammad at all.' Olague goes on to say, 'What distinguishes these etchings more than any others is their aggressive style, while in its simplicity the Islamic terminology demonstrates great reason acceptable to all believers. It is pure and exudes Islam, and its ability to effect change and spiritual mobilisation is far from revolutionary. On the other hand, the Arian term denotes a sense of religious strife: There can be no equal to God. Against who was this clarification necessary? Against the elements of the trinity [...] and the eight-sided star that defines the Arian concept of unitary monotheism, and its presence on the coins of that era confirms that the supporters of conciliatory Arian religion were in power rather than those who believed in the trinity, or the Muslims' (159–160).
9. This speech is in direct contrast to the one delivered by Abu Bakr, who said, 'I was made your guardian, though I am not the best among you'; the reason is that the latter belonged to

one of Quraish's original families, while Mu'awiya belonged to the strong Bani Umayya tribe. Mu'awiya's intent was the exact opposite of Abu Bakr's; what he wanted to say was: 'If you do not think I am the best among you at the religious level, I am the best among you at the political level.'

10. Abu Bakr belongs to the Bani Tamim tribe, a humble tribe compared with the strong tribes of Quraish.
11. Vasiliev (1934, 10–12) says, 'The Abbasids defeated the Umayyads thanks to the Khurasani Persian element. [...] In Khurasan, there was resistance against the Umayyads that was not only political in nature, but religious as well. A party virulently opposed to the religious policies of the Umayyads saw the light in Khurasan, it believed in the global nature of Islam and its slogan was, "Islam does not differentiate among peoples." We should remember here that the Umayyad Government was known for its civil nature and that religious issues got very little attention. This party, whose aim was to instil equality between different peoples under Islam, or equality between the Persians and Arabs, was known as "the Sho'oubya". It was an active and prosperous party in the Second and Third Centuries *hijri* and some of its leaders gave precedence to the Persians over the Arabs. This is why when the Abbasids came to power they considered themselves as a by-product of the Persians. In fact, at that time, the Persians were playing an increasingly significant role in the caliphate, so much so that after their victory, the Arabs had to hang down their heads in front of those they had defeated only yesterday. [...] We know full well the danger posed by the Baramika at the end of the Third Century until Haroun Al-Rashid annihilated them, although many reasons lead us to believe that this family remained faithful to the Zaradashtrian sect. [...] Moreover, all the important positions in the royal court, army, wars and administration of the provinces were in the hands of Persian officials. [...] It was not until the reign of Al-Mansour, the second Abbasid Caliph, that we saw Arabs waiting in vain to enter the gates of the palace, while the Khurasanis entered without permission, while mocking the uncouth Arabs. The war that broke out between the brothers Al-Amin and Al-Ma'moun, after the death of their father Haroun Al-Rashid, was in fact a new kind of war between the Arab and Persian "nationalities"; the Arabs were defeated again. However, in the middle of the Ninth Century, the Persians had to relinquish their favoured position to a new foreign element, the Turks, the reason being that, since the mid Eighth Century, the caliphs not only took Turkish prisoners customarily into their courts, but also into their private homes. No one suspected at the time that this custom would be a determining factor for the caliphate or that the Turks would destabilise this empire's foundations and eventually bring it to an end.'
12. Sheikh Ahlul Sunna wal Jamaa, Aboul Hassan Al-Basri, recounts what transpired at the Saqifa regarding the imamate saying, 'The first disagreement among the Muslims after their Prophet (pbuh), was over the imamate; when the Prophet of God (pbuh) was called by God to heaven and was honoured by him, the Ansar gathered in the saqifa of Bani Saada in the Prophet's city and wanted the imamate to go to Saad Bin Abada. When Abu Bakr and Omar (may God's blessings be upon them) heard about that, they went to the place where the Ansar were gathered and Abu Bakr told them that the imamate should be given to someone from Quraish. He protested their intentions and quoted the Prophet (pbuh) saying, "The Imamate in Quraish," which convinced them and made them acquiesce. The Ansar then said: "one prince from you and one from us"; then Al-Habbab Bin al-Munther drew his sword and said, "*ana juthailaha al-muhakkak wa 'uthaiqaha al-murajjab*, who will duel with me?"' (Al-Ashaari 1969, 39–41). The phrase '*ana juthailaha al- muhakkak wa 'uthaiqaha al-murajjab*' is given as an example of the individual who relies on his own opinion and seeks guidance from it. The word '*juthail*' is a diminutive of *jathal*, which is a reed against which scabby camels rub themselves; *al-'uthaiq* is the diminutive of a palm tree rich with fruit; *al-murajjab* is the object noun particular to palm, the palm being so full of fruit that there is fear that they will fall off the tree. His use of diminutive was only meant as a method of praising (Al-Ashaari 1969, 41, n. 2).
13. Abul-Hassan Al-Basri says, 'Discord took place during Ali's reign over the issue of Talha and Zubair (may God's blessings be upon them), and they fought him and fought Mu'awiya. Ali fought him until the swords of both sides broke, their spears were blunted, they had no more energy and they fell to their knees' (Al-Ashaari 1969, 60–62).

14. 'Adad al-Deen Al-Eejee summarizes various positions and reactions to these events and seditions, saying: 'As to the sedition and warfare among the Companions, the Hashemites denied that they ever took place; this is no doubt contentious, given the successive events of Othman's assassination, the Camel Incident and the Siffeen Battle. Of those who admit that it actually happened, some keep their peace because they believe it is not their business, and so be it. Al-Shafei said, "God has purified our hands from this blood, so let us purify our tongues from it, as well. If they mean for us not to know whether it took place or not, it is wrong because it definitely took place. The Amries (friends of Amr Bin Ubayd) and the Wasiliya (friends of Wasel Bin 'Ata') agreed to restore both parties' testimonies." They said that even if everyone testifies to a handful of herbs, they would not accept it. In turn, the Amries blame everyone, and the Wasiliya blame no one in particular and therefore we see no justice. What the people know is that the evil-doers are those who killed Othman and fought Ali, because they are two imams. Murder and disobedience is absolutely forbidden' (Al-Eejee 1999, 143).
15. Al-Eejee (1999) says about the imamate, 'We mention it in speech as a basis for what we accepted,' in his book *Al-Mawakif fi Ilm al-Kalam* (n.d.) Al-Ghazali (1988) says about it, 'Studying the imamate is also not one of the required tasks, and not part of the art of speech in matters of jurisprudence. It is also a root cause of partisanship, and those who stay out of the subject are saner than those that delve into it, and if he was right, how was he then wrong?! But if the intention is to no longer believe in it, then it means we want to take the usual path, for hearts are deeply repelled by the contrarian path.' Imam Al-Juweini says, 'This subject is not one of the fundamentals of belief, and the mistake that those who address it commit emanates from ignoring its roots' (Al-Juweini 1950). Al-Taftazani (1989) says, 'There is no question that the subject of the imamate belongs to the branches of the faith, because it has to do with the establishment of the imamate and qualities of those deemed fitting to occupy the post. It is not a secret that it belongs to practical rather than doctrinal rulings. Our jurisprudential books say that the ummah needs an imam that revives religion, establishes the sunna, does justice to those deprived of it, and gives each his due and puts them in their right place.'
16. The Hadith quoted by the Shia confines the imamate to the Prophet's family, particularly from outside Quraish, while the Khawarej quote Hadiths that say that any Muslim could become an *imam* (whether slaves or free men), even Ethiopians and Persians.
17. Al-Baqlani (1987, 467) says, 'If someone says "Through you will the imamate be resolved," the response was "one individual from the among the decision-makers can do that, if he decides on a man that has the right qualifications, that man would become the imam."'
18. The Hadith about the 'Imamate in Quraish' that was quoted to the Ansar was not mentioned either by Omar Bin Al-Khattab or by Abu Bakr, whether at the Saqifa Meeting or during the acclamation speech at the mosque, a day later. Sunni historians who are experts on different groups and scholars of religious fundamentals claim that this was the Hadith that Abu Bakr used as justification at the Saqifa meeting, and helped him win the Ansars' support. Al-Ashaari (1969, 41) says, for example, 'Abu Bakr justified himself by quoting the Prophet's (pbuh) statement, "The Imamate in Quraish," and thus won their obedience and support and the people returned to the righteous path.' However, Omar Bin Al-Khattab, who was a witness, details what took place at the Saqifa and quotes both parties' justification (Ansar and Muhajireen) without mentioning this Hadith. Omar is quoted as saying, 'We learned – when the Prophet (pbuh) passed away – that Ali and Zubair and their companions stayed behind at the house of Fatima (daughter of the Prophet (pbuh)), and all the Ansar went to Bani Saada's Saqifa and the Muhajirenn met with Abu Bakr. She said to him, "Oh Abu Bakr, let us all go to our brethren the Ansar." We went on our way until we met two worthy men who told us what the people had done; they said, do not approach them, and do what you need to do oh Muhajireen. I said: By God we shall go to them; so we went to Bani Saada's Saqifa. We found them gathered and among them a man who had been befriended, so I asked, who is this? They said: Saad Bin Ubada; I said: what is wrong with him? They said: he is in pain. When we sat down their preacher stood up, praised God and his family and said: We are the Ansar (supporters) of God, and Islam's battalion; and you, oh Muhajireen, you are our prophet's kinfolk (*waqad dafat daffah minkum*) *and* you want to remove us from our roots and

sideline us from what is taking place. When he fell silent, I wanted to speak – and I had edited an article that I liked – and wanted to say it in front of Abu Bakr – and wanted to indulge him a little, he who was wiser and more prominent than me. Yet, by God, he said everything I was going to say in my prepared piece, except he said it off-the-cuff, so I stayed quiet. He said, all the good you have mentioned you are party to, all that the Arabs know about this is in this quarter of Quraish: they have the highest status and relations among all the Arabs. I selected for you these two men to choose the one you like best, then took me and Abi Ubaida Bin Al-Jarrah by the hand. I did not hate what he said other than that. He was older and my throat closed and I would not like to rule over a people with Abu Bakr among them. Then one of the Ansar said: one prince from you and one from us (*ana juthailaha al-muhakkak wa 'uthaiqaha al-murajjab*), oh Quraish. So I told Malek: what does this ("*ana juthailaha al-muhakkak wa 'uthaiqaha al-murajjab*") mean? He replied as if he was saying I understand it well. He said: the clamour increased and voices rose and feared that there would be disagreement. I said: open your hand, oh Abu Bakr; so he opened his hand, and I acclaimed him as did the Muhajireen followed by al-Ansar. Omar said: By God, we found what we came for and I agree to Abu Bakr's acclamation. We were afraid that the people would not agree with us and there would not be an acclamation, and that it would happen after we left. Either we acclaim whom we like or we disagree with their choice and there will be corruption' (Al-Aashari 1969, 42–44, n. 1). Abu Bakr did not justify himself by quoting Quraish's *imams* but justified himself at length using the supremacy of Quraish: 'All that the Arabs know about this is in this quarter of Quraish.' If the Hadith was known and used at the time, Abu Bakr would not have missed the chance to use it to justify himself, especially since his words were not convincing enough; he had drawn his sword immediately after he finished speaking and the Ansar raised the slogan 'one prince from us and one from you,' and 'clamour increased and voices rose.' How does it stand to reason that the Ansar would give in when the conflict was at its height among the tribes who drew power from their past glories? What actually happened was a kind of equilibrium between the two sides that made a solution difficult. Both sides feared that the situation would reach a point of no return, whereby disagreement would be followed by chaos. Therefore, each tribe conceded one of its demands. This was an inevitable compromise solution, the most 'gentle' of solutions to avoid a senseless tribal feud.

19. The legend says: 'The discord was still ongoing between Bani Hashem and Bani Abed Shams (to which Bani Umayya belong) whereby it was said that Hashem and Abed Shams were born twins. Abed Shams was born before Hashem with the finger of one child stuck to the forehead of the other; when it was removed there was blood all over the place. People said that there will be blood between them, and so it was' (Mou'nes 1998, 38).
20. Al-Maqrizi says in this context: 'There is no disagreement among the imams who are experts in the Hadith, the critics of news or the scholars of events and history, that the Prophet (pbuh) died and was taken to Mecca by Abu Abdul-Rahman 'Attab Bin Usayd Bin Abi al-'Eis Bin Umayya Bin Abed Shams Al-Qurashi al-Umawi […] then Abu Bakr (may God's Blessings be Upon Him) accepted 'Attab until they died on the same day […] the Prophet (pbuh) had sworn in front of five men [from Bani Umayya …] and Aban Bin Said Bin al-'Aas Bin Umayya was in Bahrain by military force […] Amr Bin Said Bin al-Aas Bin Umayya was in Taima', Khaybar, Tabouk and Fadak […] and Abu Sufyan Bin Harb Bin Umayya was in Najran, and the Prophet died when he was still there. […] Said, Bin Al-Qashb Al-Azadi Bani Umayya's ally, was in Jerash, and the Prophet died when he was still there […] the Muhajir Bin Abi Umayya […] was in Kinda and Al-Sadaf, after which Abu Bakr appointed him governor in Yemen. Amr Bin al-Aas was in Oman until the Prophet's death […] and Othman Bin Abi al-Aas was in Taef […] and the Prophet (pbuh) died when he was there' (Mou'nes 1998, 71–74).
21. Like other fellow historians, Abdul-Wahed Al-Marakshi recounts the story of the conquest as such: 'The Muslims conquered Andalusia in the month of Ramadan, in ninety-two *hijri*, and the conqueror's name was Tariq Bin Ziad, also known as Ibn 'Amr. He was the governor of Tangiers appointed by Mousa Bin Nuseir, Prince of Qayrawan. It is said that Marwan Bin Mousa Bin Nuseir left Tariq there to oversee the soldiers and went to see his father for an urgent matter; Tariq took advantage of the situation to cross the sea

towards Andalusia from the Green Island side. The owner of the Green Island and its Roman districts, engaged to the daughter of the great King, angered the King who then cursed and threatened him. When he heard the news, he gathered an army and set out to the King's country, and Tariq learned that this front was clear, and took advantage of the situation. It is said that the infidel sent him a message to cross over for a reason I am aware of, which is that Roderick – King of the Island – may God curse him – had a system whereby his main leaders and princes sent their daughters to his palaces where they were taught manners and regal behavior, as they saw it. When one of them reached the age of maturity and was well behaved, he married her off to someone in the palace that he thought was worthy of her father. So the owner of the Green Island sent his daughter to him, according to that plan, where she remained until she reached the age of puberty. He saw her one day and liked her, and called her to him but she refused, and said: I will not come to you until you bring all the kings, leaders and patriarchs and marry me, after you consult with my father! He was angry at that and raped her. So she wrote to her father and told him what had happened, and this was the reason why he wrote to Tariq and the Muslims, and the conquest ensued, and God knows which of this actually happened. Tariq then crossed over to Andalusia, took his time doing what he had to do, scored a victory against the enemy and wrote to Mousa Bin Nuseir – who had appointed him governor – informing him of the conquest and his victory in Andalusia and the booty he had collected. Mousa envied him his personal gain and wrote to Al-Walid Bin Abdul-Malek Bin Marwan informing him of the conquest and taking the credit for it. He then wrote to Tariq chiding him for entering it without permission and ordering him not to advance further from where the message had reached him until he could catch up with him. He then set out towards Andalusia. [...] Tariq met him and won his acceptance and tried to quell the envy that was in his heart, and said to him: I owe you my post of governor and this conquest is for and because of you, and gave him the money he had collected as booty. This is why the conquest was attributed to Mousa Bin Nuseir, because Tariq continued and finished what was left of Mousa's conquest. [...] Upon conquering Toledo, among the objects Mousa had found was the table of Suleiman Bin Daoud (may God's blessings be upon them); it is said that it had one golden tier and one silver tier and was garnished with pearls and precious stones; he was also accompanied by Tariq. Al-Walid died when Mousa had reached Tiberias in the year ninety-six, so he took what he had with him to Suleiman Bin Abdul-Malek; it is said that when he arrived Al-Walid was still alive, but God knows the truth' (Al-Marakshi 1998, 10–11).

22. Ibn Al-Qoutiya recounts the legend of Andalusia's eternal conquest as follows: 'The Visigoth Kings in Toledo had a house with a coffin in it, and in the coffin there were four new testaments on which they swore. They honoured that house and never opened its doors, but when one of their Kings died his name was etched in it. So when Roderick became king he wore the crown. [...] He then opened the house and the coffin when Christianity had forbade him to do that, and found pictures of the Arabs *mutanakiba qasiyaha*, with their turbans on their heads. At the bottom was written: if you open that house and took out those pictures the people depicted in these pictures will come to Andalusia and score a victory' (Ibn Al-Qoutiya 1994).

References

Al-Abyari, Ibrahim, ed. 1989. *Tareekh Iftitah al-Andalus* [History of Andalusia's Conquest] (Andalusian Library 2). Beirut: Dar al-Kitab al-Lubnani and Cairo: Dar al-Kitab al-Masri.

Al-Ashaari, Abul Hassan Ali Bin Ismail. 1969. *Maqalat Al-Islamiyeen wa Ikhtilaf al-Musalleen* [Words of Muslims and Discord of the Faithful], revised by Abdul-Hameed and Mohammad Muhiyeddin. Cairo: Maktabat al-Nahda al-Masriay.

Al-Baghdadi, Abdul-Qaher Bin Taher. 1982. *Al-Farq baynal Firaq* [The Difference between the Parties]. Beirut: Dar al-Afaq al-Jadida.

Al-Baqlani, Abu Bakr Mohammad Bin Al-Tayeb Bin. 1987. *Tamheed al-Awael wa Talkhees al-Dalael* [Introducing the Basic Principles and Summarising the Evidence]. Beirut: Muassassat al-Kutub al-Thaqafiya.

Al-Eejee, 'Adad al-Deen Abdul-Rahman Bin Ahmad. 1999. *Al Mawaqef fi 'Ilm al-Kalam* [Attitudes in Rhetoric]. Beirut: 'Aalam al-Kutub.

Al-Ghazali. 1988. *Al-Iqtisad fil I'itiqad* [Economy of Belief]. Beirut: Dar el-Kutub el-Ilmiyyah.

Ibn Al-Qoutiya. 1994. *Tareekh Iftitah Al-Andalus* [History of Andalusia's Conquest], edited by Abdallah Anees al-Tabba'. Beirut: Mu'assassat al-Ma'aref lil Tiba'ah wal Nashr.

Ibn Khaldoun, Abu Zeid Abdul-Rahman Bin Mohammad. 1981. *Al-Muqaddima* [The Introduction]. Beirut: Dar al-Qalam.

Al-Juweini, Abdul-Malek bin Abdullah bin Yousef Abu Al-Maali (Imam of the two Holy Sanctuaries). 1950. *Kitab Al-Irshad* [Book of Guidance], edited by Muhammad Youssef Mussa and Ali Abd el-Mun'em Abd el-Hameed. Al-Jeeza: Matba'at el Sa'adah.

Al-Marakshi, Abu Mohammad Abdul-Wahed Bin Ali. 1998. *Al-Mu'jam fi Talkhees Akhbar Al-Maghreb* [Summary Lexicon of Al-Maghrebi News]. Beirut: Dar al-Kutub al-'Ilmiya.

Mou'nes, Hussein. 1998. *Al-Niza' wal Takhasom bayna Bani Umayya wa Bani Hashem* [Conflict and Discord between Bani Umayya and Bani Hashem] (Thakha'er al-Arab 62). Cairo: Dar al-Maaref.

Olague, Ignacio. 1991. *Los árabes no invadieron jamás España* [The Arabs Never Invaded Spain], translated into Arabic by Ismail al-Ami. London and Beirut: Riad al-Rayes.

Al-Shahristani, Abou Al-Fath Mohammad Abdul-Karim bin Abi Bakr. 1980. *Al-Malal wal Nahl* [Peoples and Bees]. Beirut: Dar Al-Fikr.

Al-Taftazani, Sa'ad el-Din. 1989. *Sharh al-Maqased* [Clarifying the Intent], edited by Abd el-Rahman Umayrah and Saleh Mussa Sharaf. Riyadh: Aalam el-Kutub lil-Tiba'ah wal Nashr wal Tawzee'.

Vasiliev, Alexander. 1934. *Al-Arab wal Roum* [The Arabs and the Byzantines], translated by Mohammad Abdul-Hadi Sha'ira, edited by Fouad Hussein Ali. Beirut: Dar Al-Fikr Al-Arabi.

The state and identity: the relationship between religion and politics – Tunisia as an example†

Salaheddine Jourchi

President of the forum group 'Al-Jahez'; a Tunisian journalist and rights activist

This paper presents the discourse, or more often the struggle, between secularists and Islamists in Tunisia relating religion and the state within the desired democratic system. The movement of 18 October is a landmark in the efforts for constructive work between different political constituents which emphasized that the relationship between religion and the state is not expected to have a ready-made formula; instead, it is the product of a social pact that interacts with politics, culture and economics. The paper looks into the basis or foundation for cooperation, the feasibility of the merger between religion and the state, the timing – before or after democracy takes hold – the focus on form and substance of democracy, its connection to laws, etc. Whereas it may be possible to separate religion from the state, it is not possible to separate it from politics as this requires a dissociation of some devout believers from their system of belief, thus denying their basic rights. There are no guarantees that within a democratic system some groups and parties basing themselves on religion will be against democracy. These groups should remain part of the political system, the solution being to honour a social pact that is based on respecting constitutional institutions, national identity, principles of the republican system and human rights.

Introduction

After the revolution brought down President Zine El Abidine Ben Ali's regime in Tunisia, a conflict broke out among the political and cultural elite on the nature of the relationship between the state and religion in the future democratic system. Since there was no peaceful and deep preparation for the ensuing debate around this sensitive issue, the discussions between the Islamists and secularists took on a sharp tone and were characterized by hard-line attitudes and mutual recriminations. The fact that it almost turned into a cold war raised fears for the future of the revolution, whose motives and slogans were as free of iSdeology as they were a social revolution with democratic dimensions.

This paper is an attempt to monitor this conflict's development and to examine its most salient aspects, after first reviewing its history, which is a necessary step given its very

†This paper was originally presented at the Symposium on Religion and the State in the Arab World, convened by the Centre for Arab Unity Studies (CAUS) and the Swedish Institute of Alexandria in Al-Hammamaat, Tunisia, October 2012.

close link to the ongoing debate on this issue that has forcefully imposed itself on Tunisia, as it did on other Arab countries going through similar changes, primarily Egypt.

The reformists after the downfall of the caliphate

When the annulment of the Ottoman Caliphate was announced, the majority of Muslims felt that the 'symbolic institution' that gave them a sense of belonging to a unified political entity was no more, and the reformists realized at that time that their attempts to save and reform the 'Caliphate State' had failed. This, however, did not end their attempts to reform the local political entities that succeeded in imposing their presence and legitimacy, while preserving in the past a pro-forma relationship with the Ottoman Sultan. These had gradually become a fait accompli and paved the way for the establishment of what became known as the nation-state or '*ummah*' (nation or motherland). The downfall of the caliphate made these separate regional entities and nation-states the only safe haven for communities and elites eager to ensure their political and economic survival, without mitigating their desire for unity and rekindling the sense of belonging to a wider entity, justified by historical ties and the need to protect the common interest. Many among the elite saw Kamal Ataturk's policies as an example for the effort to establish states based on local nationalisms, i.e. policies that entrench loyalty to the nation, meaning the individual state, and integrate this loyalty in a way which is adapted to the basics of a state.

In this context, and since the debate on the reasons behind the Muslim's underdevelopment began in earnest, the symbols of the Arab awakening failed to take on the responsibility of establishing the 'Islamic State', except for a few reformers like Mohammad Rachid Rida, who spoke about reinstituting the caliphate. However, though the Islamic State was not part of the Arab reawakening thought, it did not mean that there was agreement on the separation between state and religion. What was uppermost on the minds of the majority, in the period that preceded colonialism, was reforming the political entities that existed at the time, modernizing the army and the administration, and bridging the gap between the authorities and the people to endow the former with a minimum level of legitimacy and efficacy, by restricting its powers and attaching conditions to it. When the ugly side of colonialism became apparent, the reformers' interests expanded to include, besides political reform, a focus on distinguishing cultural and social factors such as religion, language, history and culture; on the need to protect the national wealth against foreign thievery; and on calling for independence.

The Islamists and the 'Islamic State' dream

The Islamic State concept only became a focus of debate, and an objective for some, when revivalist Islamist Movements appeared on the scene, chief among which was the Muslim Brotherhood. This banner/objective was conceived and promoted as the natural outcome of two foregone conclusions; the first was that the Prophet (ﷺ) was not content with simply establishing a society or an *ummah*, but established a state in the city as well. The second was the belief that Islam is a comprehensive system that does not require a separation between religious and political. This explains Hassan al-Banna's definition of Islam as a 'state and a religion, a *mishqf* (Quran) and a sword', a definition adopted by all those who espoused the so-called 'political Islamist' ideology that considers Islam the main reference for all issues related to state and society.

First: the Tunisian experience

When Tunisia gained its independence and the establishment of the state began in earnest; members of the Constituent National Assembly, elected to draft the country's new constitution, were soon compelled to discuss the cultural background of the new national state. It became clear at the time that, regardless of their cultural background and including followers of Al Zeitouna current (in reference to Zeitouna University), the elite had no model to emulate except the modern European-style state, in particular the French model. This is not so strange for Tunisia given that the reform project, which began to take shape in the days of Khair Eddin Pasha, centred around reforming the state based on the European model. Even adherents of the Zeitouna current, who played a major role in defending Tunisia's identity and Arabism, did not have any clear formula for a viable state based on Islam.

On the other side of the equation, and although Habib Bourguiba had an alternative ready-made model in the form of the French statehood model which he followed in form and much of its content, members of the Constituent Assembly could not bring themselves to ignore the cultural identity of the future Tunisian state. It is obvious that all states in the world are created, and develop and grow within the cultural, religious, political and geographic environment in which they exist; in other words, the state is neither established in a vacuum nor implanted in a foreign environment to which it has no connection.

However, contrary to what most people think, Habib Bourguiba, the architect of the state, did not replicate the experience of Kamal Ataturk who engaged in a direct conflict with Islam and all religion's manifestations, because he did not favour full separation between state and religion. Though it is true that he did not place religion above or ahead of the state and did not grant Islam or its institutions the status of reference above those of the state, government and parliament, he did submit religion to the state's institutional and cultural control, and made the latter responsible for managing the sacred and safeguarding the faith and its celebratory aspects. Bourguiba went even further when, in the early years of his presidency, he tried to entrench a modern understanding of Islam; he appointed himself as the religion's innovator and interpreter of religious texts and rulings, based on the state's interest and his own political agenda.

It is based on that premise that Article One of Chapter One of Tunisia's 1959 Constitution[1] says that 'Tunisia is a free, independent and sovereign state. Its religion is Islam, its language is Arabic and its type of government is the Republic'.[2] However, although this was a conciliatory formula, it did resolve the argument regarding the identity of the Tunisian state, and did not remove Islam as a reference without clearly delineating its sources and mechanisms. Moreover, regardless of whether these two characteristics (Islam and Arabism) are specific to Tunisia or to the state,[3] what is certain is that Bourguiba was careful to speak in the name of Islam, and allow the state to handle the ritualistic and symbolic aspects of religion, intervene strongly in all social and legal organizational matters, and find justification for its intervention from within the Islamic context to endow these changes and decision with a modicum of legitimacy.

This is why Bourguiba is not considered a layman, as his Islamist adversaries or secular and radical supporters say, but a pragmatist influenced by Western ideas who owes much of his cultural and political formation to France. Despite that, he was careful not to break with Islam as a symbolic storehouse, even if he seemed unconvinced by some of its positions. This became amply clear in the early 1930s when he defended the right of Tunisian women to wear the traditional *hijab* (veil), and criticized those Tunisians who supported at the time the call for Tunisian women to give it up, accusing them of confusing between 'secularism and progress'. He saw the *hijab* as part of the Tunisian personality against colonialism's attempt to obliterate this personality's salient features.

Second: the revolution's climate reshuffles the cards again

After the revolution, confusion broke out among different Tunisian parties who, under the spotlight of this sudden and unexpected earthquake, found themselves feeling their way around and trying to influence the emerging political scene after the regime's downfall. Moreover, since one of the revolution's outcomes was an increase in freedoms, it opened up new opportunities to the country's political currents, including those who were once repressed and forced to go underground.

One of the most important issues after the revolution was the relationship between state and religion. This is due to a number of factors chief among which are the following:

- The agreement among stakeholders to suspend the old constitution because Presidents Bourguiba and Bin Ali's amendments had weakened it considerably; they made many of its provisions undemocratic by granting absolute powers to the head of state, and thus laid the ground for an autocracy. Given that fact, the parties agreed to hold elections for a Constituent Assembly to draft a new constitution. This gave everyone the impression that the old consensus was no longer there, and that they now had the chance to put their ideological stamp on the country by influencing the provisions of new constitution.
- The radical wing of the secular current saw the post-revolutionary period as an opportunity to push for what Bourguiba did not dare push for, namely legally anchoring the secular nature of state and society in the new constitution; and there were several other initiatives in this regard, starting in the first few weeks after the revolution. On the other hand, the Islamists saw the absence of a coercive authority as an opportunity to 'rectify the history' that Bourguiba had 'deviated from when he became the sole ruler and monopolized decision-making after the country's independence' by reconciling state and religion and declaring Tunisia an Islamic State.
- Arguments between the factions escalated after the Constituent National Assembly's October 2011 elections brought about a new balance of power in favour of the Islamist-leaning En-nahda Party. The latter hastened to put its hand on the position of prime minister, and reserve for itself most of the other ministerial portfolios, including all the major ministries save for the Ministry of Defence. This caused alarm among secular groups who expected En-nahda, once it came to power, to reveal its true face and abandon its moderate discourse in favour of a large-scale process to Islamize the state.

Third: a priori agreement between the Islamists and secularists

Although neither the Islamists nor the secularists took part in launching or leading the revolution in Tunisia, they had tried earlier on to bridge their ideological differences on important matters, chief among which was defining the nature of the state.

The ensuing October 18 Movement is considered the main achievement in this regard.

The movement, which began with a hunger strike by a group of leading personalities from ideologically different political parties and currents, brought together representatives from the En-nahda Movement and leaders from the centre left, or the Tunisian Communist Party. Cooperation between them on a number of freedoms-related issues soon developed into regular discussions aimed at establishing the foundation of a political and intellectual front opposed to Ben Ali; it was in effect an exploratory process to prepare the stakeholders for the next stage that could usher in a future democratic state.

It was only natural for the issue of the relationship between state and religion to become the cornerstone of the discussions. At that particular period, the discussion that began in late 2005 culminated in a general statement that won the support of all those involved in the initiative, including En-nahda.[4] The statement reflected:

> the opinion of the text's authors on the status of Islam in the future democratic state, the nature of the relationship between religion and politics and the means of founding a civil democratic state that respects and secures the citizens' rights and freedoms, both individually and collectively, and preserves and protects the people's Arab and Islamic identity.

The signatories noted that, based on Tunisia's contemporary political experience, the relationship between state and religion faces three challenges:

- Tyranny of the ruling authority: one of this tyranny's manifestations is subjecting Islam to the political will of the regime in power, and the latter's constant attempts to force a particular interpretation of religion on society in a manner that serves its interests and monopolizes the religious domain. The authorities impose their control by selecting *imam*s on the basis of their allegiance, determining the contents of sermons and infringing on the personal freedoms of citizens from various religious, political and ideological backgrounds.
- Tyranny in the name of religion: it is a product of a one-sided and exaggerated interpretation of Islam that allows the authorities to intervene forcibly in the personal lives of citizens, and violate their basic human rights and freedoms and the principles of democracy.
- Tyranny in the name of modernity: it is the king of tyranny that allows the state security apparatus, from within and outside the state system, to eliminate religion arbitrarily from public life in order to provoke a clash between the state and religion. It is a vision that perpetuates the ongoing tyranny, encourages the violation of human rights and freedoms, and obstructs the democratic project.

Based on the above challenges, the October 18 Committee for Rights and Freedoms considers the following:

- The future democratic state cannot but be a civil state based on republican principles and human rights. It should derive its legitimacy from accountable and elected government institutions that enjoy a regular rotation of power system, and guarantee everyone's right to seek inspiration for their recommendations and programmes from their own sources and personal intellectual backgrounds.

- Regardless of the convictions and beliefs of the parties involved, the fact that politics is a human endeavour removes from it the halo of sanctity, and makes the political domain an arena of free dialogue and competition among the visions and programmes of political and civil elements from different backgrounds.
- The future democratic state is based on the principles of citizenship, freedom and equality. Based on that, it ensures the freedom of belief and thought and combats all forms of discrimination, whether based on religious belief, opinion, gender or social, political and regional affiliation. It will protect all basic rights and freedoms at the foundation of the democratic system.
- The future democratic state commits, in both theory and practice, to protect the personal safety of all human beings, and prevent all kinds of torture and other forms of inhuman and degrading treatment. The October 18 Committee for Rights and Freedoms vows that all its programmes will conform to these basic principles. It also commits to implementing the 1984 United Nations Convention against Torture and Other Cruel, Inhuman or Degrading Treatment or Punishment, and to all mechanisms necessary to eradicate torture from our country.
- It is the future democratic state's duty to grant Islam a privileged status, since it is the religion of the majority, without however any monopolization or personal abuse, while ensuring the rights of other religious beliefs and the freedom to practise one's own religious rituals.
- The identity of the Tunisian people was formed over a long period of time, and is still developing and being enriched through a creative interaction between the mainstays of its Arab and Islamic culture and modernity's acquisitions. Based on the above, the future democratic state undertakes to:

    - Protect the Arabic language as a national language in the administration, education and culture, and root it in society, while being receptive to other languages and cultures.
    - Immerse the Tunisian people in their Arab-Islamic culture and all its positive attributes, and develop it in manner as to accommodate humanity's modern developments. It will contribute to the enrichment of human civilization through constructive interaction, and counter all attempts to detract and control aimed at eliminating cultural diversity, and imposing a single culture and morality in Tunisia.
    - Ensure an Islamic education that cannot be exploited for political ends, within the context of an education system that guarantees the right to education and spreads the values of scientific, critical and diligent thinking. This will forge a Tunisian personality that is deeply rooted in its national identity, while remaining open to the values of modernity.

- The future democratic state will defend the just causes of the Arab and Islamic people, and support their aspirations for freedom, democracy and social justice. It will unite its efforts in the face of domestic tyranny and all forms of colonialism and foreign hegemony, to protect its right to self-determination and build its common future.

At the end, parties to the above statement underlined the fact that other people's experience has shown that the relationship between state and religion is not a ready-made formula, but a social contract that interacts with the political, cultural and economic developments in each society. This transforms it over time into a set of values and work ethics that subsequent generations internalize and develop according to their particular circumstances, and the constant need for progress, and enshrine them through representative constitutional institutions committed to the principles of republicanism, human rights and the national identity.

This important document, which was given due attention and significant parts thereof were shared with the reader, reflects the following:

- Fear among the Tunisian opposition of the time that the relationship between state and religion would deteriorate into a political issue, and act as the catalyst that causes the eruption of national unity and civil peace.
- The level of maturity among the opposition and several independent figures in the period that preceded the revolution.

They skilfully managed the issue over several years and arrived at a significant number of agreements, not only on the political level, but also on the intellectual level. This is a rare feat in an Arab world that witnessed, and is still witnessing, sharp ideological disagreements and mutual exclusion among major intellectual and political currents.

Fourth: post-revolutionary issues

Because factors and equilibriums changed radically after the revolution and directly affected the relationship among the parties involved, it is necessary to review the issues that were raised at that stage, and examine the reaction of the two main players on the political and religious scenes, to find out the extent to which they kept the promises made when they were still in conflict with the former regime.

In the past few months, the relationship between state and religion has taken centre stage in Tunisia by raising a number of interconnected issues; and although these issues vary in importance, they are all linked directly to different aspects of this key issue. The following is a sample of these issues:

- The battle over Chapter One of the Constitution: we have already referred to this particular chapter in the June 1, 1959 Constitution, in which Bourguiba resolved the argument on the nature of the Tunisian state in the early years of independence. This argument made a strong comeback after the revolution, stoked again by the ideological give and take between the Islamists and secularists, particularly on the eve of the debates on the draft of the new constitution. In the context of their response to the radical secularists who called for a secular democratic state, some of En-nahda's leaders said that the old Chapter One was not a sacred text especially since it was written during a different historical period when the balance of power allowed Bourguiba singlehandedly to delineate the nature of the state. They called for a clear statement regarding the Islamic nature of the state, despite some differences over the wording.
- The battle over Sharia: this is the very hot issue that sent different parties hastening to publicize their cause and win converts, and prompted all the Islamist political parties and movements to rally and mobilize, including the Salafists and Hizb Al-Tahrir Al-Islami [The Islamic Tahrir Party], behind the conservative Zeitouni current. The latter organized large marches to pressure En-nahda and members

of the National Constituent Council to make sure that the new constitution clearly stipulates that Sharia is the only or, at least, the main source of legislation in Tunisia. It is the first time that this kind of debate has taken place in the country.

As for the En-nahda Movement, confusion reigned among its supporters and leaders who disagreed over the issue, some of whom supported the call to include Sharia in the Constitution while others objected to that. However, a few weeks before the argument became public a copy of the draft constitution was leaked, attributed to En-nahda, stating in Chapter Ten that Sharia was a main source of legislation in Tunisia. This document was a test balloon, because once the conflict around the issue escalated, the movement's leadership washed its hands of it and said that it was unofficial.

Since the establishment of the 'Islamic Tendency Movement' on 6 June 1981, the issue of Sharia was neither part of En-nahda's discourse nor appeared in its officials' statements; even its political and electoral programme did not refer to it in any way. However, to distinguish itself from other Islamist Movements and lay aside the fears of the Tunisian elite and public opinion, in general, it defined itself as a civilian party with an Islamist background. Its leaders liked to compare their movement with Erdogan's Turkish 'Justice and Development Party', which Rached El Ghannouchi said had been influenced by his writings. It is well known, however, that Erdogan's Party differs from other political Islamist Movements on several levels, including the fact that it never called for the implementation of Sharia.

The issue of Sharia came back at this historic juncture in the democratic transition process, to revive old ghosts of the past amongst the elite who feared an intention to settle accounts with the modern current, and with the social model that established itself in Tunisia 150 years after the reform movement, and more than half a century after the national state was established. However, a series of internal, external and international issues came together at the last minute to compel En-nahda's President, Sheikh Rached El Ghannouchi, to reconsider his position and refrain from endorsing those who call for Sharia to be included in the constitution, including some high officials in the movement.

- The battle to keep mosques impartial: this is one of the hot issues that has worried many people in recent months, due to its direct association with the relationship between state and religion. Thus, a few days after Ben Ali stepped down and left the country, some groups took advantage of the ensuing vacuum and confusion to march towards several Tunisian mosques, bring down their *imams* from the podium under the pretext that they owed their loyalty to the deposed regime, replace them with loyal ones to lead Friday prayers and monopolize courses offered at these mosques. These activities escalated and grew in number to include around 400 mosques, with the majority of activists belonging to the Salafist current alongside some members of the Islamist Hizb El-Tahrir.

These activities reignited the debate around the issue of delineating the party or institution responsible for mosques and management of the sacred. Many voices were raised including Ghannouchi's calling for mosques to be independent from the state, claiming that under presidents Bourguiba and Ben Ali they were taken advantage of and turned into trumpeters for the regime. Ghannouchi went on to defend the idea that the faithful in each mosque choose the *imam* with which they felt most comfortable, and thus secure the independence of mosques from state institutions.

Though the idea might seem tempting, in practice it could open the door to religious chaos by allowing the extremists to take control of mosques and turn them into mobilization platforms that promote a religious discourse opposed to freedoms, and to Islam's message of tolerance. This is exactly what happened and turned away many of the faithful from their mosques, or provoked altercations between them and their new *imams*, which prompted the Religious Affairs Ministry to try as hard as possible to contain the phenomenon and regain control of at least some of the mosques.

Another ongoing discussion in Tunisia centres around the danger of politicizing mosques and turning them into rallying platforms for this or that current, particularly at election time. This prompted secular political parties to call for codifying the neutrality of mosques and other religious institutions and making it a provision in the constitution to prevent them from being used for political ends. However, although En-nahda supported the call and announced its commitment to the principle, several of its members refused to prevent *imams* from addressing public issues in their sermons and lessons, under the pretext that Islam does not separate between religion and people's day-to-day issues.

Fifth: the violation of public freedoms

Individual freedoms were protected in Tunisia save for the restrictions imposed by the authorities on mosques, and their attempts to limit religious freedom by forbidding female students and public sector employees from wearing the *hijab*, or detaining youths on mere suspicions such as growing their beards or regularly performing dawn prayers. However, certain events that took place after the revolution raised fears among wide sectors of the population, especially when some Salafist-leaning groups threatened girls because of their dress, attacked a number of legal brothels, violently tried to prevent the sale of alcohol in certain parts of the country, or attacked artists, cultural exhibits, cinemas and private television stations under the pretext of violating religious decorum. This generated a lot of confusion, elicited a widespread reaction and compelled many artists, intellectuals and ordinary citizens to call on the authorities to protect the freedom of creativity and culture, and prevent the recurrent attacks on individual freedoms, since democratic states are required to protect individual freedoms and prevent the use of religion to impose a particular set of beliefs on others. These incidents created a feeling among many that there was indeed an intention to change existing social patterns, and Islamize the state and society through the authorities or extrajudicial violence.

Sixth: encoding the protection of the sacred

Constitutions reflect the reference framework societies rely upon when defining the relationship between their cultural mainstays, institutions and legislation. Therefore, any research on the links between state and religion requires a return to the constitution responsible for delineating this relationship's mainstays.

The struggle in Tunisia around the issues of Chapter One and naming Sharia as a main source of legislation were referred to above. However, once these two issues were resolved, another important debate ignited around the wording of the initial draft, presented by the National Constituent Assembly's Committee and defended by En-nahda Movement, which stated that the 'State shall be the patron of religion', after abandoning inclusion of the word 'criminalise' before 'any slight to the sacred'. There was also an debate around the definition of the key term 'the sacred', which raised fears among many that the term's interpretation could be expanded to the point of imposing restrictions on the freedoms of thought, creativity and scientific research, especially by some Islamist currents that include within the sacred many subjects they consider beyond the realm of research, debate and review. Some thought it:

> right for the state to monopolize the sacred to prevent other groups from doing so themselves, since an eventual deviation by the state would be less ominous than a deviation by an individual group, given that the state is monitored by the legislative branch and is under foreign supervision.[5]

However, since the ambiguity of both the term and wording made legal confusion possible and justified the fear of a negative fallout on freedoms, the Human Rights and Transitional Justice Minister, who is also a member of En-nahda, abandoned his reserve to say: 'We do not need such a statement, and our deputies would be better off paying attention to real issues instead of wasting their time arguing over the issue of protecting the sacred or gender equality.'[6]

Seventh: questions relevant to the issue at hand

Given the ideological and political debate around the above issues, it would be necessary – in order to address the problems at hand, in particular those related to the nature of the future state – to answer the following questions: Did Prophet Mohammad (ﷺ) really found a state? Does the Islamic perspective allow for a separation between state and religion? And if separation is possible, does it necessarily involve separation between religion and politics? Asking these old/new questions is justified by the fact that now that the Islamists are in power, a number of issues have come to light again because they were resolved neither politically nor intellectually. This has again given these issues a religious dimension, and the jurisprudential debate has once again overshadowed political and philosophical thought.

The Ruler Prophet

The Prophet's journey from Mecca to Madina was not simply a geographic trip or expansion of his religious call, but also a qualitative step forward in crystallizing the message and in the manner of performance and behaviour. Historians do not disagree that the Muslim community who followed the call had gone on to establish a society and nucleus of an *ummah* (nation). However, what some have doubts about – especially since the publication of Ali Abdel Raziq's (2012) book *Islam and the Fundamentals of Governance* – is considering the entity the Prophet founded and supervised in Madina to be a state. Those who support that notion believe that denying this entity the description of statehood justifies pulling the historical and religious carpet from under the Islamist Movement's feet, since its entire call is built on this foundational stage of Islam's history.

Although it is difficult to conclude that what was founded in Madina was a state in every sense of the term, what is certain is that this entity was not simply a religious gathering but a political one as well. The Prophet did try early on to forge a contract between the religious and tribal groups who accepted to live in this entity, either through the belief in Mohammad's (ﷺ) status as Prophet or acceptance of his leadership, like the Jews of Madina did. However, regardless of this contract's nature and whether it rises to the level of a constitution, as many believe, the fact remains that Madina's

'*Sahifa*' actually delineated the relationship between groups that were never linked before by any religious or political ties within specific and expandable geographic boundaries. On the other hand, although the believers dealt with the Prophet as a spiritual guide, the citizens of Madina also dealt with him as an arbiter and reference on matters concerning the new entity's fate. These include declaring war, building an army, organizing the market, steering economic relations, regulating social relationships in and outside the family, resolving conflicts, forging alliances, and corresponding with tribal leaders and reigning monarch of the time, which many saw as diplomatic activities or akin to a foreign policy. What is certain, in any case, is that although the leaders of Qureish fought him at the beginning as a rebel against their beliefs and a destroyer of their social and religious establishment, after his migration to Yathreb they treated him like a rising king that threatens their interests and power, a fact reiterated on more than one occasion.

It is necessary, based on the above, for objective research to find a suitable formula for this entity; it was never purely ritualistic and religious in nature for, had it been so, the conflict between the rising community and its immediate and regional environment would not have developed as it did. The fact is that this new social entity crossed the boundaries of known religious frameworks, save if we concede that Islam is different from other religions in the sense that it did not stop at the boundaries that others have stopped at, meaning that it does not separate between religious doctrine and societal organization, which would not be to the advantage of those who believe in Islam's comprehensiveness.

From my point of view, what is certain is that the Madina stage paved the way for an authority that allowed the Prophet simultaneously to hold the dual roles of prophet and leader/political arbiter. At the time of his death, he left behind a collective entity capable of expanding in two different directions: either in the direction of a group with a religious message it seeks to spread throughout the world, or in that of the final configuration of statehood that governs in the name of this message, and is subject to a mechanism that allows it to expand and gain power. Subsequent well-known events have led to the fulfilment of the second scenario, when the struggle over power escalated and eventually brought to power Mu'awiya Bin Abi Sufyan, who cloaked Islam in Caesarean garb.

Religion at the service of the state

There a historical problem, though not necessarily a Muslim one, manifested in the fact that religion, which naturally involves moralistic- and value-based guidelines that lay the foundations for a non-arbitrary relationship between ruler and people, has been hijacked by families that came to power by force and deception, and misused it to achieve personal objectives, secure their interests and ensure that their king survives in power. For this reason, and contrary to common belief, never has Islam in its history imposed its control over the state, but it was the state that imposed its control over Islam and turned it into an ideological cover for its policies and practices. It is for this reason that the vast majority of religious policy scholars and other Islamic parties agreed on the need for an *imam*, or a ruler and a state, and saw it as a condition for the *ummah*'s protection and survival. However, they disagreed over the imamate's legitimacy and whether it was part of the doctrine and its pillars, as the Shia believe, or is independent of it, like others believe, in particular the Sunnis, without necessarily meaning that they separate between state and religion. As they see it, not only is the *imam* governed by Islam's teachings and guidelines, but also he draws his legitimacy from them and could lose it because of them.

The biggest failure of the Muslims has been their inability to establish a political system that draws its legitimacy from the public, and has a clear and accepted system for the peaceful transfer of power. In the first half of the twelfth century, Al Shahrestani attested to that in his book *Sects and Wrong Ascriptions* when he said that: 'The biggest disagreement among the *ummah* was over the imamate; never has a sword been drawn in Islam against any religious subject as it was at all times against the imamate.' It is also for this reason that Ibn Khaldoun tried to distinguish theoretically between the caliphate and the king, saying that 'pure justice is a legitimate caliphate'. He nevertheless noticed that the caliphate was not 'sustainable', i.e. it is not capable of surviving strong conflicts aimed at turning the caliph into a despot.

We thus conclude the following:

- The establishment of the state is a historical phenomenon by virtue of the fact that humans have a civil nature; it was therefore natural for Islam to have founded a state.
- Islam's reference texts contain general guidelines on the political authority's relationship with individuals and society.
- These guidelines never rose to the level of a clear and binding political system, because different types of governance and systems are linked to the movement of history and level of a society's development and characteristics. This is why Islam kept the political system issue open-ended, and subject to practice and general interests.
- Based on the above, there is no ready-made and agreed-upon governance system in Islam, whether now or in the past, and it remains one of the issues most open to interpretation and review, and dependent on general consensus. All that we have is an insistence on the principles of justice and *shura*, an important and vital insistence despite having historically lacked authenticity and diligence. The two principles have therefore mostly remained subject to interpretations that voided them of their meaning. The principles of justice and *shura* also lack clear mechanisms that make them binding on rulers, and instruments through which the public can fulfil its aspirations. This is why the Islamic State concept is no more than a mere presumption or supposition, rather than part of Islam as a religion or doctrine.

Could there be a separation between state and religion?

Is it possible, based on the above, to open the door to a total separation between state and religion, as the secularists want? To answer this question we should expand the discourse to talk in more detail about the relationship between the state and culture, since religion is one of culture's dimensions rather than the other way round. Here, the following remarks are in order:

- Every state is a historical and cultural product in itself; thus, if the state as we know it today is made up of territory, institutions, people and recognized sovereignty, then none of these elements was created in a vacuum. Each was born, grew and took shape within a historical context in which culture played an essential role, alongside interests, geography and human beings. This does not mean that the state and culture are static concepts whose content does not change, but the contrary: they can develop and assume more than one shape, especially culturally, compared with countries that tend to remain static and stable. However, at the core, this constant change is subject to a kind of internal continuum that links past, present and future, which is why it is difficult, if not impossible, to separate any state from the culture that gave birth to it, or was the cement that tied its individuals, groups and symbols to each other.

- The formation of the state, especially in modern times, has been linked to the concept of the *ummah*, which in turn gave rise to the 'nation-state' concept. Thus, if the state does not reflect a culturally homogenous nation, it relies at least on the cultural mainstays of the majority, and makes their language the official language and their history the common denominator among the citizens, alongside other symbols of unity like the national anthem and flag. As to minority rights, they developed slowly and are still the object of ongoing demands that keep them open to a variety of formulas, especially after the exponential increase in the number and role of immigrants in democratic countries, which is why some countries like Canada opted for a federal system that preserves unity and maintains equilibrium. However, in cases where there is no consensus on the protection of minority rights in the nation-state, conflict ensues and the weaker and more vulnerable national minorities, threatened by the tyranny of the majority, start calling for independence and a state that reflects their cultural specificities. This is what happened in the Balkans where Kosovo is on the verge of full statehood.
- The lay system is a form of secularism but not its only formula. It is also the least widespread formula in the democratic world, given its organic link to French history and nature of the struggle between church and state, particularly after the French Revolution. Other European countries, as well as the United States of America, chose other formulas than those that advocate total separation between state and religion. This is why we can speak about more than one formula for the link between state and religion, within the context of a secular project or vision.
- For example, it is necessary to take into consideration the particular characteristics of Islam compared with Christianity. In Christian Europe, there is a church that speaks in the name of religion; it has its own particular interests and a fulltime clerical staff subject to a clear organizational hierarchy. Moreover, the fact that the church has its own institutions, schools, universities, companies, and local and international relations made it possible for it to negotiate with the state, and there is a history of a certain distribution of roles between them, including in France where the church is financially, administratively and socially independent. Islam, on the other hand, has no official institution similar to the church through which to negotiate. Islam is an open and popular phenomenon that could be formed, practically, into groups, individuals, discourses, institutions, parties and a variety of interests, to the point of differences and contradictions, which necessarily forces the state in a Muslim society, or majority Muslim societies, to take a position vis-à-vis Islam and forge a relationship with it and with different groups active within it, and affiliated to it. In any case, it all comes down to three possible formulas. The first requires the state totally to sever its relationship with Islam and refrain from interfering in its affairs, which would give the faithful full prerogatives to manage their own religious affairs, including mosques; prayer

> sites; collecting *zakat* (religious tax); selecting *imam*s and preachers; establishing religious schools, including writing their curricula and choosing their teachers; establishing special tribunals that apply Sharia laws, at least in personal status issues; establish interest-free banks, and having a free hand in matters related to behaviour within the family, especially in connection to women and their social rights. If such a formula is adopted, everyone has to bear the consequences at every level, including the political level.

The second formula involves full integration between state and religion whereby religion is placed at the service of the state. This will reproduce the centuries-old tyranny since the state will be in a position to monitor everything, including people's conscience and restriction of their rights.

The third and final formula requires the state to undertake a minimum level of commitment to organizing religious life in the country, and allowing individuals and groups a wider range of freedoms in light of a constitution and laws that allow it to take into account the uppermost interests of the state and society, and prevent anyone from monopolizing Islam.

I am not in favour of either the first or second formula, since it is impossible to separate entirely between the state and religion, as it is also unacceptable to integrate them totally because this would necessarily create a theocracy no matter how much the Islamists and others claim otherwise. The most valid option would be a simultaneous system of distinctions and connections, i.e. a flexible distribution of roles bound by stringent respect for public and individual rights, alongside a commitment by the state to take care of mosques, and protect religious rites and the freedom of belief. This distinction is vital for the protection of Islam from tampering, and for preventing it from becoming a tool of deceit and tampering with people's rights.

The question that begs itself here is: What position does one take vis-à-vis the state that emerged after independence? Is it Islamist or is it inimical to religion? This was never clearly addressed by Tunisia's Islamists, though the first group that founded what will become known as the Islamist Movement cast doubt on the legitimacy of the state or, more precisely, on the legitimacy of the incumbent. At the beginning, this doubt was religious in nature since the movement considered Bourguiba an apostate and enemy of Islam and its symbols, but when the 'Movement of the Islamic Tendency' became active in politics this doubt expanded to include the political angle. However, though the term 'Islamic State' did not appear in any of the movement's literature, its Founding Statement of June 1981 said that among its objectives was the 'establishment of an Islamic order'. Moreover, a scrutiny of Ghannouchi's writings shows that he made noticeable efforts to give this desired Islamist system a modern veneer, which helped forge common discourse and demands between En-nahda and the democratic parties. However, in some of his writings and statements Ghannouchi said that the establishment of a democratic state was a necessary stage to provide the right climate for the development of an Islamist alternative, whereby the Islamic State remains the main objective of the project, and a religious duty for all Muslims. This is likely to create confusion among friends and foes, alike. In his important book *Public Freedoms in the Islamic State*, Ghannouchi (2011) remarked that his book 'does not come up with a perspective nor a programme for an Islamic party or an Islamic State, as this is an objective beyond this endeavour'. He elaborated on that in the footnotes saying that the present stage is not one of 'a struggle between the secular and Islamic State, this would also be for a later stage of the struggle; we are currently in a situation akin to a liberation struggle from colonialism'. Therefore, the present situation is confined to 'the struggle' over 'whether to be or not to be, between the supporters of the democratic state and protectors of the subservient autocratic state'.

As to the stage that preceded the current one, i.e. 'building the national democratic state' that provides an opportunity 'to think and work in the public sphere, help mature the alternatives and theories, crystallize the options, open the door to freedom of choice and public adjudication, and establish a rotation of power system through the ballot box', he believes that 'before that, there is no place for any marginal debate'.

Eighth: the Islamic State and the Democratic state

Here we should once again clarify the 'Islamic State' issue; I wish to reiterate in this context that the Islamic State concept is a trap that should be approached with extreme caution, for the following reasons:

- We already mentioned that Islamic reference texts did not specify a clearly defined system for this state, but were content with a set of general guidelines that are open – in some of their aspects – to interpretation in two different directions.
- The Islamic State that actually became reality was embodied by the caliphate, a system that many Islamists agree was autocratic in nature, and used Islamic religious texts and objectives for nefarious ends. Many have cast doubt on its legitimacy, content with only the Rashideen era, though the civil war among the Prophet's companions confirmed the lack of a clear binding mechanism, at the time, for a peaceful exercise of power.
- Based on that, the Islamic State concept automatically refers us to two different models: the first happened in the past and cannot be replicated; and the second was the object of several embodiment attempts, in the last quarter of the 20th century, notably by Iran, Sudan and Afghanistan. Although each of these two models has its own particularities, they all failed to protect freedoms, rid the country of its negative past experiences and provide a model on which consensus could be built.
- From the theoretical point of view, an Islamic State cannot but be ideological in nature, and ideological states usually have a specific social model into which they try to coerce society, whether by force or by peaceful means. However, the fact that every experience has shown that in the exercise of power the logic of statehood trumps that of revolution, or the ideological discourse, actually means that they have all fallen into the trap. They started by colliding with the opposition and ended up colliding with their own societies.
- The 'Islamic State' is upheld as an antithesis to the incumbent national state. This is why the struggle between the two above models takes on an ideological dimension, i.e. when the disagreement with the current state becomes commensurate with its Islamist credentials. This Islamization is usually linked either to the ruler's morality and his level of piety and religious performance, or to the extent of the authorities' commitment to implement Sharia, i.e. the legal character of the state. This raises several issues regarding the concept of Sharia itself, the rulings issued and how long the people will accept that they remain in effect in light of the social injustice and arbitrariness, or from the perspective of their conformity to international human rights conventions.

- If the incumbent state is non-Islamist or its religious legitimacy is in doubt, it would require, on the one hand, extensive discussions regarding the claim's validity and, on the other hand, the eventual replacement of that state by the promised Islamic State. This has led many Islamists to a strategic dilemma whereby they would have to choose either violence and total popular revolution, like in Iran, military coup d'états, like in Sudan, or civil war, like the Taliban, in order to bring down the incumbent regime. This means that raising the Islamist State banner necessarily exacerbates the contradictions between the Islamist Movement and the national state, and distances them from the reformist path that rests basically on recognizing the state's legitimacy, though it also highlights the inadequacies and helps deflect and reform them by peaceful means.
- Constant allusions to the eventual Islamic State have created a contradiction between it and the democratic state. Thus, despite the diligent efforts that these movements and some of their intellectuals have so far exerted to demonstrate that there is no contradiction between Islam and democracy, the concept of the Islamist state still has a different meaning than that of the democratic state, or that it is an alternative to it. This explains the insistence on the democratic stage as a step towards the establishment of the Islamic State, which many saw as an advanced notion compared with others. They also insisted that democracy is both form and content, and that the form, unlike the content, is not in contradiction with Islam. This is why advocates of centrism within the Islamist Movement tend to see democracy as a series of mechanisms for the peaceful transfer of power, but have reservations on aspects of the democratic culture associated with liberalism.
- Democracy is both mechanisms and content, though the content does not entirely give in to all that the liberal capitalist system advocates, as some Islamist theoreticians say today, or the Marxists have said before, to minimize the importance of the culture and practice of democracy. Here, the content is linked to a set of basic values without which the democratic system would lose its real power. Democracy is not simply an electoral mechanism but also a belief in the value of the individual; the right to be different; the protection of intellectual, political and religious minorities; the precedence of human rights over all other considerations, and in not tampering with individual freedom as long as the freedom of others is not being tampered with. This culture is a real challenge to everyone, in particular to the Islamists, for they know better than anyone else about the ambiguity of the concept of freedom in the Arab-Islamic culture, and how this ambiguity has impoverished it and defined it primarily as the antithesis to slavery. This implied that within political culture, it remained insufficiently connected to political and social liberation, a fact that kept the Islamic State concept highly ambiguous and sometimes very dangerous, as well.
- There is a problem whose importance cannot be overlooked or minimized when dealing with the issue of statehood; we are referring here to the legal dimension, or the relationship between the legislative law and the state. This is a vital issue for the Islamists who see Sharia as the core of the political system, and the source from which the state draws its legitimacy, and for the secular currents most of whom believe that laws define and help modernize societies. However, those who follow the progress achieved before and since the establishment of the national state will not fail to notice that Islamic legislations have been a proof of great flexibility in adapting and responding to new issues. In other words, we could say that considering Islamic Sharia and jurisprudential culture as the main

sources of legislation, especially in Tunisia, if not in many Arab countries, would not be an obstacle to reform or the establishment of a democratic system. What is important is to avoid establishing, outside the framework of the state, religious bodies whose authority is above that of parliament, under the pretext of monitoring laws, since this would obstruct parliament's role and create a duality that could void it of its prerogatives as an independent authority. This way, conservative Islamic parties can submit their draft laws in parliament, which would be the only authority able to accept or reject them. Moreover, intellectual life in the country should be promoted so that the debates and discussions would involve the entire population, and lead to the development of the legislative process in a manner that allows civil society and the elite to play a vital and necessary role.

Ninth: politics and religion – between separation and integration

Let us now look at the other side of the problem, namely separating religion from the state, a totally different dimension than the relationship between state and religion, given the latter's institutional nature. The more we speak about separating or distinguishing between religion and the state, the more difficult the issue of separation between state and religion becomes. These are two very different levels despite the overlap among some of their aspects. It has to do with requiring pious Muslims to give up their religious beliefs the moment they enter the political arena, which is not only unrealistic but also contradictory to the freedoms of belief, thought and organization. We all define our political positions based on our convictions, including our philosophical and religious beliefs, and it would be arbitrary to ask the Islamists to do so.

Moreover, the freedom of belief, as international human rights conventions define it, is associated with the right to practise, publicize and promote it, and to the rights of organization and participation. Therefore, since there are overlapping issues in Islam, there will be parties and groups that use religion as a reference; the latter's right to organize, publicize, take part in the elections and codify their practices should be recognized even if some of their positions are inimical to democracy.

In principle, this recognition does not negate the fact that there are problems that need to be addressed:

- Given the religious nature of our societies, Islamist parties usually create confusion in people's minds when they allude to the fact or openly say that they are the sole legitimate representatives of Islam, and therefore more entitled to rule than others. This is why some of these movements (such as the Muslim Brotherhood) are keen to raise slogans in the elections that say 'Islam is the solution' in an obvious attempt to reap political and electoral gains. This is one of ways of creating a 'mess' that prevents public opinion from maturing, and rather than help focus on the substance and on promoting the more capable candidates, gives priority to ideological affiliations. However, this problem is addressed through debate and reason, the education of public opinion and forging agreements with the Islamists on issues of morality, rather than through prohibition and alienation. What we need is a transitional period to help mature ideas, programmes and political thought, in general, and Islamic thought in particular, so that the struggle will be based on programmes rather than intentions or ritualistic manifestations.
- Islamist parties should refrain from monopolizing Islam or believing that they are the only legitimate side allowed to speak in its name.

- The need to refrain from using violence or trying to impose opinions and beliefs on the citizens, no matter the reason. The more the Islamist parties, especially those who lived in the shadow of illegality, deepen their reform option, avoid security and military attempts to infiltrate state institutions and abandon the secrecy imposed on them by past confrontations and repression, and the dual discourse associated to that, the better is the climate of trust they create and the stronger will be their contribution to strengthening the conditions of democratic transition.
- The need to neutralize mosques from all political activities, especially during election campaigns, and require *imams* and preachers to choose between political party activism and proselytization and religious guidance.
- Islamist political parties should respect individual and public freedoms, and draw a clear line between the mainstays of political activism and those of proselytization and religious activism, because mixing the two has led, and still does, to problems related to content, methodology, means and discourse.
- The need to avoid any kind of discrimination among citizens, whether based on gender or in political and civil rights, since activism in the public sphere is a right for everyone.
- The need to agree on a code of ethics or an honour code among different political parties and organizations, to improve party and political performance and protect the democratic option from any slippage or tampering that annuls pluralism or obstructs freedoms.

These necessary issues are essential for ensuring a genuine democratic transition of which the Islamists are an essential part. The Arab revolutions have unveiled the extent to which such ideas need to be entrenched, accepted and built on, and this will likely prevent these promising popular revolutions from deviating from their course, and prevent the return of autocracy under new slogans and banners.

Notes

1. It is said that Bourguiba was the one who drafted this chapter or supervised its writing.
2. See the text of the 1959 Constitution.
3. This is the object of a constitutional and legal debate among the experts due to the two different possibilities that emerge from the agreed-upon text.
4. The text appeared on 10 December 2009, i.e. a year before the outbreak of the Tunisian Revolution.
5. Mohammad Al Haddad, President of the Arab Observatory of Religions and Liberties (Observatoire Arabe des Religions et des Libertes), in Al-Shurouq, 23 September 2012.
6. Samir Dillo's translation of the interview he gave to *l'Express*, the French magazine, in the Arab Maghreb, 23 September 2012.

References

Abdel Raziq, Ali. 2012. *Al-Islam wa Usul al-Hokm* [Islam and the Fundamentals of Governance]. Beirut: Dar el-Kitab el-Lubnani lil-Tiba'a wal Nashr wal Tawzee'.

Ghannouchi, Rached. 2011. *Al Hurriyyaat el-Aammah fi-l-Dawlah al-Islamiyya* [Public Freedoms in the Islamic State]. 4th edition. Beirut: Centre for Arab Unity Studies.

Relationship between state and religion: Egypt after the revolution[†]

Tarek El-Beshry

Former Vice President of Egypt's State Council

According to Tariq Al-Bishri, it is not true that it is the Islamic current that controls the state in Egypt as a political project is in the process of crystallizing. His main proposal is for the three forces dominating the structure and dynamics of political life in Egypt – namely the army and judiciary, the Muslim Brotherhood, and liberals – to collaborate and avoid posing religion and the state as two opposing entities. Having to deal with the Shari'a as the source or reference for legislation need not be a polarizing issue as religion is being dealt with as 'the dominant culture'; moreover, much work has already been done along this line throughout the 20th century. Al-Bishri argues that democracy within a society becomes vacuous if it is detached from solving its socio-economic challenges. To this end he prioritizes four main issues: (1) freeing the Egyptian national will from American and Israeli pressures; (2) reforming and rebuilding government administrative bureaucracy; (3) organizing civil society; and (4) drafting a constitution. Al-Bishri considers that 'after Islamists assume power in Egypt' it is imperative for the existing political and cultural forces in Egypt to cooperate as none of them has enough power to negate the others or lead on his own.

This paper looks at state and religion in the Arab world, and specifically in Egypt after the 25 January 2011 Revolution, from the perspective of the status of religion and its influence on the Egyptian regime, and in the context of what is known about the rise to power of the Islamist current in that country.

Within the broader context of the relationship between state and religion in the Arab world, the focus of this paper is on Egypt. The key question with which to start is to ask whether the political situation following the 25 January Revolution has produced its own political system or is it still in the process of doing so? In fact, this initial question does not yet have a complete answer because the post-revolutionary equilibrium and characteristics of the new Egyptian system have not yet taken their final shape, though they are in the process of doing so. This system is being shaped and defined through the ongoing political struggle between different forces and currents, while the country is still experiencing a revolution as events unfold. The best we can do

[†]This article is translated and adapted from a paper originally presented at the Symposium on Religion and the State in the Arab World, convened by the Center for Arab Unity Studies (CAUS) and the Swedish Institute of Alexandria in Al-Hammamaat, Tunisia, October 2012.

now is to ascertain what is really happening on the ground, and which forces are currently interacting on the political scene, whether by force or by peaceful means: namely the forces that have emerged.

I am writing this from my own perspective on Egypt, a perspective which I could say is crystallized in a number of intellectual elements relating to the subject, i.e. to the Egyptian state, its influence on society, the impact of the national community on it, and the religious references that express the prevailing cultural conditions, as far as the Egyptian people are concerned. I refer to this issue because the guidelines set out in the letter written to me by the Center for Arab Unity Studies (CAUS) in which I was asked to write about the subject did not, in my opinion, only define the parameters in order to avoid an overlap between different topics (to be addressed by myself and others), but went beyond it to reflect a point of view that a certain current had total control over the state, and to express an opinion on this from its particular religious viewpoint. As I see it, the subject is much more complicated and complex than this perspective would imply, since there is much overlap between topics and the matter is still far from being resolved in a manner that allows a definite conclusion to be reached.

Classic stages in a revolution

As we all know, a revolution usually garners all its force in order to bring down the incumbent regime, and although this effort usually brings together disparate groups with different views, objectives and cultural outlooks, they are united by the resolve to bring down the regime. As to the regime itself, it embodies the people in power, the governing institutions, the political elite and the balance of power among its members that gives the regime its shape. In other words, the final configuration of any political regime depends on the people, institutions and equilibrium among members of its elite, and it evolves within the context of their interaction with each other.

This particular stage of the revolution, i.e. when the revolutionary forces agree on bringing down the incumbent regime, is usually easier than what follows. The reason is that despite their differences, the forces behind the revolution, which came together for this particular purpose, agree on the fact that the regime they want to bring down has become a major stumbling block or wall that prevents the changes and amendments that each sees as necessary for the good of their political group and its pressing interests, despite disagreeing on what is the good of the political group and what are its pressing interests.

The fact that revolutionary action has managed to dislodge a regime does not mean that it has destroyed all the elements and social and organizational structures that have allowed it to survive. The most important step in the process is when its infrastructure is destroyed, and the former political equilibrium and relationships among its elite are destabilized. This destabilization is measured by the extent to which the regime loses its control over political conditions in the country.

Moreover, when a regime is removed or destabilized and loses control of the situation, a political and organizational power vacuum ensues. This requires that another force take over and, as a rule that happens so often in a way that it has almost become law, namely that he who brought the regime down takes its place, whether it is a single force or a collection of forces. In reality, however, things are not as simple as this generalization implies for reasons the most important of which require examination.

The political force concerned here is that of the *organized* group and the regime concerned will be one that is able to gather information and make relevant decisions based on the prevailing political conditions in the country, and within the framework of ideas and objectives that have been agreed upon. This regime should – at the same time – have the organizational networks that will allow it to implement these decisions and through them impact on the actual course of events. This could be done by organizing and activating social, popular and unionized groups, as well as the state's apparatus, or creating a series of conditions that affect the politics and behaviour of others by supporting or dismantling them.

The fact that many forces were active in the effort to bring down the old regime necessitates an evaluation of the impact that each of these has had in that respect. This is done by evaluating the status in society of each of the several forces, such as their relations with the political parties and related groups; their links to the authorities in power that help them impact the course of events, like the military and other services; the tools that allow them to influence public opinion and elicit the right reaction, through, for example, the media; or their financial capacities, including links to politically active businessmen who use their financial assets to affect any of the above forces.

Each and every one of the forces involved in the revolution that successfully ousted the former regime will later have its own calculations regarding the role it will play in the new regime. The status of each force's participation will then depend on the equilibrium resulting from the relative weight of each force in its relationship to others.

Another complicating element is that the revolutionary conditions in Egypt were not only the result of the significant public anger that erupted in tandem with revolutionary activism of organized groups, but also they attracted large unorganized masses far larger in number than the organized forces that ignited the revolution. These masses did not come from organized action channels; some were affiliated with organized groups from outside the political sphere, became spontaneously politicized as the revolution evolved, placed their social, unionized, cultural and services networks at its disposal and thus were, without exception, instrumental in bringing down the targeted regime. Nevertheless, although this additional spontaneous force and the significant role it played in bringing down the regime will not be part of any organized configuration that will assume power after the revolution, different organized forces will always vie for its (i.e. the mass's) support, or some of its support, to gain the upper hand in the new balance of power.

What further complicates the matter is that the relative equilibrium among the groups or forces that toppled the establishment is experiencing a readjustment that also changes the relationships between these component groups, because the vacuum caused by the downfall of the old regime, and the relationship among the various elites, alters the equilibrium that once existed among these revolutionary forces. This power vacuum, and the ensuing changes in political and social relationships, are likely to also change – add, detract or amend – the old political power configuration, as far as different organized revolutionary groups are concerned. Thus, those who were effective in destroying the old regime may not necessarily be the most effective in steering the affairs of the new state and, likewise, those who were less effective in effecting the change could be better equipped to assume responsibility in the new state. Therefore, the balance of power that exists among the revolutionary forces while the old regime is being toppled is different from the one that emerges after it is toppled. There is likely to be a change in their respective size, objectives, technical abilities and expertise gained.

These complications exacerbate certain aspects of the struggle or, at least, create arguments and friction among the revolutionary forces that helped bring down the regime. It is a struggle that revolves round the revolution's objectives and each group's share in the ensuing configuration, with the aim of guaranteeing their respective objectives, and securing a place among the new elite and related balance of power. With this, we are still in the extended revolutionary process since the struggle is impacted by all the new changes, a fact that could eventually lead to clashes among the different forces involved, clashes that could well be calm and measured, but are difficult to avoid when several forces are involved in the revolution. Egypt's revolutionary history attests to that fact, from the changes wrought by Mohammad Ali in 1805, to Orabi in 1882, the Wafd in 1919, the 23 July 1952 Revolution, and we are still witnessing it in the 25 January 2011 Revolution.

The problem is that the process involved in the struggle ensuing from the second stage of the revolution is becoming increasingly fraught, more intense and long winded, and more difficult to predict due to a number of factors chief among which are as follows:

- The impact and influence of the various revolutionary forces are very similar, making it impossible for any of them to bring the new regime's affairs to a quick resolution.
- The inner and organizational strength of different revolutionary forces was not defined clearly enough, either before or after the revolution, to allow any of them to bring the situation to a quick resolution. This often happens when the spontaneous popular movement that joins the revolution after it starts is larger in size than the organized groups that sparked it. This situation makes it difficult for many organized groups to gauge their real political size, clout and independent strength to a degree that would allow them to determine the extent of their desire to play a role in the new regime.
- The revolutionary forces are unaware of how much their political position and abilities have changed after the old regime's demise, and this prevents them from knowing either their own or their partners' real independent strength. This confuses their political calculations and turns the political struggle among them into guesswork and estimations that could be very far from reality. The result is that each starts to estimate its power and that of others based on trial and error during the process of struggle, which leads to a general murky political situation devoid of accurate estimates, expectations and calculations.

The portents of revolution in Egypt

Egypt was highly charged with revolutionary zeal a few years before the outbreak of the 25 January Revolution; the ruling elite was confined to a very select group of people who included the president and his family, a number of businessmen who turned in his orbit, and a small group of non-officials who controlled the security services and the economy. Egypt became a society controlled by a very select group of people who determined its policies, disbursed its assets, dismantled its state system, and proceeded to demolish the foundations of its civilization and progress. It was a group closed-in on itself and one that had become, with time, even smaller, more isolated and virulent. To ensure its survival, this small elite began systematically to tear down every institution or organization that had the power to make decisions beyond its control, whether these were political parties, labour and professional unions, societies or state apparatus not involved in maintaining the elite's security vis-à-vis the public. This is why in recent years this elite was not unduly worried by the general public anger since it had succeeded in dismantling every organization where decisions against its interests could have been made.

In December 2010, I wrote about this particular subject, about how we could extricate ourselves from it, and what was likely to ignite the revolution's spark given the narrow space for manoeuvre.[1] I wrote:

> When we see Egypt's weak political party system and its obvious disintegration, rather than blame it entirely on internal factors, it would be only fair to admit that one of the causes behind it is the fact that the policies that have been pursued over the years, especially over the past three decades, have brought about the demise of these social institutions, because the people are no longer a tangible reality except when organised into groups, classes and coalitions. Political parties can only play an effective political role if they are connected to various organised popular centres in the country, whether these are traditional entities like tribes and sects, which do not exist in our country, or more modern entities like unions and labour, peasant and capitalist associations, without which political public opinion cannot be transformed into tangible material strength. [...]
>
> There are professional military and civilian organisations whose presence is necessary because the social and professional role they play would not be there without them. Among these are the state's civil, military and security establishments all of which are naturally able to perform on the professional and functional levels, within the national domain that defined their role. However, although these entities usually perform their prescribed duties in an orderly manner and do not deviate from them, when faced with a difficult situation or socially threatening crisis, any or some of them could use its organisational network not necessarily to perform its usual duties but a necessary and urgent task imposed by political conditions in the country. Thus, these institutions turn away from their day-to-day responsibilities to become an extraordinary tool that rectifies a wrong or saves a nation, and cases like that are well known in history.
>
> There are other entities which – despite their small size, weak political impact and the fact that they were hardly taken into account when planning the country's future – are able in times of crisis or rebellion to garner enough public support to have a significant impact on the country's political life, and there are many such examples in history. Those who know precisely what happened in Egypt in 1919 also know how people who used to gather in small limited groups soon grew closer, and coalesced into larger and stronger entities.
>
> Somewhere between the two above cases a future movement might rise under a more modern form, and using more advanced methods, though those who follow events closely cannot predict such possibilities because life's movement is far richer than the confines of past experience and knowledge, and because crises generate energies that could atrophy but soon find a way out of their predicament. Have you seen how the small green shoot finds its way to the sun and air despite all the rocks above it?
>
> Those who fight to maintain the status quo resist any movement that could go against them and, to do that, have to rely on their past knowledge and historical experience. However, though they suppress any activism that could challenge them, all they know about it is based on their past experience. As to what this new turn of events could lead to in terms of new shapes and forms, they can only be surprised by it and prevented from reacting in a timely fashion.

I have quoted this long segment to describe the crisis conditions that existed in Egypt prior to the revolution, and make the point that there was nothing tangible at the time to indicate that the hoped-for revolution was on the way. All we had were hopes that new and extraordinary ideas would eventually culminate in a revolutionary movement, a situation that impacted the revolutionary process later on, at the end of the first stage, that brought down the regime.

Revolutionary forces and roles

What actually happened was that the mass movement that ignited the 25 January Revolution, which takes the main credit for bringing down Hosni Mubarak's regime, started on the first day of the revolution and quickly grew in size to reach tens of millions of people in the main cities and regions. This rightfully earned it the title of 'revolution', given its cohesiveness, regular attendance, numbers, determination, exponential growth and consistent calls to bring the incumbent regime to an end.

However, the movement lacked the right organization and institutional leadership capable of turning revolutionary activism into an organized force with able people capable of taking over once the ruling elite was no longer in power. Officially recognized political parties were weak and had no accomplishments to their name whether in the revolution itself, in motivating the revolutionaries or in organizing them effectively. What ignited the revolutionary flame was a handful of youth groups, armed with spontaneous zeal, who managed to turn the spark into a conflagration that eventually consumed the incumbent regime. Turning a spark strong enough to light a cigarette into a flame that causes a conflagration that consumes buildings and institutions depends on the quantity of available fuel, an asset that would have been lacking had it not been for the Muslim Brotherhood. However, despite their higher numbers, the latter had neither the size nor the ability to take control of the revolution and determine its path.

There were also a number of intellectual and revolutionary leaders known for their patriotism and long struggle, especially over the past six years, i.e. since 2005, who undoubtedly played a significant role by preparing the ground for the revolution that began on 25 January and ended on 10 February. However, these leaders were not linked to organized entities through which they could help organize and motivate the people according to specific decisions and objectives. In fact, they were even incapable of helping the revolution reach its ultimate goal of replacing the old regime with a new one.

There were also popular protest movements and significant social activism by workers from Egypt's cities and countryside; employees of private businesses and members of different social groups and sects who held several protests in the six or seven months that preceded the revolution. The number of groups that gathered, protested and staged sit-ins is estimated in the hundreds, and their demands ranged from the economic field, such as better wages and employment conditions, to calling for their rights and the release of detainees, including calls for the equal rights of particular groups. This activism helped develop and spread the culture of congregating, going down into the street and protesting.

Although this activism paved the way for the big event, these events were at the time still uncoordinated and disconnected from one another. Political parties that existed at the time could not connect with them or bring them together in organized entities that could turn this socio-economic activism into the political activism of a limited number of political organizations, and thus help them get ready to replace the fallen regime.

This is why this large mass revolution that surprised everyone – including those who made it happen, with its size, exponential growth, challenge to Mubarak and insistence on the ultimate objective of removing him from power – did not have a joint leadership to express its views and speak in its name, be it one or a coalition of movements. This is despite the fact that this revolution had enough collective intelligence to unmask all attempts to rout it and see through all the false promises, and had the ability to escalate the political situation and insist on achieving its objectives, while maintaining its peaceful nature in the face of the violence unleashed by the state, that inflicted murder and injury, and retaining its ability to distinguish between friend and foe as events unfolded.

It is probably a gift from God Almighty, who blessed this revolution from the very start, that this revolution did not have a particular leader or leaders, including the already tested leaders, none of whom could have taken a decision that would have been heeded by the masses. This absence of prominent leaders helped to paralyse the government and prevent it from reaching out to specific individuals in its effort to repress, isolate or rout them, or foment sedition among the revolutionary groups. We now know that high government officials, as high as the head of intelligence who was later appointed vice president, had tried but failed to contact certain individuals whom he thought represented the revolutionaries. Among the reasons for this failure was the fact that none of the leaders or groups could claim that they were in control of the rebellious masses, or able to influence them.

It seems that what further contributed to the successful removal of the incumbent regime, despite the absence of groups capable of controlling the crowds, was the people's ability to react collectively in times of crisis, motivated by the same sentiments that resulted in a single position, or similar positions, especially in a culture where there are no major distinctions like sectarianism, tribalism and regionalism.

Once the people decided on the removal of the regime, however, other factors came into play – specifically regarding whom and what would replace this regime and the kind of policies that should be pursued. The political authority in the state is an umbrella for a collection of institutions for which it is responsible; it channels various decisions and implements them through organizational structures. There are also special agencies for collecting data and analysing facts on the ground, legal and conventional systems to study them and determine their validity, and a system for distributing and implementing responsibilities. As for the popular revolution, its ultimate aim is to control the state and its institutions, and this cannot happen in an institutional vacuum, because the state system cannot survive in such a vacuum and needs someone or something to take charge of it. As we now know, however, the revolution lacks an organized system capable of representing this mass movement singlehandedly or collectively, since even the strongest organization at the time did not have what it takes to assume this role.

This explains why the army stepped in to fill the void. The army is a formal institution subject to the state's legitimacy and decisions; in other words, it is the backbone of any state. At the beginning of the revolution, the army acted legitimately towards Mubarak's regime, for it was the regime that asked it to go down to the street and confront the revolutionaries when the police had obviously failed to do so. Once on the street, and after taking control of the main cities based on a legitimate decision by the President of the Republic, the armed forces refrained from implementing the orders they were given, and refused to use violence against the people. It is worth noting in this context that nothing in Egypt's history or culture indicates that the country's armed forces had ever used violence against the people. The result was that the rebellious but peaceful masses in the street welcomed them with open arms.

The actions the army took do not count as a transgression against the state's legitimacy because it was the state that asked it to act. As for its siding with the revolution, that was based on a decision by the Armed Forces Command to throw in their lot with the revolution, taken on 10 February during a meeting of the Higher Military Council, in the presence of the Chief of Staff but the absence of the Commander in Chief, Hosni Mubarak. The army issued Statement No. 1 to demonstrate that it took the Egyptian people's interests and achievements to heart and, on the very next day, i.e. on 11 February, it was officially announced that Mubarak had resigned.

Once it was announced that the incumbent regime had been deposed, the armed forces stepped in to fill the administrative void created by revolution and, as a state institution, took control of the movement and became a full partner in the revolution since it provided it with the institutional dimension it lacked.

The role of the armed forces

I indicated above that there were two positively linked political assumptions, namely that he who brings down the regime is likely to replace it and that the most likely candidate is the organized political force that has the necessary backbone to make decisions and implement them. It is from this dual perspective that we should view the events that followed Mubarak's political demise, since what we are witnessing now is a process of determining which political force or forces will replace him, singlehandedly or in participation with others.

The main organized force in Egypt is the state's apparatus which, it is apt to mention, had previously taken part in several Egyptian revolutions. The first was the Revolution of 1800–1805, jointly led by the Popular Movement under the leadership of people from Al Azhar, several businessmen and factions from the armed forces, led by Mohammad Ali. It was followed by the 1881–1882 Revolution jointly led by the armed forces, under the leadership of Ahmad Orabi, and the Egyptian masses, represented by what was known at the time as the National Party. Then there was the 1919 Revolution, in which the armed forces did not take part since many of the units were fighting in Sudan, between 1896 and 1899, where they remained until the British forced them out in 1924. However, Egypt's civil state apparatus did take part in that revolution by going on a total strike that prevented the British from controlling the government and country, which eventually forced Britain to recognize Egypt's independence in 1922. There was also the 1 July 1952 Revolution launched by a faction within the army, under the leadership of Jamal Abdel-Nasser, with the aim of bringing down the monarchy. Finally, there is the recent 25 January 2011 Revolution that began as a mass movement but which was resolved by the armed forces on 10 February 2011. Its aim was to build free and fair democratic institutions that genuinely represent the will of the people, and although it started as a mass popular movement, the armed forces eventually joined it as representatives of Egypt's state apparatus.

As we know, the state's apparatus in its modern configuration comprises two kinds of institutions. One is directly linked to politics from the point view of evaluating positions and making decisions, and is essentially represented by the President of the Republic, the ministers and parliamentary bodies. The other mainly performs technical responsibilities, is relatively removed from direct contact with politics, and is represented by the armed forces and the judiciary. Mubarak and his regime have systematically weakened and dismantled all state apparatuses not involved in protecting his regime because they were established under Jamal Abdel Nasser as the overall administrators of Egyptian society in matters that relate to the economy, public services and other facilities.

Mubarak's regime also tried to change the nature of these apparatuses' responsibilities and shift them to the private sector, specifically to the parasitic ruling elite, to dismantle the links between different state agencies. Autocracy requires that the sole ruler dismantle all state institutions except his own to eliminate the sources of pressure on his free will and render them more pliable. This naturally excludes the security services that came under his and his elite's direct supervision.

The institutions of state thus became disconnected and weak, and political institutions that were distanced from the political arena were kept deliberately busy with projects and activities that had nothing to do with their original responsibilities. Therefore, when Mubarak's state fell with all its political institutions, be it the presidency, the government or the legislature, what remained were the essentially non-political institutions, namely the army and the judiciary. Thus, with the appearance of the governance crisis brought about by the revolution, the army and its traditional professional leadership turned to politics to fill the ensuing vacuum. We also began to see a tendency towards political activism on the part of the judiciary in the way it handled cases it had to deal with.

It was clear that the armed forces' leaders who became active in the political domain were military professionals par excellence with no previous political experience or expertise, since they were strictly prevented from delving in politics, even expressing an opinion. These leaders were professional military men whose entire lives revolved around their field of expertise. They had assumed the highest military positions, arrived at the top of the professional ladder and their careers were nearing their end when they found themselves compelled to enter the political fray, with a revolution on their hands. They did not have the benefit of experience, or the time to acquire one, at an age where it is difficult to learn an entirely new profession through trial and error. This is why their political performance was obviously weak when they took over power, without prior notice or preparation, and were required to deal with an unexpected national crisis.

The Muslim Brotherhood and the Islamist current

The second organized force is the Muslim Brotherhood. It is the main organized force in the political non-governmental sphere from the point of view of organization and infrastructure, considered the strongest in Egypt's public arena. It is also the main force from the points of view of membership, internal organizational control and cultural coordination among its members. The Muslim Brotherhood played a significant role in the popular activities, with their participation constituting the bulk of revolutionary activism. Moreover, although they were not the ones who lit its spark or called for it originally, they eventually became very active in the revolution in a very self-controlled manner involving self-denial and readiness for sacrifice. This, coupled with their high level of organization, made their participation in the revolution more significant than that of any other political party or group.

However, the Muslim Brotherhood's role in the 25 January Revolution was not similar to that of the Wafd's in the 1919 Revolution, for although it was a more effective political force than any other, it was neither a governing power nor strong enough to lead the revolution on its own, make final decisions regarding its course or endorse a specific political position. Nor was the role of the Muslim Brotherhood like that of India's Congress Party or China's Kuomintang or Communist Party in their countries' respective revolutions, since it was neither a leader nor a ruling majority despite being an influential movement that should be taken into account. If it succeeded later on in attaining office, it would be in participation with other groups to ensure the stability of its new-found power.

In this respect, we should recall Egypt's historical experience and draw the appropriate lessons from it. The 1919 Wafd Party, a non-governmental organization, managed to win 90% of the People's Assembly seats in the first elections that took place four years after this Revolution, i.e. in 1923, based on a constitution and an electoral system drafted by its adversaries at the time, namely King Fuad I and the Liberal Constitutionalists. Despite that, the Wafd government stayed in power for only ten months after which it resigned and parliament was disbanded. In the 30 years that this constitution remained in effect, i.e. until 1952, ten different elections were held, six of which were free and fair and gave the Wafd a majority of no less than 70%, including in 1952. Despite that, the party was not able in those 30 years to hold power for more than seven years and seven months, in total, two years being their longest single term in office.

I quote this example to show that political power does not only lie in a popular majority or large effective party organization. It could equally lie in the apparatus of state that gives it its strength, as it could lie in the media and their outlets, which allow it to shape public opinion and highlight the political issues of which they are most interested, and through them sway the opinion of non-politicized sectors and determine the ensuing spontaneous or prearranged reactions. Political power could also lie in the hands of businessmen in light of the influence they have on those associated with them, not to mention their financial contributions to political activist causes.

In fact, the Muslim Brotherhood's popularity should not be measured by the outcome of the referendum on the amendments to the constitution held in the wake of the revolution, on 19 March 2011, that showed 77.2% support for these amendments and 22.8% against. The reason is that these amendments had strictly to do with constitutional provisions relevant to the establishment of democratic political state institutions, including the two parliamentary chambers and presidency of the republic, and to guaranteeing free and fair elections, including the elections of a constitutional assembly to draft a new constitution. The assembly would have the right to choose its own members democratically from either chamber of parliament, rather than staffing it with non-elected appointees. None of the provisions included in the referendum referred in any way to the state's identity or to typically Islamist slogans and demands, which means that although the 77.2% vote included the Islamists, it was not confined to their ideology's supporters, though there is no way to gauge these voters' impact on the referendum's results.

On the other hand, what can give us a real indication of the Muslim Brotherhood's popularity are the elections to the People's Assembly, held in December 2011. The elections to the bicameral parliament, the People's Assembly and Shura Council, in which the Muslim Brotherhood ran as a front comprising other smaller parties, were based on a system whereby two-thirds of the seats were allocated according to the party-list system, and the remaining one-third according to the individual candidate system. The Front won 47% of the total vote, with the Muslim Brotherhood's share amounting to 40% of the total number of seats, despite the fact that the elections took place barely ten months after the revolution.

The presidential elections were another indicator of the Muslim Brotherhood's support among the public. In these elections, a second round had become necessary when none of the candidates won an absolute majority in the first round. Thus, although in that first round the Muslim Brotherhood's candidate won the highest percentage of votes this percentage did not exceed 5 million votes, and four other candidates each won between 4 million and 5 million votes. In the second round, which pitted Dr Mohammad Morsi against former minister General Ahmad Shafiq, Morsi won the absolute majority with around 52% of the votes, i.e. around 5 million votes (turnout was lower than the 23.6 million or so people who cast their votes in the first round). Morsi became president of the republic with an official mandate, among others, to form the government.

As a matter of fact, although the post of president allows its occupant to control the state authority, it is difficult for this occupant to control an old system, or systems, whose cadres mainly comprise military and security personnel, and institutions and agencies of various ages and expertise, and have everyone defer to him and show obedience and consideration. This is especially true when that individual or individuals are from a different background to the one they are used to dealing with, particularly if they are not expert in bureaucratic management and come from outside the professional and cultural context with which the agencies' employees are familiar. This is especially true if the new incumbent's mandate is only temporary and it is uncertain whether it will last long enough to make a difference.

While reviewing the 1919 Revolution in Egypt and the events that following it, I was drawn to an amusing development, namely the manner in which the revolution was transformed into a regime and the mechanisms and struggles that made that possible. What I found was that a state apparatus and an authority as deeply rooted as Egypt's are like a fortress, and he who controls and manages this fortress will likely succeed in ruling and controlling it, because he is a native. I also learned that any outsider who enters this fortress ends up either controlling it, and in return is protected and defended by it, or is imprisoned in it and becomes its hostage. A good example is the hesitation of Saed Zaghloul, the revolution's leader, politician and seasoned statesman, to accept the leadership after his party won 90% of the seats in the People's Assembly, and his resignation barely ten months later having achieved nothing and still behaving like a member of the opposition, i.e. making statements on his position towards this or that issue without taking practical steps to address them. The fortress protects or imprisons based on the kind of relationship between the newcomer and its local residents; its agencies give the president information on which to base his decisions, and once he does that they take charge of implementing them and, by doing this, remain fully in control of Mr President.

I would also like to clarify the point that within the parameters of the Muslim Brotherhood's Islamist tendencies, one of whose members is now the president of the republic, the source of the Islamist tendencies so clearly evident in the behaviour of Egypt's government officials is not the presidency of the republic, but the predominant culture among a large majority of Egypt's society, a culture that is either Islamist in nature or inspired by Islam. This is clearly evident in the professional associations' elections which, when free and fair, favour the Islamist tendency and grant it an influential majority. As we know, professional cadres form the backbone of every state apparatus and other domains are an influential part of the associations' memberships and strike their own intellectual balance between the requirements of their profession and the surrounding Islamist-inspired culture.

Falling within this second force are the Salafists whose presence on the scene was not particularly noteworthy, nor were they known for their active participation in the early stages of the revolution that toppled Mubarak, though they emerged from it as a force whose influence should be taken into account at a later stage. However, though their initial role was to spread the religious call, this role, like that of other mainly social and cultural groups such as the Sufis and unions, was transformed by the prevailing social conditions into organized networks whose members become familiar figures on the activist scene. This strengthens their presence because it is based on an already existing well-organized system that could be reluctant to respond to some aspects of its new role, due to its novelty and their lack of expertise in this domain. The Al-Nour Party, the Gamaa Islamia, the Jihad Group and others are typical cases in point.

What allowed the Salafists to gain strength and mark their presence on the political scene was the postponement of the People's Assembly elections from June 2011 to November and December of that same year. This delay created a lax atmosphere and gave the Salafists time and opportunity to turn their religious proselytizing into political activism, allowed them to win around 25% of Assembly seats and to display considerable political clout later on.

It is clear, however, that the Salafist movement is neither homogenous nor of one mind, and generally lacks political expertise except for some groups and individuals who do not represent its main policy line. The divergent political positions within the movement were plainly evident during the presidential elections when the movement's votes were split among a number of candidates, which weakened their electoral strength and created enmities among some members. Moreover, despite their ability to mobilize quickly, the well-organized and disciplined system that could allow them to work hard, and for the long-term, is yet to be tested.

The conclusion is that despite its considerable influence, this second force has neither the size nor the ability singlehandedly to govern society or the state, despite being strong and influential enough to be an effective part of any future participatory system; there is also the fact that its expertise is more in the proselytizing rather than in the political domain. On the other hand, the military's expertise is more technical than political, and this lack of political experience by both parties has caused a considerable number of political miscalculations. The proof is that after the elections to the People's Assembly the latter tried to bring down the government but failed, and after the constitutional court's decision of 14 June 2012 that necessitated the dissolution of parliament, the elected president tried to recall the People's Assembly and also failed. It is worth noting that this political struggle is still ongoing between the two above-mentioned forces, and that the main mistake that both committed was to try to govern singlehandedly, each soon realizing that it is incapable of doing so, then trying unsuccessfully to backtrack.

The 'Liberals'

The third force is the so-called liberals – made up of political parties and independent personalities that emerged from Mubarak's rule with their popularity diminished. The proof is that their high-profile and noisy political activism did not help them develop into wide-based popular movements, even after the revolutionary atmosphere had gathered steam, beginning in 2005. This despite the fact that the protest movements had increased in size and number, which gave political parties and groups the opportunity to develop quickly their organizational skills in a manner that allowed them to stage organized popular protest.

Liberal parties and groups comprise members of the cultural and social elite that the former regime had prevented from forging ties with the public, which restricted them to launching media campaigns which they were able to do without the need for public organizing. They became active in the media, political conferences and elite gatherings, and their growing ability to ascertain what was happening politically and expose the shortcomings of the incumbent regime helped lay the ground for the 25 January Revolution, although most of their activists lacked expertise in the field of mass popular organization.

The liberals' diminished public organization skills weakened their attempt to motivate the masses during the election campaign, when they had the opportunity to do so after the revolution. Though these elections were guaranteed to be free and fair, and both the parliamentary and presidential elections were indeed so, their behaviour and demands during the campaign hurt them politically. Although they asked for the elections' postponement to allow them time to organize, their failure to garner enough public support gave the Salafists the chance to do so instead. The latter used the delay to orient their public networks towards political activism, which seems to have paid off at the liberal current's expense.

The liberals also demanded and insisted that the elections be based on the party-list system, and brought significant pressure to bear until it was decided that two-thirds of the People's Assembly and Shura Council's seats would be based on that system. In fact, this system works well when the organized parties are few in number but large in size, and enjoy a significant presence among the public in light of their prominent personalities, leaders, platforms and past records. Since none of the parties that emerged from the revolution had any of that yet, the main beneficiary was again the Salafist current thanks to its public proselytizing networks and long-established activities in the deprived areas and mosques. The proof is that, in the People's Assembly elections, the Salafists won around 15% of the one-third of seats based on the individual system and 29% of the two-thirds allocated to the party-lists.

The liberal current's strength lies in its considerable contribution to shaping the country's unorganized public opinion through its control of the media, a quasi-total control that affects not only the unorganized public opinion sector, but also the state's decision-making circles. Its acumen in the sphere of political cultural, coupled with its strong influence on the audiovisual and written media, gives it the ability to make its positions known on various issues, allows it to shape them and determine which priorities and demands are worth addressing, all of which impacts on shaping political reactions. This impact increases in strength in tandem with the discord between the two other forces.

Although the influence of this political force, which lacks the proper organizational structures and weight, does not allow it to be an independent force capable of governing through its organizational structures, it does allow it to shift its weight in favour of one of the two other forces, and strengthen one at the expense of the other. This is particularly true given that the two other forces have their own weaknesses and hesitations, due to their lack of political experience, and that none of them has clear majority support, especially since the sheer size of the unorganized masses changes the balance of power. This explains the 'Tahrir Square' phenomenon from which the liberal current has been able to benefit, given the unorganized masses' ability to rally, mobilize, attend regularly and appeal through the media.

However, one of the liberals' persistent weaknesses is that because they lack the proper organizational structures, the positions of different parties, groups and personalities affiliated to it vary and change. This makes it difficult to say that it is a single force or that the differences between these groups will not lead to serious disagreement, and thus detract from their supposed overall status and power.

The liberal current supports media outlets that are widespread throughout the country, especially those with a particular political orientation and take positions vis-à-vis various ongoing political conflicts. What happened, however, was that as soon as more space was open to the media, a specific group of prominent Egyptian businessmen took control of the main outlets, a group that had acquired and increased its wealth under Mubarak, thanks to its connections with the ruling elite, at the time. However, their wealth did not come as a result of productive agricultural, industrial or service-oriented projects, but mainly from bank loans and purchasing land earmarked for construction from the state. These businessmen steered their capital into real estate, traded in consumer products and privatized all that could be privatized of the communications sector, and many saw the establishment of a media outlet as a lucrative endeavour to be used in applying pressure on Mubarak's government to secure additional privileges.

We all know that businessman Najib Sawiris partnered in 2004–2005 with businessman Salah Diab to publish *Akhbar al-Yom* newspaper and establish the OTV (Orascom) satellite television channel, in addition to founding the 'Misriyoun al Ahrar' (Liberal Egyptians) political party, which he established after the revolution without becoming a member. There is also the audiovisual CBC (Capital Broadcasting Center) satellite television channel owned by businessman Mohammad Al-Amin, who later established *Al-Watan* newspaper, and businessman Walid Mustapha who runs the internet site 'Al-Youm al-Sabe'' (The Seventh Day) and publishes a newspaper under the same title. It is said that the latter has links to businessman Hussein Salem who was close to Mubarak and Safwat Al-Sharif; and so it goes.[2]

The liberal party scored a major success during the revolution in shifting public opinion's attention away from important and compelling issues, mainly those related to the policies that need to be pursued after the revolution, specifically those that allow Egypt to regain the free will that reflects the country's national interest in Arab and international politics. We are talking here about policies that would help Egypt regain the freedom to determine its own affairs and pursue economic and social policies that target an economic development that increases productivity at all levels, develops a good income distribution system and ensures social justice.

The media turned public attention away from all these issues to concentrate on a single issue related to the Egyptian state and whether it will be religious or civil in nature, at a time when we should all be focusing first on issues relevant to Egypt's future. As for the issue of identity, Egypt is not discovering its identity today; identity is not a matter of choice but the sum-total of all the social cultures that make up the country.

Moreover, the liberal current does not have the proper organized structure that allows it to be independent of others; what gives it depth is the political culture it advocates, the positions of its cultural majority, its influence on society and its skill in swaying public opinion. This is what makes it the third force in the country in the wake of the 25 January Revolution and, as such, should consider its role in shaping the country's future.

The conclusion, based on the above, is that the Islamist current, which is the second force in the country and the main subject of this paper, is not alone in the Egyptian scene when matters concerning the state and who controls it are at stake, or in determining Egypt's identity. Moreover, although it is neither a leading nor a ruling power, its social influence should, since we seek to build a society along genuine democratic lines, allow this current its rightful share in determining Egypt's national, cultural and social future. Genuine and effective participation should be the common standard among different Egyptian forces, so that they will draw strength from each other, and none will dominate or cancel the others.

Looking to the future

We now move to the final set of issues that are the focus of this paper, which is that none of the above forces that emerged as a result of the revolution is capable of assuming power on its own, or claims that it is the only deciding factor in rebuilding the country or determining its policies. The current struggle will undoubtedly reveal shortly that a participatory system is the only option for Egypt, not by coercion however, but by each force adjusting its position to allow participation to happen. If this is the case, it is then only apt to address the issue at the root of the ominous intellectual rift in the country in the past few months, namely the state's identity and whether it is religious or civil. This issue could be solved by these forces being aware of the need to work together, or for parts of them to work together, and we mean here the state's apparatus, the Islamist movements and parties and intellectual groups that identify themselves as liberal or civil.

In order to take stock of the problem that the 25 January Revolution has suffered and is still suffering from, we should first note that the revolution has brought down a regime that prevented people from dealing with the real challenges facing the nation and society, and it failed to adopt and implement the right policies in this regard in response to the national community's search for solutions. Therefore, the latter focus on reforms considered the main link in the chain that leads to the resolution of looming socio-political problems.

In Egypt, the main link in the chain was the issue of democracy, because autocracy was at the root of all the wrongs, shortcomings and corruption that became widespread in Egyptian society, while democracy is a political governance and social management system that leads to proper reforms, progress, justice and independence. However, democracy becomes a hollow slogan if it is not linked to, or used to help solve, the political, economic and social problems plaguing society since its ultimate objective is the institution of a governance system that expresses the will of the people. In this context, one cannot imagine such a notion not being to the people's advantage since it leads to independence, progress and the right amount of social justice that maintains a balance among different social strata. Democracy should involve all the above notions and incorporate them, intact, in its factual and concrete programmes, or it risks losing its main function.

To summarize, the following are the main issues that need urgent attention in Egypt. First, liberating the nation's will from American and Israeli pressure in matters related to internal and foreign policies. This can only be done (given what Mubarak's regime has left us with) if we implement economic policies that are self-reliant on local production, to the extent that Egypt's food and medical resources and abilities can meet local demand. The second issue is the need to rebuild or repair the state administration system, and bring it up to par, to undo the dislocation, weakness and corruption wrought by Mubarak's regime. This is the system Egyptian society relies on to keep facilities and services operating, and draws the appropriate development strategies. The third issue is the need to strengthen and support all that helps resolve issues relevant to civil society and its organization, including various institutions and all that is necessary to ensure a functioning democracy, and prevent the country from going down the path of autocracy, again. This involves the establishment of political parties, professional and labour associations, peasant and craftsmen's unions, and a wide array of societies. A constitution should be drafted in a manner that ensures a consensus-based decision-making system, and multiple implementation bodies that take expertise into account, and avoid any form of individual or institutional autocracy.

Moreover, although all of the above is part and parcel of what the revolution is all about, we were and still are surprised to see the issue of the state's identity (religious versus civil) dominate all of the above. There was an uncanny insistence, mainly by the media, on making this particular issue the focus of the written and audiovisual media's attention, and drown out the people's other concerns.

Strangely enough, this is a continuation of the policies that Mubarak's regime has been pursuing since the People's Assembly elections of 1984, the first modern elections in which the Muslim Brotherhood participated in partnership with the Wafd, against the ruling party. At that time, Mubarak's regime had insisted on placing this issue above all the other political and cultural issues of the day. We should also not forget that American policy had placed culture and civilization at the top of its strategic priorities, in its ongoing intellectual and political struggle with Iran. It happened after the 1979 Iranian Revolution, the emergence of Islamic national movements in Palestine and elsewhere, the collapse of the Soviet Union and search for alternative political and intellectual enemies, and the appearance of Samuel P. Huntington's *The clash of civilisations*. It also happened after the intellectual divisions caused by Haydar Haydar's *Banquet for seaweed* (1983), *Lajja* [Shame] by Pakistani author Taslima Nasreen (1993), and others, all of which turned the Egyptian people's attention away from issues like Sinai, Palestine and Israel, the agricultural expansion projects, artistic freedom of dramatists and other writers, and so on.

Also strange is the fact that many intellectuals and liberals, including their parties, intellectuals, politicians, individuals and groups, focused on this issue as well, and made it the centre of attention and the main cause of political polarization in the country, in the false belief that they were defending the civil nature of the state against backwardness, although this civil nature is highly achievable and autocracy is at the root of backwardness and defeat. By doing this, they also inadvertently increase the popularity of the religious current, since giving the public the choice between the religious and non-religious, regardless of the issue, is a definite vote for the religious. It would have been better for them had they put forward everyday issues that touch people's lives, regardless of their cultural affiliation. Many liberals became so deeply involved in this issue that they almost turned their backs on the concept of free and fair elections so convinced were they that the religious would win. This is why they asked that the elections be postponed to an undetermined future, and why they were actually delayed from mid-2011 to the end of 2012.

The public polarization round the issue of religious versus civil should be blamed on all those who got involved in it on both the liberal and Islamist sides, because it seems as if they had agreed on making this issue the main bone of contention and using it to polarize public opinion, although it is not a truly controversial issue. The proof is that one year after this polarization began the conflict is almost back to the old balance, since Article 2 of the 1971 Constitution states that Islam is the state religion, and Islamic Shari'a is the main source of legislation. This is the same text that is almost the object of consensus today among Constituent Assembly members.

In fact, this has never been a controversial cultural–political issue before, because most of those who speak about the 'religious' actually refer to governance systems and procedures. The religious reference is an intellectual concept relevant to the intellectual sources that makes the final determination about right and wrong, good and bad, or what used once to be called 'the beautiful and the ugly'. These are the general intellectual and cultural sources on which are based rules regarding treatment, admonitions on comportment and behaviour, the general fundamentals underlying the legitimacy of the regime's structural social and political systems, and the relationship among groups within the national community.

In this case, religious reference does not refer to rulings and systems per se, but to the prevailing cultural and religious beliefs in society, and among the national community, beliefs on which the majority agrees. This is why we do not choose religious reference as a prevalent cultural matter, but rather synthesize its nature and characteristics based on society's predominant cultural and doctrinal values. Likewise, we do not choose the language we speak but it is inculcated collectively in us through the ages, based on the manner in which most people address and understand one another; and in this context, religion is dealt with as the prevailing culture. We also do not choose the prevailing culture such as we choose between goods in shops, exhibition halls or museums; we choose the rules of behaviour and treatment as appropriate, and choose systems also as appropriate from within the prevailing cultural context.

This is why there is no real conflict in my mind between what relates to the religious reference and what relates to rulings; we choose the most suitable rulings in light of the prevailing religious reference. And when we talk about a prevailing culture, it means something that was genuinely formed, throughout the ages and in modern history, from which we gain all the intellectual sources and modern concepts that prevail among the national community, in terms of intellectual sources and new concepts, and all that the socially prevailing cultural context involves, based on the prevailing circumstances at the beginning of this 21st century. We could study this issue and disagree over it, but this would take place in an inclusive context that accepts diversity and renewal based on what the prevailing culture and new interests agree on.

Conclusion

I was asked to speak about the political and social repercussions of an eventual Islamization of legislation on, for example, women, the Copts, secularists, individual freedoms, and so on. These issues were debated at length during the entire 20th century, and many of the country's jurists and intellectuals have carefully and diligently come up with several formulas, to add up to the many opinions and interpretations that exhausted Shari'a's resources. This means that all these jurisprudential and legal efforts are out there, and all we need to do is choose from them what we can agree on.

This choice has two contexts. The first is a general cultural context in which the debate is unfettered and free, and in which several parties and institutions could take part, though it is not the subject of research today. The second is the space that will be allowed by the authorities once the Islamists are in power. This paper has been devoted to highlighting the similar strengths of Egypt's current political and cultural forces, and that none of them can govern singlehandedly or impose a certain policy line on the country. This makes participation the only option, and participation requires that the participants reach a formula on which they can all agree.

As to the issue of implementing Shari'a law, in fact statutory laws have been based on Islamic Shari'a for decades, and efforts to codify some of its rulings have produced comprehensive projects and results. Moreover, efforts exerted throughout the 20th century in this regard were mainly the work of jurists and researchers who did not belong to political Islam. However, although the latter essentially represented both Muslim and Western legal cultures, and the outcome of their efforts constitutes a real intellectual treasure trove, some of them did call for the implementation of Shari'a law, chief among whom were Abdel-Razzaq Al-Sanhouri, Abdel-Halim Al-Jundi, Sufi Abu Taleb and many others. Taking part in the effort were also different codification committees active in the 1970s, alongside jurists from Syria, Iraq, Morocco and elsewhere. This goes to show that the issue is much wider than a mere political issue, associated with a particular movement that might or might not eventually come to power, in a given country. It is a general cultural matter whose wide domain is beyond the internal equilibrium of a given authority, and its effects are felt through its general cultural impact.

Notes

1. The introduction to Mohammad Ali Khair's book that appeared at the time was published before the 25 January Revolution under the title *The Road to the Palace of Arabism*. It looked at the period that would follow the end of Hosni Mubarak's term as president.
2. Rajab Al Basel, in *Al-Hurriah wal 'Adalah* (Freedom and Justice newspaper), 19 May 2012.

References

Haydar, Haydar. 1983. *Walimah li-A'shab al-Bahr* [Banquet for seaweed]. 6th edition 1998. Damascus: Dar Ward.

Huntington, Samuel P. 1996. *The clash of civilisations*. New York: Simon & Schuster.

Nasreen, Taslima. 1993. *Lajja* [Shame]. Translation 2010. London: Penguin Books.

Islamist political movements in Yemen

Abdulmalik Mohammad Abdullah Eissa

University of Higgah, Higgah, Yemen

This article presents an overview of Yemeni society before proceeding to a detailed account of research undertaken by the author into the factors behind the rise of Islamic extremism in Yemen and its appeal, especially among the young and most deprived sectors of society. The author draws on and relates his findings to a number of theoretical works, including those of authorities such as Max Weber as well as more recent analysts, in a discussion of what drives extremist group formation and what attracts their adherents, in general terms and in Yemen in particular. The findings of a survey of public opinion in Yemen conducted by the author are recounted in some detail.

Introduction

Political Islam is today the most important subject on the minds of researchers and stakeholders interested in the Arab world and related developments. In the immediate term, it is the issue with the greatest potential to impact the future shape of Arab–Islamic societies, given the important role that religion plays in these societies from the cultural, political and even economic points of view. This being so, the fundamental challenge is how best to understand the way Arab–Islamic societies are evolving today.

The subject of the present research is to identify and track the different political, economic, social, religious, and cultural factors at work and that are constantly in flux, and to do so specifically in the context of Yemen. The intention is to identify what has led to the rise and development of religious extremism in Yemeni society and, to do this, the article focuses on, among other things, the social, political, economic, cultural and intellectual dimensions of the issue. These are the dimensions that nourished the extremist Salafist current and made it the complex social, political and cultural phenomenon that it is in Yemen today.

Without digressing into a discussion of the various theoretical approaches which may apply here, despite their importance, the author has identified the Yemeni public scene as the central object and source of evidence for this research and, to this end, the research takes the form of a field study par excellence.

Methodology

The research is based on a set of hypotheses that six factors, namely: poverty, the closed political environment, regional intervention, social discrimination, an erroneous form of religious mobilization, and the role of the leading figure of the community, account, in combination, for the emergence of the phenomenon of religious fanaticism in Yemeni society. In order to test these hypotheses, secondary questions were posed which facilitated the gathering of data. These hypotheses will be explained as the related survey results are reviewed. A combination of theoretical approaches guide the research, as will also be explained below. The research objective overall was to establish the role played by social factors in the emergence of a social environment which leads to the appearance of Islamic, social movements in general and to the phenomenon of religious extremism within the uncompromising Salafist movement in the Yemeni society in particular.

The practical fieldwork undertaken as part of the research employed two main tools. The first was a questionnaire addressed to a purposive sample of 200 units or respondents, selected from the registry of the capital, Sana'a, and the district of Thoummar. The second tool, participatory research action (PAR), was applied to six groups of approximately 54 units each, four of which are in the registry of the capital and two in the district of Thoummar. These procedures were performed in order to investigate the research hypotheses, thus substantiating or negating them. In order to uphold or refute these hypotheses, the appropriate statistical methods were applied, namely: repetitions, percentages and Pearson's coefficient of correlation (r).

The target population of this study were closed religious groups, the main groupings of Yemeni Salafist currents that are mostly centred in several identifiable districts, among these are Sana'a, Ma'reb, Sou'dah, Thoummar and Ibb. These groupings can be considered the main groupings of Salafists in Yemen where the general population count is around 21 million. Accordingly, the choice of this sample was based primarily on the researcher's experience and knowledge of these movements, him being a member of the environment where the study took place.

After studying the circumstances and characteristics of each district, the researcher chose the districts of Sana'a and Thoummar, while excluding Sou'dah and Ma'reb due to the unfavourable security situation which prevented administration of the questionnaire. The district of Ibb was excluded as the movements that exist in it are the same as those existing in the capital, Sana'a. Thus, the districts of Sana'a and Thoummar were considered sufficient for the research, and each district was represented by 100 respondents or units of research.

The research sample

A total of 50% of the main sample was selected from the registry of the capital, Sana'a, to represent the main urban centres. This amounted to 100 people representing three groups: university students and professors, clerics, Salafist students plus ordinary citizens (Table 1).

Table 1. Distribution of the sample in the registry of the capital.

Type of sample	Registry
University students and professors	30
Researchers in Islamist groups plus religious scholars	20
Salafist students and other ordinary people	50
Total	100

The specific choice of this sample was due to the line of enquiry on the phenomenon of Salafism. To this end the author referred to specialists in the Shari'a and in law, in addition to the departments of Islamic studies in Sana'a University and the views of their students. The author also sought the opinion of researchers specialized in the realm of religious groups and that of the religious scholars who do not belong to the same school. This also applies to ordinary citizens and to the knowledge and perspective of the Salafist students in the capital, which has no prominent Salafist scholars. Within the sample, the author tried to maintain a balance as much as possible. Also, a sample that represents secondary cities was drawn from the directorate of Ma'bar in Thoummar District; this comprises 100 units, which is 50% of the main sample. This is distributed over three groups: clerics, Salafist students and ordinary citizens (Table 2).

The reason behind choosing ten clerics is their small number relative to that of the students. Usually, a Salafist school has no more than two or three clerics. This is due to strong competition among them and to the fact that each sheikh founds a school of his own, a fact that is not present among students. As for the reason behind choosing this number of ordinary citizens, it is in order to attempt to find out opinions in the social environment in which the Salafists exist, and the extent of the exchange effect between the two; hence the choice of their equal number, that is, the equal number of students and citizens.

The intention was to gauge Yemeni society's tendency towards religious extremism and to understand how this society views this tendency, and its components, the reasons behind it, and factors that have impacted on it the most.

Whether religious or secular, Islamist or non-Islamist, every movement relies on certain intellectual and social tenets, a fertile and receptive environment, and external factors that allow it to survive. It is therefore important to identify what factors, ranging from poverty and foreign intervention to the local political environment and discrimination, are most instrumental; to identify, in other words, the basic elements that nourish religious extremism in any society. Extremism could take various forms, depending on the nature and constitution of a given society. In the case of Yemen's conservative society, in which the people still hold on to customs and traditions inspired by Islam's teachings, it means that extremism is essentially religious in nature.

The reasons why Yemeni society remains traditional and conservative are historical, social and economic. Because of its closed and isolated nature, Yemeni society has undergone very little structural change, meaning that it remained conservative and its customs and traditions intact throughout the centuries (Burgat 2006, 92). It is a homogenous society with no distinctive ethnic minorities[1] living outside the social norm with their separate customs and habits. All Yemenis share essentially the same ancestry: the Qahtani and Adnani Arabs, and their society remains largely tribal.

Table 2. Sample distribution in Thoummar district and Ma'bar directorate.

Type of sample	Ma'bar, Thoummar
Clerics	10
Ordinary citizens	60
Salafist students	30
Total	100

According to the 2004 census, the population of Yemen then totalled 19,685,161; it is relatively youthful with over 52% falling between the ages of zero to nineteen years (Central Statistics Organisation, Ministry of Planning and International Cooperation 2008, 72, 77); 71.4% live in rural areas and 28.6% in urban areas. There are 129,610 villages, most of which are difficult to reach, and therefore they remain quite isolated from each other and from the rest of the country (Central Statistics Organisation, Ministry of Planning and International Cooperation 2008, 72, 75).

The tribal nature of Yemeni society is deeply ingrained in people's consciousness, although the sense of tribal affiliation could be stronger or weaker depending on the particular region concerned; nevertheless, tribal identity remains strong everywhere compared with its strength in other Arab countries. In the tribal mindset, the notion of power is a wide-ranging and all-encompassing phenomenon that is not the exclusive domain of the state; tribal conventions precede and supersede the laws of the land. Yemen is also characterized by the widespread possession of weapons among the tribes, meaning that the latter have managed to maintain their role as independent fighting units that consider themselves above the law. These tribes often go to war against each other in the north and south of the country, primarily due to disagreements over land or water, a situation that often leads to revenge attacks against one other.

The political structure of Yemeni society is made-up of the country's political regime, an array of political parties and some 4723 (Central Statistics Organisation, Ministry of Planning and International Cooperation 2008, 490) civil society institutions of various tendencies, including charitable organizations, unions, social institutions, professional associations and cultural clubs, most of which are located in the main cities. It is a reflection of Yemen's commitment to a governance system based on democracy and political pluralism, and on the provisions of the Constitution and the Unification Agreement between the country's north and south.

In *A Dictionary of Social Sciences* (1969) the tribe is defined as 'a social division of a people comprising several local groupings like villages, towns and tribes; the tribe shares a common territory, speaks the same language, has a common cultural environment and adopts the same set of primitive emotions' (Gould and Kolb 1969, 729).

Many researchers and historians share the view that the state and society in Yemen are heavily influenced by the country's tribal system and that the majority of Yemeni tribes have so far enjoyed a stable existence, with a wide range of interests and customs in common with city dwellers, including housing, agriculture, trade and taxation. However, despite this consistency, the internal configuration of the Yemeni tribe is permanently changing, though such change nonetheless requires that it will still be organized along socially acceptable lines (Al-Thahiri 2004, 150).

Historically, Yemeni tribes are known as much for their culture as for their complex social, political and economic systems. According to certain researchers, there are around 168 tribes in Yemen living in different parts of the country, and which account for nearly 85% of the total population. However, despite this large number of tribes, Yemeni society is culturally homogenous overall and socially well integrated, its plurality being neither social nor ethnic.[2]

The recent spiral of events in Yemen and the onset of the revolution on Saturday, 15 January 2011, were an indication of how poor conditions in the country had become. The demonstrations were the result of a spontaneous movement mostly by leftist university students who could no longer accept the poor economic conditions or lack of job opportunities that awaited them; moreover, many had to abandon their studies due to the exponential rise in education and housing fees.[3]

The demonstrations began as a protest against the poor social and economic conditions in the country, as well as other indicators, such as an illiteracy and partial illiteracy rate of 76%, based on 2004 census figures. This total includes 45% illiterates, and 31.5% having only minimal reading and writing ability. The same census also showed that only 12% of the population had completed their elementary education, 8.2% their secondary education and only 2.3% (Central Statistics Organisation, Ministry of Planning and International Cooperation 2008, 335) held university degrees. Moreover, 52% lived under the poverty line, a condition exacerbated by the strong tribal influence.

In the course of the demonstrations the Parties that made up what is known as the Common Meeting (including the Muslim Brotherhood and Yemeni Congregation for Reform) soon jumped on the bandwagon and made the youth protest movement their own, using it in their two-year political struggle with the ruling Congress Party. They succeeded in imposing a fait accompli in the street by staging sit-ins in the Western Ring Road that stretches north of the capital, Sana'a, starting at the old Sana'a University and ending at the headquarters of the First Armoured Division led by Ali Muhsin Al-Ahmar, the military leader who seceded from the army.[4]

The youth movement put the Islamists to the test in front of a public waiting to see their reaction to the peaceful youth movement. Their response, when it came, was divided according to the interests of different groups in the movement, and their respective links to the regime in power and to various power centres in the country.

The Islamists Movement in Yemen comprises four different groups: the Muslim Brotherhood, represented by the Yemeni Congregation for Reform; Ansar Allah (God's Supporters), or the Houthis; Salafist movements of various leanings; and the Supporters of Sharia, namely Al-Qaeda.

The Ansar Allah Movement – the Houthis – is a relatively new movement compared with other Islamist groups. It was formed in June 2004 essentially as a result of the conflict between government forces and one of the Zaidi Movement's *imams*, Hussein Badreddin Al-Houthi (Al-Daghshi 2009, 148). The latter's anti-American slogan stated: 'God is Great, Death to America, Death to Israel, May God Curse the Jews, and Victory to Islam,' which is an adaptation of Imam Khomeini's slogan during the Islamic Revolution in Iran.

Many researchers believe that the tenets of Ansar Allah were born in the mid-1980s when a group of Zaidi youths decided to form an intellectual group to combat the injustices perpetrated against their sect. The sect was marginalized, unable to teach its tenets, and a ban was imposed on printing its books and teaching its tenets (Boucek 2012, 7, Al-Daghshi 2009, 34). The youths' ideas nonetheless grew in prominence and became set after unification in 1990 when the group established what was called at the time the 'Believing Youth Forum' which organized three-month summer camps during the holidays to teach the sect's principles and basic tenets.

The evidence indicates that:

> conflict arose from a complex combination of competing sectarian identities, regional underdevelopment, perceived socioeconomic injustices, and historical grievances. It is exacerbated by tensions between the indigenous Zaidi Shia population and Sunni Salafi fundamentalists who have relocated to the area. Tribal rivalries also made things worse, because the regime has recruited tribal fighters to combat the insurrection.
>
> (Boucek 2010, 8)

Soon after the outbreak of the youth revolution, the Houthi Movement occupied Sa'ada Governorate by force, wrenched it away from government control and elected a new governor there by acclamation (Ayesh 2012). It also helped occupy Al-Jouf Governorate in cooperation with forces loyal to the Muslim Brotherhood and the Yemeni Congregation for Reform, also wresting it away from government control, and appointed a candidate acceptable to both parties in the conflict, the Houthis and the Brotherhood (*Al-Watan* May 20, 2012).

The Houthi Movement rejected the initiative formulated by the Gulf Cooperation Council (GCC) to end the conflict and depicted it as an American conspiracy to circumvent the Yemeni people's revolution, and prevent it from achieving its full objectives. It called for a boycott of the presidential elections, proposed in the Gulf initiative, but agreed to take part in a national dialogue scheduled to take place soon thereafter.

For its part, the Muslim Brotherhood is one of the political movements most involved in Yemeni mainstream political, social and economic life; it has the largest popular following and greatest social impact. This is due to several factors. Chief among them is the fact that the country's most influential tribal, business and senior military leaders are all members of the party. Among the tribal leaders concerned are Sheikh Abdullah bin Hussein Al-Ahmar, his sons, Sinan and Abu Lahoum, and the latter's sons, who are all considered among Yemen's most important tribal leaders and all are members of the Yemeni Congregation for Reform, the arm of the Muslim Brotherhood Movement in Yemen. Also a member is Muhsin Al-Ahmar, a military leader who owns 50% of the Yemeni Army's assets (A-Qarawi 2011).

The Brotherhood's influence was not confined to the religious, spiritual guidance and education domains, but its presence was also felt in most state institutions including security, military, diplomatic and media institutions. When the youth rebellion began and the movement decided to throw its weight behind it, in the wake of the Al-Karama Friday massacre that took place on 18 March 2011, most of the Brotherhood's prominent members decided to secede from the government of Ali Abdullah Saleh. Among the latter were ministers and ambassadors in Arab and Western countries, the chief editors of government newspapers and of Yemen's news agency Saba', and leaders of security and military agencies. The group included General Ali Muhsin Al-Ahmar, leader of the North-Western Region and the First Armoured Brigade, whose forces took control of the northern areas of the capital, Sana'a, including the area where the youths were staging their sit-in.

Sheikh Abdullah bin Hussein Al-Ahmar's sons, in particular the eldest, Sadeq bin Abdullah bin Hussein Al-Ahmar, the main sheikh of the Hashid Tribe and member of the Yemeni Congregation for Reform, took control of government institutions situated near his home in the Hasaba area.

The Salafist Movement comprises three currents: the first is traditional and closest of the three to the ideas of the Salafist Movement's founder in Yemen, Sheikh Muqbel Al-Wad'i. Al-Wad'i was himself influenced by Salafist sheikhs in Saudi Arabia, including the Al-Jame'i current, whose founder is Sheikh Mohammad bin Aman Al-Jame'i, an Ethiopian cleric who teaches at the Islamic University, and the Saudi cleric Sheikh Rabeei' bin Hadi Al-Mudkhali (Al-Daghshi 2012, 107). The second current belongs to the Al-Hikma Society (Wisdom), which is heavily influenced by Egyptian cleric Sheikh Abdel-Rahman Abdel-Khaleq in Kuwait, and by the Kuwaiti Ihya' Al-Turath current (Heritage Revival). There is also the Ihsan Association current, which is influenced by the Syrian cleric Mohammad Srour, known in Yemen as the Syrian current.

However, because the Salafist Movement, especially the traditional and Muqbeli currents (after Muqbel bin Hadi Al-Wa'idi, founder of Salafism in Yemen), adhered to its own teachings and declared principles, in particular obedience to 'the guardian', it was the only Islamist political movement that continued to back the regime. It issued multiple *fatwas* (religious edicts) against disobeying the guardian, called on the youth to leave the streets (*'Adan al-Ghad* 2010), and continued on that track until the president's resignation, under the leadership of Yahya Al-Hajouri and Abu Al-Hassan Al-Ma'ribi.

The position of the other Salafist movements passed through two different stages. The first was when most of their statements preached against disobeying the unjust ruler except through legal means, and called for avoiding those that lead to sedition and bloodletting, such as demonstrations (al-Tagheer 2011).

The second stage followed the onset of the revolution, when their position towards political activism changed. They established the first Salafist political party despite the fact that they did not believe in political action per se, and used to criticize the Muslim Brotherhood for involving themselves in the political game. The new party, Itihad Al-Rashad Al-Yamani (Yemeni Al-Rashad Union), saw the light on 14 March 2012, and it counted among its members the vast majority of Yemen's Salafist parties hailing from all three Salafist currents. However, a number of traditional tribal Salafist sheikhs stayed away, including Sheikh Yahya Al-Hajouri, Sheikh Mohammad al-Imam and a number of others close to the traditional current (Almasdar Online 2012a).

As for Al-Qaeda in Yemen, the establishment of this new movement was announced in January 2009 under the name Ansar Al-Sharia, or Qaedat al Jihad fi Jazeerat al-Arab (Base of Jihad in the Arabian Peninsula) (Al-Daghshi 2012, 27). However, the movement had actually been in existence since the 1980s when Yemeni youths were being recruited to fight against the Soviets in Afghanistan, with the help of the US Central Intelligence Agency (CIA) and the Saudi intelligence service, and the support of local Muslim clerics such as Sheikh Abdul-Majid Al-Zaydani, President of Al-Iman University in Yemen.

For his part, Sheikh Anwar Al-Awlaki, one of the most important Al-Qaeda theoreticians, saw the Arab revolutions as a step in the right direction, and an opportunity for the *mujahideen* to breathe again after being suffocated for three long decades (Al-Qadimi 2012, 32).

For a short time in 2011, Al-Qaeda spread its control over vast territories in the Governorates of Shabwa and Abyan. This was due to the two governorates' geographic location; the fact that they are situated in rugged mountainous terrain in proximity to the sea, in particular the Gulf of Aden where smuggling is rife, made the nearby Yemeni shores accessible to Somali *mujahideen* jihadist youths from Afghanistan and Pakistan via the Indian Ocean (Almasdar Online 2012b). Moreover, the two governorates are sparsely populated: Abyan with its 500,000 inhabitants and 16,943 km^2 area is one-and-a-half times the size of Lebanon; and Al Shabwa with its 525,000 inhabitants and 42,584 km^2 area. Over and above that, the local inhabitants sympathize with leaders of Al-Qaeda who hail from their region, such as Mohammad 'Ameer Al-Awlaki and Jalal Bal'eedi, coupled with the fact that tribal influence in those areas was too weak to prevent the movement from imposing its control, unlike in north Yemen where tribal forces are well trained and operate in a densely populated region. There is also the sectarian dimension, whereby the overwhelming majority of the south's inhabitants belong to the Shafei sect (Central Statistics Organisation, Ministry of Planning and International Cooperation 2010, Yemeni Presidency's National Information Centre 2010).

However, as far as the adoption of religious ideas is concerned, and despite these superficial divisions, there is genuine religious vitality and activism rather than sectarian entrenchment in Yemen, as is the case in other Arab countries such as Lebanon and Iraq, for example. The individual in Yemen can join the Muslim Brotherhood one day and transfer his allegiance to the Zaidies the next, or vice versa, without difficulty because sectarianism is not the object of intense struggle in Yemen as it is in other countries. There is a wide scope of conviviality, tolerance and homogeneity due in part to the nature of the Zaidi and Shafei sects, to which the majority of the Yemeni population adheres. These are close to the Sunni branch of Islam because Zaidi theology is mostly Hanafi, and the Shafei sect is close to Sufism, which is known for its tolerance and acceptance of the other. Yemeni society is also flexible and beneficially pragmatic in part due to the poor economic capabilities and difficult daily life of its citizens.

It could also be stated that there are many similarities between most contemporary Islamist movements, be they Sunni or Shia. In terms of form, they distinguish themselves from other parities by adopting religious discourses, using religious terminology and purporting to speak in the name of religion. They all advocate a national revival through a return to the early origins of Islam, and call for *jihad* to defend Islam and the Arab nation's holy places; they combine sectarianism, advocacy for it and social and political activism, and declare their willingness to sacrifice in the cause of Islam, and their readiness to defy the political and religious authorities.

However, since the subject here is Islamic political movements, if one does not make sense of their ideological bases, their behaviour or manner of thinking will not be understood. Many researchers are surprised when they see the differences between different Islamist currents that sometimes reach the level of enmity and exaggerated mutual accusations of apostasy and heresy.[5]

There is often confusion between the common constants among the Muslims (the dogma of the faith) and political disagreements caused by a fanaticism that rejects the other. It could be stated in this context that the main differences between the Islamist political movements lie in the political form they take rather than the basic content. Differences emerged historically around a political issue, the imamate, and are still on-going today as a political disagreement around the issue of governance, 'and the first disagreement among the Muslims after their Prophet was the disagreement over the imamate' (Al-Ash'ari 1985, 39). However, this disagreement has taken on an ideological dimension, a fact this article will try to demonstrate by highlighting and analysing the ideological basis underlying political Islam, in general and in Yemen in particular.

It is impossible to talk about Islamist political movements as a single unit; they have different visions, plans, strategies, tactics, organizations and formations, and this plurality has gone beyond a few differences between different organizations to affecting individual organizations (Al Torabi et al. 2003, 235).

In this connection, the following list will serve as a reminder of a number of issues that all Islamist political groups, regardless of their specific beliefs and tendencies, agree on:

- All Islamist political movements see Islam both as a state and a religion, i.e. they do not accept any separation between the two and see it as a deviation from Islam. They see Islam as divine guidance on how to organize people's religious and temporal lives, and this led to the claim that 'Governance is God's alone'. In Islam, a governance system that emanates from the people and is separate from God's governance and tenets of the faith does not exist; Islam is a unifying religion while democracy is non-religious. Islam does not differentiate between the religious and the temporal, or public and private lives. Government by the people is outside the realm of religion, and is therefore seen as an attempt to share and dilute God's exclusive domain; Islam is not an isolated political practice but a comprehensive life system applicable to the family, to society, and to the economic, social and political spheres. The people inherit the earth on condition that they submit to God and to His governance, obey His laws and commit to this particular system of *khilafa* (selecting the ruler). At the first disagreement, they should return to the holy text and understand it in light of the religious legislative sources to which every individual in the nation should commit, through the intermediary of its *imams* and emirs.

- Islamist political movements consider the Qur'an and the Sunna the source of all legislation, despite certain differences in form between them, since Sunni sources based on Shia tenets are different from Sunni sources based on Sunni tenets.
- All Islamist political movements believe in following the worthy ancestors' example, despite the differences between them on certain issues; the Sunnis consider the Prophet's companions as worthy ancestors, while the Shia consider the *imams* of the Prophet's family as worthy ancestors.
- All Islamist political movements believe in building an ideal society free of moral corruption and spiritual vacuity, and in rearing a conservative Muslim family.
- Islamist political movements believe that their movement is global rather than local and specific to one country; their activism is not confined to a particular country but spreads further afield to the larger Arab and Muslim region, and the world as a whole, because Islam is global by nature.
- Islamist political movements believe that the only legitimate power in the state should rest in the hands of the *imams*; they also believe that the group needs a leader, an emir, though his title might differ from one movement to another. This title ranges from '*wilayat al-faqeeh*' (Guardian of the Jurisprudence) and the '*marje'ya*' (religious reference) in Shia Islam, to the General Guide of the Sunni Muslim Brotherhood, and the leaders of respective movements and religious *imams* in Salafist currents.

However, not all religious sects and movements support this last concept; others endorse the human option and believe that the establishment of the imamate is an intellectual process rather than a legal religious duty because they entrust civilian (or intellectual) interests to the group; this view is widespread among the Mu'tazala and Zaidi groups (Al-Mouseli 2003, 45).

Islamist political parties in Yemen were influenced intellectually by the thoughts of Sayed Qutob, a pioneer of the activist line in contemporary political Islam, who died in 1966. He was a 'genuine innovator with an independent mind whose influence is inestimable on the present generation of Islamists' (Barakat n.d., 162).

It could be said that Sayed Qutob's ideas, and those of his predecessors, lie at the foundation of political Islam in Yemen, including the Muslim Brotherhood and the wide array of Salafist groups. The only divergence with Qutob's ideas concerns the manner of presenting the ideology, or the names given to different ideas; local movements usually present them in a modern framework more in line with the particular nature of Yemeni society.

Some of these movements were also affected by the religious ideas Khomeini carried over to the political domain; these ideas became a strong incentive and a catalyst for Zaidi youths hungry for a religious culture to adopt. The latter badly needed an inspiration to galvanize Zaidi youths left out by the Muslim Brotherhood which failed to embrace them due to ideological differences, and the intellectual repression they suffered at the hands of the North Yemeni regime prior to 1990. Khomeini's movement was the closest example to them, on both the sectarian and emotional levels, especially with its use of names belonging to the Prophet's family. Khomeini's ideas became the material content and his person became the inspiration and the leadership they sought, and the resulting political activism among Zaidi youths led to the establishment of the Al-Haq (Truth) Party and the Believing Youths Movement, soon followed by the Mukabbireen (Callers to prayer) Movement, or Ansar Allah, or the Houthi Movement, after its founder Sayed Hussein Baderaddin Al-Houthi. The latter drew inspiration from Khomeini when warning against the American and Western threat using religious slogans.

Research findings: implications and some background

Looking again at religious extremism, it is clear that because it is a complex and variable phenomenon it cannot be explained by studying a single variable. Several factors and variables interact and overlap with each other and, in doing so, create an environment that fosters religious extremism and allows it to grow.

It could also be said that the above-mentioned variables might not necessarily be reasons that directly lead to religious extremism. Several indirect reasons might well have played a role as well, and one could say that these are the environments that allow religious extremism to grow, although they are not the immediate or latent constructive factors that give rise to the sort of religious extremism of concern here.

The findings of the research that informs this article may be summarized as follows.

The first hypothesis

The first hypothesis is that poverty is a basic factor in creating a social environment conducive to the rise of Salafism. In other words, the more acute the poverty, the more the environment is conducive to the rise and spread of extremist Salafism. What is meant here is the relative poverty that characterizes the living standards of the majority of Yemen's population.[6] The finding is that there is a direct positive relationship between poverty and religious extremism; the higher the poverty rate, the more acute religious extremism is. The results of testing this hypothesis were as follows:

- As far as religious extremism in general is concerned, it was found that the age groups 18–24 and 15–31 years are the most affected by it. These are also the age groups that poverty has a direct effect on, making them more vulnerable and, thence, it appears, more prone to embrace religious extremist ideologies, as Table 3 on poverty indicates.

The research showed that poverty is a major factor in the creation of a social environment conducive to the spread of extremism; the higher the level of poverty, the more severe extremism becomes. The disinterest shown by mainstream Yemeni groups in the people at large, particularly the poor, has fostered a lack of public trust in these groups' leaders. Added to that the shortage of funds in the Yemeni people's

Table 3. Covariance analysis of the correlation between poverty axis and the other variables.

Variables			Political milieu axis	Foreign intervention axis	Tribal and regional discrimination axis	Religious mobilization axis	Leadership axis	Religious extremism
Poverty axis	Gender	Male	0.662	0.534	0.549	0.512	0.193	0.766
		Female	0.501	0.525	0.503	0.589	0.355	0.720
	Age	24–18	0.591	0.661	0.547	0.541	0.384	0.782
		31–25	0.615	0.547	0.533	0.527	0.271	0.750
		38–32	0.668	0.328	0.492	0.325	–0.195	0.714
		45–39	0.099	0.032	–0.021	0.309	0.185	0.339
		52–46	0.554	0.342	0.349	0.633	0.021	0.569
		53 or more	0.298	0.347	0.580	0.587	0.268	0.962
	Marital status	Single	0.525	0.573	0.518	0.464	0.259	0.714
		Married	0.656	0.462	0.515	0.559	0.200	0.769
	Level of education	Can read and write	0.667	0.338	0.767	0.887	0.791	0.860
		Primary	0.750	0.595	0.421	0.208	0.408	0.796
		Secondary	0.866	0.726	0.663	0.590	0.340	0.843
		University level and higher	0.403	0.412	0.416	0.375	0.213	0.646
		Vocational education	0.945	–0.371	0.999	0.978	–0.999	0.949
		Religious education	0.580	0.499	0.321	0.602	0.000	0.671
	Profession	Civil servant	0.586	0.475	0.465	0.443	0.160	0.715
		Private sector	0.506	0.233	0.477	0.546	0.117	0.649
		Labourer	–0.404	0.305	0.367	–0.248	–0.591	0.191
		Unemployed	0.804	0.751	0.864	0.889	0.599	0.922
		Student	0.507	0.660	0.436	0.458	0.421	0.738
	Income (000)	20 or less	0.690	0.712	0.447	0.512	0.316	0.780
		30–21	0.320	0.258	0.770	0.729	0.778	0.852
		50–31	0.596	0.391	0.582	0.493	0.126	0.707
		100–51	0.554	0.468	0.222	0.344	–0.235	0.465
		101 or more	0.79	0.228	0.457	0.332	–0.082	0.617
	Place of residence	Sana'a	0.558	0.530	0.467	0.483	0.086	0.709
		Thoummar	0.683	0.535	0.636	0.628	0.454	0.818

pockets, lack of natural resources, increased population growth rates and the conflicts between different groups have exacerbated the plight of ordinary Yemenis. The conflicts that have afflicted Yemen over the years include the war between the royalists and the republicans (that ended in 1970), the Middle Region War (that ended in 1982), the Summer 1994 War, and the Sa'ada War (2004–2010). These factors have increased the poverty rates and destabilized the social fabric, which in turn has eroded social solidarity and, as argued by Durkheim, has weakened the social consciousness without offering an alternative. Over time this has led to an erosion of social norms, or anomie, which in turn has provoked acts of violence and, as anticipated by Oberschall (1993), a loss of the common interests that once existed between upper- and lower-class groups.

Specifically, as evidenced in the responses of those sampled in the survey undertaken as part of this research, this has led to experimentation with new ideas and the emergence of new groups on the scene thanks to the spread effect from nearby societies. This was substantiated in the answers of those surveyed, as follows:

- A small majority of the research sample either agreed, or agreed to a certain extent (58.5%), that poverty is a basic cause of religious extremism.
- A large minority of respondents either agreed, or agreed to a certain extent (42%), that poverty helped the creation and rise of the Salafist movement in Yemen.
- A majority either agreed, or agreed to a certain extent (77.6%), that giving financial assistance to the poor helped these movements increase their popularity.
- A majority either agreed, or agreed to a certain extent (61%), that the Islamist movements are the most attentive to the needs of the poor.
- A majority either agreed, or agreed to a certain extent (67.3%), that the lack of state-sponsored projects targeting the poor pushed them towards the Islamist movements.
- A small majority either agreed, or agreed to a certain extent (53%), that the children of wealthy parents are less likely to join Islamist parties.
- A majority either agreed, or agreed to a certain extent (73.7%), that the Islamist groups' social solidarity programmes enhanced their presence among the people.
- A majority either agreed, or agreed to a certain extent (83.9%), that the mass wedding ceremonies organized by the Islamist movements are important source of their popularity.
- A majority either agreed, or agreed to a certain extent (84.4%), that distributing food to the people is a positive move on the Islamist movements' part.
- A majority either agreed, or agreed to a certain extent (67.8%), that the Islamist movements are more attentive to the people's financial needs.

This outcome is all the more significant given that 55% of the Yemeni people live below the poverty line.

The political and economic regime's inability to absorb the new immigrants from rural to urban areas, and integrate them in the new society, makes these migrants more prone to embrace religious extremism. Therefore, the weakness or ineffectiveness of state programmes targeting this particular social sector means that there is a higher possibility that the poorest among them will join extremist religious groups, and that they will become the main raw material for recruitment by these groups.

Added to the above is the fact that oil exports, so necessary to the Yemeni government and which account for nearly 75% of its revenue, will soon be depleted. Yemeni oil exports dropped from 450,000 barrels per day in 2003 to around 280,000 barrels per day in January 2009, and according to the International Energy Agency (IEA), oil production dropped in 2010 to 260,000 barrels per day (Energy Information Administration 2010, 2).

Experts believe that Yemeni oil exports will entirely cease in 2017, and that the Yemeni government will no longer benefit materially from the country's oil exports. This means that the country's economy is headed towards disintegration, given that revenues from oil are the government's main source of funding. This means that it will eventually no longer be able to manage the entire territory, and will become more dependent on foreign assistance (Hedberg 2010, 53).

In light of these circumstances, it is fair to conclude that the growth of extremist Salafism is a natural consequence of Yemeni society's experience, as described above. It has been forced down the path of violence, with the Salafists taking advantage of the poor economic conditions and ever-increasing poverty rates.

The second hypothesis

The second hypothesis was that a closed political environment, i.e. the absence of democracy, creates a social environment favourable to extremist Salafism; the more the democracy, the less the extremism. This suggests there is an inverse relationship between the absence of democracy and extremism; in other words, the less democracy there is, the more religious extremism one has. The findings of the research showed the following:

- As far as religious extremism in general is concerned, the results show that the age group 25–31 years is more amenable to adhering to extremist movements than any other. From this it may be deduced that the political environment affects younger age groups because they are more vulnerable to extremist religious currents, and therefore more likely to associate themselves with them. This is evident in Table 4.

The research project showed that a closed political environment and lack of genuine democracy helped create a social environment amenable to the growth of extremism; and the more advanced democracy is, the lower the level of extremism. The quasi-autocratic policies of certain regimes against the Islamists, their intolerance towards their transgressions, and the limits imposed on the official channels available to them to participate in the political process in a natural and democratic manner has pushed these groups towards extremism. When asked about the subject, the research sample gave the following answers:

- A majority of the research sample either agreed, or agreed to a certain extent (62.4%), that the struggle over power is responsible for the rise of Islamist groups.
- A small majority either agreed, or agreed to a certain extent (56%), that the one-party system enhances the Islamist movements' popularity.
- Some respondents either agreed, or agreed to a certain extent (38.6%), that free elections help reduce the popularity of Islamist movements.
- A majority either agreed, or agreed to a certain extent (70.2%), that putting Islamist leaders in jail makes people sympathetic to their cause.

Table 4 Covariance analysis of the correlation between the political milieu axis and the other variables.

Variables		Poverty axis	Foreign intervention axis	Tribal and regional discrimination axis	Religious mobilization axis	Leadership axis	Religious extremism
Gender	Male	0.662	0.597	0.485	0.498	0.040	0.706
	Female	0.501	0.613	0.720	0.632	0.337	0.806
Age	24–18	0.591	0.541	0.459	0.468	0.108	0.608
	31–25	0.615	0.726	0.690	0.599	0.378	0.852
	38–32	0.668	0.543	0.556	0.365	–0.247	0.809
	45–39	0.099	0.306	0.172	0.342	–0.007	0.487
	52–46	0.554	0.475	0.595	0.750	0.131	0.801
	53 or more	0.298	0.862	–0.391	0.340	–0.786	0.189
Marital status	Single	0.525	0.559	0.521	0.460	0.162	0.658
	Married	0.656	0.617	0.556	0.569	0.041	0.784
Level of education	Can read and write	0.667	0.817	0.672	0.812	0.700	0.878
	Primary	0.750	0.413	0.370	0.299	0.366	0.702
	Secondary	0.866	0.669	0.549	0.523	0.248	0.762
	University level and Higher	0.403	0.551	0.618	0.522	0.106	0.739
	Vocational education	0.945	–0.655	0.929	0.857	–0.929	0.793
	Religious education	0.580	0.510	0.373	0.571	–0.196	0.634
occupation	Civil servant	0.586	0.627	0.515	0.467	0.089	0.764
	private Sector	0.506	0.554	0.465	0.494	0.135	0.664
	Labourer	–0.404	–0.792	–0.960	–0.553	–0.455	–0.792
	Unemployed	0.804	0.924	0.869	0.793	0.272	0.902
	Student	0.507	0.664	0.706	0.543	0.254	0.750
Income (thousands of riyals)	20 or less	0.690	0.645	0.526	0.507	0.158	0.723
	30–21	0.320	0.649	0.453	0.326	0.417	0.584
	50–31	0.596	0.514	0.557	0.458	0.118	0.736
	100–51	0.554	0.632	0.600	0.663	–0.138	0.808
	101 or more	0.479	0.458	0.792	0.765	0.161	0.895
Place of residence	Sana’a	0.558	0.676	0.702	0.613	–0.002	0.800
	Thoummar	0.683	0.507	0.391	0.419	0.266	0.665

- A majority either agreed, or agreed to a certain extent (74.2%), that closing newspapers detracts from the regime's credibility.
- A majority either agreed, or agreed to a certain extent (69.8%), that it is wrong to have armed clashes with the Islamists.
- A majority either agreed, or agreed to a certain extent (75.6%), that division and the tactic of the government to divide the Islamist movements led to the evolution of extremist movements. Having leaders grappling with each other contributes to the emergence of religious extremism, all of which is attributable to or exacerbated by the government. A small majority of respondents either agreed, or agreed to a certain extent (53.2%), that genuine freedom will decrease the Islamist movements' popularity.
- A majority agreed, or agreed to a certain extent (58.5%), that longer sentences for individuals mean more popularity for the Islamists.

Yemen's closed political climate is quasi-dictatorial, forbids protests of any significance against the regime and allows the opposition only the slightest of margins to voice its needs. A climate such as this usually reflects a highly centralized system, where decisions are made by a president with no serious challengers to his position. Instead of dealing with it as a political challenge, the regime in Yemen considers the opposition's call for dialogue and reconfiguration of the political system as a threat to national security.

In such a climate, the ruling party's hegemony is clear, as is its use of state institutions to safeguard its monopoly over power; there are no clear lines between the ruling party's operations and different state agencies.

It is important to note, however, that despite the narrow margin allowed officially, Yemen is nonetheless experiencing a stage of rich political pluralism; and most newspapers can raise important issues without being harassed. What this manifests is the extent of the challenge to state power posed by increasing disaffection.

In this Arab–Islamic world, the duality of power and the sword can also be noticed; and when the sacred appears on the political scene, trickery, sedition and mistakes rear their head, whereby cultural absolutes replace the religious creed, and new, hardline and deeply ingrained beliefs surface in the minds of fanatical individuals. The objective becomes the liquidation of those who do not fall in line, as a natural consequence of the accumulated emotional vacuity within man. The machinery of loyalty and obedience to the emir and leader is also still present, even if the latter is the lowest of the low; and the concept of death becomes predominant, *jihad* and *ijtihad* (independent interpretation) become heresy and apostasy, and religiously sanctioned disagreement is deemed taboo and a practice usually deserving death.

The discourse of the sword begins with God and ends with murder; God gets lost in all of this and only the killing remains, predominant on the scene and the favoured method of imposing one's opinion and making the desired change. This sort of discourse, which has been prevalent in man's midst for at least a millennium, is the discourse of power and destruction that turns the individual into the sole proprietor of the truth, meaning that everyone else should be put aside and cut down to size.

It is safe to say that even though groups which are prone to violence often disagree or go to war against each other, and the common denominator among them remains the language of violence, the main responsibility for this falls on the shoulders of the regime that uses religious discourse, the sacred, the claim to guardianship and the duty of obedience, to further its interests.

Ever since the Third World became an entity unto its own, its discourses and practices have been those of power and the sword, and underlying it all is the theme of God, obedience to the guardian and the premise that God takes away through power what He does not through the Qu'ran. Thus it transpires, in the Arab world, that the most ominous manifestation of power is when the sword and the Qu'ran join forces in a single discourse, and end up resting in the hands of a single authority.

The quasi-dictatorial policies of some regimes against the Islamists, never forgiving their mistakes and greatly limiting the official outlets that allow them to take part in the country's political life in a natural and democratic manner, could push these groups towards extremist ideologies.

If one looks at the current situation in Yemen, it is found that the governing institution accepts the presence of Islamist groups in the country as long as their activities are confined to religious proselytizing, and they stay clear of political activism – which is exactly how the regime in Yemen deals with the Salafist movement. Not only has the government attempted to control such movements and closely monitor their activities, but also it has fomented enmity between them and used the divisions politically to deal a blow to the opposition and to cut it down to size.

The Yemeni regime strove to balance various conflicts by pitting one social group against the other, and one political current against the other, without having to intervene directly. This is how it managed to exhaust the energies of various groups and control the strings of the political game (Carroll 1986, 185).

This is what the ruling party did when it used the Yemeni Congregation for Reform to deal a blow to the Yemeni Socialist Party, a move that led to the outbreak of the Summer 1994 War, and ouster of the latter party from the political equation in Yemen. The ruling party then turned its attention to the Yemeni Congregation for Reform and used the Salafist currents and religious youths as a foil, which led to the Congregation Party's departure from government following the 1997 elections. After that, it tried to deal a similar blow to the religious youths by instigating Salafist groups in the areas where the Zaidi religion predominates, thus provoking the Houthi War that began in 2004 and led to six different wars, with still no end in sight.

For a while Yemen turned away from the less despotic regimes in the region and instead moved in a direction that led to the campaign of repression launched in June 2004 against the followers of Hussein Badreddin Al-Houthi. It marked the first significant dismantlement of the old conciliatory formula that had framed relations between the Islamists and the regime of Ali Abdullah Saleh, and, perhaps due to American pressure on Yemen – as well as direct Saudi pressure – helped open to question the sensitive equilibriums involved in the reconciliation efforts between the regime, the Houthis and the tribes. For a long time this conciliation process was a key to the country's political stability, and would have allowed it to rid itself of the tensions associated with the repressive measures against the Islamist current, or even its eradication (Burgat 2006, 99).

The regime also tried to monopolize the ideological power of Islam and pull the rug from under the feet of its challengers by integrating and containing extremist Salafist groups in Thamar, Saada and Ma'reb, and use that power against its other enemies, in particular Ansar Allah, one of Badreddin Al-Houthi's supporters, against the Islah Party (The Muslim Brotherhood). It relied on the so-called moderate *ulema* that play, next to the regime, a pivotal role in the country's political life by issuing, among others, *fatwas* in support of the regime at election time or during armed conflicts.

The emergence of ideologically leftist parties and currents, like the Nasserism that informed the mindset of former Yemeni President Ibrahim Al-Hamdi, socialism in South Yemen, and certain elements of the Nationalist and Socialist Baathist ideologies, meant that popular political activism in the early 1970s involved a variety of conflicting political ideologies. However, because the collective consciousness of Yemeni society is essentially Islamic, it made it easier for the Salafist movement and Muslim Brotherhood to influence the public ideologically, and sway them in favour of political Islam.

The assassination of former Yemeni President Ibrahim Al-Hamdi in 1977 and some Nasserite parties' support for the coup d'état in the hope of reaching power, adversely affected the margin of democracy that existed in the country at the time. It made it difficult for other political parties to take part in the political process and in state institutions, and compelled many groups, especially the Islamists, to go underground and work in secret, a phenomenon that increased their tendency towards fanaticism and reinforced their hard-line attitudes.

The third hypothesis

The third hypothesis contends that external interventions played an important role in the rise and tendencies of Salafist parties in the Arab–Islamic world. The less foreign intervention there is, whether material or intellectual, the lower the level of extremism, and the reverse is also true. In other words, the assumption is that if foreign intervention in local societies ceases, Salafist movements will cease being attractive to the public, and more specifically, if Salafist movements in Yemen did not receive material and intellectual support from neighbouring Gulf countries, through the printing of books and other material, the reach of fanaticism and extremism will be more limited. The contention to be tested, therefore, is that there is a direct positive relationship between foreign intervention and religious extremism. The results of the survey indicate the following:

- In the case of religious extremism in general, the view was that the age group 18–24 years was more vulnerable to it than other age groups, meaning that foreign intervention affects younger age groups. It makes them vulnerable to religious extremism and therefore more likely to adopt it, which is what the table relevant to foreign intervention shows (Table 5).

The study revealed that external intervention plays an important role in the rise, tendencies and spread of Salafism, at least in Yemen, and presumably in other Arab–Islamic societies; this means that the less foreign intervention there is, the lower the level of extremism; and the reverse presumably also holds. However, the phenomenon could also spread from one country to another involuntarily through a knock-on effect, without prior planning. Events are contagious and spread from one system to another through the media and personal contacts, among other means, and they affect environments in their proximity where similar circumstances exist. The phenomenon could also spread voluntarily through planned and deliberate action. In this context, respondents in the study sample answered as follows:

- A majority either agreed, or agreed to a certain extent (65.9%), that the reason behind the rise of Salafism in Yemen is intervention by neighbouring countries.
- A slim majority either agreed, or agreed to a certain extent (51.2%), that the presence of other sects reinforces Salafism in Yemen.

Table 5 Covariance analysis of the correlation between external intervention axis and the other variables.

Variables		Poverty axis	Political milieu axis	Tribal and regional discrimination axis	Religious mobilization axis	Leadership axis	Religious extremism
Gender	Male	0.534	0.597	0.586	0.521	0.097	0.760
	Female	0.525	0.613	0.585	0.525	0.262	0.755
Age	24–18	0.661	0.541	0.678	0.581	0.158	0.803
	31–25	0.547	0.726	0.546	0.564	0.412	0.790
	38–32	0.328	0.543	0.446	0.171	–0.166	0.659
	45–39	0.032	0.306	0.338	–0.065	–0.072	0.610
	52–46	0.342	0.475	0.401	0.447	0.106	0.572
	53 or more	0.347	0.862	–0.211	0.727	–0.790	0.330
Marital status	Single	0.573	0.559	0.665	0.535	0.284	0.813
	Married	0.462	0.617	0.479	0.434	–0.022	0.685
Level of education	Can read and write	0.338	0.817	0.680	0.626	0.652	0.724
	Primary	0.595	0.413	0.126	0.037	0.625	0.779
	Secondary	0.726	0.669	0.789	0.618	0.373	0.881
	University level and higher	0.412	0.551	0.542	0.465	0.010	0.703
	Vocational education	–0.371	–0.655	–0.327	–0.171	0.327	–0.059
	Religious education	0.499	0.510	0.243	0.458	–0.094	0.625
Profession	Civil servant	0.475	0.627	0.407	0.382	0.041	0.674
	Private sector	0.233	0.554	0.560	0.359	–0.083	0.710
	Labourer	0.305	–0.792	0.930	0.628	0.505	0.987
	Unemployed	0.751	0.924	0.889	0.840	0.223	0.904
	Student	0.660	0.664	0.646	0.590	0.419	0.834
Income (thousands of riyals)	20 or less	0.712	0.645	0.630	0.582	0.223	0.851
	30–21	0.258	0.649	0.613	0.458	0.508	0.629
	50–31	0.391	0.514	0.634	0.467	0.189	0.760
	100–51	0.468	0.632	0.530	0.323	–0.266	0.632
	101 or more	0.228	0.458	0.328	0.480	–0.122	0.602
Place of residence	Sana'a	0.530	0.676	0.558	0.546	–0.029	0.751
	Thoummar	0.535	0.507	0.649	0.501	0.385	0.788

- Respondents either agreed, or agreed to a certain extent (75.6%), that the American War on Terror has enhanced the Islamist movements' popularity.
- A majority either agreed, or agreed to a certain extent (73.2%), that some of the Islamist groups' leaders have links with foreign countries.
- A majority either agreed, or agreed to a certain extent (62.4%), that Sunnis, Shias or other sects were never heard before in Yemen.
- Just under half the respondents either agreed, or agreed to a certain extent (49.3%), that most of the problems plaguing Yemen are due to outside factors.
- A majority either agreed, or agreed to a certain extent (58.5%), that charitable organizations belonging to Islamist movements receive foreign funding.
- A majority either agreed, or agreed to a certain extent (78.6%), that Yemeni society would be described as homogenous if foreign interventions cease.

The author believes that given the recent technological developments in various fields, especially the satellite media, the internet and mobile telecommunications, borders are no longer an isolating factor among states, a fact that makes countries vulnerable to interference by other countries in their internal affairs, especially by those closest to them. This is especially true if a country is 'beset by racial, ethnic, religious or regional divisions, since local warring factions tend to seek support and assistance from beyond the country's borders' (Hill and Rothchild 1980, 716). Research in other contexts bears out that, whether by deliberate intention or otherwise, a phenomenon can be expected to spread from one country to the other through the spillover effect or other forms of contagion (Kerbo 1978, 365).

In the case of Yemen; the direct effect on the country was the result of Saudi Arabia's proximity, and the indirect effect was a result of the Kingdom's expulsion of 1 million Yemeni workers to their home country during the Second Gulf War (1990–1991), as well as through personal contacts. More broadly, one can date the impact of these foreign influences and interventions in Yemen and the role they played in the rise and spread of religious extremism to the mid-1980s, the period in which the rise of the phenomenon became clearly evident.

In a report to the Foreign Affairs Committee of the US Congress, on 21 March 1985, Richard Murphy, Assistance Secretary of State for Near Eastern and South Asian Affairs at the time, alluded to the importance of the Yemeni Arab Republic for regional security, and to the fact that the South East Asia region, including the Southern Arabian Gulf region, is one of the most important regions for energy in the world (cited in Al-Tawil 2009, 39). He highlighted the importance of the Soviet threat to the region, and said that North Yemen acts as a buffer zone between the socialist regime in South Yemen and Saudi Arabia, whose regime is loyal to American interests. The report underlined the fact the objective of American policy in the region was to strengthen American national security in order to protect its interests in the Arab Gulf region. This reasoning was behind US policies to assist North Yemen to improve its military capability to act as a deterrent to the Marxist Yemeni forces in the south, supported strategically by the Soviet Union (Al-Tawil 2009).

In this connection, militias were formed under Islamic names in the middle part of the country, whose task was to stop the spread of socialism in the south. This contributed to what became known as the Mid-Section War, which lasted from 1978 to 1982, during which fighters from the Islamic Front waged a vicious campaign against the Democratic National Front. Tribal sheikhs declared their support for the Islamic Front, a name that the citizens and foreign media gave to the Muslim Brotherhood's fighters and those who fought alongside them against the National Front (Al-Tawil 2009).

Yemen's close proximity to Saudi Arabia was an important factor behind its high ranking on America's national security agenda that aimed at protecting its interests in the oil region by supporting *jihadists* inside Yemen against the socialist regime in the former south, or training young men to fight against the spread of Communism in Afghanistan. Saudi Arabia was the primary implementer of this policy and:

> for this reason, the United States refused to deal directly with the Yemeni Government in Sana'a at the time and asked Riyadh to manage the relationship with North Yemen on its behalf. The Americans only intervened when there was a serious threat and, even then, their intervention was neither strong enough nor consistent. The weapons that President Carter asked be delivered to Yemen did not arrive in time for the war against the South, but went instead to Saudi Arabia upon its request; and once the threat to President Ali Abdullah Saleh's regime subsided, Washington insisted on not dealing directly with Sana'a, and again handed the Yemeni file over to Saudi Arabia.
>
> (Al-Tawil 2009, 39)

Following the events of 11 September 2001, Yemen found itself in the eye of the American storm, and the Americans began to apply direct pressure on it (Burgat 2006, 99).

Over and above that, there is the issue of emigration to Saudi Arabia; taking Yemen as example, a country that exports people and has been associated with emigration since olden times, it is claimed that the 'ever increasing flow of the urbanised and politicised proletariat and petite bourgeoisie is responsible for the rise of Islamism' (Fischer 1982, 102).

It is clear that those who migrate from rural to urban areas, mostly peasants and the abject poor, are more attached than others to their cultural heritage, customs and traditions, with the result that their quick migration and urbanization has resulted in the formation of large blocks on the periphery of the main cities – blocks that usually end up marginalized and difficult to integrate in everyday urban life. This causes groups of migrants to congregate at the edge of the capital city, form poverty belts, and live in poor economic and social conditions, all of which makes them more vulnerable to various social ills such as unemployment and deprivation. This, in turn, increases their isolation and sense of injustice, makes them more receptive to extremist ideas, and turns them into ideal candidates and raw material for intervention and mobilization by Islamist groups amply financed from abroad. This leads one back to foreign intervention and the impact it has on the growing support for Salafist movements, and its links to religious extremism in Yemeni society.

This is not all: the ideological factor that begets extremism in Saudi Arabia is the same ideological factor that begets extremism in Yemen, and the best example is so-called Al-Qaeda in the Arabian Peninsula, which is a by-product of two organizations: Al-Qaeda in Yemen and Al-Qaeda in Saudi Arabia.

The Saudi and Yemeni security services have discovered that most of the funds that finance Al-Qaeda's operations in Yemen are donations from religious groups in the Saudi Kingdom (*Sharq al-Awsat* 2010). Needless to say that Saudi Arabia sees Yemen as its own backyard, and people are still heard to say, 'Yemen's security is the Kingdom's security,' a phrase that high officials in both countries often repeat. Moreover, Saudi Arabia pays monthly salaries to major Yemeni tribal chiefs and religious figures who profess loyalty to it, funds Salafist schools, and lends them material and moral support (Yementoday.net 2010).

It could also be said that among the main factors that led to the rise of religious extremism in Yemen is the widespread mobilization of Yemeni youth by Saudi Arabia and the United States. These youths were imbued with the spirit of *jihad* against communist godlessness and the Soviet Union during the Cold War, at a time when the United States, with help from Saudi Arabia, was trying hard to threaten and destabilize the Soviet presence in Afghanistan.

To this end, the Americans supported Islamist political groups, in particular those who upheld extremist views such as the Bin Ladens, and supplied them with weapons, men and money, and young Yemenis making up the bulk of the fighting force. The Cold War therefore allowed Islamist political groups with extremist views to strengthen their activities. In the words of Stephen Pelletiere:

> To understand fundamentalism, one must return to the 1970s and the period of the Cold War; the extremist fundamentalist movement sprang from the clash between rightist and leftist forces, and this particular circumstance – being a product of the Cold War – was the main catalyst for its creation and development.
>
> (Pelletiere 1995, 6)

The Cold War between the capitalist and communist blocks, represented by the United States and the Soviet Union, were key factors in propelling Yemeni youths belonging to fundamentalist religious groups towards violence and religious fanaticism. It was a direct result of their sudden abandonment on the battlefield once they had fulfilled what was required of them once the Soviets withdrew from Afghanistan.

After being the centre of the world's attention, with weapons and funds flowing in their direction, these youths suddenly found themselves by the wayside with nothing to their name, not even the right to return to their homeland where they were pursued for extremist terrorism activities. In reaction to that, they formed blocs and fighting groups to protect their interests and aspirations, a subject to which this article returns to below.

The fourth hypothesis

The fourth hypothesis was that tribal discrimination in Yemen fostered a climate amenable to the growth of Salafist extremism, and what is meant by discrimination here are the activities that prevent members of a particular group from accessing certain resources, rewards, higher social status and other privileges that others readily enjoy. These are the privileges that earn the individual a structurally inherited social status that rests on the social honour or high status that society confers on a certain group. Members of the elite enjoy positive privileges, while those not so honoured, the outcasts, are either looked down upon with contempt or treated by the majority like members of a lower caste. Discrimination here also means social exclusion involving a series of deprivations that prevent individuals and groups from fully participating in their society's social, economic or political life (Giddens 2005, 738, 744, 763). The more equality and justice there is among members of a certain society, the less its members are inclined to join Islamist political groups, especially Salafist groups. The assumption here is that the social exclusion of a particular group in society is the reason why people join Salafist groups, coupled with the fact that these religious groups treat their members equally. In other words, there is a direct positive relationship between increasing discrimination and religious extremism. The survey results showed the following.

- A tendency toward religious extremism, in general, when measured against relative income levels revealed that those earning between 21,000 and 30,000 Yemeni riyals were more inclined towards religious fundamentalism than higher earning groups. The lower the income, or when there is none, the more discrimination there is against those in the lower income group, usually the poor; and this creates an ideal climate for religious extremism to grow.

The study shows that tribal discrimination has fostered a climate that nourished Salafist extremism and helped it spread. Both decrement deprivation (the relative immobility of value expectations and absence of possibilities, on which more see below) and progressive deprivation born of aspirational deprivation have had a major impact on Yemeni society. Traditional elites in Yemen have failed to fulfil the people's hopes and aspirations, especially those of the lower social, economic and political classes. The latter were denied the opportunity to improve themselves and attain a higher social status despite the social, economic and political improvements in the country as a whole in the wake of the 1962 Revolution. These factors have together led to a decrement deprivation that eventually turned into deprivation born of thwarted ambition, and to the majority's adoption of new ideas that call for social equality and allow the individual the opportunity to attain high leadership positions within the new Islamist movements. When asked about the subject, the research sample answered as follows:

- Over half either agreed, or agreed to a certain extent (53%), that the presence of social classes is one of the reasons behind the rise of extremism.
- A majority of the research sample either agreed, or agreed to a certain extent (59.6%), that looking down on the lower social classes helps the growth of Islamist movements.
- Around half either agreed, or agreed to a certain extent (50.7%), that the Islamist movements deal with different social classes on the basis of equality.
- Slightly more than half either agreed, or agreed to a certain extent (52.7%), that the uppity attitude of the upper classes towards the lower classes has pushed people away from them, and towards the Salafist movements.
- Just under half either agreed, or agreed to a certain extent (47.8%), that the tribal chiefs who are members of Islamist movements are more religious than their colleagues in other movements.
- A substantial minority either agreed, or agreed to a certain extent (45.3%), that people join Islamist movements due to tribal discrimination.
- A small majority either agreed, or agreed to a certain extent (57.5%), that leaders of Islamist movements are humble.
- A majority either agreed, or agreed to a certain extent (63.9%), that cultural traditions associated with tribal and regional discrimination have been instrumental in laying the ground for the rise of Islamist movements in Yemen.

By recourse to Relative Deprivation Theory, to which reference was made above, it was found that deprivation leads to frustration, frustration to anger, and anger to violent behaviour. Decrement deprivation means the relative immobility of value expectations and absence of possibilities, and deprivation born of aspirational deprivation means the relative immobility of possibilities and steep increase in expectations. Progressive deprivation means the basic increase in expectations in tandem with lower possibilities.

All these types of deprivation are, in the author's opinion and as far as the theory of relative deprivation is concerned, among the main factors that lead to violence and to the rise of hard-line Salafist movements in Yemeni society.

Decrement deprivation and deprivation born of ambition have had a considerable impact on Yemeni society. For example, a deprived individual is unable to improve himself and/or become a religious scholar because he comes from a lower social class, and is therefore the object of inherited structural discrimination. Thus, an individual from Ta'iz, for example, cannot attain high political office because power is concentrated in the hands of powerful tribesmen and tribal chieftains, despite the fact that the population density in the middle section of the country is higher than in the north where power is concentrated; and the same applies to the distribution of wealth. Discrimination is widespread at all levels, structurally inherited, across regions and in tribal traditions.

One of the effects, as mentioned above, has been the adoption of new ideas that call for social equality and allow the individual to attain high leadership positions within the new Islamist movements. The leaders of the Muslim Brotherhood and Salafist movement are a good example since most of them come from areas of acute social, economic and political deprivation.

This leads one to state that the lack of social justice in the wake of the 1962 Revolution was a determining factor in pushing Islamist political groups towards extremism.

The fifth hypothesis

The fifth hypothesis tested in this study was that pernicious or exclusivist religious mobilization increases the religious extremism in religious group members. The process by which this occurs relies on a socialization method based on reaction and adjustments in behaviour, in response to a number of intermingled factors, and some groups use these factors to adjust the behaviour of individuals in the direction of their choosing.[7] The finding here is that there is a direct positive relationship between 'wrong' or exploitative religious mobilization and extremism; the more wrong religious mobilization is, the more religious extremism there is. Similarly, the more unified religious and official education among different groups and social sectors, and the more unified the supervision of mosques is, the lower the level of extremism. The results indicated the following:

- In the case of religious extremism in general, in relation to different age groups, the age group 18–24 years was more inclined towards it than others; this means that the 'wrong' type of religious mobilization affects younger people and makes them more vulnerable to different aspects of religious extremism.

The study showed religious mobilization increases extremism among religious group members, and beyond. The pace of religious mobilization is faster than the state's response to it in the social, economic and political fields, coupled with its failure to keep up with the religious groups' response to the needs of the of people due to the low rate of economic growth. This leads to frustration among the public, increases the appeal of religious extremism and raises the number of new extremist recruits. When asked about the subject, the research sample answered as follows:

- A majority of the research sample either agreed, or agreed to a certain extent (69.8%), that the religious satellite media encourage people to join Islamist movements.

- A substantial majority either agreed, or agreed to a certain extent (83.4%), that the spread of religious public lectures is an important factor in religious mobilization, and in increasing the number of supporters.
- A majority of respondents either agreed, or agreed to a certain extent (74.6%), that religious songs increase sympathy for Islamist groups among the youth.
- A substantial majority either agreed, or agreed to a certain extent (84.9%), that *imams* who deliver the sermons in mosques are essential to influencing people and winning them over to their side.
- A majority either agreed, or agreed to a certain extent (73%), that educational institutions provide the right climate for Islamist movements to grow.
- A majority either agreed, or agreed to a certain extent (75%), that Qur'anic schools have played an indirect role in children's religious education.
- A majority either agreed, or agreed to a certain extent (72.7%), that religious books have helped change the youths' ideas and attract them to extremist religious movements.
- A majority either agreed, or agreed to a certain extent (73.2%), that the employment of religious occasions for political purposes had the highest impact on individuals.
- A large minority either agreed, or agreed to a certain extent (46%), that ideological over-exaggeration by certain sects has enhanced the appeal of Salafist ideology.
- A majority either agreed, or agreed to a certain extent (61.5%), that using the concept of *jihad* in the mobilization process is important in winning supporters.

One of the factors behind these findings is that in rural areas that boast large numbers of mosques, religious congregations, summer camps and religious institutions – especially in Thamar Governorate where there are more of these than in the capital – the environment is more amenable to the spread of religious extremism. There is widespread religious mobilization in this particular governorate, and no effort is spared in that regard; this creates a climate amenable to the rise and spread of religious extremism. Looking again for insights into Max Weber's 'collective action theory', and the particular weight he attaches to ideological paradigms and ideas, it was found that Weber believes that the structure of collective action emanates in general from an initial commitment by group members to a particular kind of ideological paradigm. Ideologies have their own sense and power, meaning that collective action is the outcome of a particular ideological commitment. Moreover, social disagreements based on principles and values are stronger than other disagreements, and therefore more difficult to manage, according to Oberschall (1993), because resolving this kind of disagreement cannot but favour one side over the other, and therefore cannot satisfy both sides at the same time.

This makes one aware of the danger involved in interpretations that generate new notions that could go as far as declare war on Muslim society, using the term *jihad* in quotations taken from Ibn Tamima and Sayed Qutob. Extremist Salafist movements reinterpret texts by using different rulings in the Qur'an against apostates in Quraish and applying them to Muslim society; they went so far as say that 'the land that is not subject to God's rule is a land of apostasy and war, regardless of its inhabitants' faith' (Abdel-Ghani 2006, 280).

Because Saudi Arabia is close to Yemen, is the largest Salafist Wahabi country, has the longest border with Yemen and gives it substantial financial aid, it saw fit to consider changing the religious identity of Yemeni society using all available means at its

Table 6. Covariance analysis of the correlation between religious mobilization axis and the other variables.

Variables		Poverty axis	Political milieu axis	Foreign intervention axis	Tribal and regional discrimination axis	Leadership axis	Religious extremism
Gender	Male	0.512	0.498	0.521	0.752	0.379	0.807
	Female	0.589	0.632	0.525	0.747	0.374	0.804
Age	24–18	0.541	0.468	0.581	0.827	0.637	0.867
	31–25	0.527	0.599	0.564	0.713	0.371	0.770
	38–32	0.325	0.365	0.171	0.483	–0.153	0.558
	45–39	0.309	0.342	–0.065	0.594	0.081	0.571
	52–46	0.633	0.750	0.447	0.682	0.240	0.817
	53 or more	0.587	0.340	0.727	0.244	–0.254	0.637
Marital status	Single	0.464	0.460	0.535	0.772	0.536	0.807
	Married	0.559	0.569	0.434	0.699	0.146	0.769
Level of education	Can read and write	0.887	0.812	0.626	0.916	0.947	0.985
	Primary	0.208	0.299	0.037	0.847	0.119	0.477
	Secondary	0.590	0.523	0.618	0.808	0.673	0.821
	University level or higher	0.375	0.522	0.465	0.629	0.272	0.738
	Vocational education	0.978	0.857	–0.171	0.987	–0.987	0.994
	Religious education	0.602	0.571	0.458	0.850	0.121	0.885
Occupation	Civil servant	0.443	0.467	0.382	0.674	0.270	0.733
	Private Sector	0.546	0.494	0.359	0.343	0.393	0.703
	Labourer	–0.248	–0.553	0.628	0.632	0.796	0.719
	Unemployed	0.889	0.793	0.840	0.963	0.521	0.947
	Student	0.458	0.543	0.590	0.784	0.624	0.829
Income	20 or less	0.512	0.507	0.582	0.819	0.580	0.835
	30–21	0.729	0.326	0.458	0.863	0.769	0.887
	50–31	0.493	0.458	0.467	0.658	0.141	0.706
	100–51	0.344	0.663	0.323	0.620	–0.057	0.729
	101 or more	0.332	0.765	0.480	0.610	0.001	0.770
Place of residence	Sana'a	0.483	0.613	0.546	0.725	0.210	0.799
	Thoummar	0.628	0.419	0.501	0.787	0.573	0.817

disposal; it also tried to export its Salafist ideology to other areas of the world. The Saudis established some 1300 so-called education academies and managed to enrol 400,000 students in 2002, among which were 4600 teacher trainees ready to continue spreading the word (Walsh 2010, 99). These academies, whose expenses are paid by Saudi Arabia, accept live-in students who spend the week at the academy and go home only for weekends and holidays.

Moreover, there are millions of Yemeni migrant workers in Saudi Arabia who receive Salafist indoctrination while in the Kingdom, and once back home spread the dogma through the mass media.

This shows the extent of religious mobilization to which Yemenis are subjected, and explains why it is so easy for many to join Salafist groups. Once his needs are not fulfilled, the individual turns to extremist groups whose beliefs are more in line with what he learned in Saudi Arabia, beliefs that are based on accusing others of sin and apostasy.

Some researchers and Islamists blame extremism and violence on a wrong interpretation of religious texts; in other words, they claim that these groups' leaders interpret the Qur'an incorrectly and, as a result, accuse others of apostasy and declare war on them; this is a view often encountered in the studies and writings of contemporary Muslim scholars.

Understanding the phenomenon of religious extremism begins by understanding, analysing, and critiquing their religious discourses and mobilization methods. Imam Ali Bin Abi Taleb understood the danger of injecting the religious text into the political sphere, and warned against such interpretations; he did that as he was engaged in fighting Mu'awiya in the battle of Siffin (in the seventh century), when he said, 'we fight them based on his interpretation, as we had fought them before because of their the disbelief in Qura'an.'

In the current social climate, we find ourselves wedged between the rock of the religious text and hard place of the interpretation; when Salafist groups use the text as a weapon, conflict ensues around the issue of who has ownership of that text and who has the right to interpret and understand it, even within the same current. The fact that the religious text ends up being used as an ideological tool in the struggle between groups, makes religious interpretation and mobilization an important entryway to the study of religious extremism.

The extremely dangerous synthesis between the concept of governance and the dogma of loyalty, i.e. the marriage between two ideologies Wahabism and Quthbiya, has led to an activist and intellectual dynamic that sharpened attitudes against the other, regardless of whether or not this other is Muslim. This synthesis brought together ideological contexts, political ideologies and attitudes vis-à-vis the Muslim ruler, and turned it into a rigid cultural dogma not subject to review or discussion (Abdel-Ghani 2006, 285).

This wrong interpretation of religion found itself in a bind; it is first of all a historical interpretation of religion that returns to the first three centuries of Islam's history; it is also a selective interpretation of this history. Not only does this mindset choose the right example to follow, but also the selectivity in interpretation is in itself an exclusionary tendency that many intellectuals have adopted throughout Islam's history (Abdel-Ghani 2006, 302).

It is important to note here that the Muslim religious text is easy and clear in itself, and provides each and every social sector with logical answers to its problems; it is a discourse that easily attracts people. The increasing rates of religious mobilization are accelerating faster than the state's response to it socially, economically and politically, and its failure to keep up with the religious movements' response to the needs of the people, due to the low rate of economic growth, has led to frustration, and increased the appeal of religious extremism.

The sixth hypothesis

The sixth hypothesis was that the emir, or leader of the group, plays a pivotal role in forming the religious group's opinions and ideas by building a halo of sanctity around himself. The individual leads the group and his ideas and beliefs become their ideas and beliefs. These ideas become dogma not subject to discussion, and this leads to extremism or to what is known as 'religious ossification'; in other words, there is a direct positive relationship between the leader and religious extremism. In relation to this contention the survey results were as follows:

- In the case of religious extremism, in general, it was found that the age group 10–31 years was, more than others, linked to religious extremism, in the sense that the emir or leader has more influence on the younger people.

The study shows that the emir, or leader of the group, is an important factor in the formation of violent Islamist political groups in Yemen. The predominance of the military–security dimension of life within these groups, coupled with the leader's charismatic personality, has been instrumental in steering them towards extremism. When asked about the subject, the research sample gave the following answers:

- A majority either agreed, or agreed to a certain extent (69.7%), that obedience to the guardian is a sacred duty.
- A majority either agreed, or agreed to a certain extent (57%), that the interpretation of Qur'anic *aya*s by the *ulema* is perfectly acceptable.
- Half either agreed, or agreed to a certain extent (51.2%), that he would willingly sacrifice his life to protect the *ulema*.
- A majority either agreed, or agreed to a certain extent (61.9%), that it is not permitted to contradict the *ulema*'s views.
- A majority either agreed, or agreed to a certain extent (65.4%), that the *ulema*'s opinion supersedes that of his father and his tribe.
- A significant minority either agreed, or agreed to a certain extent (38%), that the *ulema*'s views are right for all times and places, and that there are no objections to it. This is a high percentage given the ease with which the Yemeni people willingly accept the other.
- A more sizeable minority either agreed, or agreed to a certain extent (45.3%), that they profess loyalty to the *ulema* more than anyone else.

The structure of groups and organizations established expressly for the purpose of collective action is very important, it affects their work, especially the work of groups that have an impenetrable security arm, and operates in secrecy; the latter are also more prone to use violence under the cloak of religion. According to Oberschall's (1993) Mobilization and Organization Theory, the roots of solidarity and violent collective action lie in the group's organization and formation, which clearly underlines the importance of framing and organization to the transfer of a large amount of personal interests to be actualized through the organizations and leaderships.

Charles Tilly (Tilly 2004) believes that interests, organization, mobilization and collective action increase the threat and therefore the potential for collective violent action; organization and framing become stronger as does the ability to attract ambitious new elements to the power structure. A group that faces a military–security threat is better able to mobilize its members because of the mutual interest network and strong internal organization; its use of violence is more structured.

On the basis of Oberschall and Tilly's theories, extremist Salafist groups are more prone to embrace religious extremism and use violence; Salafist groups were established thanks to foreign funding and enjoy wide international support, thus creating a situation where money has found an ally in power.

At a given time during their process of formation, these nascent organizations were abandoned to their fate, which is when Osama Bin Laden stepped in with his inspiring and charismatic leadership and rallied and galvanized the youths left by the wayside in Pakistan, Afghanistan and Central Asia. Bin Laden rallied and motivated them, united their interests, began to organize and mobilize them, created common cause among them, and found a target for their collective action, which is the protection of their threatened interests against a security and military threat in their own home countries. All this took place in secret.

The nature of the new organization was essentially based on the idea of *jihad* against apostasy, and this was the theme behind the training of the new recruits in Afghanistan, all of whom belonged to the same sectarian affiliation and had the same ideological background. Bin Laden's charismatic leadership facilitated the creation of a new global organization that found it easy to use violence and murder to announce its arrival, and that of smaller versions of it, on the scene.

Yemen contributed the largest number of young fighters to the organization, mostly youths who returned to Yemen and could not feel at home with all the social, economic and political changes that took place after the Unity Agreement was signed in 1990, especially since power was now in the hands of their former enemy, the Yemeni Socialist Party. The bloc they formed against 'the newcomers' accounts for the assassinations that took place before 1994, until war broke out later that same year.

One of the main factors behind the rise of extremist Salafist groups was the move by several influential leaders from Afghanistan back to Yemen; these eventually formed the nucleus of the fighting Salafist force. The group's leadership was a key factor in the formation of violent Islamist political groups in Yemen, and the military–security character of these groups coupled with the personality of their leaders played a defining role in their march towards extremism. The leader attempts to effect social, political and religious changes through the formation of a fighting force and, to gain legitimacy, he quotes *ayas* from the Qur'an and the Sunna and recounts incidents from Islam's history.

'Social movements – including Political Islam – rely heavily on political guidance for their survival and effectiveness' (Tilly 2004, 32) and Tilly believes that in the Muslim mind this political guide is the leader, the inspiration and the example.

Notes

1. Although both before and after Islam Yemen was settled by a variety of ethnic groups (Ethiopians, Persians, Turks), it managed to integrate them in a unified society (Alwaisi 1962, 158; quoting Al-Shurbaji 1986, 53).
2. For more details, see Al-Thahiri (2004), 198–200.

3. For details on why the demonstrations began, see the *Al-Watan* newspaper website: http://www.alwatnye.net/65153.htm; for details on the reasons behind the demonstrations, see the Egyptian Yaom al-Sabe' website: http://www.youm7.com/News.asp?NewsID=341417.
4. See Al-Wahdawi.net: http://www.alwahdawi.net/news_details.php?lng=arabic&sid=7116, dated 20 February 2011, which is the day on which the all parties of the Joint Meeting Parties joined the popular youth movement nearly a month after it began.
5. There is no need to offer proof for what is known by everyone regarding the differences between Sunni and Shia Islamist movements, or even Sunni–Sunni or Shia–Shia movements, as in Iraq, for example, not to mention the ongoing disagreements between the Salafists and other Islamist movements.
6. Based on Anthony Giddens (2005, 758).
7. A personal definition based on Giddens (2005, 744).

References

Abdel-Ghani, Imad. 2006. *Al-Harakat Al-Islamiya fi Lubnan – Ishkaliyat al-Deen fi Mujtama' Mutanawe'*[Islamist Movements in Lebanon – The Issue of Religion in a Diverse Society]. Beirut: Dar Al-Tali'a.

'Adan al-Ghad. 2010. "Foreign Policy: Failure of Islamist Movements to Integrate the Political Process in Yemen Threatens with a Sectarian War." *'Adan al-Ghad*, February 12. http://adenalghad.net/print/news/7493.htm/.

Almasdar Online. 2012a. "The Salafists in Yemen Establish the First Political Party called 'Al-Rashad Al-Yamani.'" Almasdar Online, March 14. http://almasdaronline.com/index.php?page=7article-section=17news_id=29742/.

Almasdar Online. 2012b. "The Ministry of Defence Says that the Navy Sank 10 Al-Qaeda Motorboats: The Army Controls Zanzibar the Capital of Abyan, Launches Operation 'Golden Swords' and Violent Clashes in Shaqra." Almasdar Online. http://almasdaronline.com/index.php?page=news&articles-section=1&newsid=33063&utm_source=twitterfeed&utm_medium=facebook/.

Alwaisi, Hussein Ali. 1962. *Al Yaman Al-Kubra* [Greater Yemen]. Cairo: Al-Nahda.

Al-Ash'ari, Abu Al-Hassan. 1985. *Maqalat al-Islamiyeeni* [The Islamists' Articles]. Beirut: Dar al-Hadatha.

Ayesh, Abdo. 2012. "*Itiham Iran bi 'Arqalat Al-Mubadarah Al-Khalijiya bil Yaman*" [Accusing Iran of Obstructing the Gulf Initiative in Yemen]. AlJazeera.net, May 20. http://www.aljazeera.net/news/pages/e5808e20-00db-4503-b536-c3fa13a56140/.

Barakat, Mohammad Tewfic. n.d. *Sayed Qutob, Khulasat Hayatuhu, Manhajuhu fil Haraka, Al-Naqd al-Muwajah Ilayhi* [Sayed Qutob, Summary of His Life, Methodology in the Movement and the Criticisms Levelled at Him]. Beirut: Dar Al-Da'wa Beirut.

Boucek, Christopher. 2010. *War in Sa'ada, from Local Insurrection to National Challenge* (Carnegie Endowment for International Peace – Middle East Program, No. 110, April).

Burgat, François. 2006. "*Islamism in the Shadow of Al-Qaeda, Re-Islamisation, Modernisation and Radicalism*". Translated by Sahar Said Damascus: Qadmos.

Carroll, G Terrance. 1986. "Islam and Political Community in the Arab World." *International Journal of Middle East Studies* 18, 185.

Central Statistics Organisation, Ministry of Planning and International Cooperation. 2008. *Statistical Yearbook 2008*.

Central Statistics Organisation, Ministry of Planning and International Cooperation. 2010. *Statistical Yearbook 2010*. http://www.cso-yemen.org/content.php?1ng=arabic&id=574/.

Al-Daghshi, Ahmad Mohammad. 2009. *Al-Houthiyoun: Al-Thahira Al-Houthiya, Dirasa Manhajiya Shamila* [The Houthis: The Houthi Phenomenon; A Systematic Comprehensive Study]. Sana'a: Khaled Bin Al-Waleed Bookshop and Dar Al-Kutub in Yemen.

Al-Daghshi, Ahmad Mohammad. 2012. *Al-Fikr Al-Tarbawi Li Tantheem Al-Qaeda, Al-Intishar Al-Arabi* [The Educational Ideology of Al-Qaeda, the Arab Dimension]. Beirut: Al Intishar Al Arabi Publishers.

Energy Information Administration. 2010. "Country Analysis Brief: Yemen." March. Accessed January 10, 2013. http://www.eia.doe.gov/emeu/cabs/Yemen/pdf.pdf/.

Fischer, Michael M.J. 1982. "Islam and the Revolt of the Petit Bourgeoisie." *Daedalus* 3 (1), 102.

Giddens, Anthony. 2005. *Sociology (with Arab inputs)*, translated by Fayez Sayegh. Beirut: Arab Organization for Translation Publications.

Gould, Julius, and William L. Kolb, edited by 1969. *A Dictionary of Social Sciences*. New York, NY: Free Press.

Hedberg, Nicholas J. 2010. *The Exploitation of a Weak State: Al-Qaeda in the Arabian Peninsula in Yemen* (June). Monterey, CA: Naval Post-graduate School.

Hill, Stuart, and Donald Rothchild. 1980. "The Contagion of Political Conflicts in Africa and the World." *Journal of Conflict Resolution* 30 (4), 716.

Kerbo, Harold R. 1978. "Foreign Involvement in the Pre-Condition of Political Violence: The World System and the Case of Chile." *Journal of Conflict Resolution* 22 (3), 365.

Al-Mouseli, Ahmad. 2003. *Jadaliyat Al-Shura wal Dimocratia, Al-Islamiyoun wal Mas'ala Al-Siyasiya* [The Shura and Democracy Debate: The Islamists and the Political Issue]. Beirut: Centre for Arab Unity Studies (CAUS).

Oberschall, Anthony. 1993. *Social Movements: Ideologies, Interests, and Identities*. New Brunswick, NJ: Transaction.

Pelletiere, Stephen. 1995. *A Theory about Fundamentalism: Hizbollah of Lebanon (September)*. Carlisle, PA: The Strategic Studies Institute, US Army War College.

Al-Qadimi, Nawaf Abdul-Rahman. 2012. *Al-Islamiyoun wa Rabee' Al-Thawrat Al-Mumarasa Al-Muntija lil Afkar* [The Islamists and the Applied Thought Provoking Revolutions]. Doha: Arab Centre forResearch and the Study of Politics. http://www.dohainstitute.org/.

A-Qarawi, Hisham. 2011. *Thawrat Al-Yaman: Istibdal Ali Abdullah Saleh Am Istibdal Mu'assassat Mufawata?* [The Yemen Revolution: Replacing Ali Abdullah Saleh or Replacing Defunct Institutions?]. Doha: Arab Centre for Research and the Study of Politicshttp://www.dohainstitute.org/.

Sharq al-Awsat. 2010. Leaks from Wikileaks. *Sharq al-Awsat (London)*, No. 11689, November 29. http://aawsat.com/details.asp?section=4&article=597244&issueno=11689 and http://www.almustaqbal-a.com/NewsDetails.aspx?NewsID=12267&Type=13/.

Al-Shurbaji, Qa'ed Nu'man. 1986. *A-Shara'eh Al-Ijtima'iya Al-Taqlidiya fil Mujtama' Al-Yamani* [Traditional Social Sectors in Yemeni Society]. Beirut: Dar Al-Hadatha.

Al-Tagheer. 2011. Official Spokesman of the Salafist Coalition: 'President Saleh should follow the example of Bin Ali and leave power to prevent the spilling of Muslim blood', in a conversation with Abdel-Razzak al-Jamal. al-Tagheer, May 18. http://www.al-tagheer.com/news298htm/.

Al-Tawil, Mohammad Naser. 2009. *Al-Ilaqa bayna al-Nitham al-Siyasi wal Ikhwan al-Muslmimoun fil Yaman: Dirasah fi al-Muhadidat al-Dakhiliyah wal Kharijiyah* [The Relationship between the Political Regime and the Muslim Brotherhood in Yemen: A Study of the Internal and External Limitations] (MA thesis). Cairo: Cairo University, Faculty and Economics and Political Science, Political Science Department.

Al-Thahiri, Muhsin Mohammad. 2004. *Al-Mujtama' wal Dawla: Dirasa li 'Ilaqat Al-Qabila bil Ta'adudiya Al-Siyasiya wal Hizbiya, (Al-Joumhouriya Al-Yamaniya Ka Namouthaj Tatbiqi)* [Society and the State: A Study of the Relationship between the Tribe and Political and Party Pluralism, (The Republic of Yemen as an Applied Example)]. Cairo: Madbouli Bookshop.

Al Torabi, Hassan, et al. 2003. *Al-Islamiyoun wa Al-Mas'ala al-Siyasiya, (Hawla al-Tahawol fi Harakat al-Islam al-Siyasi fil Sharq al-Awsat)* [The Islamists and the Political Issue Regarding Transformations Within the Islamist Political Movement in the Middle East]. Beirut: Centre for Arab Unity Studies (CAUS).

Tilly, Charles. 2004. *Social Movements: 1976–2004*. London: Paradigm.

Walsh, Rachel. 2010. "Education Systems and Islamic Radicalism in the Arabian Peninsula." *Madarat*Year 1 (3), 99.

Al-Watan. 2012. "*Nabbihou Al-Liwa' 115 wal Amn Al-Markazi: Al-Jouf Tasqot fi Aydi Al-Houthiyeen*" [Alert the 115th Brigade and the Central Security Forces: Al-Jouf is Falling into Al-Houthis' Hands]. *Al-Watan*. Accessed March 23, 2011. http://www.alwatanye.net/65954.htm/.

Yementoday.net. 2010. June 15. http://yementoday.net/-saleh/index.php?option=com_content&view=article&id=3157:2010-06-15-06-56-14&catid=61:2009-02-20-16-32/.

Yemeni Presidency's National Information Centre. 2010. Accessed January 10, 2013. http://www.yemen.net/gover/apyan/brief.

Relationship between state and religion in Saudi Arabia: the role of Wahabism in governance

Tawfiq Alsaif

Independent Saudi Researcher and Intellectual

This paper tracks the relationship between religion and the state in Saudi Arabia during the past 50 years. This relationship is unique in the sense that the religious power (Wahabi) together with the ruling family (Al Sa'ud) were partners in founding the Kingdom. This cooperative relationship has been degenerating into mutual suspicion. Right now there are three main variants of religious stratification in Saudi Arabia vis-à-vis the state: the traditional Salafists who back the rulers come what may – the government is gradually reducing their prerogatives; and the opposition, which in turn is divided between Sahwa (who are discontented Salafists) and Tanweeris (advocates of enlightenment). The Sahwa current with its elderly leadership believes that the state is straying away from the teachings of religion and it recommends austere adherence to it; the dynamics of their activities are possibly pushing towards taking leadership from outside the Kingdom. The Tanweeris, on the other hand, have young leaders, the popular base is young and broad, and they are strong advocates of democracy. Despite their capacity for effective social mobilization, it seems too early to judge whether this religious stream will eventually push for reform or constrain it, especially given that it has not yet resolved its position on some key issues such as different national constituencies and women.

Introduction

Religion is a main source of state legitimacy in the Arab countries, including those with secular ruling elites. In these countries a formula was worked out according to which official religious establishment and the elites work in parallel, each using its own discourse and operating within its area of interest, and neither infringing on the domain of the other.

However, Saudi Arabia is a particular case because the state has neither created nor inherited the religious establishment, like in most other countries; on the contrary. The religious elite and the politicians have worked together to establish and safeguard the state for quite a long time, which explains the overlap between the religious and political discourses and the religious clerics' rejection of certain practices deemed 'secular' instate institutions, and the leaders' personal lives and policies.

However, and as Max Weber has said, things always move towards the same end. Once the winds of modernity blow, their impact not only changes existing frameworks, but also reconfigures them in a manner that destroys the old balances of power, and the relationships that depend on them.

Although all Muslim sects are represented in Saudi society, Mohammad Bin Abdul-Wahab's school, or Salafism as it is known today, is the only one that the state recognizes and draws its religious discourse from. The Saudi religious establishment is based on Wahabism and its leaders are chosen from among the sect's senior clerics; this sect is the subject of this paper.

The paper examines the relationship between the religious and political establishments in the Kingdom over the past 50 years, and highlights the initial partnership between them that turned into an alliance during the foundational stage. This initial stage also witnessed the onset of differences between the allies who soon parted ways, so much so that in recent years their relationship has been plagued by mutual denial and suspicion. The paper aims to pinpoint the fault lines in the relationship between these two parties and their impact on the Kingdom's policies.

In the interest of full disclosure, the paper's author finds it necessary to mention his affiliation with a current that calls for political reforms involving fundamental changes in the relationship between the religious establishment and the state, and that ideas in this paper could be biased towards this particular position, or affected by its tenets.

Background note

Before I begin, I would like to mention a number of the Wahabi Salafist sect's characteristics, such as its dependence on the Hadith as a main source of religious rulings, compared with the other three sources of jurisprudence (Quran, Qiyas and Ijma'), and its acute interest in doctrine in its most basic form – at the level of the individual. Another characteristic is its cultural and historical links to the Kingdom as the sect's home country, which implicitly means that Saudi citizens are more privileged than others because they are citizens of this sect's home country. We understand this to be the case because some influential non-Saudi personalities whose help was crucial at the foundation phase of the religious establishment, have never managed to attain leadership status in the traditional religious current. These include Abdul-Razzaq Al-Afifi, Abu Bakr Al-Jazairi, Mohammad Mahmoud Al-Sawwaf, Nasereddin Al-Albani and Manna' Al-Qattan, though some of them did eventually obtain Saudi citizenship. Moreover, the Arab national element is given precedence over others, since none of the Salafist sect's main leaders or influential authors is non-Arab. Some prominent Salafist *ulema* have written about the particular characteristics of the 'Arabian Peninsula' and its contribution to religion and history (e.g. Abu Zayd 2000).

The significance of the local component lies in the quasi organic links between the Salafist sect and the Saudi state, and in the makeup of the current leadership. The sect's traditional environment gave the religious clerics a key role in social activism unlike other Arab societies such as Egypt, for example, that sees nothing wrong in giving Sayyed Qutob a more prominent status than other *ulema*. The same goes for the Muslim Brotherhood, the largest religious party in Egypt, whose leadership does not include prominent religious clerics.

First: the official religious establishment

There are no specific data on the number of religious clerics in Saudi Arabia; nevertheless, the number indicated below will give the reader a general idea about the size of this sector, most of whose members are organically and existentially linked to the state:

- The Council of Senior Ulema sits at the head of the official religious establishment; it was established by a royal decree in August 1971 and, as its name indicates, its members are supposed to be the most learned in matters of the Sharia. This, however, is not always an objective criterion because it sometimes has to do with determining who is the most learned, sometimes with administrative standards imposed by the need to forge harmonious relationships within the council itself, and sometimes with political standards relevant to the distribution of power and the state's preferences and needs that do not necessarily depend on qualifications.[1]
- The Supreme Judicial Council, established in 1975, comes next in rank in the religious leadership hierarchy. Although it was traditionally led by the highest ranking judge, in recent years the government has leaned towards taking into account the requirements of legal and administrative development when appointing its members. The council is the main reference point of the Kingdom's judges, and addresses major issues that ordinary courts are unable to address, or those that should be referred to it by law, such as cases that involve capital punishment.
- In third position come the specialized religious ministries, the most important among which are the Justice, and the Religious Affairs (Awqaf) ministries, followed by various independent religious bodies. These include the Council for Enjoining Good and Forbidding Evil, the Muslim World League, the International Islamic Jurisprudence Forum, and the World Assembly of Muslim Youth.
- There are two religious universities in Saudi Arabia: the Islamic University in Madina and the Imam Mohammad bin Saud Islamic University in Riyadh, both of which depend administratively and financially on the Ministry of Higher Education. Although traditionally senior *ulema* were consulted on the appointment of their administrative and academic leaders, there are signs that this is being discontinued, especially after the king appointed presidents for both universities from outside the usual circles, namely Dr Mohammad bin Ali Al-Uqla at the Islamic University and Dr Sulaiman Abalkhail at the Imam Mohammad University.
- In 2008, the number of religious positions, or those that fall under the supervision of clerics, exceeded one-quarter of a million, or 25% of all government positions. A newspaper report stated that the Religious Affairs Ministry planned to appoint 140,000 muezzins and mosque *imams* as full-time employees (Aljahni 2010).[2] According to Tawfik Al-Sudairy, Secretary General of the Awqaf Ministry, there are 72,000 mosques in the Kingdom (Al-Sudairy 2010)[3] and the Council for Enjoining Good and Forbidding Evil runs 470 offices in different parts of the country, with some 4400 employees.

Many religious clerics perform a variety of cultural and social activities under the aegis of the official religious establishment, and although they are nominally dependent on the state, their work is independent of it. Most prominent among these activities are the Charitable Societies for Holy Quran Memorising that operate, according to data collected by the author, a little over 25,000 memorization circles, comprising 515,000 students, and employing 26,500 teachers and staff members, excluding circles run by clerics outside the above-mentioned societies. Other activities in which religious clerics play a leading role include Al-Birr (charitable) societies, most of which fall under the jurisdiction of regional emirs, are administered by clerics and operate independently of the state.

The above activities also include the Cooperative Offices for Call and Guidance, and for raising the awareness of foreign communities, which numbered 210 offices in 2010, spread throughout the country. As their name indicates, their main function involves direct proselytization that includes lectures, lessons, the distribution of material, *iftar* banquets, and the like.

Alongside these specialized religious bodies, all the Kingdom's ministries are involved in extracurricular religious activities. The Saudi Armed Forces have a Moral Guidance Administration founded by a well-known cleric called Saud Al-Funaysan, and staffed mostly by graduates of religious colleges. The Ministry for Foreign Affairs appoints a religious attaché in many of its embassies abroad. The Ministry of Education is one of the main employers of religious college graduates, since it hires thousands of them to teach religious education; this accounted for around 31% of the entire academic effort in 2010.[4] According to the Saudi Press Agency (2010), the ministry also runs 2,077 Quran Memorisation schools; and, according to the newspaper *Al-Bilad* (18 September 2010) 'The Kingdom is witnessing a comprehensive education renaissance, 9 million Rials for the King Abdullah Bin Abdul Aziz Public Education Development Project'.

The Salafist current sees its dependence on the state for employment and daily subsistence as entirely normal, and the issue was never a matter of controversy as far as the clerics' credibility and independence were concerned. Furthermore, many religious clerics, especially from the middle and higher echelons, use their positions and relationships with prominent statesmen to strengthen their social clout and improve their status among the public.

The majority of Saudi clerics belong to the traditional Salafist current. Not only does the current call for supporting the state as the only guardian of Sheikh Mohammad bin Abdul Wahab's school and the Salafist sect, but also it considers the royal family's rule as legitimate and deserving of obedience, even if its members sometimes act reprehensively, so long as this does not involve plain apostasy. They also advise senior government officials on controversial issues, although they know that the administration does not always follow this advice.[5]

Among the new *fatwa*s (religious edicts) issued by the Council of Senior Ulema, in late October 2010, is one that bans women from working as sales personnel and countering the green light they were given by the Ministry of Labour in August of that same year.[6] As everyone knows, this *fatwa* was not universally welcomed by state officials, though the council did not criticize them for their position and will likely not make an issue of it if the ministry does not abide by this *fatwa*. It is more of a statement of general principles directed at the public rather than the state.

Second: eyeing state authority

In the 1960s, the traditionalist current had one of the strongest leaders in its history, Sheikh Mohammad bin Ibrahim Aal Al-Sheikh (1893–1969), who rose to prominence during the ten years of King Saud's rule (1953–1962). The fact that the governance system that the king had inherited was very simple and limited gave him the chance to rebuild the government administration from scratch.

It is in this context that the official religious institution saw the light and was transformed from a simple entity into an independent institution with special status within the political system and state administration. This status was embodied in the establishment of the General Presidency of Religious Colleges and Institutes in 1953, the Ifta's Administration in 1954 and the Presidency of the Judiciary in 1959, all of which were under the personal supervision of Bin Ibrahim who was by then Grand Mufti of Saudi Arabia. In 1960, the General Presidency of Girls' Education was established and placed under his supervision as well, as were the Muslim World League (1962) and the Islamic University in Madina (1971).

Bin Ibrahim used the Kingdom's transition from the foundational to the organizational stage to turn his own institution into an effective centre of power in the new system. According to Mansour Al-Nuqaidan (Al-Nuqaidan 2012, 108), the Mufti was suspicious of the government's intention to expand general education and hire Arab teachers who might have nationalist or leftist views. He was particularly worried about religious laws being sidelined and expressed his apprehension in this regard in his famous letter entitled '*Tahkim al-Qawanin*' [Enactment of Positive (non-religious) Law] – 1380 *hijri*', which later became a reference point for the Salafist current in matters of 'governance'.[7] Though the letter did not address the political authority, it argued for maintaining the law in the clerics' hands and keeping the religious domain outside the bureaucratic system.

The experience of Mufti Bin Ibrahim reveals one of the dynamics of the crisis that plagues Saudi Arabia's religious community; by that I mean the ambiguous relationship between the clerics and the state compounded by the latter's erroneous vision of what modern statehood implies, and what the transition from traditionalism to modernity involves. Just like at the beginning of the 20th century, at its end the clerics were under the illusion that their alliance with the royal family meant that the state had become their property. The notion comes from a belief that the current model, i.e. the coercive state or sultanate, is an acceptable model of good governance according to Islamic standards. However, this illusion has blinded them to the natural yearning of the state to establish itself, gain independence and create the mechanisms that would allow it to do so.

Because of this illusion, the religious current failed to develop a comprehensive vision either of modern statehood or of a more advanced state system in tune with the requirements and challenges of the times. Instead, the predominant view among the religious leaders was that safeguarding society's faith is only possible if they have the 'authority' to enjoin and forbid, and implement this authority by closely supervising academic curricula and teachers; in other words, making use of the authority already in place. This view belies the fact that the Saudi government had begun to transform itself from its early image as a traditional quasi-tribal authority into a separate central state, away from the traditions of its foundation stage and all those who were involved in it. This necessarily changes the power structure and composition of the ruling elite and its supporters and, by extension, changes the values and conventions that justify that model.

The Mufti was unaware of the real nature of the changes taking place in the country, and thought that the crux of the problem lay in the 'people' who made the decisions. For example, his insistence on holding onto the Presidency of Girls' Education was based on the traditional view that sees women as enchantresses and, as such, all that concerns them should be in safe hands to prevent corruption. The same applied to the judiciary such that instead of seriously trying to reform it and make it fairer, the clerics' focus was on keeping it under their control.

In 1992, the 'Advisory Memorandum' – which was supposed to represent the apogee of the religious current's maturity – offered the same solutions and did not deviate from the above reasoning, i.e. that the state and society were to blame for the country's problems because they strayed away from religion, and the remedy therefore lay in strengthening the clerics' supervision of all walks of life. In other words, like the Mufti in the middle of the last century, those who wrote the memorandum at the end of it saw nothing wrong either with the philosophy of the state or with the administration's methodology. As far as they were concerned, the blame lay squarely on the shoulders of administration officials who cannot be considered honest unless they are religious clerics or operated under their supervision. Had they been honest they would not have made mistakes. This overly simplistic view leads to a preoccupation with trivial issues and leaves significant ones aside. Many activists will realize later on that they wasted precious time pursuing insignificant matters and – as Salman Al-Odeh has said (Al-Odeh 2002, 49) – had drowned themselves in the parts at the expense of the whole.

In October 1975, King Khaled appointed Sheikh Abdul-Aziz bin Baz as the first president of the religious establishment to come from outside the family of the official sect's founder, Sheikh Mohammad bin Abdul-Wahab, thus making a break with a tradition that had been in existence since the establishment of the first Saudi state. To some observers this step signalled the undeclared end of a tradition that meant a 'power-sharing partnership' between the founding families of the state and the sect.

With the increase in oil revenues in 1971 and their meteoric rise in 1974, changes in the state's administrative and legal structure accelerated in tandem with an exponential increase in economic activities. This opened up the country more than ever before to international markets, and exposed it to hitherto unfamiliar ideas, ways of life and work ethics.

These changes strengthened the government bureaucracy's role, and reduced the political authority's need for religious clerics. The government's newfound wealth allowed it to bring the religious establishment under its supervision by spending more on it and financing its new projects. Of particular note in this context is King Faisal's decision, in September 1974, to establish the Imam Mohammad bin Saud Islamic University, which became the jewel in the official religious establishment's crown. However, although these projects fostered a sense of satisfaction among the religious community that saw itself grow and prosper, it increased at the same time its dependency on the state, which was the financier of these projects.

Third: the religious current emerges out of the state's shadow

The holy city of Madina has seen the first appearance of the *new* Salafist current. In 1964 a group of youths attacked photography studios and destroyed coffee houses that served *shisha* (or *narghileh*) and plastic mannequins displaying women's clothing, all of which are considered taboo in the Salafist doctrine. Among these enthusiastic youths were some destined to have a considerable impact on the course of events later on, including Juhaiman Al-'Otaibi, Abdul Rahman Abdul Khaliq and Omar Al-Ashqar.[8] The group was motivated by a deep conviction about what they learned at Madina's Islamic University and, unlike the more patient sheikhs, tried to organize themselves and eliminate evildoing (Al-Tarifi 2004).

The 'mannequins destruction incident', as it came to be known, was an initial largely instinctive reaction against commercialism and the manifestations of consumer-oriented modernity in the holy city of Madina. However, when analysed scientifically, it reveals a general sense of being under threat, or what is often described as modernity's culture shock. The country's newfound openness to international markets had led – as expected – to a gradual but obvious deterioration in the values and behaviour of a highly traditional society, a phenomenon for which the religious establishment had no answer. The fact that the latter was unable to develop a new discourse to accommodate these sudden challenges explains the reaction of the new generation, most whom were youths barely in their 30s.

Although initially basic and limited in scope, this incident sparked an idea that would have an impact for years to follow. The idea was simply that the official religious establishment was no longer capable of shouldering the responsibility of spreading the call, and that its links to the state had become a major obstacle to the latter's progress. Therefore, the solution lay in trusting the youth to find alternative ways to spread the call, from outside the official framework, an idea encouraged by Arab religious clerics who had come to teach at Saudi universities, most of whom were activists in their own home countries. Most prominent among these were Nasiruddin al-Albani, Muhammed Srour Zein al-Abdeen (from Syria), Abdul Munim Al Azzi, known as Mohammad Al-Rashed (from Iraq), Mohammad Qutob, Manna' Al-Qattan, Mohammad Mahdi 'Akef, Ma'moun Al-Hudaibi, and Kamal Al-Helbawi (from Egypt). Credible information indicates that the Muslim Brotherhood tried to establish a Saudi chapter in the first half of the 1970s (Al-Otaibi 2010, 37).

The occupation of the Holy Sanctuary (in November 1979) under the leadership of Juhaiman Al Otaibi, which took place a few months after the success of the Iranian Revolution and establishment of an Islamic state under the leadership of religious figures, coupled with the onset of *jihad* against the Soviet forces in Afghanistan, in December of that same year, were key elements for the Salafist current and its relationship with the state.

Al-Sahwa current

Although the entire religious current condemned the Holy Sanctuary's occupation, it nevertheless began to think seriously about its role, position and the nature of its relationship with the state. Shortly before this incident took place, the coming to power of religious clerics in Iran was clearly a challenge to the Saudi religious community, and many wondered, particularly the clerics and youths, whether ideally a religious cleric should be directly involved in the power structure or be simply content to eat at the sultan's table.

From 1980 to 1985, the government followed a dual containment strategy towards the religious current. On the one hand, it harshly suppressed direct political protests and executed or imprisoned all those who supported Juhaiman and his movement.[9] On the other hand, it increased its support to other religious clerics and gave them free reign at all state levels. The ensuing unprecedented increase in religious activities overextended the religious institutions, and increased demands for employment in the religious domain. As a result of that, the number of students in academic religious institutions increased five-fold in 1985, from 30,914 (or 7% of the Saudi university students in 1979) to 190,481 (or 22% of Saudi university students) (Department of Statistics 2007).

For a brief period it seemed as if the government had managed to contain the new religious current, since in the five years that followed the Holy Sanctuary's occupation the country witnessed no events worth mentioning. However, the questions and debates did not cease but simply shifted to the campuses of religious universities that had become natural incubators for the new religious current. All the present prominent leaders of the current, which will become known later on as Al-Sahwa (Awakening), were at the time students at these religious institutions.

The pressure created by these questions and debates found an outlet in the Afghanistan issue that had gradually become the focus of the religious current's attention. In his blog *Thikrayati ma' al-Ikhwan fi-l Sa'udiyya* (My Memories Amongst the Brotherhood in Saudi Arabia, http://www.som1.net/?p=3340), on 27 June 2011, Dr Mustafa Al-Hassan, who was active in the Muslim Brotherhood at the time, mentions: 'When the conversation in Saudi Arabia turns to the *jihad*ist ideology, many contentious issues are unearthed.' These issues were in fact no more than a series of discussions round the nature of the relationship between religion and the state in the Kingdom, and round the religious current's role and position towards the government's policies. Here, the sensitive question imposes itself again: is it a state for, and based on, a religious call, or is it a partner that managed to capture the religious clerics' share at a time when no one was paying attention? There was no answer to this question; questions based on vacuous assumptions do not have answers. This blocked avenue has led to a new and even more sensitive question: what is our responsibility in this regard, and what can we do as believers to rectify it?

Two strong currents were born in the context of this argument: the Muslim Brotherhood and the Militant Salafism, known locally as the 'Srouriah' after Syrian cleric Mohammad Srour Zain Al-Abdeen. Between the middle and the end of the 1980s, hundreds of Saudi youths had joined the *jihadis* in Peshawar, on the Pakistan–Afghanistan border, and while some bore arms and fought alongside the Afghans against the Soviets, others spent weeks in Mujahideen camps. According to the testimony of a former Saudi *mujahid* who had travelled to Peshawar in 1987, the trip to the Afghan border was every believer's wish:

> when I went to buy my ticket, I found many others already there trying to book their flight to Islamabad. On the same flight with me were 20 Saudi young men from different cities, a number which sometimes reaches 75 youths per trip – meaning a total of 225 young men on the three weekly flights.
>
> (Al-Bunyan 2001)

The Brotherhood and Srouriah movements managed to draw the most activist Saudi youths, and succeeded in crystallizing a position opposed to the state's or, at least, that doubted the latter's loyalty to Sharia teachings, which was one of the main differences between the traditional Salafist current and the official religious institution. Ali Al-Omaem believes that this had to do with the impact of the Arab activists who take the main credit for launching Al-Sahwa:

> The Islamist movements were neither attracted to the recent Saudi experience nor to its ideological historic base embodied by Muhammad Abdul Wahab's Salafist call. What it was strongly attracted to was the Ottoman State's experience and the Islamic Caliphate concept, of which Sultan Abdul Hamid II (1876–1909) was the last Caliph, and last pious Muslim ruler.
>
> (Al-Omaem 2011, 170)

The above description depicts the movement that rose to the surface of Saudi society until the end of the 1980s. However, another story was unfolding under the surface, one that perhaps no one had planned for and few had noticed, although its fallout would prove decisive in the following two decades. It is the Salafist sect's separation from its socio-political cocoon, i.e. the region of Najd.

The Salafist sect's separation from its social cocoon

As the income from oil increased, the government launched a series of five-year plans, the first of which was in 1971, aimed at modernizing the economy, administration and public services. Naturally, the new economy created additional opportunities for those who aspire to raise their social status and roles, through education, trade and state bureaucracy. Therefore, the country has seen the rise of numerous influential figures, many of whom came from previously marginalized social backgrounds. The large cities were the locus of economic and social transformation. Thus, it started to receive a large-scale migration of countryside youths who saw in the city life style a unique opportunity to escape poverty (Table 1). However, these young men who came looking for a new life represented fertile ground for the religious current, in its different manifestations and orientations, and found themselves – spontaneously for the most part – the object of the religious activists' attention; they later became – inadvertently perhaps – the tool that caused the sect itself to change.

In the early 1980s, the main element within the Salafist current hailed from Najd, in the Kingdom's central region. However, as public and religious education expanded, elements from other regions came to settle in the region, thus reducing the sect's identification with Najd and affecting the nature of its activism. In the first stage, the adoption of the Salafist call meant loyalty to the political regime and safeguarding its social environment (Najd), while in the second stage, the Salafist current developed as an independent entity from the state and its social milieu. It is in this context that religious leaders and proselytizers emerged from outside the central region, and that the tendency to be independent from the state and the official religious establishment became more pronounced.

Several reasons made the religious current shed its old identification with Najd, of which two in particular warrant mention:

Table 1. State budget and public employment, 1971–1980

Year	Budget (rials, millions)	Capital for projects (rials, millions)	Number of government jobs based on the budget
1971	10782	5036	141320
1972	13200	6718	162439
1973	22810	14263	177184
1974	98247	26397	192808
1975	95847	74380	217704
1976	110935	94795	242478
1977	146493	97720	244113
1978	130000	97606	272584
1979	160000	131501	326062
1980	261516	174737	n.a.

Note: n.a., Not available.

- In the 1970s and 1980s, non-Saudi religious clerics managed to erode the professional credibility of Najd's religious clerics, particularly the descendants of the sect's founder, Sheikh Mohammad bin Abdul Wahab. I am referring particularly to the influence of Syrian cleric Nasireddin Al-Albani, widely known as one of the world's experts on Hadith. Al-Albani did not hesitate to refer repeatedly to the weakness of reference sources quoted by the sheikhs from Najd, and to the fact that the latter lacked the methodological tools necessary for an accurate assessment of the credibility of an Hadith before using it as a jurisprudential reference; this is especially shameful for a school that relies on the Hadith as the main source of its teachings (Lacroix 2011).[10] Many of Al-Albani's students saw themselves as superior to the graduates of other traditional schools with no expertise in the Hadith. Among these were a considerable number of southerners who studied in Mecca and Madina, to which Al-Albani paid regular visits.[11] However, the majority of Najd's religious students preferred to pursue their education in Riyadh and Buraida, the original home of the Salafist doctrine.
- Between 1979 and 1982, the Kingdom witnessed an unprecedented economic boom; the large increase in government spending created thousands of new employment opportunities for all citizens. This economic well-being began to dampen in the following seven years, in tandem with the drop in oil revenues (Table 2). As of 1983, Saudi society began to feel the fallout from unemployment, especially when hundreds of new graduates began looking for work, but failed to find any. The Ministry of Finance had frozen all new positions and halted all construction projects whose budgets had not been allocated years earlier.

Opportunities decrease in times of scarcity; this fuels competition over what little is available, and people beg and plead to get hold of these few opportunities. Under such circumstance, the law is the only means of guaranteeing a minimum level of fair distribution of opportunities, and preventing the powerful from monopolizing them. However, the rule of law is not familiar to the Kingdom's administration. People in high places control the allocation of material and non-material benefits as they

Table 2. Budget expenditures and government jobs, 1981–1989

Year	Projected budget revenues (rials, millions)	Credit for projects in the budget (rials, millions)	Number of government jobs in the budget
1981	340 000	205 925	371 816
1982	313 400	202 814	192 120
1983	225 000	128 504	305 151
1984	214 100	130 097	328 046
1985	200 000	82 091	341 234
1986	200 000	82 091	341 234
1987	117 280	57 084	341 234
1988	105 300	32 299	342 928
1989	n.a.	37 088	344 020

Note: In 1986 no new budget was announced, but the previous year's budget was extended instead.
n.a., Not available.

please. Between 1983 and 1990, the Kingdom witnessed a period during which various ministries and departments were 'allocated' to specific persons or groups. If you were, for example, a minister, deputy minister or general secretary, the members of your tribe would expect to find employment in your department; this means that in the absence of a legitimate civil society, those who aspired to become leaders in their natural habitat, i. e. their tribe or region, used this system to increase their social capital, a practice considered normal in previous years. However, the wide availability of jobs had lowered the competition level and confined it to the higher positions, though what there is now is competition even over small jobs; Table 3, which was prepared by Al-Wardi (2006, 92), the former administrator of Al-Jawf Princedom, shows a side of that impact.

The competition spread to the religious sector like it did to all other government sectors, and what made the situation worse was the re-emergence of patronage traditions that have somewhat abated recently. In earlier years, the government used to grant senior clerics – especially from Najd – a share of the jobs available, which they in turn passed on to their relatives and friends. This system was meant to strengthen the social belt surrounding the royal family, in which religion, family, tribe and region came together to form a strong reliable security belt. Some families are known for never having to look for a job, since theirs are reserved well in advance. However, with the retreat in opportunities, these religious clerics were no longer content with their usual share, but tried to help their village and tribe members to nab some of these opportunities. In other words, the official religious establishment's clerics and senior employees were involved in discrimination, a practice that necessarily alienates all those outside the immediate circle of the person concerned, especially in times of economic hardship.

This was a highly emotional issue for the youths who had recently joined the religious current. The sheikhs preached salvation in the afterlife when people wanted salvation in this life as well, and expected the sheikh to focus on the afterlife and leave earthly matters to them. What they found, however, was the exact opposite; those who hailed from the Kingdom's southern and northern regions saw their colleagues getting comfortable positions in various ministries, in the judicial branch and in different religious organizations, without much effort, while they spent days looking for a decent job in vain. They begged the sheikh who helped educate them or whose recordings and pamphlets they once distributed to help them, but all they received in return were polite excuses. Some even lowered their expectations and were content to be taken on as a *muezzin* or an *imam*, two secondary-level positions, only to find that their colleagues from Najd had also beaten them there.

Table 3. Distribution of high officials by region based on a selected sample of government departments, 1994

Region	Population (millions)	Percentage of the total population	Number of senior employees	Percentage of the total
Western	3.62	0.294	172	0.203
Middle	3.22	0.262	511	0.602
Southern	2.41	0.196	84	0.099
Eastern	1.90	0.154	36	0.042
Northern	1.15	0.093	46	0.054
Total	12.30		849	

Although I am not entirely sure that this was what raised the ire of the religious current's youth against Najd and its clerics, what is certain is that the second half of the 1980s witnessed the emergence of young clerics from the southern and northern regions (those who failed to reserve a place in the upper echelons of the official religious establishment). Among the latter's main traits are their open and candid political views, a hitherto unfamiliar trait among religious clerics. These young clerics had transcended all the talk about Afghanistan and its *mujahideen* and were now talking about a Western plot to Westernize Muslim societies, and thus defeat Islam on its own turf, with the inadvertent or coerced participation of countries that claim to be Muslim. As usual in such cases, they were referring to Saudi Arabia. Among these clerics were Sheikh Safar Al-Hawali, 'Awad Al-Qarni and 'Ayed Al-Qarni, all three of whom hail from the country's southern region.

Fallout from the Gulf War

The Iraqi occupation of Kuwait in August 1990 unleashed a number of social crises, the first repercussion of which was the emergence of a current calling for political reform. In December 1990, a number of prominent personalities drafted a petition with a list of demands calling on the government to introduce essential reforms to the official administration, and the relationship between society and the state. The signatories included well-known intellectuals, former officials and socially influential personalities, but no religious clerics.[12]

The crises rocked the entire religious current and left it tense, hesitant and incapable of seizing the initiative. The Council of Senior Ulema's decision to endorse the government's call for the help of American forces came as a considerable shock to the Salafist current that had been in a prolonged dream and, when it woke up, found that it had to deal with a plethora of unprecedented challenges and apprehensions.[13] For years the religious discourse had insisted on the principle of '*al-walawa al-bara*' ('loyalty and disavowal') as an essential element of faith, one of whose main tenets is to forbid the reliance on non-believers and expelling them from the Arabian Peninsula, yet here was their army with an official invitation endorsed by the senior *ulema*.

The new generation of the religious current's leaders believed that the presence of a foreign military force would reorient the country towards secularism. Their fears were vindicated when, in November 1990, 47 Saudi women organized a demonstration in the streets of Riyadh calling for their right to drive a car.[14] However, though the small demonstration was quickly put down by the Council for Enjoining Good and Forbidding Evil and the local police, who arrested all the participants, the incident elicited a fierce debate and the issue became the main subject of Friday sermons during the following three months. Dr Mohsen Al-'Awajy remembers a meeting in Dar Al-Fatwa called to discuss the issue, attended by the Mufti, Sheikh Abdul Aziz bin Baz, the Emir of Riyadh Salman bin Abdul Aziz – later the crown prince – and a number of *ulema* and prominent personalities. Al-'Awji writes in this regard:

> Huge crowds of people had gathered outside the building brought together by the interest in the subject, the paucity of remedies and murky official position. It was the first time that a crowd of this size had gathered in that manner.[15]

Over the following years, the right of women to drive would become the symbol of Saudi women's struggle for liberation and equality. The religious current's position in this debate and the ensuing events reveals three fundamental problems in its discourse and activities:

- The absence of any calm and collected debate on major issues of the logic of negotiations to arrive at the best solutions and the predominance of the mobilization rhetoric over the current's discussions and pronouncements. By virtue of its very nature, the mobilization rhetoric is populist, simplistic, hard-line and imprecise.
- The fact that the religious elite, and by extension its supporters, overlooks – or maybe denies the existence of – the social change taking place in the country, particularly the rise of new forces and questions on the need to develop the country's political system in a manner that allows it to accommodate the unprecedented challenges. Overlooking these changes results from misunderstanding the relationship between the state and religion and its clerics, as indicated above. The fact that this continues despite all the deep socio-political changes helped entrench the exclusivist aspect of the religious discourse. Later on this exclusivist behaviour turned inward on itself and became the norm inside the current, when once it targeted only those on the outside.
- Believing in conspiracy theories and assuming that those opposed to the current are part of a global plot, instead of dealing with them simply as people who have different opinions with whom one could agree or disagree at different times. The total belief in conspiracy theories without diligent examination is the outcome of what could be seen as a sudden politicization that prompted some to explain major issues in light of small insignificant ones. This way of understanding politics departs from the tactical to understand the strategic, rather than the other way round, as it is supposed to be.

Neither during that particular period nor in the years that followed did any Salafist activist address the conditions and rights of Saudi women; their discourse centred entirely on two different issues:

- Intermixing between the sexes and the enchantment and corruption that ensues from it.
- When women gain their rights it means victory for the Westernized liberal current over its religious counterpart (e.g. Al-Ahmad 2011; Al-Omar 2011).

Some preachers noticed that the government did not react strongly enough to what they saw as a Westernization onslaught, but did exactly the contrary. King Fahd ordered the dismissal of the Chairman of the Council for Enjoining Good and Forbidding Evil, a move seen as a sign of the government's determination to restrict the activities of religious institutions that act without direct official orders.[16] Moreover, in an official statement, the Awqaf Ministry ordered mosque preachers not to mention the women's demonstration incident in their Friday sermons, and threatened to punish the *imams* who do not abide by the order. The President of Riyadh University, where some of the demonstrating women were teachers, did the same. Some Salafist activists wondered about the secret behind the state not dealing strongly enough with the women who staged the demonstration in Riyadh:

> Did the liberal current use the crisis to embarrass the state and conservative society, i.e., to pit the two historical allies against one other, starting with a pro-forma issue like women

driving cars, or, perhaps – as the conspiracy theory goes – America's fingers are all over it?[17]

The immediate impact of the crises was the collapse of trust and respect between the senior *ulema* and the activist religious current, and the latter's emergence from under the senior *ulema*'s mantle. The activists declared their opposition to both the government's request for American military assistance and the senior *ulema*'s endorsement of the move, and considered it evidence of the sheikhs' alienation from reality and their lack of knowledge in what they called 'the jurisprudence of reality', i.e. of politics and its reversals. Sheikh Safar Al-Hawali delivered several sermons condemning the decision and warning against its repercussions.[18] Sheikh Salman Al-Odeh did the same in a sermon entitled 'Causes of the State's Collapse' in which he said that the worst transgression is placing one's trust in non-Muslims and seeking victory through their help (Al-Khudor 2011, 180–200). This was the first time that the Kingdom's mosques turned into arenas of political debate and mobilization against the government and the official religious authority. The split drew many youths to the activist religious current (Alshamsi 2010, 86).

About half a year after the crises, the new generation of Salafist leaders succeeded in reorganizing their ranks, and believed that the crises had weakened both the government and the religious current. They believed, therefore, that the time had come to formulate a new relationship between the parties, one that would strengthen the religious currents' role in the country's decision-making circles and administration, especially its new representatives. The new idea appeared in the form of a petition drafted by a group of activists and presented to the Kingdom's Grand Mufti, Sheikh Abdul Aziz bin Baz, who in turn endorsed it in a letter to King Fahd. The fact that Sheikh Mohammad bin Uthaimeen endorsed the idea as well meant that it had the support of two of the most prominent Ulema in the Kingdom at the time. The letter, signed by 52 sheikhs and prominent Salafist personalities, was presented to the Chief of the Royal Court in May 1991.[19]

The Ulema's letter or memorandum comprised 12 demands, some of which were related to political reforms, while others underlined the need to promote the *ulema* and the institutional role of religion, in both the state and society. However, although the government did not respond to these demands, the fact that the Mufti saw the letter's sensitive political contents compelled him to reconsider his relationship with the same young proselytizers whose public activism and enthusiasm for the call had made him so optimistic earlier on. In June 1991, the Council of Senior Ulema issued under the Mufti's leadership a declaration distancing itself from the petition, although the criticism focused on having spread the petition in the media instead of treating it as confidential advice, as is customary when advising those in charge.

In March 1992, King Fahd issued three Royal Decrees in response to public demands prior and during the Gulf War. These were relevant to the Basic Governance System, which in fact meant a constitution; the Consultative Council Law; and the Regional Law which was supposed to lay the legal foundations for a decentralized administration system. However, reception of the decrees by various social groups and the religious current was tepid, and deemed far less than what the society had expected over the previous two years.

This circumvention by the government of the religious current's demands and the Mufti's refusal to continue applying pressure on it seems to have been a watershed moment for the young Salafists. Those who had struggled to ensure a key role for the Mufti and portrayed him as the father and guide of the religious current could no longer convince their colleagues who wanted to seize this historic opportunity to assume leadership of society.

The impact of this transformation became evident in June 1992 when 107 Salafist advocates and activists, from the second and third rank, signed a statement in which they called the 'Advisory Memorandum' a document they hoped would clarify the *ulema*'s petition. This memorandum, written in the form of a political party platform, was the first widespread organized political appearance by the independent Salafist current opposed to the government. Unlike its first letter whose tone was soft and pleading, the memorandum openly connected the government's religious legitimacy to its commitment to their demands. Sheikh Al-Obaikan, one of the period's activists, believes that while the first letter was a sincere reflection of the local Salafist current and its vision of reforms, the Advisory Memorandum was a reflection of a politicized activist current.[20]

In light of the above, the Salafist current emerged as an entity independent of its traditional political cocoon, i.e. the state, and of its legitimate leadership, i.e. the Council of Senior Ulema and the official religious establishment, and of course independent of its original environment, i.e. the central region of Najd. And although, like their counterparts in the traditional Salafist current, the religious leaders who hailed from the central region, in particular Al-Qaseem, kept their first rank status in Al-Sahwa, they were no longer the only leaders, nor was derivation from Najd a criterion for choosing leaders.

The Grand Mufti was angry because he did not have the chance to express his opinion on the memorandum before it was published. He gathered the Senior Ulema in September 1992 and issued a statement distancing himself from the memorandum and condemning its contents, even expressing doubts on the real intentions of those who signed it.[21]

Based on the council's position, most of the Advisory Memorandum's signatories were dismissed from their government positions, and some were prevented from leaving the country. This marked the beginning of the largest secession in the Salafist current's history, and the appearance of what become known later as the Al-Sahwa current as a distinct entity from the general Salafist current that had stayed out of the political struggle.

Crises give rise to a variety of ideas based on which new political parties are formed, and new leaders created. The Al-Sahwa current, which was born out of the Gulf War, was based on the idea of separation from the traditional Salafist current and the government, a politically motivated and self-interested idea that produced a new generation of young leaders. At the time of the crises, the average age of the Ulema Council's members was 71 years, while Sheikh 'Ayed Al-Qarni was 31, Salman Al-Odeh was 34, and Naser Al-Omar and Abdul Mohsen Al-Obaikan were both 38 years old.

The new sheikhs' discourse was embarrassing to the senior sheikhs. On the doctrinal level, it cast doubt on their insistence on obeying the ruler no matter how much he deviates from the prescribed path, which is one of the established tenets of traditional Hanbali jurisprudence. On the political level, their influence on the street was elbowing out the popularity that the senior sheikhs had diligently built over the years (Al-Omaem 2011, 164). Moreover, despite the Mufti's advice and attempts to calm down the proselytizers and convince them to avoid provoking the state, the young supporters were pushing for more radical positions, and the new leaders were enjoying their success in mobilizing the masses.

In September 1994, the government had had enough and arrested the main symbols of the new Salafist current, starting with Safar Al-Hawali, whose followers call him the 'Ibn Taimiah of his age' and one of the current's most prominent political theoreticians, along with Salman Al-'Odeh, 'Ayed Al-Qarni, Nasser Al-Omar and others (Alshamsi 2010, 126).

The end of the struggle: a new generation that transcends Al-Sahwa

When the Sheikhs came out of prison in 1999, they found an entirely different scene than before they went in; it was clear that the government had managed to absorb the shock. In 1995, when a small group from the religious current became involved in terrorist activities with Al-Qaeda, the activist religious current became suspect and its main concern was to defend itself against a fierce attack that held it responsible for furnishing Al-Qaeda with ideas, money and men.

Al-Qaeda's attack on New York City and Washington, DC, in September 2001 was another watershed moment for the religious current. The government became convinced that the impact of the 'rough curriculum' of Salafist education would not stay limited to Saudi society, and that its old wager on its ability to contain the current again had reached its limit. Many of the current's activists and leaders, especially the young generation, became convinced that the cost of the fight with the government was steeper than they could handle, and that the large masses that they had attracted to the mosques were not necessarily prepared to fight for their discourse.

This reconsideration led to serious fragmentation within the new religious current. Some of its youths developed a discourse more in tune with liberal principles and most of its clerics tried to bridge the gap with the government. In the meantime, the government took a hardline position aimed at quelling sources of extremism and terrorism, thus depriving the religious current of its political power sources.

Fourth: the siege

While in the first half of the 1990s, official and media pressure came down hard on the second generation of Salafists, or the so-called 'Al-Sahwa Sheikhs', in the second half, the traditional wing joined the list of targets. It seems that after years of placating and being courteous to traditional Salafism, the government had decided to limit its circles of influence after succeeding in cutting Al-Sahwa down to size. According to Sheikh Abdul-Mohsen Al-Abbad, former President of the Islamic University, this change indicates that the forces behind the Westernization strategy did not only comprise local liberal groups or groups opposed to the religious current. The events that followed 2001 confirm that the government was also involved in the plan, and that prominent ministers and royal family members were helping to implement it, including the king's daughter and her husband (*Al-Alouka* 2001). In the past, Al-Abbad used personally to deliver his messages to the king and major princes, but had started to publish them on the Internet when he discovered – or so it seems – that none of these officials was listening to him. His messages mainly revolved around allowing women to work outside the home and warning against their removing the veil and mixing with men (Al-Badr 6/7/1434 *Hejira*). He also severely criticized Islamic University for opening non-religious colleges and admitting women to them (Al-Abbad 2010).

In March 2002, a fire broke out at a girls' school in Mecca killing 14 pupils; the government used the incident to take girls' education away from the religious establishment and place it under the Ministry of Education. Girls' education had been under the sheikhs' control since its establishment in 1960, and was considered the fortified bastion and symbol of the traditional religious current's power. All those who presided over that sector were senior clerics and most of its employees were loyal to the religious current. Many saw it as entitlement or prerogative of the Kingdom's senior clerics, no different in that from the ministries of Awqaf and Justice, or specialized religious institutions. The Presidency of Girls' Education used to run 10,674 schools with a total of 178,276 female teachers, or 25% of the state's civil employees, in 2002 (Saudi Arabia Department of Statistics 2002).

As an example of the blow's severity, the Salafists tried to organize a sit-in in protest against the move but some senior sheikhs convinced them to postpone it, with the hope that their discussions with the crown prince would change his mind, but it seems that no one at the royal court was listening to them. It was already November by the time the activists realized that the sheikhs' efforts would likely not succeed, and a few hundred of them organized a sit-in in front of the Grand Mufti's office in the capital Riyadh, but this reaction came in what amounts to 'injury time'. The religious current no longer had its old thrust and power, and the government was no longer interested in placating it.

The Council for Enjoining Good and Forbidding Evil was the government's next target; the council was another of the religious current's fortresses and a symbol of its struggle against other currents, and until 2002 had enjoyed immunity from public criticism and various kinds of litigation. The well-known Saudi novelist Abdo Khal recounts an incident he personally had with the Council, which shows the clout it once had in the political system (Khal 2010). He says,

> I was severely beaten by the security forces accompanying the Council for Enjoining Good and Forbidding Evil that stopped me when I was driving around looking for parking outside a mall, while my wife was doing her shopping. They dragged me out of the car [...] I went with my wife to the Nazla police station to make a complaint, but the major told me 'you are crazy, who complains against the Council for Enjoining Good and Forbidding Evil [...]?' Eight years have passed since that incident and I am still waiting for the police to get in touch with me. [...] I tried to write about the incident at the time but was unable to because the Council had been granted total immunity against complaints or exposure of its members' mistakes.

This real story is a good example of the manner in which the council deals with the public, and there are several similar incidents of which very few have been recorded, most having been transmitted by word of mouth (Al-Nuqaidan 2012). In April 2004, a judge agreed to prosecute a case raised by a Saudi woman against the council's employees, whom she accused of kidnapping and terrorizing her and her daughter. The fact that the case was accepted at all was unprecedented. In the past, the courts refused all cases against the council even when the accusation was supported by ample evidence or the judge was convinced of the claimants' honesty, preferring to opt for an amicable solution between the parties to avoid bringing the council before the law.

In the same context, the past ten years have witnessed thousands of yearly dismissals of teachers and *imams* from their positions, especially those who harbour non-traditional views, and the Civil Service Commission gave the Minister of Education permission to transfer teachers to positions outside the education sector, if he receives directives to that effect from the Interior Ministry. In 2010, for example, 2,000 teachers were transferred to other jobs (Al-Awwad 2010), as were 3000 others the following year; the Minister of Awqaf said that 6000 mosque *imams* were dismissed between 2008 and 2011 because they had been 'derelict in their duties as *imams* and preachers' (Al-Naqmi 2012), meaning that they failed to abide by professional or political rules. Candidates to higher education branches having to do with the rehabilitation of judges and professors of religious colleges received the same treatment. In theory, these measures are aimed at sidelining those issuing accusations of apostasy and those suspected of sympathies with Al-Qaeda or of adhering to their beliefs, though in fact they also target activists, even reformist Salafists whose loyalty to the state or support for its policies is in doubt (e.g. Al-Thabit 2010).

Fifth: *Al-Tanweer* (enlightenment) current

Just like the attacks on New York City and Washington, DC, marked a turning point in the relationship between the state and the religious current, it became the cornerstone of the religious current's path; the Al-Sahwa current that dominated all social activities in the Kingdom for over two decades had begun to unravel. Scores of activists who had found in Al-Qaeda global discourse a model of power and pride soon discovered that the price to pay for supporting it was dearer than the hopes pinned on it. The sheikhs who for a short time dreamt about becoming national leaders discovered that the religious current was still operating within narrow confines, and that their discourse had failed to convince anyone beyond these confines. Scores of Arab activists who in the 1980s and 1990s had become the engine of the religious movement discovered that they were ultimately classified as foreigners and, as such, could be deported at any moment for security reasons, which is what actually happened. In 2002 the Interior Minister, Prince Nayef, said that many of Saudi Arabia's problems came from the Muslim Brotherhood (Nayef 2002).

When he came out of gaol in 1999, alongside other prominent symbols of Al-Sahwa, Sheikh Salman Al-Odeh found a changed world; he felt a gap between the society he knew in 1994 and the one he was then seeing. He said, in this context:

> Television has become part of the house's furniture when once local society rejected the whole idea for both the ordinary people and the sheikhs [...] his [my] student, Abdul Rahman gives him a laptop, and shows him how to connect to the Internet and access a website [...] it is the magic of information and fear of the unknown. He rediscovers things and reacts with astonishment; his memory is in an unusual celebratory condition; it recuperates its old files, recalls the spirit through which he used to look at things [...] and links them to today's feeling and emotions.
>
> (Al-Odeh 2011, 540–541)

Sheikh Odeh put his finger on the key change that had taken place at the time: the information revolution; unlike other Arab countries, the Kingdom had been closed to new ideas and currents (Article 19, 1991). The emergence of satellite television and the Internet broke the walls of isolation and brought down the borders; the extreme censorship of books and media was no longer an issue. In mid-2010, a Salafist cleric noticed that the post-Al-Sahwa generation dealt with religious ideas and symbols differently. The new generation was becoming increasingly individualistic due to its growing ability to access information directly and express itself via modern communication tools that allowed it to bypass its relationship with the clerics. The youths' knowledge of religious matters and their exposure to different ideas gave them the self-confidence and courage to dispute the *ulema*'s opinions that were once considered infallible and sacrosanct, including the option of consulting non-religious sources in their arguments with the *ulema* (Al-Buloushi 2010).

After five years of isolation from the world, Al-Sahwa's sheikhs had to choose between confining themselves to their current's old culture and politics and gaining access the wide world beyond. Each of these choices has a price, one to be earned and one to be paid. The years they spent in gaol gave them the opportunity to reconsider their positions, their relationships and the old ways they used to do things, and this reconsideration impacted on their activities during the next stage. The first impact was to break with Al-Qaeda and those who advocate violence. Although this decision would cost them a significant part of their reputation as independent leaders, it was necessary to avoid more deterioration. According to Sheikh Odeh:

> We used to despise the American discourse which said 'he who is not with me is against me', yet here we are today plagued with a discourse that says 'he who is not with me is against God'.
>
> (Al-Odeh 2003)

The decade between 1995 and 2005 was the most difficult in the religious current's history. It had to apologize to the government on a daily basis to prove again and again that it was still loyal to the regime, and turn a blind eye to the restrictions and measures aimed at liquidating its sources of power, including the arrest of many of its figures and activists. In 2011, the Interior Ministry said that 5000 individuals belonging to the current had been arrested, but political activists claim that the real number exceeds 20,000.[22]

In 2003, there were widespread calls for political reform in the country; a number of activists issued a declaration entitled 'Vision of the Kingdom's Present and Future', a statement that marked a turning point in the history of calls for reform in the Kingdom.[23] Among the signatories were six well-known activists from the religious current, although the majority stayed on the sidelines, and neither got involved in the initiative nor launched one of their own. It was clear that the religious current was no longer unified, was unable to launch initiatives similar to the one it issued in previous years, and that its leaders were no longer willing to pay the price of a confrontation with the government, which outcome was far from guaranteed.

The social influence of most religious leaders had started to retreat and terms like 'the sultan's *ulema*' began to circulate among the religious community, terms that were heard briefly during the Gulf crisis before disappearing. In fact, quite a significant number of Al-Sahwa's leaders had decided to return politically to the state's embrace and work alongside its officials without, however, regaining their former positions. Within the context of their new relationship with the state, some founded their own cultural and media institutions, while others became lawyers or advisors to different statesmen.

This elitist type behaviour was very different from the populist activism of the old Al-Sahwa. Today, the current's youths are the main absentees from the scene. Some of those who had separated themselves from their leaders developed their own intellectual and practical abilities, and now had a new vision of religion, politics and society. The latter would in time form a new elite – at least some of them – and lead a new religious current with a discourse different from Al-Sahwa's and, by extension, from traditional Salafist ideology (Al-Qudaimy 2011).

The new current was looking for a special occasion to make its presence known, and it seems that it found it in the American elections that witnessed Barak Obama's rise as the first 'African American presidential candidate of Muslim origin'.

The new current's activists seized the occasion to announce their adoption of democracy as the only option for the Kingdom's future. Dr Mohammad Al-Ahmari attacked the clerics and Al-Sahwa's followers who had previously described democracy as the product of apostates saying:

> Democracy is the highest form of governance, and all other systems are not even worth mentioning in the news, any news, except for news about the coerced and defeated among the marginal, failed or backwards groups.
>
> (Al-Ahmari 2008)

Salman Al-Odeh commented saying, 'Laawe Kana Obama Fi Balad Arabi …' (If Obama were in an Arab country you would have found him in one of the deportation centres)[24] in reference to the treatment of foreigners in the Kingdom. Al-Ahmari and Al-Odeh were implicitly announcing the creation of a new current whose discourse is different from Al-Sahwa's, adopts democracy and public freedoms, and bets on good relations with other currents and trends in Saudi society.

The announcement was met by a strong attack by Al-Odeh's former colleagues; it was clear, however, that the latter was actually wagering on a new trend whose size and influence in Saudi society was likely to grow, a trend that believed in democratic transition and public participation as a way for Saudi society to exit its accumulated crises.

Although the new current's youths have neither media nor social institutions similar to the sheikh's, they are enthusiastic, have a good knowledge of the world and harbour new ideas that have allowed them to use what Manuel Castells calls the 'Power of Flows'. This happens when ordinary people have access to information on the Internet, for example, then reproduce it and spread it around the world. Not only does this release the power pent up within them, but also it disperses the power that was once monopolized by certain groups (flow of power), and allows marginalized communities to find their own sources of power or form influential pressure groups (Castells 2001, 217). These youths would soon impose themselves and their discourse on the scene using new media outlets, and would become a considerable force that has so far managed to offer a national democratic discourse as a more attractive alternative that responds to the new generation's needs.

The current, called 'Al-Tanweery [Enlightenment] Current' since 2009, issued its first petition in the middle of 2011, delineates the separation between it and the state, on the one hand, and the traditional Salafism and Al-Sahwa, on the other. Around 10,000 citizens signed the petition, entitled 'Towards a State of Rights and Institutions', which began with a reference to the transformation taking place in the Arab world:

> The revolution that the youths have launched and the entire population participated in, in Tunisia, Egypt, Libya and elsewhere, suggests that the kingdom, like other countries, is facing a serious challenge and that the situation will head towards revolution if the state does not quickly introduce reforms, development, freedom and dignity, reverses injustice and combats corruption.

The first 50 names on the list of signatories are of particular importance; the names show a wide cross-section of support that transcends the religious current's social milieu, since among them is a number of liberal, leftist and Shia activists, both men and women, which confirms the interest of the petition's drafters in offering a discourse that represents all sectors of Saudi society. The religious discourse once described itself as the sole shaper of events and public opinion, and addressed the Saudis as an adviser and arbiter. This petition, however, presents itself as a partner in the same discourse that calls for joint objectives and offers collective solutions.

The petition pinpointed eight avenues of reform, starting with an elected parliament with full prerogatives, separating the prime minister and monarch's positions, reforming the judiciary and ensuring its independence, combating administrative corruption and abuse of power, encouraging the establishment of unions and civil society institutions, allowing freedom of expression and guaranteeing it in the law and, finally, releasing all prisoners of conscience and ensuring that the security forces abide by the rule of law in matters of state security.[25]

These days, there are three distinct warring factions within the religious current:

- Traditional Salafism, most of whose members and positions are linked to the state.
- Remnants of the Al-Sahwa current whose activities focus on combating Westernization and issues related to mixing between the genders and women's work. The latter's political position wavers between opposition to what it calls Westernization policies implemented by the state and supporting policies that strengthen religious activism and its institutions.
- The Tanweer current that calls, alongside those who advocate political reform, for transitioning towards a constitutional monarchy that ensures the rule of law, public freedoms and people's participation in political decision-making. This automatically places it among the political opposition, although it is not involved in day-to-day opposition activities.

Conclusion

This paper has addressed the relationship between the religious current and the state in Saudi Arabia, based on the dialectic of: alliance–intimidating domination–discordance. It has clarified the special status of religion within the state compared with other Arab countries, due to the fact that the religious establishment is a founding partner in the political system, which endows it with a political and social status unlike any other in the Arab world. Despite that fact, the state's openness to international markets and its adoption of the modernization option – at least in the economic sphere – resulted in a series of change dynamics within the state, society and the religious current itself, which eventually led to slow but deep changes.

Relationship between the religious current and the state

The paper delineated five different stages in the relationship between the religious current and the state, each of which begins at a particular turning point:

- The first stage began in 1961 and witnessed a change in the religious leadership that saw it develop from its old image into a strong and organized institution; it succeeded thanks to the mufti's ability to dominate all official religious activities, the judiciary and girls' education.

- The second stage began in 1979, witnessed the rise of a new generation of followers and leaders, and saw politics become a daily occupation thanks to the Iranian revolution, the occupation of the Holy Sanctuary, the *jihad* in Afghanistan and the impact of Arab activists. The religious institution doubled in size and more people enrolled in religious education. The debate expanded round the state's legitimacy, its relationship with religion and its qualifications as a model of good governance. However, the most important change at the time was the Salafist current's growth beyond its original social milieu (central Najd) when thousands of migrants from rural areas joined its ranks. As a result, Salafism lost its historic trait as a Najd-based sect and its function as an organic security belt for the royal family.
- The third stage coincided with the occupation of Kuwait in 1990, and saw the above questions change into accusations, against the Saudi state and elite, of involvement in a Western plot to control Muslim societies. The crises shed light on the new generation of clerics as the shapers of public opinion and political pundits. The stage also witnessed the rise of the Al-Sahwa current; however, before most of its leaders were arrested, in 1994, they managed to reorient the current role from guardian of the state to detractor of its legitimacy, by contradicting the old vision of the Saudi state as a model of good governance in line with religious teachings.
- The fourth stage began with the attack on New York City and Washington, DC, in September 2011; its main event was the state's decision to dismantle the sources of the religious current's power, especially those that allowed it to mobilize and play a political role. Different strands of the current were affected by the decision including the official religious establishment and traditionalist trend affiliated to the state. Also during that period, girls' education was appended to the Ministry of Education, and the Council of Senior Ulema and Higher Judicial Council had their membership changed. The immunity that religious institutions once enjoyed was lifted, including that of the Council for Enjoining Good and Forbidding Evil. Several domestic religious institutions were either cut down in size or closed, and thousands of activists were arrested, dismissed from their posts or denied promotion.
- The features of the fifth stage became clear with the outbreak of the Arab Spring in 2011. One of its most salient manifestations is the rise of the Tanweer current that openly opposes traditional Salafism and turns its back on Al-Sahwa's discourse. The current adopts democracy as a model of good governance and calls for transitioning towards a constitutional monarchy. These principles were laid out in a petition entitled 'Towards a State of Rights and Institutions' that was a turning point in the history of calls for reform in Saudi Arabia.

The religious current as a political player: does it help or impede the reform movement?

In theory, the religious current could be for or against the state; likewise, it could play a defining role in shaping public attitudes towards the government. Realistically, it is difficult to determine which way it will go, at least in light of the situation on the ground. Most people do not distinguish between a religious cleric loyal to the state and another who is not, and most clerics do not have a firm position towards the state and its policies.

This is mainly due to predominance of a fragmented view of public affairs. While a cleric supports the government because it holds prayers, spends on mosques, manages the *haj* (pilgrimage to Mecca), and respects religious occasions and rituals, he ignores economic, foreign policy and legal matters. Intellectually, the Saudi cleric tends – for the most part – to delve in generalities like day-to-day matters and people's behaviour, and has no interest in politics; he is no different in that from the vast majority of ordinary people. The lack of either a political life or a modern organized civil society in the Kingdom is a major contributor to the poverty of political culture, and impacts religious clerics and ordinary people alike.

It was stated above that all religious clerics – save for a few – are linked to the state, both professionally and for existential reasons, via the official religious establishment. However, apart from the existential aspect, many religious clerics, especially those from the middle and upper echelons, obtain their power from the positions they occupy or connections they have to various statesmen, and use it to increase their social capital. In other words, the cleric has no choice – for existential reasons or to maintain his social status – but live in the shadow of the state. In times of crisis, the state works feverishly to win the latter's support and punishes those who hesitate, which is what happened to thousands among them and among the activists over the past decade.

For those two reasons, i.e. the poverty of political culture and existential and social links to the state, the religious current was an active supporter of the state or, at least, helped thwart any serious moves by the opposition, as happened during the so-called Hanin Revolution in March 2011. A change in this position is contingent upon other factors, chief among which is the development of alternative 'circles of interest', which could happen as an outcome of changes taking place in the region. A good example is the Muslim Brotherhood and Salafists' rise in Egypt and Syria, or change in local public opinion as a reaction to the government's policies or regional changes.

Division within the religious current and its impact on short-term policies

Al-Sahwa's leaders saw the deaths of Sheikhs Abdul Aziz bin Baz (in 1999) and Mohammad bin Othaimeen (in 2001) as the end of the great Salafist fathers' era, and the end of the dream to unite different trends within the current (Al-Awajy 2002). This factor, coupled with changes in government policies and the escalating international pressure on the government to curb religious extremism – particularly by the Americans – quickly unravelled the old patriarchal-like system within the religious current and opened the door to new ideas and leaders who forge their way forward by openly stating their opposition to those in power. This change played a double role: it opened the door to radical political trends and provided an opportunity to those seeking to acquire the social power enjoyed by senior clerics by identifying with the state and forging alliances with its officials. An example of the first case is Sheikh Youssef Al-Ahmad who shifted his interest from issues like Westernization, mixing among the genders and women's work to the cause of political prisoners, organizing sit-ins in front of the Interior Ministry and calling for their release, which led to his arrest in July 2011.[26]

Positions like these force the current's followers and activists to negotiate their political positions – with or against the state. Whichever decision is made, it has to be grounded in a socio-religious justification. It was noticed, for example, that a significant number of activists who supported the state, in March 2011, and gave religious and political justifications for their choice, tended after Sheikh Al-Ahmad's arrest to voice their despair that reforms would take place in the foreseeable future, a move that placed them on the side of the opposition. On the other hand, and contrary to that, a number of clerics and activists formerly identified as reformers decided to keep quiet and focus on their professional matters when an official decision was issued preventing judges from making public statements or engaging with the media.[27]

I believe that the tendency for position-demarcation will be stronger among activists who remained loyal to Al-Sahwa, because the trend proved unable to regenerate its discourse. Its leaders are growing older and lead conservative elitist lives, with no new leaders ready to replace them; it is akin to a popular movement without popular leaders. In my opinion, a large segment of this current will give up politics in the short-term and involve itself in cultural activities aimed, first and foremost, at developing new visions capable of confronting the challenges brought about by the Arab Spring.

On the other hand, the current was highly affected by the rise of political Salafism outside the Kingdom, especially in Egypt and Yemen. What strengthened the hand of those advocating that democracy be accepted as a good governance system was the particular involvement of Egypt's Salafists in politics by democratic means. Until recently, the latter saw democracy as a Christian model and an entryway for Western culture into the minds of Muslims. In May 2012, a major faction of the current held a meeting in Doha, under the leadership of Sheikh Nasser Al-Omar and the participation of prominent activists from the Kingdom and elsewhere, in which democracy was the main topic of discussion. Such discussions will, on the one hand, lead to a wider cross-section of people believing in democracy and, on the other hand, help centralize the Arab Salafist movements at the expense of its Saudi counterparts. Both options will in the short-term widen the gap between Al-Sahwa and the government.

The Tanweer current and the limits of its impact

Although Al-Tanweer's general position places it among the ranks of the opposition, it is still too early to say that it has a major impact on political conditions in the country. The current still has major unresolved issues including its position towards other national groups, and towards women's and minority rights, although those who know the current's members believe that these issues have already been resolved. It is also clear that they avoid openly declaring their position on these issues to avoid jeopardizing their relations with the remnants of Al-Sahwa, or lose a public that is still halfway between Al-Sahwa's old discourse and Al-Tanweer's new one. The current is still a youthful social movement that expresses itself mainly though cultural activities, wages a cultural war against the traditionalists and Al-Sahwa's followers, and has not yet reached the level of a concrete and organized movement. Sheikh Salman Al-Odeh's adherence to the current is a source of strength for it since he is one of the most credible clerics today, though it is unlikely to cut corners. Many restrictions pull him back to his history and traditional sources of power, which I do not believe he is ready to forgo, unless social and political conditions in the country undergo a major change.

Given all the above reservations, the current's fast expansion tells us that it has succeeded in achieving a major breakthrough, and is becoming increasingly convincing to the new generation; this encourages the belief that it is likely to play an influential role in any future local movement.

Notes

1. For more information on the council, see Al-Dhayan (2011).
2. It is worth mentioning that the Minister of Awqaf had previously denied that the ministry was planning such a move (Aal-El-Shaikh 2006). Based on Ministry of Awqaf statistics, the actual number of mosque employees in 2008 was 78,347; for more information, see the Awqaf Ministry's website at: http://www.moia.gov.sa/Menu/Pages/%D9%8DStatistics2.aspx/. Accessed July 3, 2013.
3. Based on the Ministry of Awqaf's statistics, the number of mosques under its supervision is 55,266, in addition to 3604 prayer sites for special occasions. This number does not include mosques under the supervision of other government institutions or private individuals.
4. For more information on the percentage of those involved in religious education in the general academic curricula, see Al-Issa (2009, 23).
5. The general tendency among senior *ulema* in the Kingdom is to admit that the state has made mistakes and committed legal violations, while at the same time forbidding anyone from defaming it. The only solution in their opinion is to pursue the system of giving confidential advice to the ruler. For a collection of opinions on the subject, see the Subul Al-Salam website (http://sobolalsalam.net/).
6. The *fatwa* was issued by the Permanent Committee for Scientific Research and Iftaa' (Islamic rulings), no. 24937, on 31 October 2010. It states that: 'Muslim women are not allowed to work in a place where there exists mixing with men. They should stay away from areas where men congregate and find employment in permitted domains where they would neither seduce nor get seduced.' What was mentioned in the question (to which the *fatwa* is responding) means that it exposes women to both seduction and to seducing others and is therefore forbidden by *Shar'* (Islamic jurisdiction). 'Any company that hires her for such a position is abetting her in doing the forbidden and is therefore itself forbidden.'
7. For the text of the letter, see Aal al-Sheikh (2011).
8. For Sheikh Omar Al-Ashqar's account, see Shehadeh (2011).
9. For more details on the occupation of the Holy Sanctuary and those who took part in it, see Al-Huzaimi (2011).
10. Personal conversation with the author on this specific issue.
11. For more on Al-Albani's methodology and impact, see Shehadeh (2010, 45).
12. For more details on this petition, see Ahmad (2010).
13. See the interview of the editor-in-chief of Al-Bilad newspaper, Abdul Aziz Mohammad Qassem, with Mohsin Hussein Al-'Awajy: 'Mukashafat al-doctor Mohsin Al-'Awajy – Al-Juso' al-Awal' (Dr Mohsin Al-'Awajy's Disclosures – Part I). This interview was published in Al-Bilad on 20 Shawal 1422h, and on the interviewee website in January 2002 (http://www.mohsenalawajy.com/ar/index.php/2009-12-05-13-19-49/93–1, accessed 3 August 2013).
14. For the story about the incident, as told by Dr Aziza Al-Mane', one of those who took part in the incident, see Qassem (2007, 80).
15. See note 13.
16. The new Chairman of the Council, Dr Abdul Aziz Al-Saeed, who was appointed by King Fahd on 16 December 1999, was the first president from outside the family of Sheikh Mohammad bin Abdul Wahab, which had monopolized the post since 1903 (Al-Nuqaidan 2012, 65).
17. See note 15.
18. The most important of Al-Hawali's sermons were: '*Fasatathkuroun ma Aqoolu Lakom*' (You shall remember what I am telling you), in Jeddah, and '*Farfirou ila-Allah*' (Escape to God), in Riyadh, both of which were delivered in early September 1990. He also wrote articles and a memorandum to the Council of Senior Ulema, all of which focused on what Al-Hawali said was an international plot to liquidate the religious current and control the Middle East. For the text of the first sermon, see the website of Sheikh Dr Safar Al-Hawali (www.alhawali.com/index.cfm?method=home).
19. For the text and additional reasons for its publication, see Lacroix (2011).
20. On this, see Sheikh Abdul Mohsin Al-Obaikan's interview to *Al-Sharq Al-Awsat* newspaper (Al-Thayidi 2005).
21. See the Council for Senior Ulema's statement distancing itself from the Advisory Memorandum in *Wasiyyah, wa Nasiha Hatta la Takuna Fitnah* [Recommendation and Advice to

Avoid Strife] on the *Al-Sakina* website, dated 25 February 2011 (http://www.assakina.com/taseel/6722.html, accessed 3 August 2013).

22. In April 2011, the Interior Ministry spokesman said that there were 5056 prisoners: 'Waddaha Wa Fassala Bayan Hay'at-l-Tahkeek ...' (He Clarified the Statement of the Bureau of Investigation and Public Prosecution ...); 'Ministry of the Interior: 90% of the Detainees for Terrorist Offenses are being Currently Tried ... and Only 616 are Under Investigation'. *Al-Iqtisadiaya*, April 2, 2011. Commenting on the statement, the opposing *Harakat al*-Islah said that the real number of prisoners exceeded 27,000; 'Bayan Harakat Al-Islah Hawla Adad-l-Sujana ...' (Statement by the Islah Movement Regarding the Number of Political Prisoners in the Kingdom). *Al-Saha* website, April 3, 2011 (http://www.saudiwave.com/ar/2010-11-09-15-55-47/615-2011-04-03-09-43-40.html, accessed 4 August 2013).
23. 'Hal Yatumm Taf'iluha? Nass Wathiqat al-Islaah-l-Watani (Will it be Activated? Text of the National Reform Document). *Shu'oon Saudia*. Accessed July 3, 2013. http://www.saudiaffairs.net.
24. See the Alweeam website. September 29, 2008. http://alweeam.com; the interview was aired during the MBC's Hajar al-Zawiya programme on 27 September 2008.
25. For details of the petition, see Alsaif (2012).
26. It has been said that Sheikh Youssef Al-Ahmad was released from prison in November 2012 as part of a general amnesty.
27. Regarding this decision, see *Al-Weeam* May 6, 2010: http://alweeam.com/archives/126161/. The website was undergoing maintenance when accessed on 3 July 2013.

References

Aal al-Sheikh, Mohammad bin Ibrahim bin Abdul-Latif. 2011. "Rislala fi Tahkeem al-Qawaneen" ["A Letter on the Enactment of Positive (Non-Religious) Law"]. *Multaqa Ahlul Hadith* May 5. Accessed 3 July, 2013. http://www.ahlalhdeeth.com/vb/showthread.php?t=243738/.

Aal-El-Shaikh, Saleh. 2006. "The Minister of Islamic Affairs Denies: No Truth in the News that Imams and Preachers are being Hired to Create Jobs." *Al-Jazeera* May 25. Accessed July 3, 2013. http://www.al-jazirah.com/2006/20060525/ln59.htm/.

Al-Abbad, Abdul Mohsin. 2010. "Min Thikrayati an el-Jami'at l-Islamiyya ..." ["Some of My Memories of the Islamic University a Century after its Establishment"]. *Multaka Ahlu-l-Hadith* [Ahlu-l-Hadith Forum] June 4. Accessed July 3, 2013. http://www.ahlalhdeeth.com/vb/showthread.php?t=212894/.

Abu Zayd, Bakr Ibn Abdullah. 2000 *(1421h). Khassa'es Jazirat al-Arab* [*Characteristics of the Arabian Peninsula*]. 3rd ed. Al-Riyadh: Adwa' al-Bayan.

Ahmad, Adnan. 2010. "Al-Saudia 1990: Makhad Dawlawa Mujtama" ["Saudi Arabia 1990: A Changing State and Society"]. *Al Akhbar (Beirut)*March 3.

Al-Ahmad, Sheikh Youssef. 2011. "Kiyadat-il-Mar'at ...." ["Women Driving Cars is a Western Project and should be Resisted"]. *Al-Muslim* website, May 30. Retrieved July 23 2013 from http://almoslim.net/node/147245.

Al-Ahmari, Mohammad. 2008. "Intissaril-Dimoukratiyyahala l-Wathaniyyah ...." ["The Triumph of Democracy over Paganism in the American Elections"]. *Al-Asr*. November 10. Accessed July 3, 2013, http://alasr.ws/articles/view/10439/.

Aljahni, Hana'. 2010. "Appointing 140 Employees to Work Full Time as Mosque Muezzins and Imams." *Al-Wifaq* October 4. Accessed July 3, 2013. http://www.al-wefaq.org/news-action-show-id-12057.htm/.

Al-Alouka. 2001. "Al-Ahdaath-l-Akhira Athharat li-Wulaat ..." ["The Recent Events Revealed to the Rulers of the Country of the Two Holy Sanctuaries Who is the Advisor, the Cunning, the Enemy, or the Friend of Sheikh Al-Abbad"]. Accessed June 4, 2013. http://majles.alukah.net/showthread.php?83643-.

Alsaif, Tawfiq. March 1, 2012. "Ba'da Aamen Ala Sudurihi ...." ["One Year After its Issuance, the Declaration 'Towards a State of Rights and Institutions' is the Cornerstone of the Saudi Religious Current"]. Accessed August 1, 2013. http://www.almqaal.com/?p=1928.

Alshamsi, Mansoor Jassem. 2010. *Islam and Political Reform in Saudi Arabia: The Quest for Political Change and Reform*. New York: Routledge.

Article 19. 1991. *Silent Kingdom: Freedom of Expression in Saudi Arabia (Article 19 Country Report)*. London: Article 19.

Al-Awajy, Mohsin. 2002. Interview with *Al-Bilad* newspaper, January 4. Accessed 3 July, 2013. http://mohsenalawajy.com/ar/index.php/2009-12-05-13-19-49/93–1/.

Al-Awwad, Mut'eb. 2010. "Ib'aad Akthar Min 2000 Mu'allem Nasharu-l Fikr-il-Mutatarrif an-il Tadreess" ["Dismissal of Over 2000 Teachers that Spread Extremist Ideas from their Teaching Positions"]. *Okath* July 12.

Al-Badr, Abdul Mohsin Al-Abbad. 6/7/1434 *Hejira*. "Majmou'at Makalaat al-Sheikh Abd el-Mohsen …" ["The Collection of Articles on the Internet by Abdul Mohsin Al-Abbad Al-Badr"]. *Al-Sheikh l-Waled Abd el-Mohsen al-Abbaad l-Badr*. http://al-abbaad.com/index.php/articles/105-1434-07-16. Accessed July 3, 2013.

Al-Buloushi, Majed. 2010. "Jeel Ma Baad al Sahwa" ["The Post Sahwa Generation"]. *Lojainiat* website June 22. Accessed August 1, 2013. http://www.saaid.net/arabic/344.htm - and https://groups.google.com/forum/#!topic/azizkasem/GuOHzqIHW8U.

Al-Bunyan, Hasen. 2001. "Aqdam 'Al-Afghan Al-Arab' fil Saudia: Shahidtu Milad 'Al-Qaeda' wa Fikratil Tantheem Massriyya: Al-Surayhilil-'Shark el Awssat' Kuntu Imaman Limasjed Bin Bazwa Thahabtuila Afghanistan bi-Ttalab min al-Outhaymeen" ["The Oldest Saudi 'Arab Afghani': I Witnessed the Birth of 'Al-Qaeda' and the Idea Behind the Organization is Egyptian: Al-Suraihi to the 'Sharq Al-Awsat' I was the Imam of Bin Baz Mosque and I Went to Afghanistan Upon Uthaymeen's Request"]. *Al-Sharq Al-Awsat* November 25.

Castells, Manuel. 2001. "Information, Networks and Identities." In *Keys to the 21st Century*, edited by Jérôme Bindé, 214–23. Paris: UNESCO Publ./Berghahn.

Department of Statistics. 2007. *Al-Kitaab al-Ihsa'i al-Sanawi* [The Statistical Yearbook]. Riyadh: Department of Statistics.

Al-Dhayan, Sulaiman. 2011. "Hay'at Kibar Al-Ulama's fil Saudia: Al-Ta'sis wal Wathifa" ["The Council of Senior Ulema: Formation and Function"]. In *Hirasat Al-Iman: Al-Mu'assassat al-Diniyah* [Guarding the Faith: The Religious Institutions]. 3rd ed., edited by Turki Al-Dakheel, 71–101. Dubai: Al-Mibsar Centre for Research and Studies.

Al-Huzaimi, Nasser. 2011. *Ayam ma' Juhaiman: Kuntu maa 'Al-Jama'a al-Salafiya al-Muhtasaba'* [Days Spent with Juhaiman: I Was With the 'Referee Salafist Group']. Beirut: Al-Shabaka l-Arabiyyalil-Dirasaatwal-Nashr.

Al-Issa, Ahmad. 2009. *Islah Al-Ta'leem fi-l Saudia* [Reforming Education in Saudi Arabia]. Beirut: Al-Saqi.

Khal, Abdo. 2010. "Su'-l-Than Bucilat Rijal-il-Hai'ah" ["Council-Men Always Assume People's Ill Intentions"]. *Okaz* March 16.

Al-Khudor, Abdul Aziz. 2011. *Al-Saudia: Sirat Dawla wa Mujtama* [Saudi Arabia: The Course of a State and a Society]. Beirut: Arab Network for Research and Publishing.

Lacroix, Stéphane. 2011. *Awakening Islam: The Politics of Religious Dissent in Saudi Arabia*. Translated by George Holoch. Cambridge, Mass: Harvard University Press.

Al-Naqmi, Ali. 2012. "Seeyanat al Massajed Lam Nanjah fi Halliha Fala Touharrek Shujooni: Aal-il-Shaikh …" ["We Could Not Handle the Maintenance of Mosques, So Do Not Ask Me to Sympathise: Aal-il-Shaikh in a Speech to Makkah Notables"]. *Al-Madina* February 22.

Nayef, 'Al-Amir (Prince). 2002. "Fi Hadith …" [Prince Nayef in an Interview with the Kuwaiti *Al-Siyasa* Newspaper: 'We Are Not frightened by the Animosity in the American and British Media, Yet, it is Bothersome"]. *Al-Riyadh* November 28.

Al-Nuqaidan, Mansour. 2012. *Al-Mulouk Al-Muhtasiboun: Al-Amrbil Maarouf wal Nahi 'an al-Munkar 1929–2007'* [The Referee Kings: Enjoining Good and Forbidding Evil in Saudi Arabia 1929–2007]. Dubai: Markaz-l-Misbarlil Dirasaatwal Buhuth.

Al-Odeh, Salman. 2002. *Al-Ighraq fil Juz'iyat* [Getting Drowned in Partialities]. Riyadh: Dar Al-Iman.

Al-Odeh, Salman Bin Fahd. 2003. "Tafjirat Al-Riyadh … Rasm Turok al-Khalas" ["Riyadh Bombings … Drawing the Path to Redemption"]. *Al-Jazeera* November 12.

Al-Odeh, Salman Bin Fahd. 2011 (1432*h*). *Tufulat Qalb: Doona-l-Tathakkor Fawqa-l Nisyan* [Childhood of a Heart: Less than a Full Memory, More than Forgetfulness]. Al-Riyadh: Mu'assassat-l-Islam-l-Yawm.

Al-Omaem, Ali. 2011. *"Shay' minal Naqd Shay' minal Tareekh: Aaraa' fi l-Hadathah wal Sahwatwa fi el-Liberaliyyatwal-Yassar* [A bit of Criticism, a bit of History: Opinions on Modernity, Al-Sahwa, Liberalism and the Left]. Beirut: Jadawel.

Al-Omar, Sheikh. 2011. "Mouhathiran min Tahaluf …." [Warning Against an Alliance between the Secularists and the Rejectionist Women … Sheikh Omar: The Country of the Two Holy Sanctuaries is Targeted and the Issue of Women Drivers has Ulterior Motives]. *Al-Muslim* website May 23. Accessed August 1, 2013. http://www.almoslim.net/node/146827.

Al-Otaibi, Abdallah bin Bajad. 2010. "Al Ukhwan Al-Muslimounwal Saudia: Al-Hijrawal 'Alaqa" [Muslim Brotherhood and Saudi Arabia: The Relationship of Migration]. In *Al Ikhwan el-Muslimunwal-Salafiyyunfil-Khaleej* [Muslim Brotherhood and the Salafists in the Gulf], edited by Turki Al-Dakheel. Dubai: Al-Misbar Centre for Studies and Research.

Qassem, Abdul Aziz. 2007. *Mukashafat* [Disclosures]. Riyadh: Maktabat Al-Obaykan.

Al-Qudaimy, Nawaf. 2011. *Al Muhafithounwal Islahiyounfil Hala Al-Islamiya Al-Saudia* [The Conservatives and Reformists in the Saudi Islamic Situation]. Beirut: Al-Markaz l-Thakafi l-Arabi.

Saudi Arabia Department of Statistics. 2002. (1422–1423*h*). *Statistical Yearbook*. Al-Riyadh: Department of Statistics.

Saudi Press Agency. 2010. "The Kingdom is Witnessing a Comprehensive Education Renaissance, 9 Million Rials for the King Abdullah Bin Abdul Aziz Public Education Development Project" [in Arabic], *Al-Bilad* September 18.

Shehadeh, Marwan. 2010. *Tahawolat al-Khitab Al-Salafi: Al-Harakat al-Jihadiya – Halat Dirasa (1990–2007)* [Transformation of the Salafist Discourse: Jihadist Movements – A Case Study (1990–2007)]. Beirut: Al-Shabaka al-Arabiyyalil-Abhaathwal Nashr.

Shehadeh, Usama. 2011. "Juhaimanbayna al-Takfeeriyeenwal Salafiyeen." [Juhaiman between Apostasy Accusers and Salafists]. Alghad newspaper website, May 13, 2011. Accessed August 3, 2013. http://www.alghad.com/index.php/article/473550.html.

Al-Sudairy, Tawfik. 2010. *Al-Da'wa* March 21. http://www.aldaawah.com/?p=3110/.

Al-Tarifi, Adel bin Zayd. 2004. "*25 'Aamanala Hadithat al-Haram.*" [25 Years Past the Incident of the Holy Sanctuary]. Al-Riyadh newspaper website. March 10, 2004. Accessed August 3, 2013. http://www.alriyadh.com/2004/03/10/article16480.html.

Al-Thabit, Saeed Muhammad. 2010. "Kissa Wakiyya! Fi Jami'at el-Imam … Touthabbatwa Turadd" [A Factual Story! At the Imam University … Gets Confirmed then Denied]. *Lojainiat* October. Accessed 3 July, 2013. http://lojainiat.com/c-47625.

Al-Thayidi, Mashary. 2005. "Ad'u li Tashkeel Lajna Ulya …" [I Call for the Formation of a Higher Committee to fight Takfiri Ideology and Would Like to Debate Usama bin Laden, Al-Maqdisi and Fares Al Shawil]. *Al-Sharq Al-Awsat* May 15.

Al-Wardi, Hamad. 2006. *Al-Burocratiawal-Tamtheel al-Burocratiwal Takafo' fil Mamlaka Al-Arabia Al-Saudia: Dirasa Tahliliyalil Mukhasasat al-Maliya* [Bureaucracy and Bureaucratic Representation and the Parity of Opportunity in the Kingdom of Saudi Arabia: An Analytical Study of Financial Allocations]. Introduced by Matrouk Al-Faleh, translated by Hana' Maatouq and Dalia Hamdan. (Doctoral Thesis No. 55). Beirut: Centre for Arab Unity Studies (CAUS).

Islamists in power: the case of the Muslim Brotherhood in Egypt

Hesham Al-Awadi

Department of History and International Relations, Faculty of Arts and Sciences, American University of Kuwait, Kuwait City, Kuwait

The article examines the Muslim Brotherhood in power in Egypt, 2012–2013, and how they dealt with the multifaceted challenges. The main argument is that the Brotherhood benefited from their past populist legitimacy to fill the vacuum created by the collapse of the Mubarak regime, but that this legitimacy waned when they did not consolidate this legitimacy with a tangible national achievement. The Brotherhood were unable to count on Egyptians' sympathy for their endurance of rough treatment at the hands of the previous regime over many years, because the 25 January Revolution changed the Egyptian people's expectations and spread knowledge of how to punish rulers who fail to meet these expectations: with sit-ins and street demonstrations. Despite Muhammad Morsi's victory in the presidential elections, and the forceful curtailment of his four-year term by the army, this leading member of the Muslim Brotherhood failed to translate his legal legitimacy into a wider populist legitimacy based on tangible achievements.

No one imagined that the revolution of 25 January 2011 would topple the Hosni Mubarak regime in 18 days and then bring the Muslim Brotherhood into power in Egypt's first free presidential elections in May 2012. Even Mubarak and the Brotherhood themselves could not have expected that a spontaneous, non-politicized, youth-led demonstration could morph into a popular revolution forcing the army to deploy in the streets and impose a curfew, nor that chants of 'Bread, freedom, and human dignity' on 25 January would soon change into the Tunisian slogan of 'The people want to overthrow the regime.' This groundswell of popular protest led to Mubarak stepping down from the presidency on 11 February 2011, after having ruled Egypt for 30 years, with events unfolding so quickly that neither Mubarak nor the Brotherhood was able to keep up, their reactions being tardy and fitful. Even more remarkable was the ousting by the Egyptian military of Muhammad Morsi, Egypt's first elected president, on 3 July 2013, after only one year in office. Despite Morsi's victory in presidential elections, and forceful curtailment of his four-year term by the army, this leading member of the Muslim Brotherhood failed to translate his legal legitimacy to a wider populist legitimacy based on tangible achievements.

During the brief course of the revolution, Mubarak gave speeches on 29 January, 1 February and 10 February offering superficial, piecemeal reforms, suggesting that he was either being intransigent or was actually unaware of what was happening in the streets. Mubarak formed a new government, appointed the 75-year-old veteran head of intelligence Omar Suleiman as vice-president, and promised not to seek a sixth term in the presidential elections slated for September 2012. In his speeches, the president reminded Egyptians of his accomplishments and sacrifices, and the role he played in the October 1973 war with Israel, but his emotion-charged rhetoric was unable to placate the angry demonstrators or stop their revolution. The security forces' heavy-handed attempts to break up the protests, particularly with the bloody assault on Tahrir Square by pro-regime thugs on 2 February 2011 (known as the Battle of the Camel, since some thugs charged into the fight against the protestors on horses and camels), backfired by erasing any remaining faith in the government's promises, and strengthened the demands for Mubarak's resignation. Although everyone knew it was a distortion of a complicated reality, Mubarak steadfastly accused the Brotherhood of being behind the revolution and of responsibility for the deaths of protestors in Tahrir Square.

The Brotherhood and other political movements had been aware that popular discontent was surging in Egypt, with the emergence of protest movements such as the Kifaya (Enough) movement in 2005, the April 6 movement in 2008, and 'We are All Khaled Said' in 2010. From 2005 to 25 January 2011, some 5000 demonstrations took place, not only in Cairo and Alexandria, but also throughout Egypt's 27 governorates. Both the rapid growth of these movements and the sheer number of protests were unprecedented. Most of the demonstrations were comprised primarily of youth and were non-politicized, such as the 'Youth for Change' offshoot of the Kiyafa movement in 2005, which had limited economic and social demands related to higher wages, equal opportunity, social justice, etc. (Zahran 2012, 138–150). With time, these disparate grassroots movements began to join ranks, and their demands came to focus explicitly on political change.

The Brotherhood supported some of these protests, although they did not envision the protest movement leading to Mubarak's downfall, and instead hoped for at most that the government would undertake more reforms. When the Tunisian revolution erupted on 17 December 2010, the Brotherhood issued a statement calling on the Egyptian government to avoid similar protests by making reforms, specifically to end emergency law, hold free and fair parliamentary elections, and to amend the more restrictive constitutional items in the constitution (Articles 5, 76, 77, 88, and 179) (Muslim Brotherhood 2011). As the first demonstrations in Cairo took place on 25 January, the Brotherhood officially refrained from participating, fearing a confrontation with security forces and believing that the results would be limited, although youth members took part on an individual basis, according to Mohammad Al-Qassas, an advocate of Islam and activist.[1] The movement had long since lost hope of any imminent change, and had no clue that the demonstrations would snowball and drastically alter the destinies of both the Mubarak regime and the Brotherhood.

The Brotherhood and the revolution

The 25 January Revolution was a spontaneous, non-religious, unpoliticized mass revolt, which the Brotherhood neither organized nor even participated in initially. The only link between the Brotherhood and the protests was through the youth who were simultaneously Brotherhood members and part of the independent protest movements which had been growing since 2004, and in which they took part on an individual basis. The Brotherhood had distanced themselves from the calls for street protests, fearing that others' participation would be merely symbolic and that the group would find itself targeted directly in the security services' response. The increasing government crackdowns since the mid-1990s had led the Brotherhood to adopt a strategy of 'seeking refuge in society' and avoiding sticking their neck out by leading any protest movements. Rather than stake a claim to lead the protest movements, the Brotherhood preferred to seek to remain indistinguishable from the other opposition groups.

The Brotherhood dismissed the seemingly remote chance that the calls for demonstrations overlapping with Police Day on 25 January 2011 would resonate, and chose to stay on the sidelines as usual. According to Ahmad Rami, a mid-level leader:

> The group believed that the 25 January demonstration would not be a mass event, and that if it participated in full force at the forefront, this would give the demonstration a certain nature, provoke the security forces, and give an excuse to single [the Brotherhood] out and drag their members through the streets without fearing the West and international opinion, which was already prejudiced against Islamists.[2]

This belief is what prompted the Brotherhood to make only a token show of participation, spread out over stages. The Brotherhood assigned some of their more visible members (parliamentarians, journalists, members of the labour syndicate boards, etc.) to take part, without officially approving or ordering other members to do the same. As of 20 January 2011, the Brotherhood posted on its official English website '*MB's Statement on Tunisia's Uprising and the Demands of the Egyptian People*', which said that only days before the revolution, the group had been specifically warned by Mubarak's security forces against joining the demonstration, and chose instead to assert its independence by announcing it would neither require nor forbid its members from demonstrating (Muslim Brotherhood 2011). When the Brotherhood realized belatedly that 25 January was unlike any other previous protest movement, in terms of both numbers (an estimated 20,000 in Tahrir Square) and the diversity among the demonstrators, including a large number of women, it decided to go forward with officially endorsing participation in the demonstrations from 28 January until Mubarak's resignation on 11 February.[3]

The youth

There is no youth division within the Brotherhood organization, but rather a student division coordinating between the central organization and its university student members. This division is overseen by recent graduates in their late 20 s and early 30 s, part of a Brotherhood generation that stands out for its openness towards other ideological currents, stemming from friendly relations with their classmates of varying political affiliations, and which solidified with the anti-regime protest movement starting in 2005. The Brotherhood youth were influenced by the non-violent means used by the more secularist groups to protest government policies, such as strikes, marches and sit-ins.[4] They saw civil disobedience or non-violent resistance as an effective middle ground between violent confrontation with the state and avoiding any activism out of fear of government repression.[5] Some Brotherhood activists received hands-on training on how to organize civil disobedience campaigns and offered their experience to the group's leadership, which replied unenthusiastically. This did not deter the Brotherhood's student division from airing their argument before the Guidance Bureau in 2010 that as the presidential elections scheduled for 2011 approached, the movement should launch a sweeping pro-change campaign called 'New Egypt' utilizing civil disobedience and mass protests – a proposal which was again vetoed by the central leadership. According to Al-Qassas – an activist who helped draft this proposal:

> We offered a clear, written proposal, an integrated plan of action on the national level, mentioning phrases such as civil disobedience, strikes, and revolution. We said that change would be in Mubarak's hands, that genuine change would require a direct confrontation with the regime, and that any indirect confrontations would be of no use, but the Guidance Bureau turned down the proposal, and emphasized that we should be concerned with missionary and educational work, not confrontation, because the Egyptian regime was repressive and clashing with it would be useless.[6]

The gap continued to widen between the two generations of Brotherhood members: a younger generation believing that Egypt was witnessing a growing mass anti-government movement which the Brotherhood should lead or at least play an active role in, and an older, traditionalist, conservative generation resolute in its belief that the regime was still too strong to be shaken by popular discontent and that the Brotherhood should avoid triggering a government crackdown. The leadership's refusal did little to deter younger Brotherhood members from individually joining youth protest movements and becoming active in wide-reaching youth networks, whether on the ground or online.[7] The most prominent groups in this network were the Change Youth Coalition, which called for the 25 January demonstration, then the Revolutionary Youth Coalition, which was formed in Tahrir Square on 25 January, incorporating socialists, liberals and independents (Badawi 2011, 64–65).

Thus, the Brotherhood youth were a step ahead of their leaders, bolder and more ready for change. It is not known how many Brotherhood youth participated as individuals in the first three days of the revolution, but their ranks swelled when the organization officially endorsed the protests from 28 January onwards. The Brotherhood youth played a very prominent role in the 2 February Battle of the Camel, mounting a courageous defence of the revolutionaries against the assault launched by pro-regime thugs. Thousands of Brotherhood youth also poured into Tahrir Square from other governorates, bolstering the morale of the protestors and putting their management skills to use in organizing the protestors. However, this did not heal the rift between the youth and their leaders.

The disagreements can be divided into two types: one related to the Brotherhood's stance towards the 25 January Revolution, and another, more far-reaching in its implications, related to the youth's status within the organization. There was a widespread impression among young members that the leadership did not rise to the occasion during the revolution, with overly cautious, plodding decisions and demands that were far too modest.[8] A case could be made for its traditional organizational principle of 'compliance and obedience' while living under dictatorial regimes, but the youth-led revolution set the stage for political openness, which in the youth's view required reshaping its organizational model to allow for dialogue between the leadership and the youth. There was a growing feeling that youth were marginalized within the movement, and that the leadership, specifically the Guidance Bureau and the Shura Council, was deaf to their voices, despite the fact that it had been the youth who brought about political change in Egypt.

> There are no representatives for youth, students, women, or professionals within the Guidance Bureau or the Shura Council, and the organisational structure needs to be

> developed, even if this means the organisation expanding the number of Shura Council members so that it includes these marginalised groups

said Al-Qassas.[9] According to the same source, by individual initiative the Brotherhood youth held an internal conference with about 400 members who demanded that organizational promotions be based on competence, and emphasized the importance of involving youth and women in the decision-making process. A second internal conference was held, this time sponsored by the organization, in which the youth also called for modernizing both the organizational structure and decision-making process, while evolving from a secretive into an open organization (Abdul-Latif 2013, 231–232). The Brotherhood responded with promises to make changes and put Khairat El-Shater in charge of instituting reforms, but there have yet to be any changes since 2011. Subsequent defections from the organization by frustrated members have included not only revolutionary youth, but also some upper-level leaders.

Islamists' defections

During and shortly after the revolution, several well-known, veteran leaders in the Muslim Brotherhood were either dismissed or stepped down. Defections are hardly a new phenomenon, and have been taking place since the days of the movement's founder, Hassan El-Banna, but carried special significance after the revolution. The rapid unfolding of events in late January and early February 2011 forced the leadership to make difficult choices that were bound to be unpopular with some of its members. With the Mubarak era, which had tended to unify the Brotherhood ranks in opposition to the government, now over, and because the organizational leadership has limited conflict management skills and has historically relied instead on 'compliance and obedience', there was a series of high-level defections. Shura Council member Ibrahim El-Zaafrani stepped down in April 2011, citing the lack of any meaningful reforms since the revolution, followed by Kamal El-Halbawi in March 2012 in protest of the Brotherhood's decision to field a candidate in the presidential elections, while Abdel Moneim Aboul Futouh and Mohammed Habib quit the Guidance Bureau (*Al-Misriyuun* 2012). Regardless of the details, the overriding reason for resignations was dissatisfaction with the way in which the organization was being run.

In an interview with the author, Aboul Futouh declared that he had resigned to protest the Brotherhood's initial decision not to field a presidential candidate, while announcing his own candidacy as an independent.[10] However, the deeper reasons originated more than ten years previously, when he began to become disillusioned with the group's administration.

> When I left prison in 2000, I found that the group was being run with an exclusionary organisational mentality. Clashes began to take place between myself and the administration which has been in place since that time. I disagreed with the leadership about two key issues: the first was that I wanted the group to legalise itself, which the leadership did not want. The second was for the group to separate between its work in party politics and its overall religious missionary work, a need which the leadership rejected.

Aboul Futouh had suffered at the hands of the Mubarak regime, having been arrested and imprisoned several times since the 1990s on charges of belonging to an illegal organization, and he believed that the only way for the Brotherhood to avoid these charges was to seek legal status as a civil society association. The senior leadership argued that inclusion under the Associations Law would belittle the Brotherhood's weight in society, seeing the organization as more comprehensive and larger than a mere association. Aboul Futouh also criticized the group's function in party politics and vying for power.

Mohammed Habib, another veteran leader in the Guidance Bureau and former Deputy supreme guide, who chose to resign in July 2011, did so protesting the lack of consultation in the decision-making process within the organization, and the tyrannical rule of a small minority. Despite the fact that Habib himself was a prominent member of the Guidance Bureau, he had become marginalized within the bureau controlling the decision-making process. Habib was particularly shocked by a powerful faction within the Guidance Bureau determining who should succeed the former Supreme Guide Mehdi Akef, before the entire Guidance Bureau met officially to choose the supreme guide, meaning that the internal election process was only a formality. Habib also cited other authoritarian decisions such as the group agreeing to join negotiations with Mubarak's Vice-President Omar Suleiman during the revolution to discuss the constitutional amendments drafted by the army in February 2011.

Undoubtedly, the defections of leaders such as Habib, Aboul Futuoh, El-Zaafrani and others had an impact, but the effectiveness of the movement as a whole was not significantly changed. Its strict disciplinary values remained in place, with a spiritual and ideological conviction that the organization has divine support, and so its destiny is not reliant on individuals, regardless of the celebrity status they enjoy. Instead, the departure of reformist and more liberal leaders has worked to consolidate the influence of the group's traditionalist, conservative wing, while the exit of a number of ambitious, intelligent youth will deprive the organization of the newer generation's abilities to modernize the movement.

Political party

The transitional period in which the army was in power after Mubarak's resignation led to amendments to the political parties law, allowing the Brotherhood to form the Freedom and Justice Party (FJP) in June 2011. The FJP won a plurality of the seats in parliament (216 out of 508) in the People's Assembly elections later that year, qualifying the FJP Secretary-General Saad El-Katatni to become Speaker of the People's Assembly in an unprecedented development. There are many reasons for the Brotherhood's sweeping victory, including the fact that the post-revolutionary elections were free and fair compared with those under Mubarak, particularly the 2010 elections which had been boycotted by the opposition. With the National Democratic Party out of the picture, the Brotherhood's high level of organization allowed them to mobilize more quickly than their rivals, some of whom were hampered by the public mistrust of the traditional political parties, in addition to the fact that the Brotherhood already enjoyed broad popularity thanks to their provision of social services (Rabia 2012, 369–379). The People's Assembly was, however, dissolved by a constitutional court ruling in 2012, voiding the election laws as having been biased towards party candidates over independent candidates.

The FJP's platform kept Sharia as a point of reference, while asserting its belief in democracy, an elected president and the *umma*, or Islamic community, as the source of authority (Rabia 2011a, 27–28). The FJP's stated goals are political reform, improving the economy, enhancing security and Egypt reclaiming its pioneering role. Party membership is open to all Egyptians, including Coptic Christians (such as Rafiq Habib, who became the FJP's vice-president in June 2011). The FJP provided legal cover for the

Muslim Brotherhood, since all members of the latter organization (men and women) with a membership card in the party could if necessary avoid the traditional charge of 'membership in a banned group'.

The establishment of the FJP – the first time in the Brotherhood's existence since 1928 that they were allowed to found a political party – set off a heated internal debate. Abdel Moneim Abul Futouh argued that this betrayed the intentions of founder Hassan El-Banna, who had refused to mix religious missionary advocacy with party politics: 'The freedom to form parties in Egypt was guaranteed in the 1930s, and El-Banna could have formed a political party for the Brotherhood, but he did not do so.'[11] Abul Futouh questioned the leadership's claims that the Brotherhood and the FJP were organizationally autonomous, stating his belief that the FJP was no more than a front organization, and that the Guidance Bureau was calling the shots behind the scenes. Top FJP leader Essam El-Aryan acknowledged the existence of a joint committee between the Brotherhood and the FJP to coordinate decisions related to the state, and that the group's leadership was naming the leadership of the FJP on an interim basis until complete separation between the two entities was a reality.[12] The movement bans its members from joining any party other than the FJP with the threat of expulsion, meaning that any autonomy is incomplete. In line with other analysts, Diaa Rashwan, a prominent Egyptian journalist, voiced his doubts as to whether the Brotherhood's political party experiment would evolve as the Islamist parties in Jordan, Morocco and Turkey did, such that the party's organizational relationship with the movement which created it is severed.[13]

The Morsi regime

Instead of dying down with the dismantling of the Mubarak regime, popular discontent continued unabated and even grew through the beginning of Mohammed Morsi's rule, with 2012 alone witnessing some 558 demonstrations, 514 strikes and 500 sit-ins (Egyptian Center for Social and Economic Rights 2012).[14] But the most serious were the mass demonstrations on 30 June 2013 calling for Morsi's resignation, on the back of which, on 3 July, the army forced the elected president out of office, in what amounted to a military coup. Morsi had won the first free presidential elections, albeit by only a narrow margin, over his opponent Ahmed Shafiq, the last prime minister under Mubarak, with only 51.7% of the vote. Yet, only a few months after Morsi came to power, disappointed by his performance the opposition began to call for the army to step in and hold new (early) elections.

The Brotherhood's decision to take part in the 2012 presidential elections was a surprise, coming after explicit statements that they would not do so.[15] Morsi was not the group's first choice, but was the backup candidate derisively referred to as the 'spare tire' after Khairat El-Shater's candidacy was overturned by the Higher Elections Board. Morsi does not possess El-Shater's charisma, but does have substantial experience accumulated since joining the Brotherhood in 1978 and its political department in 1992. Morsi served in the People's Assembly in 2000, was in charge of the organization's political affairs under former Supreme Guide Ma'moun El-Hudeibi, was a member of both the Guidance Bureau and the Shura Council, and became president of the FJP in 2011. Morsi's electoral victory can be attributed not only to his personal abilities of course, but also to the Brotherhood's mobilizational competence.

A comprehensive, detailed evaluation of Morsi's performance is difficult as it was short-lived and forcefully interrupted. However, overall it was rated as unsatisfactory, particularly in tackling the challenges of the economy and security. Morsi inherited a struggling economy, but this does not exempt him from responsibility for the continued rise in unemployment and inflation in Egypt. The president was relying on securing a US$4.8 billion loan from The World Bank, which would saddle his government with more debts without even sufficing to cover the budget deficit.[16] His challenge was to generate economic growth benefiting the lower and middle classes (33% of the people), if he wanted to establish genuine popular legitimacy.[17] The deteriorating security situation can be traced to the mutual mistrust between the public and the security services since Mubarak's rule, the lack of political and security coordination, and the existence of militias within the Ministry of Interior loyal to Mubarak-era leaders. The opposition came broadly to the assessment that the Brotherhood's leadership – the supreme guide and the Guidance Bureau – had managed to attain control of the system, and was hard at work 'Brotherising the state'.[18] This belief led to demonstrations in March 2013 in front of the Brotherhood's headquarters in the Muqattam district of Cairo that set off bloody clashes which left ten dead and more than 200 injured.

Morsi was faced by challenges too overwhelming for his limited political experience. Regionally, there was the diminishing of Egypt's traditional clout as non-Arab countries like Iran and Turkey and smaller Gulf countries such as Qatar expanded their influence, and the struggle to balance relations with Israel (in keeping with the Camp David Accords) and the Brotherhood's ideological ally Hamas. Domestically, Morsi failed to deal with the mounting economic challenges that include the gaping budget deficit, high unemployment, inflation outpacing wage growth, street children (around 3 million), crime, and entrenched holdouts from the Mubarak regime in key institutions such as the Ministry of Interior and the army. More importantly, Morsi failed to convert his legal legitimacy into broader basis of popular legitimacy and antagonized the opposition and the masses by his unpopular policies, such as tightened state media controls and, more disturbingly, his November 2012 constitutional declaration that granted him unlimited powers.

Though their ascendancy was short-lived, during that time it became clear to the Muslim Brotherhood that the practical requirements and dynamics of being in power are very different from the dynamics of opposition, and that sharp disagreements and confusion among Islamists once in power is not unprecedented – it happened in Sudan in the 1990s and in Tunisia after the Arab Spring.[19] Moreover, Egypt's domestic and foreign situation has imposed constraints on Morsi very different from those faced when the Brotherhood was in the opposition from the 1980s.

The tanzim

The organization or the *tanzim* of the Muslim Brotherhood is a central concept and remains a main source of the movement's power. When I visited Egypt after the revolution to research this article, I sought a meeting with Mahmoud Ezzat to investigate the developments that had taken place in the Brotherhood's organization since I last wrote about the significance of tanzim over eight years ago (Al-Awadi 2004, 111–139). Ezzat's official position is the Deputy supreme guide, and he is known as the Brotherhood's organizational theorist. He joined the movement in 1962 as an 18-year-old student in the Faculty of Medicine, and was jailed under both Nasser and Mubarak: ten years in prison after Nasser's mass arrests of Brotherhood members in 1965, and five years after Mubarak's military trials in 1995. I met Ezzat in his office at one of the Brotherhood's charity hospitals in Cairo to discuss recent developments in the Brotherhood's organizational structure.

The Brotherhood's organization is characterized by a complex hierarchy starting at the lowest level, that of the 'family', and ending at the top with the Guidance Bureau. None of the Brotherhood likes to speculate on the total number of members, but estimates range from 100,000 to 500,000 (Tammam 2012, 35). The average size of a Brotherhood 'family' is five people, headed by a captain, who meet on a weekly basis and pay monthly dues calculated as a fixed percentage of a member's income. The 'section' is made up of several families in a certain geographical region within one of Egypt's 27 governorates, and is the smallest administrative unit at the governorate level. The sections elect a Shura Council for each governorate, which consists on average of roughly 30 people, but varying according the governorate size, and represents all the governorate's members at the national level. Alongside the Shura Councils, in each governorate there are multiple administrative bureaus managing local organizational affairs, such as the offices for students, missionary work, parliament, etc. Each governorate's Shura Council elects members to represent their governorate at the national Shura Council, which is the Brotherhood's legislative body for Egypt. The national Shura Council has about 118 members, representing all the governorates, serving a maximum of two six-year terms. The Shura Council in turn elects 17 of its own members to comprise the Guidance Bureau, which is the most powerful body in the organization, and is equivalent to its executive branch.[20]

The Guidance Bureau is headed by the supreme guide. The Brotherhood have had eight supreme guides since the group was founded in 1928, who up through the fourth supreme guide, Hamed Abu Al-Nasr (1986–1996), were elected for life. Under the fifth incumbent, Mustafa Mashour (1996–2002), the supreme guide's term became six years, with a 12-year term limit. Mehdi Akef (born in 1928) was then the first supreme guide to not even seek a second term.[21] Under Mohammed Badie (2010–present), the Brotherhood were wracked by controversy following Morsi's election to the presidency of Egypt, and questions were raised over the nature of the relationship between the Egyptian president and the supreme guide.[22] At the very least, the balance of power between the two remains ambiguous and unresolved.

The relationship between the Guidance Bureau and the Shura Council within the Brotherhood's organization is equally opaque. Although the resolutions passed by the Shura Council are theoretically binding for the Guidance Bureau, since the Shura Council is the legislative body, in practice the Guidance Bureau carries much more weight. The supreme guide, who is head of the Guidance Bureau, has enjoyed historical legitimacy since the days of Hassan El-Banna, and consequently has substantial moral authority over the other organization members, including the members of the Shura Council. The Brotherhood's bylaws include clauses consolidating the Guidance Bureau's power, such as giving it the right to appoint 15 members of the otherwise elected Shura Council, and the stipulation that all Guidance Bureau members concurrently serve in the Shura Council as full voting members, besides the fact that the supreme guide himself is head of the Shura Council. Even more significantly, the Guidance Bureau alone was setting the organization's policies for years without the Shura Council's input, when the latter was refraining from meeting due to frequent arrests under President Mubarak. Mohammed Habib, a former Brotherhood leader, said:

> The last time the group's Shura Council met was in January 1995, and it did not meet again after that until after the revolution, on 10 February 2011, the reason being the

> security raids and the fact that, by meeting, members of the Shura Council found themselves on trial by military tribunal. The Shura Council members [therefore] no longer met, and its powers practically *de facto* moved to the Guidance Bureau, which damaged the culture of participation and turned the group into a monolith, moving wherever the leadership moved, without discussion.[23]

The dominance of the Guidance Council over the Shura Council accompanied another equally significant development, namely what is believed to be the attainment of greater influence by hardline 'Qutbists' at the expense of 'moderates' within the Guidance Bureau. The term 'Qutbists' has become common parlance when referring to Brotherhood leaders heavily influenced by the ideas of Sayyid Qutb, and who tend to be obsessed with maintaining a strictly hierarchical organizational culture and are sticklers for following regulations and upholding the principle of 'compliance and obedience'. The Qutbists are also called 'the 1965 Organisation' after a secret organization formed by some Brotherhood members based on Qutb's ideas, whether with or without the approval of the supreme guide at the time, Hassan Al-Hudaibi (1951–1973). The 1965 Organisation was known for shutting itself off from society and the government, while possessing a sense of moral superiority over others, believing themselves to be what Qutb (2009), in his groundbreaking work *Landmarks*, called 'the vanguard of believers'. The Qutbists carry more weight than the moderates in the Guidance Bureau, particularly after the departure of two leading moderates, Abdel Moneim Abul Futouh and Mohammed Habib. According to Abul Futouh, the 1965 Organisation is now effectively in charge, and impeding the Brotherhood's evolution:

> Those present now in the Guidance Council are Sayyid Qutb's pupils, and I do not disagree with most of Qutb's ideas, but he had opinions and ideas which do represent neither Imam [Hassan] Al-Banna nor the Brotherhood's school, and so the 1965 Organisation was like a foreign body when it entered the Muslim Brotherhood's body, becoming tantamount to an organisation within an organisation, impeding the evolution of the group as a whole.[24]

According to Mohammed Habeeb,[25] the Qutbists include Supreme Guide Mohammed Badie, Mohammed Ezzat and disqualified presidential candidate Khairat El-Shater. There are several challenges facing the organization. These include: its duelling factions; the question of who is in control of both the decision-making process and decision-making itself; establishing a separation between the Guidance Bureau and the Shura Council as exists in Muslim Brotherhood organizations in other Arab countries; giving better representation in the Guidance Bureau and Shura Council to the range of demographic groups within the Brotherhood, most importantly youth and women (there being no women on the Guidance Bureau or the Shura Council); and calls to amend restrictive regulations, once necessitated by having to operate under a ban during dictatorship, once that was removed.[26]

The greatest challenge, however, that will determine how much populist legitimacy the movement can attain, lies in transforming its trademark culture of secrecy – which was justified under Nasser, Sadat and Mubarak when the Brotherhood were driven underground – into a culture of transparency and openness more appropriate for an Arab Spring generation that no longer trusts in clandestine organizations. The same applies for the international Muslim Brotherhood organization as a whole, given the ascent of the Brotherhood not only in Egypt, but also that of the Muslim Brotherhood-inspired al-Nahda Party in Tunisia, and fears that the organization is plotting against the ruling regimes in the Persian Gulf (Pargeter 2010, 96–132).

Conclusion

Following the revolution the Muslim Brotherhood reclaimed their legal legitimacy, missing since the group was formally dissolved by Nasser in 1954. In March 2013, the Brotherhood officially registered as a civil society association under the Mubarak-era Civil Association Law. Prior to that the Brotherhood had refused to legalize their status through such means for a number of reasons: they argued that a civil association was too narrow a category for their comprehensive movement, since it was involved in politics as well; and under Mubarak they were understandably hesitant about coming out into the open and exposing themselves to a future crackdown, with their funds overseen by the Ministry of Social Affairs made vulnerable to confiscation. But with the Brotherhood's rise to power, the group realized that its destiny was in its own hands, and legalization was more of a foregone conclusion than a sudden break in policy or historical achievement. Once no longer haunted by their lack of legal legitimacy as in the past, after coming to power the Brotherhood then began to worry about their endangered popularity.

The debate in Egypt is now about the Islamists' track record in power, and not their legal legitimacy per se (though that too may be denied them again). While the Brotherhood's social performance in the 1980s in the trade unions, student unions and neighbourhoods was certainly impressive, generating public enthusiasm for continued Brotherhood rule has certainly waned. While spending decades underground under authoritarian (Nasser) and semi-authoritarian (Sadat and Mubarak) regimes, the movement did not fully help develop democratic mechanisms, neither did it convert its legal legitimacy into populist legitimacy based on performance.

While the Mubarak regime may have fallen, the collapse of a semi-authoritarian regime should not be understand automatically to entail a blooming of democracy. The real challenge before Morsi was not whether he was able to achieve full democracy under his short-lived term; instead, it was whether he was able to put the building blocks in place to create a somewhat democratic system, able to continue evolving after his departure. Most challenging for Morsiwas to re-establish a base of popular support and thence legitimacy by making tangible economic and social achievements, which did not occur. Whether one likes it or not, Egyptians are still in a revolutionary mood, and are impatient to see the change for which they paid such a dear price, and accordingly are being very strict in judging their post-Mubarak rulers. And the anti-Morsi demonstrations on 30 June that led to Morsi's ousting after only one year in power were a vivid manifestation of that Egyptian mood.

Notes

1. Interview between Mohammad Al-Qassas and the author in Cairo, 10 September 2012.
2. Interview between Ahmad Rami and the author in Cairo, 9 September 2012.
3. Various publications have chronicled the revolution, including Rabia (2011b) and Al-Munawi (2012). For the Brotherhood's attitude towards the revolution, see Abdul-Latif (2013), 218–256.
4. By the Brotherhood youth, I am referring to those under the age of 35 years who comprise an estimated 35–50% of the organization, or 210,000–245,000 members based on estimates of the Brotherhood's overall size as 600,000–700,000 (Martini, Kaye, and York 2012, 9–10).
5. Reference is being made here to the same personal interview with Ahmad Rami in Cairo, 9 September 2012.
6. Interview with Al-Qassas.

7. The youth used their familiarity with the internet to create websites and blogs criticizing the police state, with the Facebook page 'We are All Khaled Said' becoming very popular and being the first website to call for protests on 25 January 2011. The killing of Khaled Said, aged 27, by plainclothes police outside an Alexandria internet café set off a furious reaction that began to break down the Egyptians' longstanding fear of the security forces. For more on the role of this Facebook page in the revolution, see Majdi (2011).
8. While the youth were perfectly clear about their opinion that the revolution should continue until the Mubarak regime fell, the leadership was willing to come to a mutual understanding with the government to achieve political gains. The senior leadership gave a green light to negotiate with Mubarak's Vice-President and intelligence chief Omar Suleiman over withdrawing its youth from the demonstrations in exchange for the state recognizing the Brotherhood's legitimacy, over the indignant protests of the Brotherhood's youth themselves, who refused any withdrawal from the streets.
9. Interview with Al-Qassas.
10. Interview between Aboul Futouh and the author in Cairo, 11 September 2012,
11. Interview with Abul Futouh.
12. Interview between Essam El-Aryan and the author in Cairo, 10 September 2012.
13. Interview between Diaa Rashwan and the author in Cairo, 12 September 2012.
14. This figure is separate from the protests and violence that wracked Port Said that year.
15. The Brotherhood's statement that they would not field a presidential candidate was made on 5 February 2011: http://www.ikhwanonline.com/Article.aspx?artid=78757&secid=212. Accessed June 22, 2013. The group decided to participate as a result of the existence of what it labelled a threat to the revolution, democratization and the transfer of power to a civilian government in a reference to their rejection of the military maintaining power. See the Brotherhood's statement of 31 March 2012: http://www.shorouknews.com/mobile/news/view.aspx?cdate=31032012&id=01c9d3c1-3242-422d-af01-fd857ff13530. Accessed June 23, 2013.
16. Egypt's foreign debt stood at roughly US$35 billion in early 2013, its domestic public debt totalled another 962.3 billion Egyptian pounds, and the payments to service the foreign and domestic debt totalled roughly 210.9 billion Egyptian pounds (110 billion in interest and 100.1 billion to repay the principal). In the first six months of his rule Morsi borrowed roughly 112 billion Egyptian pounds, which made analysts speculate that if he continued to borrow at this breakneck rate in his term he would have borrowed more than the Mubarak regime did over 30 years (*Al-Quds Al-Arabi*, 22 March 2013). (1 Egyptian pound = $0.14516.)
17. Among the proposed economic reform measures were tax reform to increase taxes on the wealthy, on bank interest, and on oil and gas companies according to hydrocarbon prices; in addition to reforming the sales tax collection system to reduce tax evasion or non-payment (there is an estimated 63 billion Egyptian pounds due from high-income taxpayers who are late in making the payment) (*Al-Quds Al-Arabi*, 22 March 2013).
18. After coming to power, Morsi chose Brotherhood loyalists to fill the positions of eight ministers, five governors and 13 advisors to the governors (*Al-Masri Al-Yaum*, 14 February 2013).
19. In Sudan, the nature of the relationship between the party's Secretary-General Hassan Al-Turabi and Omar Al-Bashir was changed when the latter became head of government, as was the means of managing state policy. In Tunisia, Nahda Party Secretary-General Hamad Al-Jibali and Nahda leader Rashed Al-Ghannouchi fell out over how inclusive to be towards the secularist parties and whether to allow them to join the ruling coalition.
20. All this is according to Mahmoud Ezzat in a interview with the author in Cairo, 10 September 2013.
21. According to Akef: 'I made it conditional for the group that I would step down when I turned 80, because a person's performance changes after the age of 80, and I believe that the supreme guide should not be above the age of 70'; personal interview with Mehdi Akef in Cairo, 8 September 2012.
22. When I asked Akef, former supreme guide (2004–2010), who was more powerful, Morsi or Badie, he said: 'Definitely Morsi, because he's the head of state, and the supreme guide is part of the Egyptian state, and this is clear to both Morsi and Badie'; personal interview with Akef.

23. Interview between Mohammed Habib and the author in Cairo, 12 September 2012.
24. Interview with Abul Futouh.
25. Interview with Mohammed Habib.
26. Khairat El-Shater is known to be in charge of structural development, and sweeping changes had been promised in the wake of the revolution, but more than a year after the Brotherhood came to power, there were virtually no changes.

References

Abdul-Latif, Omayma. 2013. "Al-Islamiyuunwa al-thawra" [Islamists and the Revolution]. In *Al-thawra al-misriyya: al-dawafi' wal-ittijahatwal-tahaddiyat* [The Egyptian Revolution: Motives, Trends and Challenges]. Beirut: Arab Center for Research and Policy Studies.

Al-Awadi, Hesham. 2004. *In Pursuit of Legitimacy: The Muslim Brothers and Mubarak 1982–2000*. London: I. B. Tauris.

Badawi, Mohammed. 2011. "25 and 28 yanayir ... al-tariqila al-tahrir" [25 and 28 January ... the road to Tahrir]. In *Yawmiyat al-thawra al-misriyayanaayir 2011* [Diaries of the January 2011 Egyptian Revolution], edited by Ahmed Hussein, 64–65. Beirut: Arab Scientific Publ.

Egyptian Center for Social and Economic Rights. 2012. *2012 Report*. Cairo: Egyptian Center for Social and Economic Rights.

Majdi, Amr. 2011. "Kulluna Khalid Sa'id, shahidyarhalwasha'byab'ath" [We are all Khaled Said: a martyr passes away and a people is resurrected]. In *Yawmiyat al-thawra al-misriyayanaayir 2011* [Diaries of the January 2011 Egyptian Revolution], edited by Ahmed Hussein, 39–61. Beirut: Arab Scientific Publ.

Martini, Jeffrey, Dalia Kaye, and Erin York. 2012. *The Muslim Brotherhood Youth: Generational Divides and Implications for US Engagement*. Santa Monica, CA: RAND.

Al-Misriyuun. 2012. "*Ashhar al-inshiqaqat fi tarikhjama'at al-ikhwan al-muslimin*" [The Most Famous Defections in the History of the Muslim Brotherhood's Organization]. *Al-Misriyuun (Cairo)*, 8 May.

Al-Munawi, Abdul-Latif. 2012. *Al-ayyam al-akhira li-nidhammubarak, 18 yawm* [The Final 18 Days of the Mubarak Regime]. Cairo: Lebanese–Egyptian Publ. House.

Muslim Brotherhood. 2011a. *MB's Statement on Tunisia's Uprising and the Demands of the Egyptian People*'. January 20. www.ikhwanweb.com/article.php?id=27890. Accessed September 11, 2013.

Pargeter, Alison. 2010. *The Muslim Brotherhood: The Burden of Tradition*. London: Saqi.

Rabia, Amr Hashim. 2011a. *Al-ikhwanwa al-barlaman: dirasa fi al-fikrwa al-suluk* [The Brotherhood and Parliament: A Study of Ideology and Behavior]. Cairo: Al-Ahram Center for Political and Strategic Studies.

Rabia, Amr Hashim, ed. 2011b. *Thawra 25 yanayir: Qira'a Awaliya wa Ru'iya Mustaqilla* [The 25 January Revolution: An Initial Analysis and Independent Vision]. Cairo: Al-Ahram Center for Political and Strategic Studies.

Rabia, Amr Hashim, ed. 2012. *Intikhabat Majlis al-Sha'b 2011–2012* [The 2011–2012 People's Assembly Elections]. Cairo: Markaz al dirassaat al Siyassiyya wal Strateegiyya - Al Ahram.

Tammam, Hussam. 2012. *Al-ikhwan al-muslimun: Sanawat ma Qabla al-Thawra* [The Muslim Brotherhood: The Years before the Revolution]. Cairo: Dar Al-Shurouq.

Qutb, Sayyid. 2009. *Landmarks on the Pathway*. Beirut: Mu'assassat al-Rissalah al-Alamiyyah.

Zahran, Jamal Ali. 2012. "'*Al-Ihtijajat al-Manatiqiyya wa 'alaqatuha bil-Markaz Ibban al Thawra* 25 yanayir fi Misr" [Regional protests and their relationship with the center during the Egyptian 25 January Revolution]. In *al-Thawra al-misriyya: al-dawafi' wa al-ittijahatwa al-tahaddiyat* [The Egyptian Revolution: Motives, Orientations, and Challenges], by multiple authors. Qatar: Arab Center for Research and Policy Studies.

The relationship between religion and the state: the institution of 'Commandment of the Faithful' in Morocco†

Ahmed Al Khamlichi

Dar Al-Hadith Al-Hasaniyyeh, Ministry of Endowments and Religious Affairs, Rabat, Morocco

The term '*Amir al-Mou'mineen*' (Commander of the Faithful) and 'caliph' were first bestowed on Omar Bin al-Khattab who became the successor of the Prophet (Peace be upon him) two-and-a-half years after he passed away. By virtue of the political and religious connotations of the term, the title conveyed overarching political authority – a kind of absolute power. The notion of Commander of the Faithful facilitated oppression of those who held different views, directly or indirectly, through employing *fatawa*, that is religious interpretations and edicts, in addition to mobilizing religious followers and devotees. This excess of political power is based on the definition of *Imarat al-Mu'mineen* (Commandment of the Faithful) or *the Caliphate* common in religious jurisprudence. This definition was coined by Ibn Khaldoun, and may be translated as: 'making people abide by the view of Shar (the Law of God in Islam) regarding their temporal and afterlife interests'. Morocco has been no different from the rest of the Islamic world over the centuries, and now two distinct phenomena are apparent. First, the emergence of different groups, each with its own ideology and claims to be defending religion and pursuing its implementation. Such groups consider all other ways of thinking as apostasy that must be eliminated; while juxtaposed to them, there exist intellectual currents calling for the continued separation of religion and the state and its laws. During the past two decades this phenomenon has led to tragic situations in a considerable number of Islamic states, whose prospects now seem very gloomy. Second, a tight regulation of state institutions, together with constitutional guarantees of individual rights and freedoms, can prevent the manipulation of the state in the name of religion, and its use for tyranny and the oppression of individuals and minorities, be it in the name of Commandment of the Faithful or any other term. It seems that Morocco is aware of the power of these two phenomena, especially after it faced social unrest in 1992 and 2001, which almost destroyed its stability.

Introduction

I have been asked to prepare a research paper addressing the relationship between religion and the state in Morocco as embodied in the central foundation of the ruling

---

†This paper was originally presented in the Joint Symposium on 'Religion and State in the Arab World' convened by the Center for Arab Unity Studies and the Swedish Institute – Alexandria in Hammamet, Tunisia, 15–17 October 2012.

regime, the 'Commandment of the Faithful',[1] its role in the management of religious affairs, and the extent of identification or differentiation under that regime between temporal and religious authority – a topic which is steeped in ambiguity and confusion arising from the divergence between theory and practice.

Theory still confers upon the Commandment of the Faithful an indicative load that comes close to rendering it entirely contradictory to the concept of a modern state and its institutions. Yet, in practice – in the case of Morocco at least – it does not seem to present an obstacle to building a civil state based on the principle that the *Umma* (nation) is the authoritative reference in administering the public affairs of the state, whilst ensuring the basic rights of individuals and equality between them, regardless of sex, colour, ethnicity or creed.

'The Princedom of the Believers' in history and in theory

History tells us that the first ruler to be called 'Commander of the Faithful' was Omar Bin Al-Khattab (May God be pleased with him). Its connotation was no different from that of the term 'caliph' (successor), or the Caliph of God's Messenger (the Prophet), which was the title of Omar's predecessor, Abu Bakr (May God be pleased with him). So, how were the religious and political connotations of these two terms formed, especially after the advent of hereditary rule, before the end of the first half of the Hijri century? This concept relates to the inauguration of the caliph or the 'Commander of the Faithful' and to his role, obedience and area of competence.

Inauguration

If the inauguration and appointment of the caliph was made through a 'Pledge of Allegiance' (Ibn Khaldoun 2005, 356–357; Abu Yousuf 1987, 3)[2] by the nation or by the people of power and authority, it was usually quickly attributed to the will of God. For example, it is reported that Abu Yousuf addressed Haroun Al-Rasheed saying:

> O, Prince of the Believers, God – praise be to Him – has installed you in a great office; its reward is the greatest reward, and its punishment is the greatest punishment. God has assigned you to be in charge of the interests of the Nation. Therefore, you are working day and night for the interests of the masses to whom God has made you a guardian, whom He has left with you as a trust, and He has put you to the test regarding the way you manage them, and assigned you to be in charge of their interests.
>
> (Abu Yousuf 1987, 5)

Historical sources abound with such statements as well as with others with clearer indications attributing the appointment of the caliph to God.

It was common practice before and after the advent of Islam, and among Muslims and others, to make a connection between the appointment of a caliph and God's will. It seems that the adoption of this attitude by most Muslim scholars was facilitated by the culture inherited by the peoples who entered into Islam, as well as by the doctrine that attributes all acts of man to God (May He be Glorified and Exalted), in addition to the desire of the ruling caliph for a hereditary succession.

The role

Al-Mawardi summarizes the role of the Commander of the Faithful by stating that the 'Imamate (leadership)[3] is there as a successor to prophecy in guarding religion and administering everyday life' (Al-Mawardi 1982, 5).[4] Daily activities should be regulated in accordance with the teachings of religion, i.e. in order to implement the written religious guidelines, and should never contradict these commandments. Al-Mawardi adds that the imam or the Commander of the Faithful, having received the pledge of allegiance, should first of all:

> safeguard the religion with its established principles and as collectively agreed by the *Umma*'s forefathers. And if a contriver appeared or if a suspected person went astray, he would explain the evidence to him, show him the righteous way and would make him aware of his duties and the extent of his obligations so that religion remains guarded against any defect and the *Umma* immune to faults.
>
> (Al-Mawardi 1982, 15)[5]

Therefore, the job of the President of the Islamic state does not go beyond watching over religion and the application of its provisions as set forth or derived from its stipulations in all fields concerning the lives of individuals and the *Umma*'s interests.

Obedience

Islamic scholars unanimously agree that the duty of obedience is obligatory upon the *Umma*, arguing that obedience to the Prophet is indisputable and the Holy Quran associates obedience to the Prophet with obedience to God, confirming that 'He who obeys the Prophet obeys God' (Surat Al-Nisa', verse 80). Thus, since obedience to the Prophet is obligatory, His successor also deserves obedience, not only by way of succession and deputyship, but also according to these injunctions from the Holy Quran: 'O, ye who believe! Obey Allah, and obey the Messenger, and those charged with authority among you' (Surat al-Nissa, verse 59),[6] and from the Hadiths (Sayings) attributed to the Prophet (PBUH) that expressly decree that the prince or imam should be obeyed and which couple that to the obedience and disobedience of God and the Prophet (Abu Yousuf 1987, 9).[7]

The scope of obedience includes, on the one hand, the imam's decisions concerning all matters relating to both the individual and society as a whole, noting that all details of these affairs are governed by the Islamic Sharia and that the application of the teachings of the Sharia is entrusted to him; and every decision related to the management of the situations of the individuals and the groups shall be in accordance with the Sharia from which none of the acts of those who are obligated (to give worship) deviates.

On the other hand, obedience is also due to the imam or prince of the believers, in his capacity as the 'successor' of God's Messenger (*Salla Allahu Alayhi Wasallam*), and is decreed in the Holy Quran as well as in the Hadiths of the Prophet. Obedience to whatever he decrees becomes imperative, because he is one who applies the Sharia teachings and may give discretionary judgments where no stipulation is available.

Does obedience have limits?

It is not possible to give a definitive answer to this question, for two reasons, namely:

- There is a jurisprudential difference on this matter. One view requires absolute obedience on the basis of the traditional quotation 'even if he seized the money and whipped the backs', as patient endurance in the face of an unjust tyrant is considered less harmful than arousing commotion by protesting against him.

Meanwhile, others are of the opinion that obedience to the ruler is obligatory, even in worship (Ibn Aabdeen 1900, 559).[8]

- The absence of a party or institution that may be entrusted with taking decisions on managing the ruler's actions and judging whether they were 'virtuous actions' – where obedience becomes imperative, or 'vices' – where the *Bay'ah* (Pledge of Allegiance) should be dispensed with and he should be ousted, even by the sword.

Yes, it was said that judgments on whether an action was good or unacceptable might only be made by a 'jurisprudent' (*Mujtahed*), while others could only receive such judgments and implement them.[9] However, this idea of discretionary judgment appears to have been discontinued after the fourth century and the term 'scholars' has since replaced the term 'discretionary interpreters'. By virtue of the large numbers of these 'scholars' and the uncontrollable elements or qualities of their work, various contradictory *fatwa*s have been issued and it became easy for the 'guardian' (person in charge) or his opponents to get the *fatwa* or judgment they sought. Thus, the ability to distinguish between the concepts of 'good' and 'unacceptable' in relation to the ruler's actions was lost, along with the ability to distinguish between rulings that should or should not be obeyed. No lessons were learned from the great strife that followed the assassination of the third caliph – instead of seeking to establish a sound conceptual basis for enjoining that which is right and forbidding that which is wrong by peaceful and collective means, authority remained with individuals and their inconsistent opinions and execution by the sword was legalized.

Jurisdiction

The uncertainty referred to in the discussion of obedience becomes clearer when we turn to the subject of jurisdiction. In his capacity as a successor to the Prophet and a discretionary interpreter,[10] the caliph or the Commander of the Faithful enjoys a general jurisdiction that covers all affairs of the *Umma*, both individuals and groups, stemming from the provisions of the religion that cover all realities of life. As Al-Shafe'i says: 'Whatever plight afflicts the people of God's religion has a guidance in Allah's book to direct towards the path of truth therewith' (Al-Shafe'i n.d., 20).[11]

Therefore, according to Al-Mawardi, if the imam received a *Bay'ah* and was made known: 'the whole *Umma* has to delegate all public affairs to him without derogatory remarks or opposition thereto, so that he can carry out what he is entrusted with in terms of interests and management of affairs … ' (Al-Mawardi 1982, 15). However, the scholars did not recognize the discretionary interpretations of any of the 'imams' other than the four caliphs and Omar Bin Abdul Aziz. They acknowledged competency for discretionary interpretation only amongst those who had theoretically fulfilled its requirements, such as those who had studied the fundamentals of jurisprudence, even going so far as to say: 'The Kings are the rulers of the people and the Scholars (not the discretionary interpreters) are the rulers of the Kings' (Al-Ghazali 1967, 17).

Consultation (*Shura*) was also discussed, and mention was made of the absence of agreement on whether it is obligatory or otherwise, and about whom amongst those with power and influence should be consulted, and so forth, in respect of theoretical discussion in the absence of the means of resolution, and thence application. This left conditions on the ground subject to the law of 'winners and losers', and to the complexities of the influence of the concerned parties: the imam or ruler, the *Ulama* or scholars and power seekers.

This is confirmed by the historical accounts of cases of killing and persecution which befell caliphs, *Ulama* and revolutionaries who sought to challenge evil, all of which took place in the name of religion, in the fight against heresy and sedition … and to promote virtue and to prevent vice.[12]

The Commandment of the Faithful in the Moroccan experience

A distinction can be made between two phases, one preceding constitutionalization and the other following thereafter.

Pre-constitutionalization phase

The independent political authority/state in Morocco was founded at the hands of Idris Bin Abdulla Bin Al-Hasan Bin Ali (May God be pleased with them) after Islam was introduced to the country in the late second century AH (172 AH). Seemingly due to the short duration of the state he founded and the scarcity of documentation and research on the period, it remains unclear whether he, or his son, Idris II, was named caliph or 'Prince of the Believers', but what is certain is that statehood was established on a religious basis by the same means and for the same goals as the caliphate state. Moulay Idris and his son spread Islam to most regions and amongst most of the tribes that were either still heathen or Christians or Jews.

One of the speeches attributed to him began thus:

Greetings,

1. I am inviting you to follow Allah's book and the Sunnah of His Prophet, peace be upon him.
2. And to be fair with the people and to treat them equally, to lift injustices and to support the oppressed.
3. And to revive the Sunnah, to put an end to heresy and to apply the rulings of the Holy Quran to relatives and non-relatives.[13]

Since Idris I was given *Bay'ah* in 172 AH, the term '*Bay'ah*' was repeatedly used at the inauguration of the kings of Morocco, regardless of which of the various ruling families they emerged from, and the king was referred to as 'Commander of the Faithful', a description that often appeared on the stamp placed by the king at the top of the royal decrees he issued.

In view of the means of communication and transport available at the time, the *Bay'ah* was made at each of the various towns and locations of the tribes, and ranged in length from less than 100 words to more than 2,000, whilst maintaining all the basic elements required by jurisprudence. In addition, obedience was the norm in cases of agreement and disagreement, and on the basis that it was a religious duty for which no mitigation was allowed. Often this verse from the Holy Quran was cited: 'O ye who believe! obey Allah, and obey the Messenger and those charged with authority among you.' Some *Bay'ah*s were extensive, including Hadiths and showing evidence of the obligation of the *Bay'ah*, and prohibiting any revocation thereof, this being restricted exclusively to *Quraysh* and the family of the Prophet.[14]

As such, the term 'Commandment of the Faithful', with all its religious connotations, covers all actions of the king who embodies the 'state'. Therefore, the relations between the two institutions, or, rather, between the two terms, were relations of intermingling and correlation in decision-making, as well as in implementation.

The constitutionalization phase

The first constitution was issued in Morocco in 1962, and was amended in 1970, 1972, 1992, 1996 and 2011. There appear to be substantial differences with respect to the foundation of 'The Commandment of the Faithful' between the constitution of 1996 and those preceding, on the one hand, and the 2011 constitution, on the other.

Constitution of 1996 and earlier

Chapter or Article (19) of the 1962 constitution reads as follows:

> The King is the *Commander of the Faithful*, a symbol of the unity of the nation, guarantor of the permanence and continuity of the state, protector of religion, vigilant in respecting the Constitution: He safeguards the rights and freedoms of the citizens, groups and organizations, and is the guarantor of independence and the country's possessions of real rights.

In subsequent constitutions, the same article was repeated, with the same wording, but the words 'the supreme representative of the nation' were added, to read: 'The King is the *Commander of the Faithful*, the supreme representative of the nation, the symbol of its unity and the guarantor of the continuity of the state', with the article being split into two paragraphs.

What is important with respect to this matter is:

- The combination of the two roles of the king: The Commander of the Faithful and the Head of State, in one article.
- The use of the term '*Umma*' in place of the 'state'.

Hence, all decrees issued under Chapter 19 can be considered to be within the authorities of the 'Commandment of the Faithful', although their absolute majority comes within the powers of the king in his capacity as Head of State/*Umma* and the one who is vigilant in respecting the constitution. Because of this, it has become difficult to distinguish between the religious authority and the temporal power the king exercises in accordance with Chapter 19, but these may be merged together explicitly.

As an example the decree issued on 10 April 2001 reorganizing the Advisory Council for Human Rights is cited, the preamble of which reads as follows:

> As safeguarding the rights and freedoms of the citizens, groups and institutions, and securing the exercise thereof, is considered a constitutional trust which lies at the core of our superior missions in our capacity as Commander of the Faithful, and it is an embodiment of the foundations of our civilization, culture and tolerant Islamic values as well as of our international commitments relating to the protection, safeguarding and promotion of human rights taking into consideration that each of these constitutes a reference authority in this respect ....[15]

The reality is that the concern for these rights and freedoms is carried out through the state's temporal authority rather than through its religious powers. For this reason, the

2011 Constitution, in Chapter 71, stipulated that the law relates to 'legislation' in the following fields:

- 'The fundamental rights and freedoms provided for in the Foreword and in other chapters of this Constitution … .'

Even before the 2011 amendment to the constitution, the royal decree issued to establish the National Council for Human Rights (1 March 2011) as successor to the Advisory Council for Human Rights made no reference to any of the titles: 'Commandment of the Faithful' or 'Guardian', but instead affirmed that the establishment of the council was:

> an embodiment of Our Majesty's firm commitment to safeguarding the rights and freedoms of the citizens, both individuals and groups, and guaranteeing the exercise thereof, it being a constitutional trust at the core of our superior missions. It is also an embodiment of the Kingdom's fulfilment of its international obligations in the field of human rights protection and promotion so that our country remains in line with the values of its age, true to its international obligations in the field of human rights, qualified to meet the challenges of transformations and societal changes and to face all forms of extremism, fanaticism, terrorism, exclusion, discrimination and hatred, in complete harmony with the rich history of Morocco, and its cultural traditions which are based on the virtues of fraternity, tolerance, moderation, openness, solidarity and justice, prohibition of injustice as well as on the international principles and values of freedom, equality, peace and democracy, in embodiment of the Divine honouring of humans.

The decree's failure to refer to the titles of 'Commander of the Faithful' and 'Guardian' affirms that the king issued it in his capacity as 'Head of State', rather than as 'Commander of the Faithful', despite the fact that its issuance was based on Chapter 19 of the 1996 Constitution.

To sum up, no legislative text was issued under the title 'Commander of the Faithful', provided for in Chapter 19 of the Constitution to organize any of the legal fields assigned by those constitutions to the parliament.

The most important requirements issued by the king in his capacity as Commander of the Faithful include the following:

- Establishing Mohammad VI's Award for Islamic Thought and Studies (Decree of 22 June 2012).
- Establishing Mohammad VI's Award for Quranic Centres (Decree of 23 July 2002 amended by the Decree of 17 July 2012).
- Organization of the Ministry of Awqaf and Islamic Affairs and Identifying its terms of reference (Decree of 14 December 2003).
- Creation of the Supreme Scientific Council which is composed of the heads of the regional Scientific Councils (Decree of 8 April 1981 amended by Decree of 22 April 2004).
- Reorganization of Dar Al-Hadith Al-Hasaniyyeh for Higher Islamic Studies Foundation (Decree of 24 August 2005).
- Creation of the Regional Scientific Councils (Decree of 12 July 1981).
- Reorganization of 'Al-Rabitah Al-Muhammadiyyeh for Scholars' (Decree of 14 February 2006).[16]
- Creation of Mohammad VI's Award for Quran People (Decree of 30 November 2007 amended by Decree of 17 July 2012).

- Creation of Mohammad VI's Award for the People of the Hadith (Decree of 23 May 2008 amended by Decree of 17 July 2012).

In very rare cases, the king issued orders in his capacity as Commander of the Faithful, under special stipulations, not in the form of legislation as published in the official Gazette, but as a speech as published through the public media. These are examples:

- King Hasan II's speech on 7 September 1975 addressed to the officers, non-commissioned officers and soldiers of the armed forces, which states:

> And yet, we, the *Commander of the Faithful* and Supreme Commander of the Royal Armed Forces, have decided to exempt from fasting in this month of Ramadan all members of our armed forces who shoulder direct military responsibilities that require full vigilance and caution and all elements of intellectual competence and physical ability in accordance with the content of the *fatwa* that we ordered our Scientific Council in Fez to issue on the subject.

- The speech of 5 November 1975 addressed to participants of the 'Green March' to the Western Sahara, which was then under Spanish occupation, which included:

> As a father and guide to you, as Commander of the Faithful and as Commander of your politics, I will provide you, my dear people, with some advice. Firstly: My dear people, as soon as you cross the borders, you must make *tayammom* on the immaculate sand, then stand up facing the *kiblah* and make a prayer of two *Rake'h*s with your footware on because you are fighters, as a thanksgiving to God. For, as the Scholars have said, 'if goodness comes by, kneel on the ground in submission and reverence, as it is obligatory to kneel as a thanksgiving.

On the other hand, Mohammad VI requested a *fatwa* from the Supreme Scientific Council with respect to 'the relationship between the public interest and the public affairs causes', and on the occasion of opening the first round of the proceedings of the Supreme Scientific Council in Fez on 8 July 2005, the king's speech included the following:

> In this context, we have decided that the first proceedings of the Supreme Scientific Council shall be to assign the Council, in its enlightened jurisprudential scholarly wisdom, the responsibility of educating the people in the fundamentals of the Maliki creed, with special emphasis on its unique attitude of adopting the law of public interests, which has always been followed in the Kingdom of Morocco, to keep up with the changes taking place in all aspects of public and private lives, through the enlightened discretionary interpretations of our great ancestors and early scholars. It is the basis upon which are built all legal and religious harmonious and integrative provisions that are enacted by the State under our leadership as King and Commander of the Faithful in response to recent developments and in order to serve the country's interests, ward off evil, safeguard rights and perform our duties.

The council's response to this request for a *fatwa* was as follows:

... The interference of the Imam in legislation may extend to include three areas as a minimum, namely:

1. Where there is no text.
2. What has been the subject of jurisprudential non-agreement.

3. Where a genuine interest can be achieved Islamic law regulated the interest, identified it with clear features and distinguished the valid ones from the unsound ones before it allowed its usage.

> If attainment of the interest is an issue that Sharia is keen to achieve, the Grand Imam, with his mandatory rulings and ability to give discretionary interpretations, remains the party qualified to regulate that which achieves genuine interests and wards off the evils that might demonstrate themselves in the form of interests … .

I will return to this issue at the end of this discussion.

The 2011 Constitution

Chapter 41 of the 2011 Constitution stipulates as follows:

> The King is the *Commander of the Faithful*, the protector of religion and the guarantor of the free exercise of religious affairs.
>
> The King, as Commander of the Faithful, chairs the Supreme Scientific Council that studies the issues presented thereto.
>
> The Council is the only party which is competent to issue fatwas to be officially adopted regarding all issues referred thereto, on the basis of the provisions and principles of the Islamic faith and its magnanimous purposes.
>
> The terms of reference of the Council, its composition and the way it is administered shall be defined in a decree.
>
> The King exercises his religious powers with respect to the Commandment of the Faithful and which are exclusively assigned to him, under this chapter through Decrees.'

Chapter 42 stipulated:

> The King is the head of the state, its supreme representative, the symbol of the unity of the nation, the guarantor of the permanence and continuity of the state and the supreme judge between its institutions. He is vigilant in respecting the Constitution and the proper functioning of the constitutional institutions, for safeguarding the democratic choice and the freedoms of the citizens, males and females, and the groups, as well as for honouring the Kingdom's international commitments.
>
> The King is the guarantor of the country's independence and of its possessions of real rights. He exercises these functions under decrees, through the powers conferred expressly upon him by the text of the Constitution.
>
> Decrees shall be countersigned by the head of government, except for those stipulated in Chapters 41 & 42 (Para. 2), Chapter 47 (Paras. 1 & 6), Chapters 51, 57, 59, and 130 (Paras. 1 & 4) and chapter 174.[17]

As such, the 2011 Constitution is distinguished from the preceding ones in:

- separation between the two titles of the king: 'Commander of the Faithful' and 'Head of State'; and
- the use of the term 'Head of State', which had no existence in the preceding constitutions.

This wording, in my belief, is of utmost importance. On the one hand, it removes the confusion created by the issuance of legislative texts under Chapter 19 that combined the two roles of the king. On the other hand, the use of the term 'Head of State' assures us that we are dealing with the application of the Constitution and the interpretation of its statements in the sense prevailing in contemporary constitutional jurisprudence.

It is true that Chapter 41 did not precisely specify the areas of the powers of the Commandment of the Faithful, but in assigning 'legislative authority' to the Parliament in Chapter 70 and detailing the scope of legislation in Chapter 71 it confirms that the Commandment of the Faithful is but a symbolic institution and that its scope of authority is the spiritual and ethical security of the religious life of the society, not the daily realities of human co-existence, or managing the interests and dealings of the political community, competition among its members, its human and class components, and its quest for betterment.

The current Constitution was put into effect on 29 July 2011 and, as of the end of October 2012, three decrees had been issued under the aforementioned Chapter 41. These decrees amend former ones that govern the organization of the following:

- Mohammad VI Award for the People of Quran.
- Mohammad VI Award for the People of Hadith.
- Mohammad VI Award for Quranic Schools.
- Hassan II's Mosque Institution in Casablanca.

The first three are dated 17 July 2012, with the most recent, related to the Hassan II Mosque Institution in Casablanca, issued on 17 September 2012.

In 2009, The Ministry of Awqaf and Islamic Affairs issued a book entitled *The Commandment of the Faithful in Ten Manifestations* (compiled by Hassan Al-Mir 2009) in which it explained that the manifestations of the Commandment of the Faithful 'in history and its present concern' are responsible for the following:

- The Quran and Hadith.
- The Ulama (Scholars).
- Imams of Mosques.
- Mosques.
- Traditional Education.
- Religious Discourse and the Media.
- Commemoration of the Days of God (such as *Lailat Al-Qadr* [Night of Revelation] and the Prophet's birthday).
- Culture, heritage, thought, publications and libraries.
- Pilgrimage and its historical caravan.
- Mysticism and sponsoring charity values.

This shows that the Commandment of the Faithful is concerned with the religious feeling of the nation and supporting it, but without approving of it being completely decoupled from the political activity undertaken by the king in his capacity as Head of State. The historical connotation of the term has formulated a culture that makes the status of the king, who was given *Bay'ah* as Commander of the Faithful, distinct in social awareness and in accordance with the model established by jurisprudence and consolidated by practice. This also shows the status of the 'Head of State' who is elected in the manner specified in the constitution of each state.

The most important of these distinctions is that the king who has received a *Bay'ah* is regarded as far beyond the effects of political parties, ideologies, sects or ethnicities. This is explained by historical events related to the sovereignty of his judgment.[18] Even jurisprudence recognized the power of his judgment when it said: 'the Guardian's opinion puts an end to any dispute'.

The role of the 'Commandment of the Faithful' in the complicated relationship between the religious and the political

It seems necessary to distinguish here between the intellectual heritage with its historic circumstances, on the one hand, and the developments that have shaped present-day reality, on the other hand.

Intellectual heritage and its circumstances

Any meaningful discussion of intellectual heritage should take account of the circumstances that previously allowed no room for debate about temporal authority and religious authority in the community/state.

This inability to conceive of a role for anything other than religion in managing both individual interests and the affairs of the *Umma* appears to be the reason for the lack of clarity in drafting theories relating to the powers of the 'Commandment of the Faithful', 'the guardian' or 'the caliph'.

So, what were the theories that were used to introduce the powers of the 'Commander of the Faithful'? And were those theories ever put into practice?

Theorizing

The description 'Commander of the Faithful', the 'imam', 'caliph' or 'guardian' has been attached to the assignment to manage all the affairs of the *Umma*. No distinction was drawn between the religious and the political, and the heritage makes no reference to any field or facility within the community that was dealt with in isolation from religion and that which was ordained by the Sharia.

The expression 'guarding the religion and administering everyday life' does not mean that they were to be considered as separate from each other. Neither could living be managed away from the provisions of religion. On the contrary, this policy has no aim other than the protection of religion.

Consequently, Islamic constitutional jurisprudence did not address the diversity of the areas of activities of the Muslim ruler, or discuss the competencies limited to the 'Commandment of the Faithful', because it considered that there were no powers beyond this capacity, or the capacity of the guardian. And if the actions that the guardian is empowered to take are restricted to those achieving the interest at stake, then the guardian himself is the only one who will identify what is meant by the concept of 'interest', for as Shafei says: 'The status of the Imam before the people is the same as that of the custodian to the orphan' (Al-Soyouti 2007). The custodian exclusively assesses the orphan's interests because of the orphan's innate inability to discern what is good or what is bad for him.

This argumentation is still valid within jurisprudential theorizing. Al-Mawardi says that the imam:

> has his word listened to, his order obeyed and his decision effective as long as the *Umma* places trust in him. In that case he may keep for himself the right to reject the views of all [Shura] council members where he believes that they are contrary to the truth.
>
> (Al-Mawdoudi 1958)

When jurisprudence attempts to identify the power of the 'Commander of the Faithful', it is expressed in general terms, namely: guarding religion and life, or in relatively detailed form, by saying that he provides:

- judgment on all incidents on which there is no text;[19]
- judgment as to what will achieve the interest (of all); and
- the opinion that should be implemented in case of disagreement between discretionary interpreters.

The judgments he gives in these cases are not based on reasoning or politics but are instead issued in the name of the Sharia in his capacity as the representative of the Owner of Sharia and on His behalf.

Ibn Khaldoun, for example, says that the management of the politics of the crown/state may be achieved by power or force or through laws 'imposed by the wise people and the prominent people of the state' or may be 'imposed by Almighty God through legislation … '. What was made through oppression and conquest or by the wielding of power in anger is injustice, aggression and something detestable by him, and whatever was done through politics and its provisions beyond the legislator's guidance is detestable also because it came contrary to God's light ('And he for whom Allah has not appointed light, for him there is no light'; Holy Quran, Sura al Noor, verse 40). This is because the legislator better knows the interests of all people in what is not revealed to them of the issues of their other life. All people's acts belong to them in their destiny, but the provisions of politics govern the affairs of this life only. ('They know but the outer (things) in the life of this world'; Holy Quran, Surat al-Rum, verse 7).

The legislator's intention towards the people is to ensure them good in the afterlife. Therefore, it has become imperative that the whole community adheres to the principles of the Sharia in the conduct of their affairs for this worldly life as well as for the afterlife. This judgment was for the people of the Sharia, who are the prophets and whomsoever replaces them, such as the caliphs.

That has been manifested clearly from the significance of 'caliphate' – and natural royalty or rule involves judging all on the basis of purpose and lust, while political royalty or rule means judging people on the basis of reasoning to attain worldly interests and ward off harm. Caliphate (succession) is to judge all people on the basis of Sharia opinion, in the interests of their afterlife and the worldly interest related to that. Thus, all worldly conditions, for the legislator, are judged on the basis of their relations to the afterlife, which is in fact being done on behalf of the legislator in guarding religion and running the worldly life therewith (Ibn Khaldoun 2005, vol. 1, 326–328).

It is clear that this conception of the Commandment of the Faithful or the Guardianship, which has prevailed for more than 13 centuries, and is still promoted in accordance with the principle that says: 'Jurisprudence is transmitted, never reasoned', cannot be in harmony with the state of modern institutions, and can play little part in resolving the problematic issue of religion and state.

If we were to return to the fundamentals of jurisprudence, we would find no mention of the 'Commander of the Faithful' or the 'Guardian'. The discretionary interpreter alone was the one who 'revealed'[20] the stipulations of God or 'God's judgment' according to his opinion.[21] Then, the discretionary interpreter was replaced by the 'Mufti' (One who issues *fatwas*) who is a reporter from God, just like the Prophet. He represents the Sharia in witnessing the acts of worshippers as he finds fit, like the Prophet. His word carries the authority of the caliphate's declaration, like the Prophet. Hence, they were called guardians and obedience to them was coupled with obedience to God and His Messenger (Al-Shatebi 1999, 245).[22] There are also other terms, the meanings of which are indeterminate, such as: the scholar, jurist and sheikh. Any person giving himself one of these titles speaks in the name of Islam, and provides assurance that his opinion is right and all others are erroneous. This attains under an inherited culture that maintains:

> A layman has to follow the mufti, as consensus has stressed that it is the obligation of the common folk to follow the mufti whether he lied or was faithful, made a mistake or hit the mark. We say whatever the mufti says. Whatever has received consensus is an obligation, and it is an acceptance of an opinion with a proof, not an imitation at all.
>
> (Al-Ghazali 2008)

The theories of political or authoritative jurisprudence and the fundamentalist jurisprudence, although contradicting each other, have absented the *Umma* or the community which is characterized by religious and intellectual plurality. Therefore, together they complicate the relationship between religion and the modern state.

Application

If theorizing conferred upon the 'Commander of the Faithful' unlimited powers and competency to produce Sharia principles in all cases where no text had been given or where he could achieve interest in his capacity as a caliph (successor) to the Prophet or a deputy thereto, practical application of these powers went in another direction.

Jurisprudence did not recognize the religious legitimacy of the judgments made by the 'Commander of the Faithful' or the guardian, except for those of the five caliphs, namely: the first four and Omar Bin Abdul-Azeez. Thus, their decisions and their interpretations of a text are considered as 'Sharia provisions' which the nation is obliged to follow.

For other than those five caliphs, we do not find in the jurisprudential reference books of all the Sunni creed 'Sharia Provision' for formulation thereof attributed to any 'guardian', whether those who were called caliphs or those who gave themselves independent authority in the various Islamic provinces. If jurisprudence in general maintained its use of terms like 'Guardian' and 'Commander of the Faithful' and maintained the obligation of obedience to such figures, there was prudential consensus not to document those provisions in its codes of 'Sharia' judgments. Moreover, in order to completely preclude them gaining such legitimacy, it was said that the orders of the caliphs or the guardian ended with his death, in contrast to the opinions of the 'discretionary interpreter' which nobody may cancel, not even the nation itself. With such confusion in the concepts that were recorded relating to the powers of the 'Commander of the Faithful', both in theory and in practice, it is not possible to make use of these provisions in the crisis that we are experiencing in the relationship between the religious and the political.

In light of developments on the ground

The following 'real-world' developments are related to the 'Commander of the Faithful' and cannot be ignored:

- The emergence of the state of institutions that represent the highest achievement of human political thought to date, and which is still developing in form and in content and is being sought all over the world.
- The state of co-existence that embraces citizens of diverse creeds, opinions and ethnicities. Human awareness has moved, or is about to move, from building the state upon religious or ethnic unity, for example, to adopting citizenship or co-existence, and establishing a culture of co-existence, despite the plurality of faiths and opinions.
- The nation (*Umma*) is no longer described as a 'flock' (subjects) obliged to practice obedience (to the ruler) even if he whipped backs and seized property. Instead, the state emerges as something that secures the rights and freedoms of individuals and protects them in the sense universally agreed upon. At the same time, the scene has been set for the intervention of international community organizations and their monitoring of the respect of those rights and freedoms.
- The birth of intellectual trends that believe in giving religion, as they understand it, full authority to govern all activities of the state, being the sublime constitution that forms its governing terms of reference. Although each of these trends adheres to its own interpretation of Islam, they all describe legislation issued by the constitutional institutions as 'temporal law' which is 'contrary to Islam'.[23]
- There are other intellectual trends that call for estrangement between religion and the state which should be concerned with the immediate interests of the society aside from the religious beliefs of the individuals.

Against this reality – which is experienced by all Muslim societies, including Morocco – what is the solution with the least disadvantages and that responds most closely to the wishes of the highest percentage[24] of the members of the society – especially those societies in which there is only a very limited presence of non-Muslims?

- Is it a complete separation between religion and the state, which means an absolute disregard of religion and its values and stipulations in the state's basic and organizational arrangements and legislation, and in the management of social facilities and running the affairs of its individuals, whilst leaving the religious creed, its rituals and orders as private issues that concern the individuals themselves, with the state having nothing to do therewith?

This solution does not seem viable because the justification for creating a state is to care for the common values and to manage the uncompromising with the principles of co-existence. It would be unwise for the state to see itself as wiser than the community and to deceive itself by repeating the words of the Pharaoh of Egypt, who said: 'I [do not] but point out to you that which I see myself; nor do I guide you but to the path of righteousness!' (Holy Koran, Surat Ghafir, verse 29). What happened in South Yemen and in Somalia in the 1970s may yet overtake us, and the infamous consequences of those events linger on.

In view of this, it would be unwise for those who manage public affairs to disregard the values and wishes of the majority of the community, who find the spirit of their existence in their religious creed, and require them to abandon everything passed down from their fathers and forefathers.

- Is it by leaving the issue to the religious trends, that are headed in the following three basic directions?:
  - Satisfaction with generalities, such as stressing 'Islamic terms of reference' or 'application of the Sharia Law' or at least considering this as the 'major source' of legislation.
  - Avoiding talk about the institutions of the state, preferring instead to discuss the application of the Holy Quran and the Sunnah, and whatever was done by the good ancestors, together with terms such as 'Imamate', 'Caliphate', 'Guardianship' and 'consultation' which political jurisprudence dealt with in the early centuries of the Islamic history.
  - Make reference to some of the components of the modern state, but in a conceptualization that whilst appearing to be full of compassion is yet filled with torture and destructive tyranny at heart.[25]

There have been a few instances where Islamic trends with strong designs to 'apply the Sharia' have taken power, but this has resulted in the division of the state. Some authors have interpreted this as an application of the argument 'Islam is the solution', meaning by 'solution' the division and break down of the state. I do not agree with this analysis, but still, one must be cautious and learn from this.

The fundamental problem with the groups commonly described as 'Islamists' is that they strongly believe that their view of Islam and its stipulations is the indisputable truth and that everything else is deviation and aberration, and, to some militant groups, blasphemy. This sometimes leads to violence between groups, each claiming to be acting in defence of 'true' Islam. The interpretation that each group adheres to with respect to its views of religion is the source of the dangers because by excluding all dissenting views such groups are similar to the groups that believe in a total separation between religion and the state. Both rule out the 'legitimacy' of the other view and, therefore, it becomes impossible to build up a state of co-existence.

- Is it by delegating all religious affairs to the state that everything gets corrected?

The answer seems to be in the negative when we look into the historical reality that extends across all time and all faiths. However, the state we are talking about now is the 'state of institutions' and the institutional system is the most effective means whereby the human community manages to protect itself from the tyranny of the state, whether this tyranny takes place in the name of religion or under the pretext of achieving higher interests for the nation, or for the host of other excuses that are well established in the lexicon of the authoritarian ruler, both ancient and modern.

The proper building of the state institutions, the commitment to their development and the pursuit of the ever-renewable facts of life serve to preclude tyranny in the name of religion, or under other pretexts. This also directs all activities of the state towards intensifying the principles and culture of co-existence among all citizens, no matter what their religious or ideological belief, colour, ethnicity or social upbringing. For this reason, nobody can challenge the fact that the state is the party empowered with safeguarding the individual's rights and freedom according to the standards agreed upon in the modern society based on co-existence. Thus, it is possible to avoid any collision between the social groups and the various intellectual trends in the interpretation of the concept of individual rights and freedoms, and in its application to the conflicting facts of an individual's activity and his relations with others.

In other words, both the groups calling for the separation of religion and the state and those calling for the Islamization of the state – however they choose to conceptualise 'Islamization' – seek to provide their own ideas to improve the functioning of state institutions and to prevent deviation from the goals set for them in the constitutional system, whether written or otherwise.

However, it is not sufficient to warn against the utilization of religion by the state for the purposes of oppression and deviation. What is happening is that each group embraces only its viewpoint as a system for life and bars other viewpoints from participating in the management of public affairs. For this reason we argue that the intervention of the state, and its institutional system, in religious affairs constitutes a protection of religion and the system of co-existence which is rejected by those groups that either exclude religion totally or restrict it to the teachings they provide to their followers.

To return to the institution of the 'Commandment of the Faithful': considerations long associated with this institution might be raised.[26] Is it sufficient to concentrate on this issue? Or should focus be directed towards correcting these defects by discarding the negative symptoms and strengthening the positive elements of the heritage?

When Omar Bin Al-Khattab was given the title of 'Commander of the Faithful', there was no immediate change in the structure and function of the state, although this did not last for long. This was due to the fact that jurisprudence did not differentiate between the presidency of the state and the Commandment of the Faithful, the powers of which have expanded to cover all functions of the state, including the faiths of individuals, whenever it was challenged for aberration and deviation, and the notion 'obedience even if backs are slashed and money is seized'. He who did not adhere to this notion did not necessarily offer practical ideas to prevent oppression and the monopoly of decision-making.

Now, in light of the developments already referred to, neither jurisprudence nor what is called 'political Islamic thought' achieved the desired outcome, which was to expose the defects and offer practical means to correct them in light of the progressive developments affecting all institutions of the modern state. Instead, like their opponents who called for the separation of religion from the state, they were not satisfied with criticizing the 'Commandment of the Faithful' institution and its responsibility for the oppression and the corrupted political regime without citing examples experienced by Islamic countries where extremist Islamic or secular groups assumed authority.

The 'Commandment of the Faithful' in Morocco

By virtue of Morocco's maintenance of its political independence from the caliphate, first that in Baghdad and thereafter that in Istanbul, the Moroccan kings were given the title of 'Prince of Muslims', then 'Commander of the Faithful' (in the general sense of the term and with the formalities used for the ruler in the capital of the caliphate on the basis of what political jurisprudence established in *Al-Ahkam Al-Sultaniyyeh*

(Al-Mawardi 1982)) thus maintaining the title with its religious symbolism attached and with a cultural load that included politics in its formulation.

If the mid-20th century was a remarkable milestone in the history of the West with respect to the rights and freedoms of the individual and gender equality, the same period also marked a turning point in the Arab and Muslim world as the debate about the religion-and-state dilemma manifested a clear link with human rights and its different variants. This development saw the emergence of movements calling for the application of the 'Sharia' by various means. The features common to these movements included:

- Disregarding the state of institutions and then taking a hostile attitude towards it and resisting its so-called 'man-made' laws. Also making fun of much of what is written about the state of institutions, as well as human rights and freedom.
- Considering as Sharia what the people of old times said in interpreting texts and what they implemented in their private and public life, including seeing the caliphate as a 'political system' for all 'Muslims' living on the globe.
- Each of them believes that they alone understand the true Islam and all other groups are perverse, misguided or infidels, the killing of whom and expropriation of their property should be declared lawful.
- Considering the current Arab regimes to be the parties responsible for corruption and 'disrupting the application of Sharia'. Therefore, they should be ousted and 'Islamic regimes' should be established in accordance with the philosophy each group adopts.

By contrast, there were also groups calling for the complete exclusion of religion from the state, its organs and its various activities, and demanding that they be built on rational, pan-national, liberal or socialist bases that achieve interests. Groups of both types managed to take hold of authority in a number of Islamic countries, and the results are well known and need not to be mentioned here. All these ideological trends moved to Morocco following its independence in the 1960s. As time passed, and as a result of developments affecting the Arab world and the Third World in general, limited collisions took place between the state and radical groups with support from one party or another. Also, student factions appeared at universities with sometimes violent clashes taking place from time to time.

Now, did Morocco benefit from the 'Commandment of the Faithful' in facing these scorching political crises? Did it achieve any progress in establishing a state of institutions, in consolidating human rights and freedoms or in trying to solve the 'man-made law' dilemma?

The political crises

In the last two decades, Morocco has witnessed social–political shocks that could have given rise to the sort of violence and instability seen in more than one Arab or Muslim country. Blood was shed and the two primary parties known as Islamists and Secularists reciprocated 'victory' and 'defeat'.

(a) The Personal Status Code

At the beginning of 1992, the Union of Women's Action launched a campaign to collect 1 million signatures in support of a call to change the Personal Status Code of 1957. The petition to be signed included:

- Considering the family an institution built on the basis of equality and solidarity between the husband and wife on an equal footing.
- Looking upon the woman the same as the man. She becomes fully competent upon reaching the legal age of maturity.
- Giving the woman the right to get married without the need for a guardian upon reaching the legal age of maturity.
- Developing texts giving equal rights to both husband and wife.
- Leaving divorce to the judiciary and developing texts giving equal rights to man and woman to apply to the judiciary for divorce.
- Prohibition of polygamy.
- Giving the woman the right to be guardian for her children like the man.
- Considering work and education an inalienable right for the woman that the husband is not entitled to usurp.

The petition provoked strong opposition and some 'scholars' disseminated *fatwas*, memoranda and brochures accusing its supporters of blasphemy and abandoning their faith. They were to be requested three times to repent and if they failed to do so, their killing would be announced as lawful.

In a bid to avoid worse, on 20 August 1992 King Hassan II announced in a speech from the throne the necessity of reviewing some articles of the Code, especially those derived from jurisprudential interpretation. He requested the women's associations and all concerned parties to put their proposals to the Royal Court. The court received no more than nine proposed amendments which were put before an appointed committee. Several proposals were approved and, as a result, three Royal Decrees were issued on 10 September 1993.[27] All parties accepted the outcome of the king's arbitration, and the tempest faded away.

(b) The National Plan for the Integration of Women in Development

Following the amendment to the Constitution in 1996, the government, formed by the opposition and dubbed the 'government of rotation', announced a social–political project in favour of women entitled 'The National Plan for the Integration of Women in Development'. This plan included amendments to some articles of the Civil Status Code.

This project provoked much stronger opposition than the Union of Women's Action in 1992. A huge demonstration was organized in Rabat in support of the plan, which motivated a larger counter-demonstration in Casablanca condemning the plan and those who drafted it. Thousands of petitions were raised to the Royal Court, both in favour of the plan and against it. *Fatwa*s were issued calling for the plan to be rejected as representing 'deviation from faith in God', 'in contradiction with His Sharia', and 'changing God's provisions', while condemning all those who 'drafted it, supported it and were behind it'.

On the occasion of Woman's Day on 8 March, the king received female representatives of associations and organizations interested in the debate taking place about the national plan and promised that he would intervene to prevent the situation becoming more dangerous. He appointed a committee of 15 members, including three women in addition to its head, and installed the committee in the presence of the representatives of the three above-mentioned associations. In the inaugural address, he said:

> Since we acceded to the throne of our great forefathers, we have undertaken to carry on improving the condition of the Moroccan woman in all fields of national life, and to

> remove all forms of injustice that she suffers from, out of our capacity as Commander of the Faithful and Protector of religion, in full adherence to the Islamic Sharia in all that is legalized, prohibited or permitted, and in implementation of the consolidation of values of justice and equality between men and women. That cannot be achieved except with a creative union between adherence to our enduring religious principles which constitute the core of our identity and in full harmony with the spirit of our time which is characterized by the global nature of human rights, within the framework of the discretionary interpretation you are assigned to exercise, and for achieving the purposes of magnanimous Sharia in giving priority to achieving the common interest among the members of the family within the scope of a precise balance between rights and duties in the application of the verse of the Holy Quran: 'And women shall have rights similar to the rights against them'. In this context, the committee is requested to listen to all concerned parties, open all doors for them to provide their views, consider their demands carefully, with insight and patience … .

The committee listened to more than 70 associations and organizations of the various orientations and ideological directions and formulated a draft code for the family in September 2003; minor amendments were introduced thereto and the king presented it at the inaugural session of Parliament on 10 October 2003. It was passed by the two Houses of Representatives and Advisors. It is to be noted that the most important proposals of the National Plan for the Integration of Woman in Development were included in the new family law.

The year 2010 witnessed the beginning of unrest and popular uprisings in several Arab countries, at the forefront of which were Tunisia, Libya and Egypt, which resulted in the change of regimes in these countries. This had a bearing on Morocco where popular demonstrations started on 20 February 2011 in various cities and urban communities demanding an end to corruption in government bodies and calling for reform, freedom and human rights. All segments of society, from the extremist radical left to the Islamic anti-monarchy groups who call for an Islamic Caliphate, took part in the demonstrations.

On 9 March 2011, the king delivered a speech in which he announced an extensive review of the Constitution, especially in the fields of consolidating the institutionalized system of the state, human rights and protection of freedoms. Once the new Constitution was ratified and its institutions began exercising their functions, the 20 February movement receded and came close to disappearing. Thus, Morocco managed to avoid the painful negative developments that are still troubling a number of Arab countries.

In conclusion, the 'Commandment of the Faithful', with all its religious symbolism and historical heritage, helped at critical moments to avoid disputes, to maintain stability, and to thwart the ideological and doctrinal alignment that has had such profound consequences elsewhere.

The state of institutions

I do not claim that Morocco has achieved all that is meant by the term 'state of institutions' in the theory of contemporary constitutional thought, as well as in the advanced practices of this theory. Yet, I emphasize that it walked this path at a progressive pace from the Constitution of 1962 to the most recent constitution which was ratified in the referendum of 1 July 2011. With this progressive trend, which has extended over half a century, with political stability and non-exposure to ideological coups with all their painful effects, it can be said that Morocco has laid down significant bricks in the edifice of the state of institutions.

In the most recent constitution, the elements of the state of institutions appeared with all their terms of reference clearly defined, subject to mutual monitoring in accordance with the Montesquieu principle that power may be checked only by power. One of these new institutions is the Constitutional Court which is entrusted with monitoring the constitutionality of laws. These institutions need good application, and this application is linked to a culture and behaviour that still lack complete maturity both in the individual and collective consciousness.

Rights and freedoms of the individual

With respect to rights and freedoms of the individual several developments deserve mention:

- The numerous reforms introduced into the Family Law.
- The individual's right to dispute the constitutionality of the law to be implemented thereon.
- Ratification of the most important international agreements in the field of human rights, including:

    - The International Covenant on Civil and Political Rights.
    - The International Covenant on Economic Social and Cultural Rights.
    - The International Convention on the Elimination of All Forms of Racial Discrimination.
    - The International Convention against Torture and Other Cruel, Inhuman or Degrading Treatment or Punishment.
    - The International Convention on the Elimination of All Forms of Discrimination Against Women.
    - The International Convention on Children's Rights.
    - The International Convention on the Protection of the Rights of All Migrant Workers and Members of Their Families.
    - The Optional Protocol to the Convention on the Right of the Child on the Involvement of Children in Armed Conflict.
    - The Optional Protocol to the Convention on the Rights of the Child on the Sale of the Children, Child Prostitution and Child Pornography.
    - The International Convention on the Protection of the Rights of Persons with Disabilities.
    - The International Convention for the Protection of All Persons from Enforced Disappearance.[28]

These achievements, which point to the smooth co-existence between the religious and the political, were attained by virtue of the distinguished status of the Commandment of the Faithful, as confirmed by the approval given in the referendum by all parliamentary groups to the family law, which included almost all of the recommendations of the National Plan for the Integration of Women in Development which had been opposed by large segments of the society. The import of these achievements is also confirmed in what was written about the international conventions, especially the agreement on the Convention on the Elimination of all Forms of Discrimination Against Woman, whether at the time of ratification with some reservations in 2000 or when these reservations were lifted in 2011.

It is true that the road to the safe shore of peaceful co-existence between the various creeds and conflicting opinions is still long because the issue is related to an age-old individualistic and collective culture and replacing it will require extensive intellectual effort and a significant period of time.

The 'Positive Law' dilemma

The most complicated issue in the state–religion relationship dilemma is the description of all that the state enacts as 'positive law', such as the constitution, regular laws and the various organizational measures and decisions. This is a cause of suffering for all Muslim societies and forms the basis on which all groups that claim the 'application of Sharia' rely. It leads to criticism of the state for 'neglecting' religion and denial of the 'legitimacy' of its institutions. Some groups have gone so far as to hold the society as a co-partner in bearing the responsibility for accepting rule other than by that which God has revealed. This trend is consolidated by the insistence of 'Islamic' education institutions all over the world that jurisprudential interpretations which were offered centuries before and under different circumstances and social conditions are 'Sharia provisions' established to organize Muslim society and the relations between its individuals, and that the laws enacted by the state are 'positive laws', i.e. man made, and therefore contrary to the law established by God.

Had the 'Positive Law' problem been resolved, the conflict resulting from the state–religion dilemma would have come to an end. In view of this, I believe that the question that the King addressed to the Supreme Scientific Council in Morocco on 8 July 2005 had a deep significance, namely proving that:

> the [concept of] interest is the principle upon which all Sharia and legal, harmonious and integrative provisions are based … which comes in response to the contemporary developments, and commitment to take interests and warding off evils into account, safeguarding rights and carrying out duties, and especially that the order to implement the provisions of the law is issued by the King who also carries the title of 'Commander of the Faithful'.[29]

What the council should have done was to study the question within its correct framework, whatever the outcome that would have portended, whether:

- by approving the content of the question, i.e. the availability of procedures for drafting the texts of laws and issuing them with guarantees for taking interest into account, especially given that the council stated in its reply that interest is that 'which once it is presented to the minds, the minds will accept it';
- by non-availability of these guarantees and showing proofs of this statement of opinion and providing an alternative; and
- by proposing objective or formal requirements (or both together) for issuing laws, so that no deviation from the interest that is the base for the provisions of Sharia takes place.

Anyway, the reply that 'The position of the Grand Imamate, with its mandatory decisions and ability to unify the discretionary interpretation, remains the party eligible to codify that which achieves genuine interests and to ward off the evils that could counterfeit as interests' is not applicable as the institution competent for legislation is determined in the Constitution (the Parliament). The intent of the question was not to produce a *fatwa* that goes beyond the Constitution and affects the competencies of its institutions.

Conclusion

- The problem is not simply between the state and religion, but it is deep and complicated and it lies between the way the religion is perceived and the ideological perceptions of the state. These perceptions were created and are still sponsored by:

  - Continued personification of the state by jurisprudence in 'the caliph' or 'the guardian' and conferring upon him inclusive and unrestricted power on behalf of the legislator to guard both the religion and the worldly life, as Ibn Khaldoun says. And the Commandment of the Faithful and the caliphate in this conceptualization never begot a praiseworthy history. Hence, those who are aware of this history have the right to have worries in this respect in the age of the state of institutions.
  - Training at Islamic Studies institutions which insists on stipulating that jurisprudential interpretations on managing the affairs of the society and the relations between its members are laws prescribed by Sharia and that all that is issued by the state is 'positive law', which is contrary to the provisions of the Sharia, and has no relation whatever thereto.
  - The opposite call for a complete separation between religion and the state and its facilities. This makes the blood of the overwhelming majority boil, especially in Moroccan society where the religious culture inherited through generations constitutes the basic element of the components of its individual and collective living.
- Morocco has benefited at critical points in time from the religious and social symbolization it attaches to the Commandment of the Faithful. This has helped the country to maintain relative stability, by comparison with the geo-political environments surrounding it, and to achieve solid steps in the gradual construction of the state of institutions and the installation of the individual's rights and freedoms. I believe that the development of awareness at these institutions and contributing to upgrading these institutions and their improved performance constitute the factor that is capable of building a state of co-existence. By contrast, the rhetoric promising a utopia, with all its exclusionary formulas, has brought much suffering since the middle of the past century. What is really painful is that this rhetoric is still the prevailing master of the field and captivating ideas and minds.
- What will rescue us from the damaging effects of what we mistakenly see as a war between religion and the state, or a competition for influence, is the abandonment of the chauvinistic opinion, whether in understanding religion or in the system of life on the ground. At the same time, the belief must be retained that the difference in creeds, in understanding the details of the provisions of religion and in the philosophy of managing life's affairs, is but an inherent law of life with which men and women are obliged to co-exist.

Achieving accord on these principles will facilitate the drafting of principles of co-existence between religion and the state and the achievement of mutual interest between them.

Notes

1. Editor's note: The literal translation of *Amir al-Mou'mineen* is 'Prince of the Believers', yet the term is not translated as such because the title 'Prince' implies a hierarchy where there exists a higher authority, which is the 'King'. *Amir al Mou'mineen* denotes the top of a political hierarchy where legitimacy is basically derived from leadership of the community of believers.
2. Ibn Khaldoun identifies *Al-Bay'ah* (Pledge of Allegiance), saying:

   > Let it be known to you that *Al-Bay'ah* is a pledge of obedience. The person giving allegiance would pledge to his Prince (Commander) that he submits to his Prince's decisions on all his affairs and those of all Muslims, a non-disputable allegiance, and to accede to whatever the Prince assigns him to, whether to his love or otherwise. If they made a pledge of allegiance to the Prince and concluded a convention with him, they would shake hands with him. This is similar to what a seller and buyer do, and was, therefore, called '*Bay'ah*' which is, in Arabic, the noun of 'Bay'h' (selling). Thus, the *Bay'ah* (pledge of allegiance) is performed by shaking hands.
   >
   > However, the most well-known *Bay'ah* for this reign is the greeting of Khosrau Kings which involves kissing the ground, the hand, the foot or the back. This was called *Bay'ah*, which is a pledge of obedience as this submission in showing respect and adherence to good manners is a part of the requirements of obedience and its entitlements. This form of salutation prevailed and became a customary reality that outlived the original salutation by hand-shaking. (Shaking hands with anybody was seen as something humble and commonplace, unbefitting to presidency and the maintenance of the Royal Status.) However a small number of kings would not do that, especially those who wished to remain modest in dealing with their retinues and the prominent religious figures amongst his subjects.'

3. The imamate, caliphate and Commandment of the Faithful all have the same connotation in Islamic political jurisprudence.
4. A significant number of Muslims believe that the caliphate is part of the creed and the fundamentals of the religion, not merely a scholarly and discretionary issue. Therefore, the caliph is appointed by God, as the people have no authority to do this, and his job is 'to complete the Sharia', not just to apply it.
5. Note the last statement: 'The *Umma* is immunized against faults', which implies that the *Umma* is unable to control its behavior and to differentiate between good and evil. For this reason, it is in need of someone to control it and to determine what its members may or may not do. In jurisprudence, this is expressed by stating that the Caliph's custodianship of the *Umma* is similar to the custodianship of the legal guardian over minors, both of which mean exclusive disposal and guardianship of the interests of 'those who are under custodianship' and preventing them from practising any conducts or behaviours that the 'guardian' sees as harmful to the minor.
6. Where 'those charged with authority' means those in charge of the affairs of the *Umma*, at the forefront of whom is the caliph or the guardian.
7. 'Al-A'mash told us reporting from Abi Saleh reporting from Abi Hurayra saying: The Prophet (Peace be upon him) said: He who obeyed me has obeyed God, and he who obeyed the Imam has obeyed me, and he who disobeyed me has disobeyed God and he who disobeyed the Imam has disobeyed me.'
8. Ibn Aabdeen is quoting from Al-Hidayeh on the topic of the number of *Takbeers* in the two *Rak'ahs* of the feast. Nowadays people usually do seven in the first *Rak'ah* and six in the second because the Abbasside caliphs so ordained. In Al-Zaheereh, he said, in an interpretation of that which was quoted from Abu Yousuf and Mohammad, that they did so because Haroun ordered them to do as his grandfather (Abdulla Bin Abbas) did, and they did so out of obedience, rather than out of doctrine or belief. In al-Mi'raj (the date of the Prophet's journey to the seven Heavens) he said obedience to the imam is obligatory as long as it involves no guilt. In volume 4, of the same book (p. 344), quoting Al-Hamawi, 'Saheb Al-Bahr mentioned quoting our Imams that obedience to the Imam is obligatory where it involves no guilt, even if he ordered fasting one day, this becomes imperative.'

9. Ibn Rushd (1994, 144) says: 'People are of two types: one with a habitual practice of imitation.' This category of people includes the average person who has not reached the discretionary judgment rank referred to above. The second category includes the fully fledged (qualified) discretionary interpreters. He then states (p. 92): 'The credible in unanimity are the discretionary interpreters, even if they were two or three, as long as they are the only interpreters, but the average people are not the subject of consideration because they are always followers of the interpreters and are in agreement with them, as such is their disposition.' It is to be noted that from a practical point of view, nobody recognizes the discretionary judgment issued by anybody after the third century in the sense referred to by Ibn Rushd. Imitation has become well established but with discretionary judgment within the limits of 'the fundamentals of the creed' and its reference books attributed to those who were described as the founders of the creeds in the second and third centuries.
10. The theoretical pre-qualifications of the imam include: 'the knowledge that is conducive to discretionary interpretation of misfortunes and provisions' (Al-Mawardi 1982, 6).
11. In Al-Mahsoul by Al-Razi (1988, 504), we read: 'Almighty God has given a specific judgment of each incident and there is an apparent proof of that not a decisive one.'
12. Of course, the 'guardian' or 'the ruling power seekers' were not alone in going to extremes with regard to the concepts of 'virtue', 'vice' and the 'protection of religion', as many historical incidents showed, but this took place through jurisprudential *fatwa*s issued in response to the desire of the ruler, or because of the narrow-mindedness of those who issued them. For example, in 1860, Spanish forces occupied Tetouan in northern Morocco and the area that separated it from the sea. An agreement was then concluded stipulating that Morocco should pay the sum of 20 million gold Riyals in exchange for a Spanish withdrawal. The king requested a *fatwa* from the scholars and a number opposed the payment on the grounds that it helped strengthen the 'infidels', insisting that his duty was to wage Jihad against them and expel them from Muslim lands. However, such judgments failed to consider the social, political and military conditions in Morocco following the defeat of the Moroccan Army by the French in 1844 at the Battle of Esli on the Moroccan–Algerian border.

    On 24 August 1901, King Abdul Azeez issued a daring Royal Decree that laid a solid foundation for steps towards reform and modern state-building. Under this decree, the king decided to levy a general tax in the name of 'arrangement'. It is a well-known fact that the causes underlying the poor relationships between ruler and ruled in Muslim societies, the ruling authorities' lack of care of facilities for these societies, and the absence of considered planning for the present and future stem from the lack of resources for *Bayt Al-Mal* (the treasury). Such funding comes solely from 'infidels' as Muslims are obliged only to pay *Zakat*, which is distributed to beneficiaries and never goes to *Bayt Al-Mal*. This situation caused rulers to collect money from the people arbitrarily, thus creating widespread grievance and injustice. It was this situation that Abdul Azeez attempted to correct with his decree issued on 24 August 1901, the significant points of which were as follows:

    > It defined precisely the 'tax' pot and the amounts imposed on properties, cattle, trees, and farmlands, whether irrigated or dry. This was to replace the former situation where collection of monies was delegated to governors and leaders, who used to exercise full authority over money as well as over the people's dignity. It cancelled the privilege whereby certain categories were exempted from taxation, including those enjoying the protection of foreign states, the sheriffs, corner owners, and people of power and those holding Royal Decrees for reverence and respect. It also stated that 'the honored, the sheriff, the strong, the weak, even he who was a worker, a sheikh, a caliph, or the like, will all be treated in the same way as other people, so much so that nobody is excluded from the coverage of this order nor from the inclusiveness of this measure.
    >
    > It also abolished what was known as 'storage costs', the assessment of which was left to governors and leaders: 'As to governors, they have been left with no authority to impose on you or to collect from you anything, not even a trimming of a fingernail. We have decided this because we have allotted to them salaries which they receive from Bay Al-Mal, May Allah keep it prosperous, providing that they stop laying their

hands on the belongings of anyone of the tribe or make an assault to take something greedily or by deception.

However, rather than endorsing the king's proposal and looking into developing and improving its content, the scholars of Fez issued a *fatwa* dethroning Abdul Aziz for having violated the Sharia provisions by issuing the 'Arrangement' Royal Decree. At the same time, they gave *Bay'ah* to his brother, Abdul Hafiz, as his successor and attached to the *Bay'ah* pledge a condition to cancel the tax arrangements imposed by the dethroned king. (No reference is provided as these historical facts are accepted in Moroccan society as common knowledge.)

13. For the full text of the speech, see Harakat (1915, 116). He was not viewed as an imam for Muslims like the other imams, but many extraordinary capabilities were attributed to him. For example, Al-Kitani (2004, 72) quotes Abi Al-Abbas Al-Muqri: 'that he had writing between his shoulders, meaning by God: There is no God but Allah, Mohammad is the messenger of God. Mashallah. There is no power but in God. All matter is in God's hand. This is a descendant of Prophet Mohammad "peace be upon him"'. He adds that Rashid Bin Minasseh educated him in the best of manners and taught him the Holy Quran (such that he memorized the Quran when he was eight years old – some say seven), taught him the Sunnah, jurisprudence, the Hadiths, grammar, poetry, literature, the proverbs and wise sayings of the Arabs, kings' biographies and politics, told him about peoples' history, trained him in horse-riding, archery and military strategy, all of which he had mastered by the age of 10 or 11, although historians differ on this.
14. For example, see the *Bay'ah* of the people of Fez' to Sultan Abdul Malek Bin Isma'il dated 8 Sha'ban 1140 AH (corresponding to 20 March 1728) (Simo 2011).
15. The decree stipulated that the Advisory Council for Human Rights raise its proposals to the 'guardian', i.e. the king, which is a term that includes in its significance the Commandment of the Faithful and management of all the worldly affairs of society.
16. Its preamble states: 'In application of the trust assigned to us in our capacity as Commander of the Faithful, and as entailed by the General Imamate to guard the religion, to ensure performance of its rituals and implementation of its codes and to consolidate its values and provisions … .'
17. None of the decrees mentioned in this paragraph could be issued under the title 'Commander of the Faithful' without countersignature by the head of the government, except those related to the religious field, and these are the ones based on Chapter 41. But those decrees referred to in other chapters shall be issued by the king in his capacity as king, i.e. head of the state.
18. I will refer to examples of these judgments from contemporary Moroccan actuality.
19. There are too many, not only in our present time, but also formerly. Examples include what jurisprudence states about the responsibility of the guardian to specify the acts and conducts that are punishable and specifying their punishment by public censuring, except for the crimes of *Hudud* and *Qasas* which hardly exceed the number of fingers on one hand.
20. As the Mukhatti'ah school of jurisprudence believes.
21. As the Musawwibah school of jurisprudence believes. Both Al-Mukhatti'eh and Al-Musawwibeh agree that the 'discretionary interpreter' should be imitated, as people are of two types: discretionary interpreters and common folk. The latter are obligated to imitate, according to Ibn Rushd. Nobody was ever acknowledged as an discretionary interpreter after the death of Ahmad Bin Hanbal in the mid-third Hijri century (Ibn Rushd 1994, 92, 144).
22. The Mufti's jurisdiction covers all affairs of the individual and the *Umma*. The closing statement of the Global Conference on Fatwa and its Controls, which was held by the jurisprudential compound of the League of the Islamic World in Mecca, on 17–20 January 2010, included this line: 'The Mufti is the one who transmits God's judgment with a proof to those who ask for it. Scopes of the *fatwa*: the *fatwa* covers all people's conduct, and no creed or a statement or an action ever goes beyond it. This includes the relation between man and his God, with himself, with others, with the state where he is living, and the relations of the state with other states at times of war and peace. That is, the *fatwa* is related to various

fields: the creed, worship, dealing, money, economics, the family, politics, judgment, the judiciary, etc.' One of the most prominent contemporary figures of *fatwa* said, 'It is supposed that jurisprudence is what governs all, and all people refer to it. Our ancestors are reported to have said: The Kings are rulers of the people and the scholars are rulers of the Kings.' The latter statement was quoted by Al-Ghazali (2010).

23. I mean theorizing in political or authoritative jurisprudence, but as to general jurisprudence, I have pointed out the theorizing adopted in the fundamentals of jurisprudence that completely ignores the term 'caliph' or 'Commander of the Faithful' and the role of the authoritative jurisprudence attributes thereto in the interpretation of the texts of the Sharia and in formulating its stipulations.
24. What is possible does not exceed the positive points outweighing the negative points.
25. For example, the political programme of the Islamic Salvation Front in Algeria included the following:

> As a guarantee of the freedom of the nation, and of its right to express its will in the most correct and safe methods both religiously and legitimately … the election laws will be reviewed, and an immature person, such as the stupid, the minor and he who is lacking legitimate justice, may not be empowered … C- the right to elect and to run for election and to participate in the management: Islam is a religion of freedom … and on the basis of this deep humanitarian perspective for man, Islam makes man responsible, and in accordance with this responsibility, man deserves the following rights:
>
> 1. The right to vote for or to choose the leadership
> 2. His right to vote authorizes him to run for election as long as he meets the following criteria:
>
> Islam – justice – good example – competency or merit … .

This is in addition to the contents of a book entitled *Shura and Democracy* published by the sheikh of a group in Morocco with a considerable standing in the community. When he discussed the Verse in the Holy Quran that says 'those who conduct their affairs by mutual consultation' (Surat Ash-Shurah, verse 38), he said:

> who are those who deserve to be consulted regularly and who are empowered to determine what is important and what is more important? Are they any group of wise people who have agreed on a certain form and a certain system for running their affairs? Or consideration is dropped down in the account of Islam when conditions fall down for the participants? Are they believers responsive to God? Making their prayers? … to all other terms of the context. The difference between a *Shura* based on the principles of Islam and a democracy built on the basis of a social contract is a substantial one … . (34)

He confirmed that

> the context that includes the Shura judgment, as presented by Almighty God in Surat Al-Shurah, has male and female believers following its path. These believers:
>
> 1. Realized, after faith entered into their hearts and settled and became deeply rooted, that what a human being is given in this worldly life is but a pleasure … .
> 2. Realized that what God keeps for the life hereafter is better and more everlasting.
> 3. Realizedthat the good God keeps for the hereafter will be obtained by those who put their full trust in God.
> 4. Refrained from committing sins, vices and immoral acts.
> 5. Having good control of themselves, are not provoked to individual anger by an unjust act.
> 6. Acceded to Almighty God, fully and in trust.

7. The seventh feature in the context is prayer-making.
8. The eighth item in the context is the *Shura*. It is the option of life, a commitment between receivables at an attitude related to the life hereafter you believe in.
9. The ninth requirement in the context of *Shura* is to give of that which God has bestowed upon us, i.e., payment of the Zakat, which is complemented by charity doing.
10. The tenth requirement in the context of *Shura* is resisting oppression, injustice and control of our destinies without our consent. (14–38)

We leave it to readers to comment on these two texts and what they mean regarding the application of Islam, the 'Religion of freedom', resistance to oppression, injustice and control of our destinies without our consent.

26. In the spring session of 1983, the constitutional period of the parliament ended, but King Hassan II (may God bless his soul) called for a general referendum to have the members of parliament to continue in office for an additional year. The referendum took place, with the leftist parties boycotting, and the proposal was approved. When the new parliamentary period came due in October 1980, the Socialist Union Party announced its decision to boycott the session that they deemed unconstitutional, and the king threatened that if they did so he would consider that as 'departure from the group' (a piece of information that was a common subject in Moroccan newspapers at the time; no reference). The judgment of 'departure from the group' or 'from the Imam' is well known in jurisprudence. The actors are to be 'invited to go back to the true path, if they do, it will be accepted of them and they will be left, but if they refuse, they will be fought and killing them will be announced as lawful … ' (Al-Kalbi 2006). So, jurisprudence laid the groundwork for the excesses that have been committed throughout the ages by stressing that opposition to the ruler, even in thought, constitutes a 'departure' against the imam or the guardian. The opposer shall be invited 'to go return to the true path' or face execution.
27. The king did not issue these decrees in his capacity as 'Commander of the Faithful', but on the basis of Chapter 101 of the 1992 Constitution that had a stipulation that 'until a House of Representatives is inaugurated, as provided for in this Constitution, the King shall take the necessary legislative measures for the establishment of constitutional institutions, for the functioning of public authorities and for managing the affairs of the state' (Official Newspaper of the Moroccan State 1992).
28. On 12 November 2012, the Council of Ministers, chaired by the king, endorsed three draft laws approving international conventions in the human rights field, concerning: (1) The Optional Protocol to the Convention against Torture and Other Cruel, Inhuman or Degrading Treatment or Punishment; (2) The Optional Protocol to the Convention on the Elimination of All Forms of Discrimination against Women; and (3) The Optional Protocol to the International Covenant on Civil and Political Rights. (The ratification of these laws by parliament has been published in the newspapers. At the time of writing (autumn 2013) these protocols were being presented to the Board of Counselors.)
29. Lawmaking with the purpose of achieving interest is not limited to the areas or details regarding which there are no written texts, but it also includes issues for which there are written texts, but realities and circumstances changed and necessitated an alteration to the provision on the basis of two principles: a provision moves with its cause, both in existence and in absence, and taking the outcome into account in lawmaking.

References

Abu Yousuf, Ya'coub Bin Ibrahim. 1987. *Kitabul Kharaj*. Beirut: Dar el-Ma'rifah.

Al-Ghazali, Abu Hamed Mohammad Bin Mohammad. 1967. *Ihya' Uloum Al-Deen* [Reviving Theology]. Vol. 1. Cairo: Mu'assassat al-Halabi wa Shuraka'uhu.

Al-Ghazali, Abu Hamed Mohammad Bin Mohammad. 2008. *Al-Mustasfa min Ilm Al-Usoul* [Selections in the Study of Principles]. Vol. 2. Beirut: Dar al-Kutub al-Ilmiyyah.

Harakat, Ibrahim. 1915. "From the Age of Prehistory up to the End of the Era of Al-Muwahhideen." Chap. 1 in *Al-Maghrib Abr Al-Tareekh: Ard Ahdaath al-Maghreb …*

[Morocco throughout History: A Presentation of Morocco's Events and Developments in the Political, Religious, Social, Developmental and Intellectual Fields from the Era before Islam until the Present Time]. Introduced by Mohammad Al-Fasi. Casablanca: Dar Al-Salam.

Ibn Aabdeen, Muhammad Omar. 1900. *Hashiyat Ibn Aabdeen*. Vol. 1. Beirut: Dar Ihya' al-Turath al-Arabi.

Ibn Khaldoun, Abu Zaid Abdul-Rahman Bin Mohammad. 2005. *Al-Muqaddimah* [14th century]. Vol. 1. Edited, introduced and annotated by Abdu-l-Salam Al-Shaddadi. Casablanca: Bayt Al-Funoun wal-Uloum wal-Aadaab.

Ibn Rushd, Abu Al-Waleed Mohammad Bin Ahmad. 1994. *Al-darouri Fi Usoul Al-Fiqh* [The Essentials of Jurisprudence]. Beirut: Dar Al-Gharb Al-Islami.

Al-Kalbi, Abu Al-Qasem Mohammad Bin Ahmad Bin Jezi. 2006. *Al-Qawanin Al-Fiqhiyyah*. Beirut: Dar Al-Kutub al-Ilmiyyah. Accessed October 1, 2013. http://elma3arif.ba7r.biz/t1264-topic/.

Al-Kitani, Mohammad Bin Ja'afar. 2004. *Salwat Al-Anfas Wa Muhadathat Al-Akyas Mimman UqbiraMin Al-Ulama' Wa Al-Sahaba bi Fas* [A Documentary on Intellectual and Graceful People from Fez]. Part 1. Casablanca: Dar al-Thakafa.

Al-Mawardi, Abu Al-Hasan Ali Bin Mohammad. 1982. *Al-Ahkam Al-Sultaniyyah*. Beirut: Dar al-Kutubl-Ilmiyyah.

Al-Mawdoudi, Abu l-A'la. 1958. *Nizamul-Hayat fil-Islam*. Damascus: Dar al-fikr.

Al-Mir, Hassan. 2009. *Mohamed Al-Sadess: Emarat Al-Mou'mineen fi 'Asharat Tajalliyaat* [Mohamed Al-Sadess: Commandment of the Faithful in Ten Manifestations]. Rabat: Ministry of Endowments and Religious Affairs.

Official Newspaper of the Moroccan State. 1992. Number 4172, 14 October.

Al-Razi, Fakhruddin Mohammad Bin Omar. 1988. *Al-mahsoul Fi Ilm Al-Usoul*. Vol. 2. Beirut: Dar Al-Kutub Al-Ilmiyyah.

Al-Shafe'i, Mohammad Bin Idriss. n.d. *Al-Risalah*. Edited and interpreted by Ahmad Mohammad Shaker. Beirut: Al-Maktaba al-Ilmiyyah; repr. of 1940 ed. Cairo: Maktabat wa Matba'at Mustafa al-Babi al-Halabi.

Al-Shatebi, Abu Isshaq Ibrahim Bin Mousa. 1999. *Al-Muwafaqaat Fi Usoul Al-Ahkamlil Shatibi* [Consensus on the Fundamentals of Rulings]. 4th ed. Beirut: Dar al-Ma'rifa.

Simo, Bahjat. 2011. *Al-bay'ah Mithak Mustamirr* [Al-*Bay'ah* An Ongoing Covenant]. Rabat: Manshurat Ukath.

Al-Soyouti, Jalaluddin Abdul-Rahman Bin Abi Bakr. 2007. *Al-Ashbah wa-Al-Naza'er* [The Similar and the Identical]. Beirut: Al-Maktaba al-Assriyyah lil Tiba'ah wal Nashr.

Representations of religion in secular states: the Muslim communities in Sweden[†]

Rickard Lagervall

Center for Middle Eastern Studies, Lund University, Lund, Sweden

The presence of Muslim populations in Western European societies is a relatively new phenomenon which is raising questions about how these societies treat religious minorities. This article considers the situation in Sweden, beginning with a brief history of the development of the Swedish state from one based on the Lutheran faith to today's secular society in which state and religion are officially separated. It moves on to discuss the emergence of a sizable Muslim population in the latter part of the 20th century and considers the ways in which the secular character and religious neutrality of the state offer such religious minorities space to practise their religions. However, as Swedish society, politics and law are still premised on certain Christian notions of what religion should be, Muslims and more particularly Islamic organizations in the country have to find ways to adapt themselves to these pre-existing religious structures. Thus the presence of a large Muslim minority has affected the mindset of the members of this minority as well as the Swedish host society.

Muslims, state, and the public in Europe: the case of Sweden

This paper will focus on the subject of Islam and Muslims in Sweden which I believe to be of relevance to (this conference on) the on-going transformations of states in the Middle East. One measure of a democratic system is the way it treats minorities; however, there is no blueprint showing exactly what a democratic system should look like. A superficial glance at the various European states is enough to reveal that each has its own unique system, which is the result of historical developments. For example, in Sweden, as in other European states, religious education is regulated by the principle of religious freedom, which is enshrined in the constitution, and thus has to consider the fact that pupils have different faiths and worldviews. However, while states such as Finland, Germany and Austria offer separate curriculums for education in (rather than about) the major religious traditions (Catholic, Protestant, Jewish, Islamic), Sweden has opted for a system in which all pupils follow the same religious education curriculum. This has been compulsory since 1997 and provides no possibility for exemptions.[1] Likewise, while the display of religious, especially Islamic, symbols

[†]This paper was originally presented in the Joint Symposium on 'Religion and State in the Arab World' convened by the Center for Arab Unity Studies and the Swedish Institute – Alexandria in Hamamat, Tunisia, 13–17 October 2012.

in the public sphere is viewed with suspicion in France, it is considered as a fundamental part of freedom of religion in Great Britain, Sweden and several other countries.

Despite significant differences between various European states, notably between those with and without colonial pasts, their Muslim communities became established in broadly similar manners: the 1960s saw a labour immigration of single males who were expected to stay temporarily before returning home with their savings. This ceased with the oil crisis in 1973 but was followed by refugee immigration and, from the late 1970s, family immigration. Whilst the Muslim populations of many European states are dominated by specific groups (North Africans in France, Belgium and the Netherlands; Turks in Germany; South Asians in the United Kingdom, etc.), Sweden is characterized by a very heterogeneous Muslim population, the composition of which has changed constantly according to geopolitical events.

I will begin by outlining the historical development of Sweden into today's secular society before moving on to provide a brief history of Islam in Sweden. Then I will give an account of the public debate on Islam and Muslims in Sweden, as this affects not only how Muslims are perceived by the surrounding society but also how individual Muslims see themselves and their place within that society. Finally I will discuss the role of Islamic organizations and imams in Sweden.

The development of the Swedish political system

Sweden is by all accounts a secular state. In 2000 the state and the Swedish Church were finally separated. This was a happy separation, desired by parliament as well as the Church, the latter having concluded that its status as the official religion did more damage than good to its credibility. The parting was the culmination of a long historical process. After the Swedish Reformation in 1523, the Swedish Church became Lutheran in faith, independent of Rome and controlled by the king. The role of the Swedish king as guardian of the Lutheran faith, and leader of the Protestant forces in Europe against the Catholics in the Thirty Years' War (1618–1648), made the Lutheran faith an essential component of the state's legitimacy. Hence a royal decree in 1685 and a canon law the following year banned the practice of all other faiths in the kingdom, making it illegal for a Swedish subject to belong to any other religion. Local priests were tasked with interrogating their parishioners in order to check their knowledge of, and adherence to, the correct doctrine of the State Church (Karlson and Svanberg 1997). This prohibition affected not only Judaism and Catholicism but also other varieties of Protestantism. Various piety movements had begun to emerge in the 17th century and, as they grew stronger, some split from the State Church and founded independent churches known as 'Free Churches'. Lay people belonging to such movements, both outside and within the State Church, often assembled in private homes to read and discuss the Bible and this was considered so threatening to the Church's monopoly of religious interpretation that such meetings were eventually banned in 1726.

In the late 17th century a liberalization of this religious policy began, with royal decrees permitting foreigners to practise other Christian faiths, as well as Judaism, as long as they did so discretely. The interdiction of private prayer meetings was lifted in 1858 and, in 1870, citizens were allowed to belong to recognized religious communities other than the State Church. Finally, in 1952, it became permissible for a Swedish citizen to belong to no religious community at all, probably because Sweden had by then signed the United Nations' Convention on Human Rights in which freedom of religion is defined as including freedom from religion (Karlson and Svanberg 1997).

Thus, in what may seem a somewhat paradoxical situation, the independent Christian movements, most of which would be labelled fundamentalist by today's standards, had a huge impact on the development of the contemporary secular state in which religion is considered to be a private matter. The decoupling of religious identity from citizenship and from national identity was a response to growing sectarian strife. When these movements gained legitimacy in the 19th century, they were able to create more solid structures as Free Churches and eventually establish independent institutions for educating their own pastors (Sanders 1995). In 1963 members of these movements, notably the Pentecostal Church, created the Christian Democratic Party in order to fight against the increasing secularization of Swedish society. However, as the party won seats in parliament and then participated in a centre-right government in the 1990s, it gradually moved to the centre, making its Christian identity increasingly diffuse.

Thus, when a noticeable Muslim population began to settle in Sweden from 1960 onwards, they arrived into a religious context characterized by the gradual disestablishment of the State Church, and several Free Churches of various sizes.

A brief history of Islam in Sweden

The first Muslims to arrive in Sweden were Ottoman creditors who followed the indebted Swedish King Charles XII when he returned to the country after seven years in the Ottoman Empire, an ally of Sweden during the wars of the 17th century. They left no discernible traces in the country, returning home once they had been paid. It was not until the end of the Second World War that a group of Tartars from Russia and the Baltic countries arrived in Sweden, via Finland, and settled in Stockholm. Here, in 1949, they founded the first Islamic organization, known as the Turk–Islamic Association, although it later changed its name to the Islamic Association in Sweden. One of its members, Osma Soukkan, became what is considered to be the first imam in Sweden in the 1950s. The Tartars were also the first group to seek permission to build a mosque, but were always refused. Their association was active until the 1970s, but gradually lost its Tartar identity due to labour immigration from Turkey and Yugoslavia (Otterbeck 1998). By the 1970s, the Muslim population of Stockholm had grown so much that it that it began to divide along ethnic and linguistic lines.[2]

In order to illustrate how new Islam is as a Swedish religion, it is useful to demonstrate the development of the Muslim population:

- 1930 (the last time religious affiliation was registered in a census and hence the only reliable number): 15 Muslims.
- 1953: Approximately 500.
- 1966: 6000.
- 1970: 9000.
- 1980: 30,000.
- 1992: 100,000.
- 2000: 250,000–300,000.
- 2010: 350,000–400,000.

As illustrated by the figures for 2000 and 2010, these estimates are highly approximate. Religious identity is not registered and it is not possible simply to look at countries of origin because a disproportionately high number of immigrants from the Middle East belong to religious minorities (as Christians, Mandeans and Yazidies are often especially vulnerable in conflict situations). Whilst labour immigration until 1973 had brought Muslims mostly from Turkey, Yugoslavia and other Balkan countries, the 1970s and 1980s saw an influx of refugees. These included those escaping the civil war in Lebanon, Palestinians, and, in the aftermath of the Iranian revolution and subsequent Iran–Iraq War during the 1980s, refugees from both these countries. New waves of Iraqi refugees came after the American attacks in 1991 and 2003; and Afghans arrived after both the Soviet and American occupations. Somalis have formed another important group since the implosion of the Somali state in 1991. At present, the largest numbers of new arrivals are Somalis and Syrians.

Only a minority of the Muslim population appears to be religiously active. One way of estimating the number of practising Muslims is to consider the membership of Islamic congregations recognized by the Commission for State Grants to Religious Communities and the latest figure from 2010 suggests there are 110,000 (Nämnden för statligt stöd för trossamfund 2012). However, not all congregations are recognized, as registration is not compulsory and certain criteria must be met in order to achieve recognition and hence entitlement to state grants. In 2009, The Centre for Middle Eastern Studies in Lund made an inventory of Islamic associations in the twin cities of Malmö and Lund in southern Sweden. They identified 38 associations in Malmö, a city with a population of around 300,000, but managed to contact only 24 of them (Lundqvist and Stenberg 2009). It is unclear how many of these associations could be considered as Islamic congregations as most were small, unofficial and located in cellars or industrial buildings. These findings were soon out of date because some congregations closed while new ones opened.

The first purpose-built mosque in Sweden was constructed in 1976 by the Ahmadiyya community in Gothenburg, the second largest city, but did not attract other Muslims. The first non-Ahmadiyya purpose-built mosque in Scandinavia was inaugurated in Malmö in 1984. The foundation behind it, The Islamic Centre, was established mainly by people from the Balkans, but its staff and users comprise many ethnicities. Its ambition is to welcome and represent all Muslims in southern Sweden, regardless of denomination. Although the majority of its visitors are Sunnis, the centre stresses that it is open to all Muslims and, at least in recent years, it has arranged *Ashura* celebrations for Shias. There are, of course, also small Shia congregations in Malmö (in 2009 there were two). From a national perspective, the inauguration of the Stockholm Mosque in 2000 was a landmark event, and there are now at least four other purpose-built mosques in Sweden with construction plans for several more. Yet, it is only in Malmö that both the Ahmadiyya community and the Islamic Information Association have advanced plans to build great mosques.

One legal obstacle that Muslims in Sweden face, along with the Jewish community, is an animal-protection law forbidding slaughter without prior stunning. However, as the import of halal and kosher meat is permitted, this appears to present few practical problems. As in some other European states, there has been debate concerning the circumcision of young boys in Sweden, with some demanding a ban on the grounds that it constitutes physical abuse (female circumcision is already banned). Yet the major political parties have not adopted this idea and it seems unlikely that parliament will vote on it in the near future. Both the existing prohibition of halal slaughter and the proposed ban on circumcision of minor boys are justified on the grounds that religion is about what people believe, not what they eat or their bodily practices, and hence, the argument continues, such bans do not violate freedom of religion. This conception of religion as a private matter, located in the *forum internum*, is of course a Protestant idea which is often taken for granted in a Lutheran, albeit secularized, society such as Sweden.

The Swedish business community is only just beginning to identify the growing Muslim population as a potential target group. In recent years some banks have experimented with offering interest-free loans but, to my knowledge, these attempts have been short-lived due to lack of people's interest. Shopkeepers have now noticed Ramadan, but are yet to fully realize its commercial potential.

Media debates on Islam in Sweden

The public debate on Islam and Muslims in Sweden circulates around similar issues to those in other European states. However, in each country the problems identified and the solutions proposed by state authorities vary according to each state's particular history, legal system and institutional setting. The Swedish authorities' positions on different kinds of veil, for example, are clearly different from those of the French authorities. While France justifies its ban on 'ostensible religious symbols' in state schools on the basis of the principle of secularity (or *laïcité*), understood not only as an obligation of religious neutrality on the part of the state but also on the part of its citizens,[3] Swedish authorities consider the right to wear religious symbols as an essential part of religious freedom.[4]

In 2002, Swedish state television banned a television host from appearing in a *hijab*, only to retreat after a public debate on the issue. In 2006, the Swedish Police Union decided to accept the *kippah*, turban and *hijab* as part of the uniform. In December 2011, the first *hijab*-wearing woman to join the police academy appeared on the front cover of the police magazine wearing her uniform with the new official *hijab*. The headline was 'Cop in Veil. Donna became the first police trainee with a hijab.'

The right to wear *hijab* in state schools has not been questioned, but the status of the full-face veil is more uncertain. According to a directive from the National Agency for Education in 2003, each school may decide whether it is practical to allow it or not (Skolverket 2003).[5] This means that while there is no official ban on full-face veils in state schools, wearing it is not considered to be an essential part of the inviolable freedom of religion. Unlike France, where the identification of the veil as a religious symbol justifies its prohibition in public schools, in Sweden it is precisely this possible identification of the full-face veil that renders a ban more difficult. Schools may only forbid it for practical reasons, for example, the difficulty of identifying an individual during an examination, problems of communication with a person hiding her face, for safety reasons in laboratories, and, in the case of professional education, the waste of money educating someone who is unlikely to be employed.

Another interesting debate occurred in 2006 when a Muslim man who had been denied employment at a factory after a trial period was refused unemployment benefit on the grounds that he had not made enough effort to secure the job. The Public Employment Service argued that he did not secure the position because he had refused to shake the hand of his female boss (instead raising his hand to his heart as a sign of respect), something she denied. The Public Employment Service was finally ordered to pay 60,000 kronas (US$8500) in damages in 2010

(Diskrimineringsombudsmannen (DO) 2010). This resulted in a debate on the limits of religious freedom which, according to my interpretation, circulated around the question of what it means to be a Swedish citizen and how much diversity a society can contain without tearing apart. One side in this debate (with which I identify) argued that the willingness to shake hands with the opposite sex should not be seen as a prerequisite for the enjoyment of full civil rights, whilst the other side maintained that a man's refusal to shake a woman's hand was a violation of her human dignity and that hand-shaking formed part of the social contract of Swedish society.

The most recent debate, and perhaps the most interesting for the purposes of this paper, was stirred by an investigative television report in which two Arabic-speaking female reporters, dressed in *niqab* and equipped with a hidden camera, visited ten mosques in several Swedish cities. One of the reporters pretended to have marital problems because her husband had taken a second wife. This, she continued, affected their intimate life and her husband maltreated her because she did not want to have sex. Most imams answered that while it may not be good for a man to marry more than one wife, this is his undeniable right and she should, therefore, suffer this patiently in the hope that he would improve or, if not, she should await reward for her virtue in the next life. She was also told that it was her duty as a wife to have sex with her husband, irrespective of her own will and, lastly, that she must not report the violence to the police (interestingly, it was only a Salafi imam who told her, in entirely unambiguous terms, that she absolutely should tell the police). In discussions of the issue, in the television report itself, and in the ensuing public debate, accusations were made that the imams were guilty of misconduct and had violated Swedish law. While this would be true of a social worker, who is obliged by law to report domestic violence, as imams have no official status and are thus considered as private individuals from a legal perspective, it is hard to see what regulation they violated. The television report was also accused of fomenting Islamophobia. I myself have avoided such accusations because the report confirmed what I already suspected after having spoken to imams, that is, that the fragile institutionalization of Islam in Sweden has resulted in the imams' incapacity to solve difficult issues.

More problematic was the exclusive focus on Islam and imams in this debate. Some recent reports have concluded that the perception of domestic violence as a private matter to be dealt with without recourse to the authorities is also present in Eastern Orthodox Churches, as well as in some Swedish Free Churches (Älgamo 2009; Ungdomsstyrelsen 2012). Furthermore, the perception of domestic violence as a public concern, as opposed to a private matter, is a fairly recent development, the result of decades of campaigning by activists for women's rights. I raised these issues in an op-ed that the editor entitled 'Swedish imams need education' (Lagervall 2012). Although I was not happy with the patronizing tone of the title, it did lead the way towards the possibility of establishing a Swedish Islam by creating a national education programme for imams.

The discussion of a Swedish education for imams

In 2008, the then Minister of Higher Education ordered a report on the need for a Swedish education for imams. The motive he presented for this initiative, which was most frequently highlighted in the media, was that it could halt the radicalization of Muslims. If imams were to be educated in Sweden, Islamic congregations would no longer depend upon imams from abroad, notably from Saudi Arabia. There is a widespread perception in Sweden, as in the rest of Western Europe, of the pervasive and noxious influence of Saudi Wahhabism on some Muslims. In other words, it was the security argument that received most attention. Much less was made of his second reason, which was one of fairness. He argued that Swedish Muslims should have the same opportunities to educate their religious leaders as other, historically more established, denominations. The report, which was published in 2009, was written by three prominent Swedish scholars who interviewed 102 imams as well as lay members of Islamic congregations (Amnå, Brundin, and Larsson 2009). Their findings showed that of these imams only nine were educated in Saudi Arabia, thus contradicting the widespread idea of Saudi dominance. Instead it was Turkey that had educated the greatest number of imams (47), probably due to the Turkish policy of dispatching state-salaried imams to those Turkish congregations in Europe which were willing to receive them. Ten imams were educated in Bosnia-Herzegovina, seven in Jordan and Iraq, four in Britain and three in France. If we consider Turkey to be a European state, then the majority were actually educated in Europe. According to the report, the Islamic organizations estimated the total number of imams at between 250 and 300. Of these, Turkish imams are usually under the authority of the Turkish Ministry of Religion (*Diyanet*), Bosnian imams are governed by the Grand Mufti of Sarajevo, while other imams operate under the authority of the local communities that employ them.

The report also considered the ability of imams to govern the Muslim population. This idea is recurrently expressed both by Swedish authorities and Islamic organizations, the latter using it to stress their own importance to integration and for preserving social peace. The report cautioned against overstating the importance of imams as instruments for integration and attempting to give them roles for which they lacked a mandate amongst their congregations. It argued that it was not suitable for a democratic state to attempt to co-opt religious organizations which should be seen as part of civil society:

> [T]he Swedish constitution contains, formally as well as in practice, a great measure of associational policy based on the principle of freedom of association. In practice it may be difficult to draw a line between the state and these organizations. In a formal sense, the so-called 'civic associations' have been co-opted by state powers for different purposes. In a more subtle sense, the development of the association policy of the state and the communes also entails the risk that the organizations become more and more dependent and hence uninteresting or plainly counterproductive to those democratic values for which they are praised and for the dissemination of which they receive state funding. (Amnå, Brundin, and Larsson 2009, 98)

The report concludes that the proposal of a Swedish education for imams comes close to crossing an important line whereby the state risks engaging organizations and their leaders in tasks for which they lack a mandate within the autonomous organizations (Amnå, Brundin, and Larsson, 2009).

The report also argued that as the majority of Muslims in Sweden are not religiously active, integration should take place in other areas of society and across confessional borders. It therefore expressed 'doubts about placing too strong an emphasis on people's assumed religious belongings'. Another merit of the report was its refusal to consider Islam as an exceptional case. Instead it drew explicit parallels with the long process whereby the independent Churches developed their own educational institutions outside the control of the Swedish State Church, concluding that the institutional establishment of such religious organizations is the result of historical processes that take time to develop. It also pointed to the fact that it is not only Islamic congregations that depend on foreign-educated religious leaders as the same is true of Orthodox and Eastern Orthodox Christians, as well as Jewish congregations.

Although the majority of Muslim leaders and imams interviewed were positive about a Swedish education for imams, this was on condition that the advanced study of *fiqh* would take place only within Islamic organizations. The report therefore concluded that, at present, there is no great demand for a Swedish education for imams, that Islamic organizations are unlikely to unite around a shared education, that they are not interested in any teaching on Islamic matters delivered by non-Muslims, and that they are suspicious of the state's attempts to interfere in their interpretation of Islamic law. What was of interest to Muslim organizations and imams was a supplementary education in the Swedish language and Swedish society and law for imams already active within the country. The imams themselves stressed the need for training in Swedish family law as several imams are licensed to conduct official marriages.

One legal obstacle to the establishment of a state-run education for imams is the fact that teaching in state schools and universities is legally obliged to be non-confessional and open to students of all faiths or none. One of the institutions with which I am affiliated, the Centre for Theology and Religious Studies at Lund University, was rebuked some years ago by the authorities after starting a class for student priests with collective prayer. The confessional part of a priest's education is required to take place at the pastoral seminary which is run by the Swedish Church independently of the state. Similarly, the confessional part of an imam's education would have to take place within an independent institution.

Imams, sharia and parallel systems of law

One of the most contentious issues in European debates on Islam today is that of the implementation of sharia law in European states and its threat to democratic and secular systems. Of course, Islam is not the only religion with a strict legal code – Islam, Judaism and Christianity are often referred to as 'law religions'. However, in the current debate in Europe and North America, Islam is often described as the law religion par excellence. The fact that Christianity and Judaism have faced similar challenges in the context of emerging modern states since the 18th century is often forgotten.

I myself gave a course at the Centre for Middle Eastern Studies at Lund University in Sweden called 'The Implementation of Sharia in Sweden and the EU'. The title was deliberatively provocative in order to attract potential students. It also garnered some media attention with speculation that I was going to 'defend sharia' and promote its implementation in Sweden (including the *hudud* punishments). In a newspaper interview I responded that it was not a course *in* sharia but *about* sharia, that is, the purpose was not to teach future imams how to interpret sharia in order to implement it but to offer a non-confessional course which explains how the Islamic legal tradition operates in a minority situation within modern European national states (Sjögren 2011).

In the introduction to the course I told the students that I would not be offering them a clear-cut scientific definition of sharia because one of my main points was precisely that sharia is a contestable concept which means different things to different individuals and groups. In the debates that arise whenever Muslim representatives in Europe demand official recognition for sharia rules there is often confusion as to what sharia actually means. Does it mean the right for European Muslims to partition inheritance according to the Islamic tradition, which is problematic in itself because of the unequal shares allotted to male and female relatives? Or does it mean the application of corporal punishments? I would argue that this ambivalence of the term 'sharia' is its essential characteristic.

A related point that I stressed during the course was the manner in which the position of Islam and sharia changed fundamentally as a result of the rise of the post-colonial national states in the Middle East. Important developments include the codifications of the personal status laws, the introduction of European laws in other areas (most notably the *Code Napoléon* in penal law), and the expanding grip of the state over the religious field (such as taking control of the *awqaf*, thus virtually transforming the *'ulama* into state-employed functionaries, and monopolizing the interpretation of Islam by establishing state muftis or supreme *'ulama* councils (see Zeghal 1996 on Egypt; and Zeghal 2005 on Morocco). Such actions by Middle Eastern states bear some interesting similarities to the efforts of European states to establish Muslim councils to represent (and control) their Muslim populations, and to establish national educations for imams with the, often explicit, purpose of creating a cadre of domestic imams preaching loyalty to the state.

One consequence of the migration of large populations from the Middle East and North Africa to Europe is that European legal systems now encounter various forms of Islamic law. In certain circumstances, for example, in the case of a dispute between a married couple, European courts may be required to take foreign laws based on the Islamic tradition into consideration within the framework of international private law. In other instances, marriage and divorce are conducted in European mosques without being officially recognized by the state. This can give rise to the phenomenon of 'limping marriages', for example, when a civil divorce is recognized by the state but not by the Muslim community or the country of origin (on the Swedish case, see Arvidsson 2009).

So what are the consequences of all this for Muslims in Europe? It means that when questions related to sharia are raised, it may be related to a foreign positive law, that of personal status. But it can also be related to a fluid idea of Islamic law as interpreted by local Muslim representatives.

Authorities

Imams in Europe, generally, and in Sweden in particular, do not typically consider themselves capable of interpreting the law. They are neither *mujtahid*s who practice *ijtihad*, legal reasoning, nor muftis who issue *fatwa*s. Often they have a reified view of Islamic law as an ahistorical and unchanging entity. Their advice to Muslims may deviate from this perceived law, but they do not regard this as reinterpretation of the law but rather as a pragmatic accommodation to the prevailing circumstances. If they require religious justification for their advice, they tend to follow authorities based in the Muslim world. There are different types of authorities but we may, for reasons of simplicity, use the labels 'enclavists' and 'accommodationists'.

Amongst the enclavists we may count salafi sheikhs who consider European secular legal systems as inherently impious. Hence their advice to Muslims is to avoid contact with such systems, not even registering marriages or divorces. They consider men's right to be married to up to four women simultaneously as God-given and thus not to be denied by human intervention. This category of sheikhs sometimes advocate the same enclavist tendency for Muslims living in the Middle East, for example by advocating unregistered marriages (*zawaj 'urfi*), because they consider the legal systems in these countries also deviate from what they regard as authentic Islamic law.

Amongst the accommodationists, which in my estimation constitute the majority of imams, we may count a number of sheikhs who sometimes represent an *Ikhwani* tendency, although they are not necessarily formally affiliated to the Muslim Brotherhood. Here we find The European Islamic Council, of which Yusuf al-Qaradawi and Rachid Ghannouchi are prominent members, and shi'a authorities such as the recently deceased Lebanese Ayatollah Fadlallah or the Iraqi-based Iranian Ayatollah Sistani. All these represent conservative family values by comparison with the dominant norms of Swedish society but they urge European Muslims to participate in the societies in which they reside and to abide by state laws. Muslims should therefore follow civil procedures to register their marriages and respect the interdiction on polygamy. Al-Qaradawi is a proponent of minority *fiqh*, an interpretation of Islamic law adapted to Muslims living in minority situations, which eases some religious obligations in order that state law is not infringed. This minority *fiqh* may be seen as theological justification for an existing practice among many imams in Europe.[6]

Conflicts between Swedish private law and foreign private laws are not restricted to laws based on the Islamic legal tradition. The process of European integration has intensified efforts to address legal disputes with transnational legal implications. However, the differences between various European legislations pertaining to marriage and divorce are relatively minor, as all are based on a Christian conception of what constitutes a marriage. The same cannot be said of Islamic law. One major difference is that a Muslim man is permitted to be married to up to four wives simultaneously. Another is that, in principle, only men have a unilateral right to divorce as, within the classical Islamic legal tradition, a woman can only obtain a divorce with her husband's consent.[7] According to the Maliki legal school, which prevails in North Africa, a judge may proclaim a divorce in the husband's name (*tatliq*) if the woman can prove that the husband has caused her undue harm. Although modern legislation has attempted to restrict men's ability to exercise these prerogatives, as the area of family affairs is now the only field in which Islamic rules still have legal force in most Muslim states, albeit in modernized forms, such rules have been bestowed with an almost sacral dimension for many Muslims.

Legal dimensions

European Muslim couples involved in marital disputes therefore often have to consider several legal dimensions: the Codes of Personal Status of their countries of origin, European imams' unofficial interpretations of the Islamic tradition, and European laws.

One problem that can arise is the so-called 'limping marriage', that is, a marriage that is recognized in one legal system but not in another. For example, an Egyptian couple move to Sweden where the woman obtains a divorce in a Swedish court but which the man refuses to accept. He may do this because he simply does not want to divorce, but he may also be attempting to avoid the risk of being forced by an Egyptian court to pay the dower. The divorce may thus have legal force in Sweden but not in Egypt. If the woman visits her relatives in Egypt, Egyptian authorities may hand any children over to the husband, or even detain the woman herself if she does not have her husband's permission to leave the country.

The second dimension is that of a marriage conducted in a Swedish mosque. A Muslim couple may marry in a Swedish mosque, but their marriage might not be legally recognized. If they go to an imam who has no licence to conduct marriages, the union has only religious validity but is not recognized by the state. Whilst this is not illegal, it means that the marriage does not exist according to Swedish law. Of course, this religious ceremony may simply be a supplement to the civil procedure. However, if they neglect, or refuse, to register their marriage, they enter into a partnership which has no legal status according to the Swedish authorities.

This creates a grey area which the Swedish legal system finds difficult to negotiate. How should it treat a man with more than one wife when none, or only one, of these marriages is recognized by the Swedish authorities? While Swedish law forbids polygamous marriages, having several extramarital relations is considered a private matter and is perfectly legal. Another question is that of minors. While the forced marriage of minors, even if it is not officially recognized as such, is equivalent to forcing minors into a sexual relationship and is thus punishable, a religious marriage between teenagers may simply be a way of giving religious legitimacy to an ordinary teenage relationship. In the latter case, rather than being an example of honour-related structures, it could be considered as a pragmatic accommodation of religious norms to social realities in Sweden.

Most imams I have talked to express an accommodationist stance, that is, they seek to accommodate religious norms within the prevailing legal system. Whilst a licensed imam may legally marry a couple in Sweden, no imam has official authority to divorce a couple as, in order for a divorce to be lawful, it must go through the Swedish authorities. The fact that many ordinary Muslims, and even some imams, are unaware of this has resulted in couples in Sweden believing that they are legally divorced but whose marriage still exists according to Swedish law. However, even though Swedish mosques have no officially sanctioned authority to divorce people, they can still play an essential role. Firstly, they can give religious legitimacy to a civil divorce. Several imams have told me that they routinely give women who have legally divorced a certificate confirming that the divorce is religiously valid, even if the husband refuses to accept it. One imam supported this practice based on a *fatwa* issued by the *fatwa* section of The European Islamic Council. Secondly, they can mediate between the Swedish legal system and a foreign one. For example, Lebanese authorities often require a certificate from some kind of Muslim authority before they will recognize the dissolution of a marriage concluded in Lebanon. Lebanese Muslims living in Sweden therefore have to consider two authorities, Swedish and Lebanese, mediated by unofficial Muslim authorities in Sweden. There is thus, in practice, a system of parallel laws in Sweden, a situation which Muslim representatives in the country have not necessarily striven for but which they seek to accommodate by serving as intermediaries between disputing couples and foreign authorities.

This situation may not cause couples additional inconvenience beyond the supplementary measures required to ensure their divorces are recognized in their countries of origin. However, one party involved in a dispute might deliberately seek to play the different systems off against each other in order to obtain the best possible outcome. For example, if a husband refuses to accept a divorce, an imam can try to dissuade him in the hope that his religious credentials will prevail. However, if the husband refuses to agree, the woman will still be considered to be married to him in Lebanon, and often among their relatives in Sweden too. If she goes on to marry again, this marriage will be legally valid as far as the Swedish authorities are concerned, but she risks being considered a bigamist by Lebanese authorities and punished as such if she visits that country. The man, on the other hand, can remarry without fear of prosecution for he will be considered legally married in a monogamous union by Swedish authorities, and legally married to two wives according to Lebanese authorities. This conscious use of conflicting laws is called 'forum shopping' (Mehdi *et al.* 2008).

Women also have opportunities to use this strategy, for example, by demanding the payment of the dower after a divorce. European legal systems have found it notoriously difficult to translate the Islamic legal category of dower, *mahr*, into a familiar legal institution. Hence, there have been cases in which Swedish courts have not accepted a Muslim woman's claim to the payment of the dower but her rights have been recognized by a Lebanese court, with the help of a certificate from a Swedish imam. As a result the former husband risked being compelled to pay the dower, which can amount to very significant sums, if he were to visit that country. A media report in 2002 drew attention to just such a case (*Sydsvenskan*, June 9, 2002). A Lebanese man, who described himself as not especially religious but who had accepted a Muslim marriage in Sweden because of demands from his wife's family, found himself, after the divorce, faced with a claim for a dower payment of 70,000 kronas (US$10,000). His former wife had contacted The Supreme Muslim Council of Scandinavia, which despite its ambitious name appears to be a local body in Malmö,[8] which had concluded that, by virtue of having taken the initiative to divorce, the man was responsible for it and therefore obliged to pay the specified dower. The council sent documents confirming this to Lebanon and the man was summoned to court proceedings there. His lawyer advised him not to go in order to avoid the risk of being detained if he could not pay. According to the President of the council, Adly Abu Hajar, while a Swedish civil divorce is not recognized by Lebanese authorities, they do accept documents from the council, as do Syria, Jordan and Iraq. The council's actions were criticized both by Swedish politicians, who accused it of acting as a parallel court, and by the President of the Islamic Centre in Malmö who stated that it was not the task of Muslim representatives to pose as lawyers.

The council's actions are without doubt problematic. For example, in countries in which the Code of Personal Status is based on Islamic tradition, the dower can function as a financial security for the wife if the marriage is dissolved. If a high sum is specified in the marital contract, it may serve to deter the man from divorcing his wife without a legitimate reason and, if he does so, she will have some financial recompense. However, in this case, the Lebanese man was already obliged to pay monthly maintenance to his wife as a result of the civil divorce, something the council did not take into consideration. It probably considered the dower as a religious obligation and the payment of the sum agreed upon in the marital contract as an issue of contractual obligation. Yet, when the council acts as a parallel court, it bridges a gap between the Swedish and Lebanese authorities. This empty space is not of its own making but results from a lack of coordination between the two authorities. Such actions are not necessarily the results of an ambition to build up a parallel legal system to compete with the official Swedish one, but rather an attempt to provide much needed mediation between the Swedish and the Lebanese legal systems.

These realities confront the Swedish legal system and Swedish authorities with challenges they are often unwilling to face. When the social democratic MP Luciano Astudillo was made aware of the problems of 'limping marriages' and 'forum shopping' during a visit to the Islamic Centre in Malmö, he addressed the Swedish Parliament in an interpellation in 2006, suggesting a law that would require men residing in

Sweden to provide documentary evidence that they were not already married. This would be in addition to the already obligatory enquiries into impediments to marriage. Admittedly, the suggestion was not without complications, for example, a refugee who may have strained relations with the authorities of his country of origin might well have difficulty obtaining such a certificate. However, the conservative foreign minister chose to oppose the idea on the grounds that it would harm the credibility of Swedish law because it presumed the recognition of foreign law.[9]

The fact that Muslims consider foreign laws in addition to those that govern Sweden is not necessarily due to religious fervour or nostalgia for the home country. It may just as well be a practical need beyond the individual's volition. Similarly, the interventions of Muslim representatives in these matters are not necessarily motivated by an ambition to set up a parallel legal system to compete with the Swedish one. They may just as well be a pragmatic response to the dysfunctional overlapping of Swedish and foreign legal systems. If these responses sometimes prove inadequate, then these Muslim representatives are not the only ones to blame. Most of them are amateurs, without adequate knowledge of either Swedish law or the civil laws of the various Muslim states, and often have limited understanding of the Islamic legal tradition. However, these individuals are frequently the only ones who try to deal with these issues. Equally responsible are the academic researchers, jurists and politicians who neglect these questions, or who are unwilling to address them. This unease is probably due to the spectre of multiculturalism evoked by the thought of parallel legal systems. The existence of this parallel system is in some instances a deliberate enclavist choice, but it is just as often an unintended consequence of life-histories stretching between different countries. Using the oft-repeated slogan 'One law in one state' to urge Muslims in Europe to integrate is simply inadequate; instead it is necessary to consider what that principle implies when foreign laws continue to affect their former subjects long after they emigrate.

Conclusion

From a historical perspective, the Muslim presence in Sweden is still quite new. Most adult Muslims were born abroad, although many arrived as children, received a Swedish education and speak Swedish as a first language. When I began to study Islamology in the 1990s, most Islamic organizations still used Swedish female converts as spokespersons because the male leaders were unable to express themselves properly in Swedish and lacked knowledge of Swedish society. That has now changed and several individuals who are active in Islamic organizations are also active in non-Muslim ones. Most political parties in parliament have MPs with Muslim backgrounds (with different degrees of Islamic identity). However, Islam in Sweden is still in the process of institution-building and has yet to catch up with the historically more established Christian and Jewish congregations. Swedish authorities are still trying to find out with whom to negotiate and are yet to notice the complex legal realities for citizens who hold dual nationality.

Notes

1. For an overview of religious education in various European countries, see Kuyk *et al.* (2007).
2. For a useful, although now somewhat dated, overview of Islam in Sweden in English, see Sanders (2004).

3. The French Professor of History and Sociology of Laïcité, Jean Baubérot, has criticized this conflation of the religious neutrality of state institutions and the obligation of citizens to appear as religiously neutral in public. He also notes that the concept of *laïcité* in France during the 1980s was transformed from a slogan of the political left, against the Catholic Church, to a slogan of the political right, mainly directed against Muslims (Baubérot 2000, 2009).
4. For a brilliant overview of the perception of Muslims in Swedish politics, see Cato (2012).
5. In this first directive the agency laid the responsibility for allowing or banning a full face veil on the headmaster of the school; in a new directive from 2012 it laid the responsibility on the individual teacher 'with support of the headmaster' (Skolverket 2012).
6. On the influence of the Muslim Brotherhood in Europe more generally, see Gräf and Skovgaard-Petersen (2009) (on al-Qaradawi) and Maréchal (2008). The latter effectively debunks more sensationalist descriptions of the Brotherhood as a uniform international organization with a coherent agenda.
7. The Tunisian Law of Personal Status is, of course, an exception in both these respects.
8. I have only ever heard of this institution in relation to this affair. Hence, the possibility cannot be excluded that it consists of a single individual.
9. The interpellation and the response from the minister are available from the website of the Swedish Parliament: http://www.riksdagen.se/sv/Dokument-Lagar/Kammaren/Protokoll/Riksdagens-protokoll-2006077_GU0978/. March 20, 2007.

References

Älgamo, Kicki, ed. 2009. *Hedersrelaterat förtryck och våld i Stockholm stad* [Honour-Related Repression and Violence in Stockholm City]. Stockholm: Stockholm City.

Amnå, Erik, Pia Brundin, and Göran Larsson. 2009. *Staten och imamerna. Religion, integration, autonomi. Betänkande från imamutbildningsutredningen* [The State and the Imams. Religion, Integration, Autonomy. Report from the Imam Education Commission]. SOU 2009: 52. Accessed 9 May, 2012 from Swedish government website. http://www.regeringen.se/sb/d/11358/a/127317/.

Arvidsson, Matilda. 2009. "Shari'a from the Bench: Court Culture, Judicial Culture and a Judge-Made Discourse on Shari'a at a Swedish Court." In *Shari'a as Discourse: Legal Traditions and the Encounter with Europe*, edited by Jørgen S. Nielsen and Lisbeth Christoffersen, 97–116. Aldershot: Ashgate.

Baubérot, Jean. 2000. *Histoire de la laïcité en France* [History of Secularism in France]. Paris: PUF.

Baubérot, Jean. 2009. *La morale laïcque contre l'ordre morale sous la Troisième République* [Moral Secularism Against the Moral Order in the Third Republic]. Condé-sur-Noireau: Archives Karéline.

Cato, Johan. 2012. *När islam blev svenskt. Föreställningar om islam och muslimer i svensk offentlig politik 1975–2010* [When Islam Became Swedish. Representations of Islam and Muslims in Swedish Public Policy 1975–2010]. Lund: Lund University.

Diskrimineringsombudsmannen (DO) [Ombudsman of Discrimination]. 2010. *AF diskriminerade mannen som inte ville skapa hand med kvinnlig chef* [The Public Unemployment Service Discriminated Against the Man Who Refused to Shake Hands with Female Boss]. February 15, 2010. Accessed May 7, 2010. http://www.do.se/sv/Press/Pressmeddelanden-och-aktuellt/2010/AF-diskriminerade-mannen-som-inte-ville-skaka-hand-med-kvinnlig-chef/.

Gräf, Bettina, and Jakob Skovgaard-Petersen, eds. 2009. *The Global Mufti: The Phenomenon of Yusuf al-Qaradawi*. London: Hurst.

Karlson, Pia Minganti, and Ingvar Svanberg, eds. 1997. *Religionsfrihet i Sverige: om möjligheten att leva som troende* [Freedom of Religion in Sweden: On the Possibility of Living as a Believer]. Lund: Studentlitteratur.

Kuyk, Eliza, Roger Jensen, David Lankshear, Elisabeth Löh Manna, and Peter Schreiner, eds. 2007. *Religious Education in Europe. Situation and Current Trends in Europe*. Oslo: Iko.

Lagervall, R. 2012. "Genuskoll. Svenska imamer behöver utbildas [Gender Check. Swedish Imams Need Education]." *Sydsvenskan*, May 19.

Lundqvist, Erica Li, and Leif Stenberg. 2009. "Muslimska föreningar i Malmö och Lund – en ögonblicksbild." First published at http://www.islamologi.se/, but no longer accessible online. English version on Spyros Sofos' blog *Exploring Muslim Identities in Europe*: "Muslims Associations in Malmö and Lund – A Snapshot." December 11, 2010. Accessed 7 May, 2012. http://european-muslims.blogspot.se/2010/12/muslim-associations-in-malmo-and-lund_11.html/.

Maréchal, Brigitte. 2008. *The Muslim Brothers in Europe: Roots and Discourse*. Leiden: Brill.

Mehdi, Rubya, Hanne Petersen, Erik Reenberg Sand, and Gordon R. Woodman, eds. 2008. *Law and Religion in Multicultural Societies*. Copenhagen: Djoef.

Nämnden för statligt stöd för trossamfund [Commission for State Grants to Religious Communities]. 2012. "Statistik 2012." Accessed September 4. http://www.sst.a.se/statistik/statistik2010.4.59d35f60133a8327d7980001l925.html.

Otterbeck, Jonas. 1998. "The Baltic Tartars: The First Muslim Group in Modern Sweden." In *Cultural Encounters in East Central Europe*, edited by Karin Junefelt and Martin Peterson, 145–153. Stockholm: FRN.

Sanders, Åke. 2004. "Muslims in Sweden." In *State Policies Towards Muslim Minorities. Sweden, Great Britain and Germany*, edited by Blacke Anwar and Åke Sanders, 203–374. Kempten: Parabolis.

Sanders, Hanne. 1995. *Bondevækkelse og sekularisering. En protestantisk folkelig kultur i Danmark og Sverige 1820–1850* [Peasant Awakening and Secularization. A Protestant Popular Culture in Denmark and Sweden 1820–1850] Stockholm: Stads- och kommunhistoriska institutet.

Sjögren, Alf. 2011. "Sharia på schemat väcker ilska" [Sharia on the Schedule Raises Anger]. *Sydsvenskan*, March 17.

Skolverket [National Agency for Education]. 2003. *Flickor med burka i skolan* [Girls with Burqa in School]. Dnr 58-2003: 2567. Accessed 8 June, 2012. http://www.skolverket.se/polopoly_fs/1.6017!/Menu/article/attachment/burqa_utredning.pdf/.

Skolverket [National Agency for Education]. 2012. *Elever med heltäckande slöja i skolan* [Pupils with Full Face Veil in School]. Accessed 3 September, 2012. http://www.skolverket.se/polopoly_fs/1.165937!/Menu/article/attachment/Mer%20om%20Elever%20med%20helt%C3%A4ckande%20sl%C3%B6ja.pdf/.

Ungdomsstyrelsen [The Swedish National Board for Youth Affairs]. 2012. *Äkta makar* [Husband and Wife]. Ungdomsstyrelsens skrifter 2012: 1. Accessed June 2012. http://www.ungdomsstyrelsen.se/sites/default/files/publikationer_uploads/aktamakarexterna_v2.pdf/.

Zeghal, Malika. 1996. *Gardiens de l'islam. Les oulémas d'al-Azhar* [The Guardians of Islam. The Ulama of al-Azhar]. Paris: Presses de Sciences Po.

Zeghal, Malika. 2005. *Les islamistes marocains. Le défie à la monarchie* [Moroccan Islamists. Challenges to the Monarchy]. Paris: La Découverte.

Religion and the state in Turkey and Iran: a comparative overview[†]

Refat Sayed Ahmad*

Expert on the study of Islamic movements and Director-General of Markaz Yafalil Dirasaatwal Abhaath (Jaffa Centre for Studies and Research), Cairo, Egypt

The question of the relationship between religion and the state in the Islamic world is as old as Islam itself. The experiences of Turkey and Iran during the past 30 years qualify among the most instructive applications of the relationship. In these two cases, the interaction between the systems of governance, on the one hand, and the Islamic cultural and legislative heritage, on the other, represents a common factor, whereas they differ in terms of the doctrinal reference on which each of these experiences is based. They also differ in perspective, application mechanisms and their relations with the West. The present research can be encapsulated, in broad outline, under five main headlines which raise questions more than provide answers: (1) the historical background of the relationship between religion and the state in the Turkish and Iranian models; (2) the effect of the ascent of revolutionary Islam in Iran, after the revolution of 1979, on the problematic of state–religion relations; (3) from 'well-being' to 'justice and development': limitations and prospects of a historical compromise between religion, secularism and the state; (4) points of controversy and commonalities in the Turkish and Iranian experiences from the 1980s to the end of 2012; and (5) looking into the relationship of each of these two models with the Arab Spring revolutions: are they determinants of these revolutions or investing in their development?

Introduction

The problematic relationship between religion and state in the Islamic world is as old as Islam itself, though it has acquired particular significance in the present milieu. Perhaps the constitutional experiments made in Turkey and Iran during the past three decades stand out in particular as marking a clear implementation of two distinct notions of the relationship between religion and state. Both have the Islamic legal and cultural heritage as their common denominator, even if rooted in different religious traditions. They share a common philosophy as the basis of their experiment, the mechanisms for its implementation and their adaptation of Western principles, institutions and laws. Yet the Turkish model tends to emulate more the West in politics and political behaviour, while the Iranian model tends to follow more the traditional pattern, though of a particular sectarian character (The Shiite School).

[†]This paper was originally presented in the Joint Symposium on 'Religion and State in the Arab World' convened by the Center for Arab Unity Studies and the Swedish Institute – Alexandria in Hamamat, Tunisia, 15–17 October 2012.

To reiterate, despite their religious and political differences and the relative social and sectarian complexities involved in both experiments, they have certain common denominators in so far as the origin of the two experiments is concerned that need to be understood and clarified. Yet they diverge theoretically and in terms of their respective religious classes, Sufi orders and the former (military) dictatorships both have experienced, each of these playing different roles in the development of the two models. Moreover, if the Turkish model can be attributed in part to a close relationship with the West and, up to a point, the Zionist entity, the Iranian model rejects them both.[1]

Today this comparison between the Turkish and Iranian experiments, in so far as their approach to the place of religion in culture, politics, legislation and governance is concerned, has assumed critical importance in view of the phenomenon that has come to be known as the 'uprisings of the Arab Spring'. This is because the latter have seen the pro-Islam forces catapulted into seats of power and authority in the Arab world for the first time in recent history, particularly in Tunisia, Libya and Egypt.

This development has placed the Turkish experience – which introduces itself as a new and contemporary Islamic model, as an alternative to the Iranian model – the Shiite dimension of which somewhat distorts its image in the eyes of the post-uprising Arab regimes. However, this revolutionary face places Iran as a model that may be followed by some of the Arab Spring revolutions, or, at least as a player with which to build up political relations, so as to benefit from its experience and support. Alternatively, and strikingly, Iran may rank in the hostile camp, aligned with the enemies of the revolution, as in the case of the so-called 'Syrian Revolution'.

We are therefore facing an extremely complicated situation that bears great import and inspiration in the new circumstances facing the Arab world. The better to examine the lessons to be drawn from the Turkish and Iranian models of state–religion relations, the following discussion has been divided into four sections dealing with, first, the historical background; second, the Iranian model; third, the Turkish model; and, finally, a comparison between the two.

First: state–religion relations in Turkey and Iran from a historical perspective

The Iranian model

When discussing state–religion relations in Iran, the specialized historical studies indicate that a host of economic, political, historical and geographical factors have played a role in creating an overlapping relationship between the two, and in driving the country into an 'Islamic Revolution' that would accord religion a central role and empower it to become an arbiter in matters of state. This all came about through the leadership of Imam Khomeini in the 1979 Revolution and the factors that drove this development warrant examination.

Geographical and historical factors affecting the state–religion relationship and the revival of Islam's role in Iran

Iran occupies a unique geographical location that has regularly, through successive historical periods, brought it into competition and conflict with its neighbours over regional security in general and over the freedom of movement and navigation in Gulf waters and surrounding areas that represent the gateway to the Indian Ocean. What adds to Iran's importance is not only its wealth of natural resources within but also the role of its peoples and rulers in the history of Islam. The history we mean is the history of Islam's accession to authority and the forms of conflict between the former indigenous religions and Islam, the legacy of which was still manifest in the period immediately preceding the revolution, from the accession of the former shah to the throne on 17 September 1941 until his fall in 1978 (Shokry 1985, 121ff.).

In historical retrospective, we find that by the year 1978 Iran, having passed through successive crises, had reached a stage wherein the Shah became a victim of the interplay of the forces of geography and history. On the one hand, geography (and thence constant threats from other powers) had inclined him to adopt a policy of absolute centralization, with the consequent migration of an impoverished rural population to the cities and deterioration of the living conditions of the urban population. On the other hand, history, as represented by Iran's Islamic complexion and the leading role of the Shiite clergy in society, led to the emergence of the leading clerical authority Ayatollah Ruhollah Khomeini after 1963. These twin factors of geography and history turned the Shah into a 'figurehead presiding over a sprawling state that could be pulled down by a light strike of a rebellious axe' (Heikal 1987, 5–6; also Saghiyyeh 1978, 17–20). This was what actually happened. However, other political and economic reasons interacted and contributed (internally and externally) to consolidate the religion (scholars, organizations and ideas)–state relationship. The revolution of 1979 was the culmination of a popular uprising against the Shah.[2] The political and economic causes of this revolution may be summed up thus:

- Authoritarian rule and policies of the Shah.
- Failure of the plans for economic development.
- The corruption of the governing elite.
- The corruption of SAVAK (the state security service) and the military and their failure to implement the policies of the regime.

From a reading of the political and economic causes that led to an intensification of the role of religion in the running the state, culminating in a revolution, it can be concluded that what is required to overcome an economic crisis facing a state is a social base and the support of the majority of its population. However, even though he could draw on very substantial revenues from oil exports, the Shah failed to create the necessary social base. He failed not only to win the support of the intellectuals and the proletariat, but also of the rural poor. The failure of his social and economic policies led them to swell the ranks of his opposition. Moreover, in 1975 he embarked upon a course that brought him in direct confrontation with the urban merchant class and the powerful religious establishment. Thus when the country faced an acute economic crisis during 1975–77 the regime found itself isolated and encircled on all sides. The Shah himself summed up the tragedy of the collapse of his rule on 1 December 1978 when he was asked by a foreign correspondent: 'Where are your supporters?' He simply shrugged his shoulders and replied: 'Search me' (Abrahmia 1980, 114).

It was natural that this state of affairs would impact the religious establishment whose strength at the time of revolution was estimated by some at 150,000 Shiite theologians spread throughout the country and bonded together by strong spiritual and organizational ties centred on the city of Qum. It was inevitable that they would react in the face of the crisis, and it was also to be expected that their attitudes towards it were shaped by the Shiite tradition that would in turn portend a special relationship between religion and the state (Abrahmia 1980, 113; Heikal 1982, 175–176).

The Revolution and its aftermath

Since the Islamic Revolution of 1979 there has been a spate of books dealing with the relationship between religion and state. Most of them have nothing new to say with the exception of a few like *Al-Fikr el Islami l-Mu'asser fi Iran* (Wasfy 2001). This important academic work presents the thesis that religious government in Iran[3] is a natural culmination of an Islamic revolution, in its contemporary setting, and involving a nation of 60 million people with the youth constituting a majority. The government (revolutionary leaders) and nation work together on the twin bases of *religious Islamic* and Iranian nationalism while also caught up in the processes of modernization and globalization. The point to emphasize here is that the impetus for this cooperation between government and people came, in the first place, from religious thought, not from any political theory or ideology of government.

The Turkish model

According to many studies of the historical origins of the religious state in Turkey, there are many factors to take into account. The most significant of them is that Turkey is a secular state and that there exists no official religion of the state. At the same time, the Turkish Constitution guarantees freedom of religion, worship and belief. The overwhelming majority of the Turkish population is Muslim. Statistics show that Muslims constitute 99% of the country's inhabitants, although some research centres estimate the percentage of Muslims as ranging between 97% and 98% of the whole population. About 85–90% of them belong to the Sunnite sect; and between 10% and 15% to the Alawite (or Alevi) sect, i.e. between 7 million and 10 million persons (for more on the minorities, see Held and Cummings 2011, 552–554). The Christians, mostly Orthodox, constitute 0.1%; and the Jews 0.04%. At the beginning of 20th century Christians constituted about 20% of the Turkish population, but their number has kept dwindling to this day. Other minorities constitute about 5.6%, including the Aizadis, Manawis, Mundane star-worshippers, etc. Article 24 of the Turkish Constitution of 1982 declares that the matter of faith, worship and belief belongs to the personal sphere of an individual's life. Hence the constitution does not grant any special status or privileges to any religion or religious establishment. The secular character of the Turkish state, based on the separation of religion and state, is rooted in the political thought and policy of Mustafa Kamal Ataturk, founder of the Turkish Republic.

The Turkish political system

The Turkish political system resembles the Western democratic model in that it consists of three separate branches of government: legislative, executive and judicial. After years of military rule, democracy was restored under the military-sanctioned Constitution of 1982 which created a Grand National Assembly composed of 550 deputies directly elected by the people for a term of four years. The highest political authority in Turkey is the head of state who is elected every seven years by parliament. After each parliamentary election the president (head of the state) appoints the leader of the majority party in parliament as prime minister (head of government) and invites him to form his government. The president has the right to accept or reject the names of ministers presented to him. The highest judicial authority is the constitutional court that pronounces on the constitutionality of laws passed by parliament.

The modern Turkish Republic was founded on the ruins of the former Ottoman Empire, which was a multi-religious, multicultural, multi-ethnic and multi-linguistic domain with Islam as its official religion. The Ottoman Empire accommodated and managed these diversities with a number of procedures, practices and institutions until the emergence of modern nation-states. The disintegration of the empire during the First World War led to the emergence of more than 30 national states in the Balkans, the Middle East and North Africa, all of whose regions had come under Ottoman suzerainty for centuries prior to the gradual incursions of the European powers that preceded the Ottoman collapse.

The Turkish model of a secular state was developed over many years, according to Turkish researcher Talip Kucukcan, who believes that the First World War marked the final end of Ottoman Turkey and its succession by the modern Turkish national state which was declared under the leadership of Mustafa Kamal Ataturk on 29 October 1923, opening a new chapter in the life of the Turkish nation and non-Muslim minorities by establishing the modern secular Republic of Turkey (Kucukcan 2011). The new state was recognized by the Western powers by the Lausanne Treaty signed on 24 July 1923. It was an important treaty as it incorporated guarantees for freedoms and rights of Turkish religious minorities.

The idea of creating a strong secular national state reflected the ideological orientation of the republican elite to rebuild the state and its institutions on the basis of the secular model that was imported from the West. The political, economic, social and religious developments in modern Turkey have been influenced by the ideas of modernization and secularization. In retrospect, it appears that the Turkish elite tried voluntarily to implement their secularization project in Turkey, unprecedented in any other Islamic country. The democratic project was considered to be secondary in importance as compared with the state's primary concern for secularization.

Broadly speaking there exist three contending approaches regarding the nature of the secular state and the status of the religious establishment in Turkey. According to Kucukcan (2011), the first approach, held by some liberals, secularists and some religious minorities, for a variety of reasons, holds that the mere existence of a religious establishment as a public institution is in complete contradiction with the principle of secularism which entails the neutrality of the state towards all religions and faiths. Some religious groups demand that the state should cease to control the religious establishment and make it an autonomous institution free from state control. Also demanded, in this approach, is that the state keep away from all religious activities or maintaining a religious establishment. At the same time, some secularists insist that the state should not make financial grants to the religious establishment as in this case both Muslims and non-Muslims will be financing this establishment. Apart from that, the Alawites vehemently oppose the maintenance of a religious establishment and its financing out of the state budget, maintaining that it serves the Sunni majority and does not serve the other Muslim sects. The second approach, adhered to by the Kemalists, conservative secularists and the military establishment, is that the state should constitutionally maintain the religious establishment under its supervision, that its functioning in this manner keeps the state in control of all religious activities, that religious activities must be monitored and that freedom of worship must be overseen by the state so that it can protect and maintain its secular nature. The third approach sees no contradiction between the secular state and the existence of a religious establishment side by side. This approach prefers that the religious establishment should be broadly based to accommodate pluralities and diversities, and demands that the state should have minimum control over religious affairs. This is the historical background of the relationship between religion and state in Turkey that has survived to this day, though in a modified form, as discussed below.

Second: the impact of the rise of revolutionary Islam in Iran after the Revolution of 1979 on the problematic issue of state and religion and the provisions of the Iranian Constitution.

Imam Khomeini, who was born on 24 October 1902, managed through the 1979 Revolution to achieve the first strong and close correlation between religion, represented by its scholars, institutions and body of thought, and the state. This direct relationship between religion and state resulted in the formulation of the Constitution, which was approved in a popular referendum on 29–30 March 1979 by an affirmative vote of 98.2%. This constitution became the highest law governing the state–religion relationship.[4]

The Constitution of the Islamic Republic of Iran (2010) is based upon a key notion that 'Imam Al-Mahdi, who descends from Prophet Mohammad (PBUH), will inevitably reappear to restore justice in a world filled with injustice.' For the sake of this (notion-creed), the constitution paved the way for the reappearance of the 'hidden Imam', and considering this Imam to be the highest and ultimate source of legislation in all matters related to the affairs of religion and the world. All laws, constitutions and practices previously passed are subject to change or amendment upon his reappearance, which is unspecified in terms of time.

During the period of the Imam's 'disappearance', which has lasted for more than 1000 years, the Iranian Constitution stipulates in Article (5) thereof, that:

> During the Occultation [period pending the reappearance] of the Wali al-Asr (may God hasten his reappearance), the wilayah and leadership of the *Ummah* devolve upon the just ('adil) and pious (muttaqi) *faqih* [religious scholar], who is fully aware of the circumstances of his age; courageous, resourceful, and possessed of administrative ability, will assume the responsibilities of this office in accordance with Article 107.

Accordingly, the absence of 'Wali al-Asr' thus presents no obstacle for the theological elite in Iran. In accordance with the content of Article (5) of the Constitution, the right to lead the state devolves to the '*faqih*' (religious scholar) – with some elastic requirements such as that he be 'courageous', 'resourceful' and 'fully aware of the circumstances of his age'.

Article (1) of the Constitution declares that the form of government in Iran is that of '*an* Islamic Republic', and Article (2) states that '*The* Islamic Republic' is a system based on belief in six tenets, the first of which is: 'The One God (as stated in the phrase 'There is no god except Allah'): His exclusive sovereignty and the right to legislate, and the necessity of submission to His commands.' The second belief is in: 'Divine revelation and its fundamental role in setting forth the laws.' The Constitution of Iran may be especially rare in its stipulation (third tenet) that the Republic is based on belief in 'the return to God in the Hereafter, and the constructive role of this belief in the course of man's ascent towards God', and the belief in 'the justice of God in creation and legislation'. Also spelled out is belief in 'continuous leadership (*imamah*) and perpetual guidance, and its fundamental role in ensuring the uninterrupted process of the revolution of Islam'.

Article (7) is one of several that refer to verses of the Holy Qur'an – in this particular case on the subject of consultation – effectively giving political ideas the credence of having derived from the Quran itself. Thus Article (7) states: 'In accordance with the command of the Qur'an in the verse 'Their affairs are by consultation among them' (sourat 'Al-Shura', verse 38) and in the verse: 'Consult them in affairs' (sourat 'Al Omran', verse 159), Iran's consultative bodies such as the Islamic Consultative Assembly, the provincial councils, and the city, regional, district and village councils are designated the decision-making and administration organs of the country.

Article (8) of the Constitution stipulates that the call to do good deeds, enjoining what is commendable and forbidding what is reprehensible, is:

> a universal and reciprocal duty that must be fulfilled by the people with respect to one another, by the government with respect to the people, and by the people with respect to the government. The conditions, limits, and nature of this duty will be specified by law.

This stipulation is in accordance with the Qu'ranic verse: 'The believers, men and women, are guardians of one another; they enjoin the good and forbid the evil' (sourat Al-Tawba, verse 71).

In the Constitution the notion of the Velayat-e Faqih (the Guardianship of the Jurist), which was developed by Khomeini, informs the depiction of the state–religion relationship. Article (12) states:

> The official religion of Iran is Islam and the Twelver Ja'fari school [in usual Al-Din (religion) and *fiqh*], and this principle will remain eternally immutable. Other Islamic schools, including the Hanafi, Shafi'i, Maliki, Hanbali, and Zaydi, are to be accorded full respect, and their followers are free to act in accordance with their own jurisprudence in performing their religious rites.

The article adds: 'These sects enjoy official status in matters pertaining to religious education, affairs of personal status […] and related litigation in courts of law.' Article (13) specifies 'Zoroastrian, Jewish and Christian Iranians' as 'the only recognized religious minorities' who are free to perform their religious rites within the limits of the law and 'to act according to their own canon in matters of personal affairs and religious education'.

The third section or chapter of the Iranian Constitution is dedicated to 'The Rights of the People'. Owing to the fact that at the time of the formulation of the Constitution the main charge raised against the Shah was 'repression', those who drafted the constitution were keen on having a 'human rights revolution' that would look much more advanced than the situation during the reign of the Shah. Accordingly, Article (19) stipulate as follows: 'All people of Iran, whatever the ethnic group or tribe to which they belong, enjoy equal rights; and colour, race, language, and the like, do not bestow any privilege.' However, the article makes no mention of equality in case of different religions.

Article (20) states that: 'All citizens of the country, both men and women, equally enjoy the protection of law and enjoy all human, political, economic, social and cultural rights, in conformity with Islamic criteria.' Concerning the status of women, Article (21) stipulates that: 'The government must ensure the rights of women in all respects, in conformity with Islamic criteria.' This article then identifies five goals related to women, including:

> [to] create a favourable environment for the growth of woman's personality and for the restoration of her rights, both the material and the intellectual; the protection mothers, particularly during pregnancy and childbirth, and the protection of children without guardians; and establishing competent courts to protect and preserve the family.

Articles (22) and (23) deem inviolate, except in cases sanctioned by law, 'the dignity, life, property, rights, residence and occupation' of the individual; and forbid the investigation of individuals' beliefs or molestation or reproach of any individual 'simply for holding a certain belief'. Article (24) emphasizes the freedom of the press, 'except when it is detrimental to the fundamental principles of Islam or to the rights of the public', as specified by the law. As for demonstrations and gatherings, they are allowed, provided 'arms are not carried' and that they are 'not detrimental to the fundamental principles of Islam' (Article 27).

In spite of some restrictions, the provisions for the freedom of citizens are in many ways expansive. For example, Article (32) states that:

> No person may be arrested except according to and in the manner laid down in the law. If someone is detained, the subject matter of the charge, (with reasons for bringing it) must immediately be communicated and explained in writing to the accused. Within at most 24 hours the file on the case and preliminary documentation must be referred to the competent legal authority.[5]

Moreover, Article (34) stipulates that: 'it is the indisputable right of every citizen to seek justice by recourse to competent courts [...] and no one can be barred from courts to which he has a legal right of recourse'. Article (107) spells out how the Supreme Leader of Iran shall be selected and that he shall be deemed 'equal with the rest if the country in the eyes of the law'.

The foregoing shows that recognition of the role and rights of the people in the Islamic Revolutionary experience in Iran, as represented in the Constitution, marked a milestone in the evolution of thinking about political power and constituted a success for the revolution, that is worthy of careful attention. Today popular sovereignty and popular participation form the basis of successful democracies. In such democracies the people are regarded as the source of authority and legitimacy. However, many developing countries are suffering from internal difficulties because they have marginalized the role of their people and suppressed their ordinary rights (Karim 2008).

In this context we may explain the relationship between religion and state in Iran as follows (Al-Mo'min 2004, 144):

- *Supreme Authority (the Leader)*: this office supervises and coordinates among the three powers (executive, legislative and judicial); appoints the head of the judiciary; approves the election of the President of the Republic and removes him; nominates the clerics of the Guardianship Council; and appoints the members of the Board of the Identification of the Expediency System.
- *Executive Power*: its head (the President of the Republic) presents his government to the Shura Council for approval, while the council is empowered to remove the President of the Republic. (This happened with President Abu Al-Hasan Bani Sadr in 1980.) The president may monitor the authorities and coordinate between the Executive Authority and the General leadership of the Armed forces.
- *The Legislative Authority*: approves the members of the government and may remove them; and votes on the legal experts nominated by the Head of the Judicial Authority as members in the Guardianship Council.
- *The Judicial Authority*: proposes the legal experts for membership of the Guardianship Council, to be approved by the Islamic Shura (Consultative) Council;

and has organs for monitoring the Executive Authority financially and administratively. In addition, the constitution granted the Judicial Authority broad powers in order to apply the principle of the rule of law. As evidence to that, there is Article 156 that states that the judiciary is an independent power, the protector of the rights of the individual and society, and responsible for the implementation of justice.

The state administration is accountable to the views of the people and their votes. This is effected through the election of the President of the Islamic Republic, members of the Shura Council, members of the other municipal councils and so on, or through a referendum. Therefore, in the Iranian case, the distribution of power does not remain confined to a theoretical framework. Instead, the framework devised by the intellectuals and politicians of the Iranian regime presents applied and practical models developed within the field of national participation in the Islamic Republic during the first 20 years of the revolution (Shahi 2010, 223).

Third: the state–religion relationship in Turkey and its impact on the Turkish Constitution

The Turkish model of the state–religion relationship is complex, with overlaps between the two domains, particularly following the rise of political Islam with the Welfare Party, which developed into the pragmatic and progressive Justice and Development Party currently in power. Arab thinker Sadeq Jalal Al-Azm was correct when he described the Islam presiding in Turkey today, in its relation to state policy, legislation and governance, as the 'Islam of Business', as represented by the nature of its projects, reforms, aspirations, and internal and external policies at all levels. This party defines its basic ideology as 'Conservative Democracy', in a very practical indication that the broad popular and electoral base for its rule is to be found in central Anatolia, which is developing quickly in business, commerce and industry – in accordance with globalization – at the same time as it is conservative in political, social and religious terms.

One of the remarkable signs of the success of the Justice and Development Party's version of Islam is that its conservative tendency does not dissipate its energies in the trivialities of 'enjoining what is commendable and forbidding the reprehensible' in matters of dress, food, drink, religious schooling, swimming and the daily conduct of the people. Instead it has shrewdly preserved the Kemalist and secular institutions of the Turkish state and its basic constitution as it developed and served the Turkish national interest throughout the 20th century. It does not appear that this brand of Islam will ever neglect the enormous modern and quality achievements of contemporary Turkey, such as the following:

- The quickly developing Turkish civil society with all its organizations, institutions, and rules and regulations of conduct.
- The high level of democratic participation exercised by Turkish citizens, even though this may not exceed 60–70%. This presents a sharp contrast to the democracy of communities, sects and tribes, referenda held by single ruling parties, prearranged power-sharing among groups, and whatever else we Arabs are notorious for, which put strains on our lives every moment.
- A high and advanced level of separation of legislative, executive and judicial authorities, especially in comparison with any other given society with a clear

Muslim majority. It may be noted here that the famous Kemalist separation of religion and the state came as an extension to the principle of separation of authorities, a continuation of it and of its practical applications. And what if the secularization of the state in countries such as ours would involve *five* separate authorities instead of the three common authorities: the legislative authority, the executive authority, the judicial authority and the fourth authority, which is the independent press and free media, in addition to a fifth authority which is concerned with the affairs of religions, sects, religious endowments and shrines and with various other religious affairs in the same country?

- Independence of the judiciary even if it has not yet reached the advanced levels that ideally it should in Turkey.
- Public freedoms, most importantly freedom of the press and media in general, the freedom of circulation of information and data, the freedom of opinion, expression, conscience, protest and peaceful opposition.
- The numerous legislative reforms that have been accomplished recently in the direction of further Turkish commitment to the legitimacy of international human rights, and greater respect for the rights of the citizen and citizenship at home.

In other words, what the 'Business Islam' of the Justice and Development Party promises is 'further reform and modernization' rather than 'Islam is the Solution', according to Sadek Galal El-Athm (El-Athm 2011–12).

Experts were right when they came to the conclusion that the main system of the Turkish state is a secular system, though the majority of inhabitants are Muslims, since there is clear separation between religion and the state. For this reason religion, the institutions and the religious groups do not have any influence on the legislation process which depends only on civil, secular procedure, and religion is not a source of law in a state that aspires to become a full member of the European Union. And to realize this objective, Turkey has adopted a number of comprehensive modifications to the Turkish legal system to bring it in line with the standards of the European Union. Such reforms have positively contributed to the expansion of religious freedom for both the Muslim majority – including the non-Sunni groups – and non-Muslim minorities.

The political orientation of the current government paves the way for the emergence of progressive and liberal opinions that help ward off the danger to faith and call for the return of liberties and all rights to religious groups. Even so, according to some Turkish experts, there are still problems that need to be addressed urgently, such as removing the total ban on the *hijab* in universities and allowing parents to obtain the official religious education they want for their children at a very early stage instead of waiting until they reach the age of eight. Not only is the issue of primary education considered a problem, but so too is the fact that the Turkish legal system does not have a procedure for religious minorities to register themselves and acquire a legal identity, as has been noted by the Venice Commission of the Council of Europe. Furthermore, some demands by the Alawite sect have to be met in order to reach some sort of consensus and mutual understanding between sectarian and religious minorities, on the one side, and the Sunni majority in the country, on the other (Kucukcan 2011).

These issues and concerns are reflected in the modified Turkish Constitution, which seeks a balance between 'Business Islam' and the secularism of the state, and ensures that it remains integrated and does not break down or move away from the Kemalist model.

Turkey has modified the constitution of November 1982 some 13 times and in 2013 a cross-party commission was set up to draft a new constitution. Prime Minister Recep Tayyip Erdoğan has presented a number of constitutional reforms, some designed to curb the power of the army, but also to address the question of religion and the state. However, those reforms have not disturbed the core principles of Kemalist secularism integral in the Constitution, and by the end of 2013 it looked as though the redrafting commission had run into insuperable problems agreeing a new one.

The Turkish Constitution starts with a preamble stating that the document embodies the concept of nationalism, reform and the principles introduced by Ataturk, the founder of the Republic of Turkey, and affirms the existence of the Turkish nation, the home of the Turkish ancestors and the unity of the Turkish state.[6] The preamble stresses several principles, most importantly: democracy, the separation of authorities, the prohibition of providing protection to any activity that is inconsistent with Turkish national interests, the principle of keeping Turkey intact, adherence to the key principles of Ataturk, and that 'sacred religious feelings shall absolutely not be involved in state'.

As for the first articles of the General Principles Section that heads the constitution, Article (2) states that the Republic of Turkey is 'a democratic, secular state governed by the rule of law, within the notions of public peace, national solidarity and justice, respecting human rights, loyal to the nationalism of Ataturk, and based on the fundamental tenets of the preamble'. Article (4) states that the provisions of the first three articles on the republican nature of the state, its characteristics and the indivisibility of the Turkish state, nation and territory may not be amended or their amendment proposed.

Article (14), as modified in 3 October 2001, prohibits abuse of the fundamental rights and freedoms embodied in the Constitution, including endangering 'the democratic and secular order of the Republic'. Article (24) says that 'everyone has the freedom of conscience, religious belief and conviction' and that 'acts of worship, religious rights and ceremonies, shall be conducted freely'; but adds 'as long as they do not violate the provisions of Article (14)'. It goes on to say, however, 'no one shall be compelled to worship or to participate in religious rites and ceremonies, or to reveal religious beliefs and convictions, or be blamed or accused because of his religious beliefs and convictions'.

On 31 May 2007, in a step designed to increase the distance between the military and politics, the Justice and Development Party announced constitutional amendments concerning the office of and procedure for electing the president. This was just before Abdullah Gul attained the presidency on 28 August 2007. According to these amendments, the powers of the president, elected for a five-year term, include: appointment of the prime minister; acceptance of his resignation; appointment and dismissal of ministers upon the suggestion of the prime minister; in addition to power to decide to mobilize the Turkish armed forces, appoint the chief of staff; and to call upon the National Security Council to convene and preside over it. Meanwhile, Article (117) of the Constitution states that: 'The office of the Commander-in-Chief is inseparable from the spiritual existence of the Grand National Assembly [parliament] of Turkey and is represented by the President of the Republic.' As for the Chief of the General Staff, commander of the armed forces, 'in the time of war he exercises the duties of the Commander-in-Chief on behalf of the President of the Republic'. The same article also establishes that the Chief of the General Staff 'shall be appointed by the President of the Republic following the proposal of the Council of Ministers'. Further: 'His/

her duties and powers shall be regulated by the law' and the 'Chief of the General Staff shall be responsible to the Prime Minister in the exercise of his/her duties and powers'.

Regarding military justice, provision is made in the section of the Constitution dealing with the judiciary as follows:

> Military justice shall be exercised by military courts and military disciplinary courts. These courts shall have jurisdiction to try military offences committed by military personnel and offences committed by military personnel against military personnel or related to military services and duties. Cases regarding crimes against the security of the State, constitutional order and its functioning shall be heard before the civil courts in any case. Non-military persons shall not be tried in military courts, except during a state of war.

Article (118) indicates the formation of what is called 'The National Security Council'. As modified on 3 October 2001, it reads:

> The National Security Council shall be composed of the Prime Minister, the Chief of the General Staff, deputy prime ministers, ministers of Justice, National Defence, Internal Affairs, and Foreign Affairs, the commanders of the Land, Naval and Air Forces and the General Commander of the Gendarmerie, under the chairpersonship of the President of the Republic.

It further provides:

> The National Security Council shall submit to the Council of the Ministers the advisory decisions taken with regard to the formulation, determination, and implementation of the national security policy of the State and its views on ensuring the necessary coordination. The Council of Ministers shall evaluate decisions of the National Security Council concerning the measures that it deems necessary for the preservation of the existence and independence of the State, the integrity and indivisibility of the country, and the peace and security of society.
>
> [and] The agenda of the National Security Council shall be drawn up by the President of the Republic taking into account the proposals of the Prime Minister and the Chief of the General Staff.

So much for the provisions for civil political control of the military. For the bottom line on the Turkish model when it comes to the relationship between religion and the state, we can turn to an extensive study conducted by an Egyptian researcher (Habib 2010) who concluded that many questions arose from the first big victory of the Justice and Development Party in the elections of 2002, most importantly: can democracy prevail in an Islamic state? He answered the question thus: the experience of the Justice and Development Party that rules Turkey, concerning its perception of the relationship between religion and the state, is based on giving preference to the idea of the group (*al-jamaa*) rather than the idea of '*shari'a*' (Islamic legislation), i.e. it starts from the principle of bringing Islam to the people and trying to reform on the basis of where the people stand. With this approach it expresses what is called 'civil Islam' rather than 'political Islam'.

Habib's analysis of the experience of the Justice and Development Party and how it separated itself from the experience of the former Welfare Party leader Erbakan to establish itself as a new generation with a different approach. The ideology it espoused includes a form of 'conservative democracy' based on the idea of harmony and coexistence rather than struggle and duality, and it refrains from using religion as a tool in the socio-political struggle. Moreover, the middle generation in the Turkish Islamic movement represented by Erdoğan, Gul and their group presented a formula of compromise based on the idea of the historic intermediate solution that respects the beliefs of the Islamists and their right of expression, and acknowledges a form of secularism that accepts the rules of democracy and diversity – including recognizing the cultural diversity of the Kurds (Habib 2010). The party expresses the mainstream in Turkish society: it is not confined to the Islamists only but includes various segments of youth, women, leftists and liberals. The party is considered an expression of transcending the classical streams in Turkish political life, whether Islamic, national or Kemalist secular. It establishes what has been called 'The Third Republic' based on the idea of transcending the polarization and attempting to build a new comprehensive stream expressing segments of new generations that have entered the Turkish political marketplace.

Fourth: comparison between the Turkish and the Iranian models – a preliminary attempt to understand the issues in conflict

Having reviewed the most important components of the relationship between religion and the state in both the Turkish and Iranian models, and the political application of this relationship whether on the terrain of political reality or within the articles of their constitutions and the legislative policies, we note that the only really common feature between the two models is the high dose of democracy. As for the differences, they are greater, and thus form the basis of the remainder of this discussion. The most important issues of conflict between the two models may be summarized as follows.

The two models certainly differ when it comes to the relationship between religion and the state: religion as a philosophy, point of reference and system of government constitutes the main feature of the Iranian model. As for the Turkish model, religion is just a tool among various tools to reach political objectives, within the context of the political performance of a state whose rulers do not disdain to assert its secularism, claiming they are sons of such stable secularism.

The Turkish model also differs from the Iranian in the scope accorded religion in the external struggle; Iran sees its international and regional relations and alliances from the perspective of religion to a greater and more radical degree, in comparison with Turkey. The latter deals with religion in an essentially pragmatic way in the scope of its international relations. In this context, we can understand the centrality of Iran's hostility to the United States and Israel, and how it can turn to religious hostility. In contrast, we see Turkey allying with Israel and the United States – even if this works against Arab and Islamic interests – as long as this achieves the overriding Turkish interest. This political expediency is almost the ruling factor in the relationship of religion and the state in the context of Turkish foreign relations. Though Iran does appear to work for the national interest of the country, it makes calculations in its discourse and positions on external political matters that place it in confrontation with the enemies of Arabs and Muslims generally, and with the United States and Israel in particular. This extends as well to its stance regarding the Arab and Islamic resistance movements: in particular Hizbollah, Islamic Jihad, Hamas and the rest of the groups of Arab resistance against the Zionist and American occupations.

According to Mohammad Noureddin, the role Turkey is playing within NATO has not changed since it joined the organization in 1952 (Noureddin 2012). This role was in keeping with its Western-style approach to foreign policy, whereby it became the first

Muslim country to recognize Israel – three years after its establishment in 1948. Governments changed, military coups took place and the military, secularists and Islamists rotated in power, but nothing changed in Turkey's firmness in its loyalty to the organization that depicted Communism as its absolute enemy, until Communism collapsed and, in the views of many, Islam took its place as the enemy. The colour of the 'enemy' changed from red to green, but the colour of Turkey's foreign policy did not change. The recent developments in the region clearly showed that Turkey's openness to the neighbouring countries in recent years was but a 'midsummer night's dream', as the policies followed by the Justice and Development Party confirm that 'more indulgence in the Atlantic game is the only guarantee for the Party's continuation in power, facing the secularists, Kurds, Leftists, and even the nationalist Turks' (Noureddin 2012).

No one can, according to Noureddin, understand the Turkish foreign policy in isolation of its role in NATO. This has always been a reason for doubting the provenance of Turkey's seemingly 'positive' steps towards the states and forces that are hostile to the Zionist Project or those opposing the Western policies in the region. Abdulhamid Balgy, the Islamist writer in the Turkish paper *Zaman*, claims Turkey's loyalty 'precluded the transfer of the Atlantic into a crusader alliance'. However, through its participation in the war in Afghanistan, for example, Turkey did not make the Atlantic forces aware of the sensitivities of the Islamic society the better to avoid inciting religious fanaticism. On the contrary, it was 'the cover under which the Atlantic forces concealed all abuses there'. How many a time did the NATO soldiers cause the deaths of civilians and commit rape, desecrate holy places, and violate sanctities and ethics? Did such things not take place while Turkey was part of the Atlantic presence in Afghanistan? What did the government of the Justice and Development Party do in order to prevent those violations? Or, what attitude did they take in condemnation thereof at least?

Most recently, Turkish policy shifted 180 degrees, and Iran and Russia became the first two foes. Thus writes the secular writer Murat Yetkin, for example, in *Radikal* newspaper, stating that 'The transfer of the management of the radars at Malatya from the United States' to NATO will strengthen Turkey's position in facing Iran and Russia' (Noureddin 2012). He believes that the West is waiting for Turkey to restore its normal relations with Israel and Greek Cyprus, and even with Armenia. In the end, Noureddin claims in the article cited above the greater is Turkey's role within the NATO, the more it moves away from the public sensitivities in the Muslim world.

Other areas of disagreement between the Iranian and Turkish models include some manifestations of political despotism, still apparent in Turkey's case, despite the Justice and Development Party's claims of democracy. Such manifestations, surprisingly, are not seen in Iran despite the false picture typically provided by the international media about the two states. It is true that the regime in Iran is not an ideally democratic one, but still it is not as dark as that presented in reports in international and Arab media on the question of freedoms in Iran. Nor is democracy in Turkey as clear and bright as in the picture presented by the same media or promoted by large segments of the Arab elite. In an opinion piece entitled 'Dear Arab Brothers: Yes You May Borrow Our Prime Minister!' the well-known Turkish writer Burak Bekdil asserted that Erdoğan is but a 'tyrant' oppressing his people and that he presents a false media image of himself (Bekdil 2011). He is not pro the Arab revolts, but he believes in stealing these uprisings and converting them into revolts in the interests of the United States and NATO. As an example, he gives cites Erdoğan's attitude towards Syria, and concludes: 'Anyway, Dear brothers, my offer is valid forever, and I add an attractive gift: with each Erdoğan you get, we will gladly present to you Foreign Minister Ahmet Davutoğlu!'

As a Lebanese writer specialized in Turkish affairs, Noureddin wrote another article about Turkey (Noureddin 2011). This important piece is based on documents and evidence from inside Turkey and I will not summarize it here. Noureddin's message was as follows:

> Against this rosy picture of economic development in Turkey, the picture of Turkey's 'political development' is overcast with thick shadows, especially by the European Union whose recent report on Turkey was full of criticism of Recep Tayyip Erdoğan's government policy on political and intellectual freedoms. Within the context of tightening restrictions on the activities of the PKK, the Turkish government launched a wide campaign of detentions of intellectuals, artists, trade unionists and political activists on charges of collaboration with the PKK and support of terrorism. Those who were detained included film directors, prominent writers, university professors and women. Turkish sources estimate the number of detainees who can be considered as political prisoners at more than three thousand persons, which represents a very large number in a country that raises the slogan of democracy and is involved in direct talks to win EU membership. It has become a common and regular issue to compare the press and political freedoms during the reign of the Justice and Development Party to that during the eras of the military guardianship.
>
> Erdoğan's message on the 63rd anniversary of the adoption of the universal declaration of Human Rights was at variance with what is happening in Turkey, so much so that writer Semih Idiz of *Millit* newspaper doubted that Erdoğan was talking about Turkey, but about another country. In his message, Erdoğan said: 'With each passing day, Turkey takes the position of the model in the region and in the world in its attachment to democracy, human rights and the rule of law'. On this Idiz commented: 'It is really tragic to see Erdoğan, who received the "Muammar Gaddafi" Human Rights prize and did not return it at the height of the Libyan crisis, talking about this issue.'

Idiz went on:

> In order for us to understand our position in the human rights field, there is need to read all the reports issued by the international rights groups, the most recent of which is the official annual report of the European Union.

He explains that Turkey ranks second in the number of complaints received against it by the European Court for Human Rights, with the number received last year reaching 15,200 complaints, and in 2011 this number increased to 16,800 complaints. The European Court has ascertained 90% of the cases they have studied so far. He adds that 'the verification of the situation of press freedom in Turkey should not be carried out by the government, but by free media'.

This is Turkey under Erdoğan, who is being followed by a segment of our elite and politicians who are completely fascinated with him and are convincing themselves that he is supporting the Arab revolts for God's sake, while in fact he is no more than a 'glove' for Washington and the West against our Arab peoples and the unity of our countries.

As for Iran, in spite of the drawbacks that accompanied its democratic experience, and although it is not a completely perfect experience, it remains, within the context of thought and political experience of Shiite Islam and the political Iranian format, an experience more democratic and less oppressive than the Turkish regime and, of course, many of the Arab ruling regimes. This becomes evident when we objectively compare the international human rights reports on Iran with those issued on Turkey in 2011 and 2012 only.

With respect to the Arab Spring revolts, these two experiences tend in general to show support to these revolts in their entirety except in the cases of Syria and Bahrain, where disputes over how to handle either are acute. Iran looks upon what is happening in Syria, for example, to be no more than a 'guerrilla war' and a Western/Gulf Cooperation Council (GCC) conspiracy to undermine the resistance front led by Syria and Hezbollah against the American/Zionist Project, and believes that the very fact of American, Israeli and French support for the so-called Syrian Revolution leads to the distortion of this revolution, and even warrants condemnation of it. By contrast, Turkey sees exactly the opposite and regards what is taking place in Syria as a revolution. When Erdoğan personally failed to convince Syrian President Assad to change policy, Turkey hastened to support the revolution, even by building camps for refugees and fighters, and providing arms and large-scale logistic support to the so-called the Free Syrian National Army which constitutes the military arm of this revolution. However, what is striking is that despite this clarity in the difference between the two countries towards the Syrian crisis, they have not directly collided with each other, but co-existed with the crises and entered into dialogue. This could have happened because both countries realize that controlling the dispute is more beneficial to them within the context of the current regional and international environment, and due to the fact that the two countries are essentially on a par in terms of their military and political power and the internal popular multitudes, and thus enjoy strategic balance in relation to one another. This no doubt led the leaderships of the two countries to think very carefully before proceeding to any confrontation, at least not at the level of armed action.

The dispute in views with respect to the Arab Spring revolutions also extends to Bahrain where Iran talks about a popular revolution with fair demands, and they do not conceal their support thereto, politically and through the media and sometimes by *fatwa*s and money, while Turkey follows the Gulf States in describing what is happening as a sectarian Shiite phenomenon, not as a comprehensive revolution.

Disagreement between the two countries may extend to attempts to exploit the other Arab Spring revolts in the region, starting with Tunisia, proceeding with Libya and Yemen, and ending with Egypt, all countries which Erdoğan visited in 2011, along with over 100 businessmen, with a view to opening markets and building alliances. As for the Iranians, they remain hesitant about fully embracing those revolutions seriously and strategically, and satisfy themselves with providing moral and political support from a distance, maybe for historical, sectarian or strategic considerations and sensitivities related to the presence of 'NATO' behind some of these revolutions.

Anyway, Iran and Turkey will remain strategic players in the region. How close or how far they choose to be from the political quake that has affected the region and has been termed the Arab Spring will remain a defining factor in their own trajectories. The implications of this quake and its aftershocks will affect the level of reconsideration accorded to the political and economic freedoms in both Iran and Turkey and their attitudes towards the historical enemies of each nation. It is to be expected that the future will witness a change in policies and attitudes and even attempts from the outside to ride the Arab revolts and replace them with 'NATO revolutions' and the rebuilding of a New Middle East, all be it with an Islamic form, but with an American spirit. These attempts may fail, however, especially in the countries where the revolts have acquired their own momentum (such as Egypt and Tunisia), and as the peoples are now themselves manufacturing their future, rather than Washington and its allies.

The future regarding the relations of Istanbul and Tehran with the region and their impact therein, and how they are themselves affected by developments, has become open to all possibilities. And these make the problematic issue of the 'religion–state' relationship but one facet in what are likely to become more inclusive relations connected with the destiny of the homelands themselves. Whether the countries of the Arab Spring are prepared for this ambiguous future is another matter!

Notes

1. Among the most accurate studies on the geography and history of Iran, see Wilber (1981, 3–73).
2. Among the good literature that deals with the political and social preludes to the revolution in Iran, see Green (1982, 10–45).
3. For the distinguished critical review by Wahid Bahmardy of this book, see *Al-Hayat* May 8, 2001.
4. The extracts of the Iranian Constitution quoted here come from a translation located at: http://www.iranonline.com/iran/iran-info/government/constitution.html/. Accessed December 25, 2013.
5. For this extract, see: http://www.alaviandassociates.com/documents/constitution.pdf/. Accessed December 25, 2013.
6. For the full text of the Turkish Constitution (in English translation), see, for example, http://global.tbmm.gov.tr/docs/constitution_en.pdf/. Accessed December 25, 2013.

References

Abrahmia, Yervenda. 1980. "Asbaab Thawrat 1978" [The Causes of the 1978 Revolution]. In *Iran, 1900–1980*, edited by Nubar Hovsepian. Beirut: Mu'assasat al Abhaath al Arabiyyah.

El-Athm, Sadek Jalal. 2011–12. "Al Dawla-l-Ilmaniyya wal Mas"ala al Diniyyah" [The Secular State and the Religious Issue: Turkey as a Model]. *Minbar Ibn Rushd Journal* no. 12 (Winter).

Bekdil, Burak. 2011. "Dear Arab Brothers. Yes You May Borrow Our Prime Minister!" *Hurriyet Daily News* September 15. Accessed December 30, 2013. http://www.hurriyetdailynews.com/default.aspx?pageid=438&n=dear-greek-brothers-you-too-may-borrow-our-prime-minister-2011-11-22/.

Constitution of the Islamic Republic of Iran. 2010. Beirut: Markaz l-Hadara li Tanmiyat al Fikr l-Islami (Civilization Center for the Development of Islamic Thought). Retrieved from www.iranonline.com/iran/iran-info/government/constitution.html

Green, Jerrold D. 1982. *Revolution in Iran: The Politics of Countermobilization*. New York, NY: Praeger.

Habib, Kamal El-Said. 2010. *Al Deen wal Dawla fi Turkiyya: Sira'-l-Islam wal Ilmaniyya* [Religion and the State in Turkey: Struggle of Islam and Secularism]. Cairo: Maktabat al-Ousra.

Heikal, Mohamed Hassanein. 1982. *Madafi' Ayatollah: Kissat Iran wa Thawrat* [Canons of Ayatollah: The Story of Iran and the Revolution]. Beirut: Dar El-Shurook.

Heikal, Mohamed Hassanein. 1987. "Shah Iran al Akheer" [The Last Shah of Iran]. *Akhbar El-Youm* February 2.

Held, Colbert C., and John T. Cummings. 2011. *Middle East Patterns: Places, Peoples and Politics*. 5th Ed. Boulder, CO: Westview.

Karim, Ali Abdullah. 2008. *Constitution of the Iranian Islamic Republic: Kira'a fi Anasser l-Tajdeed wal Hadathah* [Analysing the Elements of Renovation and Modernity]. Beirut: Markaz l-Hadara li Tanmiyat al Fikr l-Islami (Civilization Center for the Development of Islamic Thought).

Kucukcan, Talip. 2011. "Khibrat Turkiyya ma l-Ilmaniyya wal Kanoon wal Deen" [The Turkish Experience in Secularism, Law and Religion]. *Shark Nama Journal* (Cairo) no. 7 (January).

Al-Mo'min, Ali. 2004. *Al-Nitham al Siyassi al Islami al Hadeeth* [Modern Islamic Political System]. Beirut: Dar El-Hady.

Noureddin, Mohammad. 2011. "Erdoğan Yatahaddath an Balad Akhar" [Erdoğan Talking about Another Country]. *Al-Safeer* December 15.

Noureddin, Mohammad. 2012. "Al-Laun el Atlassi li Turkiyya" [The Atlantic Style of Turkey]. *Al-Safeer* May 24.

Saghiyyeh, Hazem. 1978. *Sira" al-Islam wal Betrol fi Iran* [The Struggle of Islam and Petroleum in Iran]. Beirut: Dar El-Tali'a.

Shahi, Sayed Hady Khesru. 2010. "Al Democratiyya wal Dawlah: Alakah am Tabayun?" [Democracy and the State: Relationship or Contrast]." In *Mawsu'at al Fikr il Siyassi Inda-l-Imam-l-Khomeini* [The Encyclopaedia of Iman Khomeini's Political Thought]. Beirut: Markaz el Hadara Litanmiyat-l-Fikr-l-Islami (El-Hadara Center for the Development of Islamic Thought).

Shokry, Nabil. 1985. "Revolutionary Change in Third World Countries: Case Study of the Iranian Revolutionary Movement." PhD diss., Faculty of Political Science, Cairo University.

Wasfy, Mohamed Reda. 2001. *Al-Fikr el Islami l-Mu'asser fi Iran: Jadaliyyat el Takleed wal Tajdeed* [Contemporary Islamic Thought in Iran: Arguments of Tradition and Innovation]. Beirut: Dar l-Jadid; Dar El-Mahja El-Bayda'.

Wilber, Donald N. 1981. *Iran, Past and Present: From Monarchy to Islamic Republic*. Princeton, NJ: Princeton University Press.

What changes have taken place in US foreign policy towards Islamists?[†]

Fawaz A. Gerges

Department of International Relations, London School of Economics (LSE), London, UK

American foreign policy does not seem to have undergone radical changes in its position towards Islamists. Instead, Islamists seem to display willingness to make a transition and cater for vital American interests in the Arab world - mainly with regard to the following four points: political economy; relations with Israel; the War on Terror; and issues related to identity, especially in the case of minorities. Islamists appear to have proven malleability towards the US in relation to the economic system and foreign policy. Some Islamist leaders have pointed out that the price of this adaptability is expected to be the respect of the US for Islamic ethos, added to the Islamists' autonomy on domestic, social and cultural issues. In conclusion, the relationship between Islamists and the US seems to be in the course of being shaped, but meanwhile, Islamists seem to adopt a realist stand on American foreign policy and national security whereby they do not seem to have quit the approaches of those regimes that have just gone.

The critical question that should be asked is not whether US foreign policy has undergone a radical shift towards the Islamists, but rather what shifts have the Islamist parties undergone to bring them closer to the American foreign policy priorities? What are some of the promises and pledges that Islamist parties, particularly the Muslim Brothers and Ennahda, have made in order to engage with the United States? There are four key areas in which Islamist parties have shown a willingness to accommodate US vital interests in the Arab region: political economy, relations with Israel, the War on Terror, and identity issues, in particular the status of minorities. It is only by understanding what changes in approach have taken place in these four issues that one can really appreciate the new subtle shifts in US foreign policy towards the Islamists.

First, however, some historical context is important. For the last two decades Western governments, particularly the dominant US foreign policy narrative, viewed religious-based movements such as the Islamists as absolutist and regressive in nature, possessing no capacity or will to evolve and accommodate themselves to changes in society at large; they could not shed their ideological inheritance and hostility to the West as well. As a result, America and its European allies shunned engagement with mainstream Islamists, believing in a binary model of the Middle East, in

[†]This article is the basis for a more extended study to appear in *Political Science Quarterly* later in 2013.

which religious fundamentalists were seen as the only alternative to pro-Western autocrats. There existed an implicit assumption among Western officials that there was no third way, no public opinion, only an 'Arab street' – code for the notion that Muslims, if allowed to vote, would make the wrong choices, and that democratic forces, untried and unknown, would not be as accommodating to US interests in the region as the autocrats. The late Jeane Kirkpatrick, who served as US Ambassador to the United Nations, famously quipped about Arabs and democracy: 'The Arab world is the only part of the world where I've been shaken in my conviction that if you let the people decide, they will make fundamentally rational decisions' (Kirkpatrick 2012).

Up until the Arab popular uprisings, the upper echelons of US foreign policy, including President Barak Obama, looked at most Islamists as intrinsically anti-Western, cannot be trusted, will not respect peace treaties with Israel, and will seek to build illiberal states based on the *shariahor* Islamic law. When Obama was asked before the Arab revolts whether the United States should engage with the Muslim Brotherhood, his answers were revealing. He stated that the Muslim Brotherhood was untrustworthy, harboured anti-American views and would not honour the Camp David Peace Treaty with Israel. His response typified the deeply suspicious attitude to the Islamists at the highest levels of US government. In particular, 9/11 poisoned the attitudes of American policy-makers toward the Islamists and prejudiced their views. What was troubling to US officials were the Islamists' uncompromising position on Palestine–Israel and their hostile rhetoric against American foreign policy.

A qualification point is in order here. On the whole, the US foreign policy community was not united in opposition to the mainstream Islamists. Long before the Arab uprisings, a major foreign policy debate had unfolded in the United States about whether to engage with Islamists at all, and, if so, how far to go. A segment of the US foreign policy establishment – primarily made up of liberal think tanks, such as the Carnegie Foundation and the Brooking Institute – had argued that Islamists' parties had migrated away from their absolutist roots. Parties like the Muslim Brotherhood, they argued, had shed their old anti-Western colours and were willing to play by the rules of the political game; Islamist parties were some of the most influential actors in Arab and Muslim societies and were not going away any time soon. The question of whether engaging with the Islamist parties would confer legitimacy on them was irrelevant, liberals argued, because they had already been legitimized by the support of their constituents. In short, the United States must engage with the Islamists, as there could be no democratic transition in the Arab world without them.

Until the Arab uprisings, however, these views held little sway. The September 11 attacks reinforced the apprehensions of the US foreign policy establishment about all Islamists and the alternative to pro-Western authoritarian rulers. Since 9/11, fear of Islamism in general, not just of al-Qaeda, has taken hold of the Western imagination. Pro-American, Arab autocrats, such as Hosni Mubarak, used and abused the Islamist threat as a scare tactic in order to avoid being pressured by their superpower patron to open up the closed political system. They exploited this imaginary fear by portraying themselves as partners in the fight against 'extremists', such as the Muslim Brothers. Until his last day in power, when millions of Egyptians called for his departure, Mubarak used the menace of the Brotherhood to warn the United States of what lay ahead if he should go. As the political crisis reached a climax at the end of January 2011, Obama telephoned Mubarak and tried to find a way for him to leave the scene gracefully. A White House official summarized the response as: 'Muslim Brotherhood, Muslim Brotherhood, Muslim Brotherhood.'

Secretary of State Hillary Clinton acknowledged as much in a November 2011 speech about Washington's response to the Arab uprisings that toppled several US clients. 'For years, dictators told their people they had to accept the autocrats they knew to avoid the extremists they feared. … Too often, we accepted that narrative ourselves.'

The Arab uprisings and Washington's recalibration of its approach

Immediately after the ousting of Mubarak, the US government used its connections (and substantive military aid) to the ruling generals to demand assurances that the Muslim Brotherhood's role would be limited in any future government, as well as continuity in relations with Israel. In July 2011, the US House Appropriations Committee earmarked US$1.55 billion to Egypt on the condition that such aid should in part be used for 'border security programs and activities in the Sinai' in order to ensure Israel's security concerns. The House Appropriations Committee directed that the US Secretary of State certified that the Government of Egypt 'is not controlled by a foreign terrorist organization, or its affiliates or supporters, is implementing the Egypt–Israel Peace Treaty, and is taking steps to detect and destroy the smuggling network and tunnels between Egypt and the Gaza strip'. This was a humiliating demand made on a supposedly democratically elected government in Cairo. For example, when the Egyptian authorities acceded in May 2011 to the demand by the Egyptian public to open the Rafah crossing and ease the blockade on Gaza, the crossing was closed again within just three days because of US and Israeli pressure. The status of the Rafah crossing is not currently very different from what it was in the Mubarak era, with only minor improvements.

However, as Islamists won a majority of seats in the new parliaments in Tunisia, Morocco and Egypt, the Obama Administration reversed two decades of hostility and disengagement towards mainstream Islamists and acknowledged the new political reality in the region, though the George W. Bush administration had established limited contacts with the Muslim Brothers. What brought the sudden shift in the US position? As the Arab uprisings removed two of Washington's close clients, Mubarak and Ben Ali, the Obama Administration suddenly found itself at the mercy of the new social forces that had burst onto the scene, and had little choice but to engage with the new political realities in the region. After 9/11 US influence has declined considerably, culminating in the debacle in Iraq, which marked a low point for America in the region. It would not be an exaggeration to note that America's 9/11 war marked the beginning of the end of its hegemony in the region – a theme that I explore fully in my new book, *Obama and the Middle East: The End of America's Moment?* (2012). Obama and his senior advisors have a vivid sense of American relative decline versus other rising geostrategic and geo-economic powers, particularly China, and that the United States had overextended itself in the Middle East far and beyond what its primary interest necessitate. They believe that America's future lies in the Pacific, not in the Middle East. Accordingly from the outset, the Obama Administration has begun to shift its economic and foreign policy priorities towards the East Asian and Pacific region – away from the non-oil producing Gulf states.

With the Arab uprisings removing key pro-Western rulers and allies, the Obama Administration found itself forced to reengage in the region against its will. Its foreign plate was full and its main focus was on bettering a weak economy and deterring Iran from developing a nuclear weapon and preparing the way for the exit of US troops from Afghanistan. The lens through which the Obama Administration viewed the Arab uprisings was Iran and Israel: will Iran gain political advantage out of the turmoil in the Arab world, and how will the fall of Mubarak impact Israel's security? Since the US Administration did not have the desire or the will to invest major political capital in the Arab arena because it ranked low on its foreign policy priorities, the decision was made to engage the Islamists. It had little choice but at least to explore engagement with Islamists in Egypt and Tunisia. Obama aides therefore decided to find out where the Islamist parties stood on key US foreign policy issues: the Camp David Peace Treaty with Israel; their political economy; and the fight against terrorism and extremism.

In a marked historic shift of US foreign policy, Hillary Clinton said that the United States would work with the ascendant Islamist parties in Tunisia and Egypt if they played by the rules of the political game. Ever since, a stream of US officials has visited leaders of the Brothers, including Deputy Secretary of State William Burns and top US policy-makers, together with European officials. In April 2012, a Brotherhood team visited Washington and met with White House officials, policy experts and others apparently to dispel increasing worries about the group's agenda.

After Mohamed Morsi's election as President, the contacts have deepened and expanded on multiple levels.[1] This process has involved contact at the highest levels, not only between the Obama Administration and the Islamist parties, but also involving US politicians from both parties. To their extreme surprise, US officials discovered that the Islamists were willing to play by the rules of the political game and to compromise on most of the United States' key foreign policy and national security issues.

Foreign policy and national security

A relative consensus has now emerged in the Obama Administration over engagement with the Muslim Brotherhood in Egypt and the Ennahda party in Tunisia. The prevailing view is that now these parties exercise a moderating influence on their societies, that they are willing to pursue realist foreign policies that accommodate US vital interests, and that they can be trusted to maintain the status quo both internally and regionally. Furthermore, many now see the more mainstream Islamist parties as a countervailing influence against ultraconservative Salafi groups and a source of stability in a turbulent region.

Now there is recognition that despite the importance of culture, including identity and religion, in the Islamists' worldview, their international relations will most likely be realist and cautious, based more on the interests of their movement and the geostrategic balance of power than on ideology. Seeking to allay the fears of the Western powers, particularly the United States, Islamists, most of whom are centrist, have already sent reassurances that they will not pursue confrontational policies towards Israel and that they would respect diplomatic treaties signed by the previous regimes (the Camp David Accords). In particular, the Brotherhood's leadership has gone on a charm offensive to convince American policy-makers that they have nothing to fear from their party coming to power. The Brothers' message has found receptive ears among both senior American Democratic and Republican officials.[2]

After the Brotherhood fielded Khairat Shater for President and provoked a storm of protests at home, the group redoubled its efforts in a bid to promote his presidential nomination and allay the West's fears. Shater assured a visiting US Republican Party delegation about his commitments to human rights, women's rights and maintaining peace with Israel. To drive the message home to US officials, a Brotherhood delegation to Washington stressed the group's priorities as developmental issues and downplayed foreign policy.

While the Brotherhood's rhetoric on Israel and US foreign policy does not differ much from that of its nationalist and leftist counterparts, it has nevertheless gone out of its way to entertain a significant degree of 'moderation' when dealing with the Arab–Israeli conflict. Even the Salafis, not known for their diplomatic skills, said that they would not take unilateral actions and that they would submit any decision to revise the Peace Treaty with Israel to a referendum by the people. Islamists' stance on the Camp David Peace Treaty is another sign of subordination of ideology to interest. They are becoming more constituency driven and are gradually shedding some of their ideological luggage. In a similar tone to that of the Brotherhood, Tunisia's Mohamed Ghannouchi has addressed Israel's supporters in the United States, while also telling the Western powers that they have nothing to fear by the rise of the Islamists to power.[3]

Western diplomats and politicians have taken note of these critical changes and concessions made by Islamists. 'Very impressive,' said Senator Lindsey Graham, a hardliner Republican of South Carolina, who met with Shater along with a group of mostly Republican law-makers in March 2012. Washington's subtle shift towards the Islamists stems from this recent intense diplomatic engagement with them, an engagement that has produced a set of promises and positions by the Islamists that have somehow reassured American policy-makers about their future conduct while in power.

However, it would be misleading to suggest that relations between Islamists and the United States will be smooth and friendly. Regardless of their orientation, Islamists are deeply suspicious of the West's designs on the region and will pursue independent, assertive foreign policies that differ from those of the ancient regime. They will go to great lengths to show a different foreign policy style from that of the old pro-Western Arab rulers. It will take many years to overcome the bitter legacy that exists between the constituency of Islamists and the Western powers, particularly the United States, a legacy whose root causes go back to the post-First World War peace settlement and colonialism.

There is a real danger that by underestimating the importance of Palestine for the newly revitalized Arab civil societies, the United States, along with its European allies, might find themselves in confrontation with the Arab peoples. As the Arab revolutions establish a new order, Palestine, far from fading away, will come to play a more important part in Arab politics. As constituency driven movements, Islamists will prioritize the Palestine cause because their supporters demand a tougher line on Israel. For example, in their first meeting with Deputy Secretary of State William Burns, after they had won more than 40% of the seats in Egypt's parliamentary elections, leaders of the Freedom and Justice Movement called on the United States to pursue a more balanced approach toward the Arab–Israeli conflict and stressed the significance of Palestine in the US–Egyptian relationship. In his first speech to the United Nations General Assembly in September 2012, Egyptian President Morsi said that the first issue which the world must exert all its efforts in resolving is the Palestinian cause. He demanded that the United Nations grant membership to the Palestinians, with or without a peace agreement with Israel. 'The fruits of dignity and freedom must not remain far from the Palestinian people,' he said, adding that it was 'shameful that UN resolutions aiding the Palestinians are not enforced.'

The likelihood of an escalation of tensions between Israel and Arab countries should not be overlooked, even though there is no appreciation in Washington of the critical importance of Palestine in the Arab imagination. The status quo will be difficult to maintain, and it will likely strain relations between the United States and the rising Islamists. But for now the Islamists have succeeded in allaying concerns and fears by the United States, a development that shows how far they have travelled, as well as the divide that exists between their rhetoric and actual policies. Israel's war against Hamas in 2012 was a test case whereby the Muslim Brotherhood did not disappoint. Morsi and the Brotherhood exercised restraint and impressed on Hamas to show restraint as well. In fact, the Obama Administration was impressed by Morsi's positive role in the conflict, particularly the pressure he exerted on Hamas in order to accept the conditions for a ceasefire.[4]

The new capitalists: the political economy of the Islamists

Western and American officials have been pleasantly surprised by the Islamists' friendly attitude toward the free-market economics and wealth accumulation in contrast to their leftist and nationalist counterparts. A consensus exists in Western capitals that Islamism is a bourgeois movement consisting mostly of middle-class professionals, businessmen, shopkeepers, petty merchants and traders. If there is a slogan that best describes Islamists' economic attitude, it would be: 'Islam is good for business.' Many Arab Islamists admire and wish to imitate the example of Turkey, even though they know little about the complexity of the country's economy and lack Turkey's strategic economic model. What impresses them is Turkey's economic dynamism, especially the dynamism of the religiously observant provincial bourgeoisie who have turned Anatolian towns such as Kayseri, Konya and Gaziantep into industrial powerhouses driving the growth of the Turkish economy.

For example, the Muslim Brothers have assured the Western powers of their commitment to free-market capitalism. The architect of the Brothers' economic policy, the millionaire businessman Khairat al-Shater, has silenced voices within the organization that call for a more egalitarian, socialist approach. Although he does not hold elected office, in April 2012 he met the International Monetary Fund (IMF) team which is negotiating a US$3.2 billion loan facility with the Egyptian government. The IMF has said it wants broad political backing for the deal. After the Brotherhood confirmed Shater as a presidential candidate (the Election Commission subsequently disqualified him), the group intensified its contacts with the Western powers, with Shater meeting and reassuring US diplomats and economists visiting Cairo.[5]

In an interview with Al Jazeera, Shater said economic development would be the most pressing priority for his administration and would be based on structural reforms and growth. 'They [the Brothers] tightened the screws on anyone who had different ideas about economics,' said Mohamed Habib, a former Deputy Supreme Guide of the Brotherhood.

Although centrist-Islamists are generally for free-market economy and have always been, they are likely to seek religious legitimation for their economic policies. For example, Islamist parties have publicly vowed to promote social justice and have stressed their long record of social work among the poor. Most have chosen names like 'Justice and Development' or 'Freedom and Justice', a choice which shows their concerns, if not their priorities. In this sense, some Islamist-specific economic measures and ideas will be introduced to complement free-market capitalism. The Muslim Brothers, along with the Salafis, who are less enamoured with the free market than the Brothers, have already called for the introduction of an index of companies that comply with Sharia law as part of a wider move toward an 'Islamic' economy.[6] Designed to appeal to their base and to attract investments from the Gulf Arab region, where a *sharia*-compliant economic system exists, the idea does not alter the basics of Islamists' preference for free-market capitalism.

Similarly, according to one of the architects of Ennahda's economic programme, Ridha Chkoundali, 'The banking system will be diversified and the Tunisian financial market will therefore be made up of traditional and Islamic banks. … As a result, there will be more competition between the banks.' In Morocco as well, sensing the importance of addressing economic issues after being designated Prime Minister, Abdelilah Benkirane stated: 'We will do everything to encourage foreign and domestic investment to create a climate of prosperity.'

Now Western officials feel at ease because there is nothing in Islamists' current statements and ideas that show them to be socialist oriented, though most readily accept the Keynesian model – active state intervention in the economy. With minor variations, the dominant Islamist approach to the economy is free-market capitalism. In Egypt, Tunisia and Morocco, the Brotherhood, Ennahda and Justice and Development Party have sufficient interests to deal with global financial institutions such as the IMF and The World Bank; they do not have the luxury or ideological commitment to be insular because their countries do not have access to huge rents and raw resources, especially petroleum. This is sweet music to the ears of US policy-makers.

Culture and values

In contrast to foreign policy, national security and political economy, culture and values may prove to be a sticking point between the Islamists and Western powers, though not central or an impediment to their nascent relationship. While the Islamists have made many concessions on foreign policy and national security, they are far less willing to bend to the United States in the social and cultural spheres and the moralization and control of the public space. Islamist leaders have indicated that the price of cooperation on Israel, terrorism and political economy is that the United States respects Islamic values and their independence on internal social and cultural issues. It remains to be seen to what extent these issues will be overcome, or prove a major point of strain in relations between the United States and Islamists.

Nevertheless, Islamists are making a concerted effort to engage the Western powers and chart a new relationship based on the logic of statecraft and mutual interests. In Syria and Libya, Islamists, including the Muslim Brotherhood in Syria and the Libyan Islamic Movement, welcomed Western military intervention there, signalling a sea change in their attitudes. As the Syrian crisis rages, Syrian Brotherhood leaders said that they had spoken with officials from the Obama Administration, but that the United States remained wary about who might triumph in Syria, particularly groups of al-Qaeda variety, expressing their deep disappointment with US foreign policy.

The shift in the US–Islamists relationship would have been unthinkable before the eruption of the Arab popular uprisings. Both camps had kept their distance from one another and expressed reluctance to engage fully. As pro-Western rulers collapsed in Tunisia and Egypt, Washington has begun to take a second look at the Islamists who, in turn, have shown themselves willing to accommodate its vital interests in the region. Realism trumpeted ideology. That goes to show that significant developments, such as revolts and revolutions, do serve as catalysts that change deeply entrenched attitudes. Time will tell if the recent change in Islamists' attitudes will be translated into a rapprochement with the Western powers.

Conclusions

A qualification is in order. The nascent relationship between the United States and the Islamists is in flux, unfolding before our eyes. At this early stage, it is difficult to make definite judgement, though the writing is on the wall. The relationship is fragile and fraught with risks for both camps. After the riots in Cairo and Benghazi, when the US President was asked if he considers Egypt an ally under Morsi, Obama said that he considers Egypt neither a friend nor a foe, a revealing answer that speaks volumes about how the US government views the rising Islamists and the durability of mistrust and suspicion. If the Republicans win back the White House four years from now, there would be consequences. Conservative hardliners would fight tooth and nail to exert more pressure on the Islamists and keep their feet to the fire.

Nevertheless, the Obama Administration has managed its relations with the Islamists constructively. Both camps have stressed national interests over ideology and identity. Despite repeated calls by the Egyptian opposition and US politician as well, the Obama Administration has refrained from publicly criticizing Morsi's authoritarian tactics and has called on the opposition to sit down with Morsi and reach a political compromise. The administration has also provided financial aid to the Egyptian government and has called on the IMF and Egypt to act swiftly and sign a deal for a loan of almost US $5 billion. There is a case to be made that the US approach to Egypt has changed much after the ousting of Mubarak. It is driven by similar considerations of national security and geostrategic considerations, particularly the health of the Peace Treaty with Israel.

Regardless of what happens in Washington, the Islamists have already boxed themselves in and have made major concessions on foreign policy and national security. They are playing on Washington's terms. Although it is early to pass a final verdict on the Islamists, they lack a strategic vision and experience in foreign affairs. They have not engaged in an open and transparent national debate at home about foreign policy and national security and have not assembled a broad-based coalition that allows them to construct a new foreign policy doctrine(s) for the post-ancient regime; their tactics share many of the weaknesses of the old regime which had been overthrown by the popular uprisings.

In the post-Arab Spring countries, real change has not yet come to foreign policy.

Notes

1. For example, this can be exemplified by recent visits by Western officials (particularly from the United States) to the Brotherhood headquarters in Cairo (Ezzat 2011; Dawood 2012).
2. The truth is that Egyptians of all persuasions feel that their country must reclaim its leadership role in the Arab arena and resist Israel's oppression of the Palestinians. As a result, Egyptians are questioning the utility of the Camp David Accords with Israel. However, few Egyptians call for the Accords' abrogation. More than 70% of Egyptians who were recently polled by the New York-based International Peace Institute stated their preference for maintaining the agreement with Israel. This finding is corroborated by polling conducted by Egypt's leading al-Ahram Centre for Political and Strategic Studies (2011).
3. Ghannouchi refuted Israeli reports that the Tunisian constitution would condemn Zionism (Smith 2011; *Arabs Today* 2011; Alfajr News 2011).
4. Mohammad Morsi urged the United States to 'reconsider' its policies in the region, favouring people's choices as reflected by the Arab uprisings instead of dictatorial regimes, because that proved to be 'not in its best interest' (El Deeb 2012; Abdelminhem 2012; Islam 2012).
5. For a detailed account of the Brotherhood's economic plan and the kind of projects they intend to launch, see al-Waziri (2012). Also, for Ennahda's speedy efforts to pass a draft budget plan, see Ben Barik (2012). Similarly, for Morocco's economic reform plans, see Maghress (2012).
6. Of all Islamists, the Salafis are most attracted to the idea of state intervention in the economy and forcefully call for the adoption of distributive measures to address rampant poverty in society, especially among their poor urban and rural base.

References

Abdelmon'em, Rehab. 2012. "Morsi: Meets Burns and Patterson … and Asks to Change Obama's Politics in Relation to the People of the Arab Spring" [in Arabic]. Accessed January 12, 2012. http://digital.ahram.org.eg/articles.aspx?Serial=765201&eid=1476

al-Ahram Centre for Political and Strategic Studies. 2011. "Public Opinion in Egypt." Cairo: al-Ahram Centre for Political and Strategic Studies, International Peace Institute. September 19. http://www.ipacademy.org/images/pdfs/egyptpoll-september2011.pdf/

Alfajr News. 2011. "Ghannouchi: We Will Not Condemn Israel and We Will Allow Freedom of Belief" [in Arabic]. Accessed December 7, 2011. http://www.alfajrnews.net/

Al-Amin, Esam. 2011. "The Tom and Jerry Show: Back to Tahrir Square". *Counterpunch* November 24. http://www.counterpunch.org/2011/11/24/back-to-tahrir-square/

Arabs Today. 2011. "Tunisia's Ghannouchi Reassures Israel Amid Security Fears." *Arabs Today*, December 7.

Ben Barik, Khamis. 2012. "Tunisia Prepares a Complete Draft Budget Plan" [in Arabic]. Accessed March 20, 2012. http://www.aljazeera.net/

Boston Globe. 2012. "In UN Speech, Mohammed Morsi Assumes Major Role in Middle East." *Boston Globe*, September, 27.

Cole, Juan. 2009. *Engaging the Muslim World*. New York: Palgrave Macmillan.

Dawood, Ahmed. 2012. "Carter Visits the Headquarters of the Brotherhood and Freedom and Justice Party" [in Arabic]. Accessed January 12, 2012. http://www.masress.com/

El Deeb, Sarah. 2012. "US Raises Outreach to Egypt's Muslim Brotherhood." Associated Press, January 11.

Djerejian, Edward. 2008. *Danger and Opportunity: An American Ambassador's Journey Through the Middle East*. New York: Threshold.

Ezzat, Hani. 2011. "US Delegation Visits Brotherhood Headquarters to Talk About Latest Developments in Egypt" [in Arabic]. Accessed October 19, 2011. http://www.ahram.org/

Gerges, Fawaz A. 1999. *America and Political Islam: Clash of Cultures or Clash of Interests?*. New York: Cambridge University Press.

Gerges, Fawaz A. 2012. *Obama and the Middle East: The End of America's Moment?*. New York: Palgrave Macmillan.

Islam, Osama Abdel. 2012. "Dr Birr Urges America to Abandon its Discrimination Against Muslims" [in Arabic]. Accessed January 24, 2012. http://www.ikhwanonline.com/

Kirkpatrick, David. 2012. "Keeper of Islamic Flame Rises as Egypt's New Decisive Voice.", *New York Times*, March 12, 2012. Retrieved from http://www.nytimes.com/2012/03/12/world/middleeast/muslim-brotherhood-leader-rises-as-egypts-decisive-voice.html?pagewanted=all

Lizza, Ryan, 2011. "The Consequentialist: How the Arab Spring Remade Obama's Foreign Policy." *New Yorker*, May 2.

Maghress. 2012. "Benkirane Confirms his Government Intends to Push Reforms that Will Cut Economic Rent" [in Arabic]. Accessed March 15, 2012. http://www.maghress.com/

Morocco News Agency. 2012. "Morocco Embraces Democracy as King Mohammed VI Appoints New Cabinet." Morocco News Agency, January 3. http://morocconewsagency.com/democracy-embraces-morocco-king-mohammed-appoints-new-cabinet-1-3-12.html/

Saleh, Heba. 2012. "Egyptian Officials Look to Set Up Islamist Index." *Financial Times*, February 1.

Al Sherbini, Ramadan. 2012. "Brotherhood Courts the West." *Gulf News*, April 5.

Sieff, Martin. 1992. "New Challenge for West: Islamic Fundamentalism." *Washington Times*, February 16.

Smith, Lee. 2011. "A Tunisian Islamist Looks to the Future." *Weekly Standard*, December 1.

al-Waziri, Hani. 2012. "Al Masri Al Youm Publishes Details of the 'Brotherhood's Renaissance' Plans: Economic Restructuring According to Islamic principles … and 100 National Projects" [in Arabic]. Accessed April 26, 2012. http://www.almasry-alyoum.com/

Ziki, Anas. 2012. "Al-Shater: We are Competing for President Because of a Plot to Make Us Fail" [in Arabic]. Accessed April 12, 2012. http://www.aljazeera.net/

Towards an intellectual and political understanding of the question of religion and the state

Panel discussion*

Ghassan Ben Jeddou†: It is not by chance that the organizers decided to hold this seminar in Tunisia; for from here was launched the Arab Spring's intifada and revolution that brought autocracy in this country to an end. Democratic elections, in every sense of the term, have been held – elections that brought new faces to political power and were emulated in more than one Arab country. The paradox is that one-and-a-half years after the Arab Spring a new debate about the relationship between state and religion has begun, although the issue itself is not new and has been raised on several occasions in the past few years, if not decades. However, returning to this issue at this extraordinary moment in time is highly justified because some of the old activists, i.e. the Islamist political movements, are now in power. When we speak of Islamist movements, we are actually talking about their culture and practices and the programmes they have gradually begun to implement. Among these is the relationship between state and religion, the subject of this seminar.

In fact, because the debate over the past three days has been mostly theoretical, we would like this final session, which we have devoted to the al-Mayadeen Programme, to be firmly grounded in reality rather than confined to the intellectual and theoretical levels. We want this discussion to address the possibility of reaching an understanding, or striving to reach one; we therefore call upon you to work towards reaching an intellectual–political understanding of the state versus religion issue. What are the common denominators upon which you can all agree in the relationship between the state and religion in the Arab world, both today and in the future? How can the commonalities overcome the differences? How could the parameters be drawn such that these disagreements do not lead to conflict but remain purely intellectual? We

*This panel discussion (with the audience participating throughout) concluded the Symposium on Religion and the State in the Arab World held in Hamamat, Tunisia, on 15–17 October 2012. The symposium was a joint endeavour between the Centre for Arab Unity Studies (CAUS) and the Swedish Institute Alexandria (SwedAlex). The moderator of this discussion is a well-known Arab journalist, Ghassan Ben Jeddou; and the audience comprised the different speakers at the symposium and various participants therein – amounting to around 65 people. The following discourse – with minor contributions omitted – seems to engage with the crux of the problematic relationship between religion and the state; the main question being where to draw the line between them, or, for some, whether such a line should exist. Though this question may seem obsolete to some European peoples, in the Arab World – especially during the ongoing transitional period – it seems a divisive as well as a decisive issue.

†Chairman of the Board of Directors, Al-Mayadeen Channel.

will address this all-embracing vision if it develops at all. Naturally, rather than approach this issue from a purely theoretical perspective, we want to link theory to actual practice.

***

Ben Jeddou: We will begin with Sheikh Rached Ghannouchi who will speak about the relationship between the state and religion; he will give us his opinion on the relationship's main principles, principles that could form the basis of consensus amongst all concerned, including the nationalists, Islamists and democrats, and perhaps spare us the arguments and issues that prevail today.

Sheikh Rached Ghannouchi*: In the name of God and His Prophet, peace be upon him (ﷺ). Whenever the relationship between the state and religion is raised, a series of other issues are raised as well, including the relationship between religion and freedom, religion and secularization or secularism, and religion and democracy – since, today, democracy is the best-known expression of modern governance for guaranteeing public and personal freedoms, an independent judiciary and a free media. What we can confirm in this context is, firstly, that the concept of politics is rooted in Islam, since Islam has been a political movement from the very beginning. History shows that Islam first took hold in the city where the Prophet (ﷺ) combined two positions into one – his role as a herald of God, like all other prophets, and his political role as ruler, judge and army commander. Although these multiple roles, which he held personally (ﷺ), were proof of Islam's unity, they varied over the years as legislative roles and, later, political roles developed and were assumed by politicians, imams and army commanders. As this nucleus expanded, diversified and grew into an empire, so independent judicial roles were created, making it necessary to separate these functions in a manner that clearly distinguished the religious aspect (or religious system that involves doctrine and religious laws, i.e. the fundamentals of religion) from all that is interpretational within the practical world. Therefore, in addition to being a religious system, Islam is a social, cultural and political system. However, while the religious aspect is constant and defined by doctrinal texts, such as the number of prayers and the ways to practise them, temporal dealings are based on self-interest because Islam came to help people achieve their interests both in this life and in the afterlife. This is why Imam Abu Ishaq al-Shatibi reached deep into Islam and highlighted the fact that its objectives comprise the protection of religion, souls, minds, family, extended relationships and financial assets.

Ben Jeddou: Sheikh Rached, when you said at the beginning that politics is a core principle of Islam and that later on a series of roles involving legal, military and legislative functions were added; how is politics a core principle of Islam? Is there a text, or was it practise that rooted it firmly in Islam?

Sheikh Rached Ghannouchi: Politics is rooted in Islam, in the sense that Islam came into being to organize all aspects of life; however, while one of these aspects is organized by established religious texts, the larger part is either subject to interpretation or

*President of the Tunisian Ennahda Movement.

belongs to the domain of intellectual activity. Yet, this intellectual activity evolves within a fixed set of values, within a framework of objectives that contemporary scholars, like the esteemed Tunisian scholar Mohammad Al-Taher bin Ashour, have expanded to include issues such as justice and ensuring its implementation. Because Islam came to do justice, all that ensures justice is part of Islam. This is why some scholars have said that God supports the just state even if it is not Muslim, and does not support the unjust state even if it is Muslim, since Islam in its entirety revolves around justice.

Another objective to be included was freedom, since Islam came in the form of a comprehensive liberation revolution aimed at liberating people's minds from superstitions and illusions, people's bodies from pressure, and society from poverty and disease. Some scholars added another objective, if not several other open-ended objectives, such as protecting the environment – a very important objective of Islam. Therefore, when we say that Islam is both a state and a religion, we do not mean that the Muslim mind, or Islam, includes legal domains; we do not need to open the Quran or the Sunna to find a ruling regarding an issue. No; Islam is a state and a religion in the sense that the Muslim should behave according to Islam's objectives in every aspect of his life. Some of Islam's teachings are constant, clear, partial and precise, and have to do with faith and doctrine, and the others have to do with temporal dealings. The Muslim mind is guided by these general meanings, such as the protection of souls and minds, ensuring justice, and instituting freedom among the people. This is why we could say that secularism has no place in all this, especially secularism in its general sense, as Dr Abdul-Wahab Al-Massiri, God rest his soul, has said, which actually means removing religion from one's life; not a single aspect of Islam involves removing religion from one's life. Yet, does this mean that Muslims do not need to work hard and use their minds? Of course they do! Here, there is an important meeting of minds between Islam and democracy, because democracy is not a religion but a set of arrangements designed to prevent decision-making affecting the community being monopolized by a single individual or group.

The Islamic state, i.e. the state that evolves within the confines of Islam's objectives, is not a theocracy; its only legitimacy comes from the people based on a clear contractual agreement. This is where Islam and democracy coincide, namely the fact that the Muslim state is a civil state that draws its legitimacy from the people. It is also a pluralistic state because Islam has no official spokesperson and no one church or body that reflects its views single-handedly; this means that there is freedom of interpretation in Islam and, by extension, political pluralism, which means a wide variety of political parties, societies and opinions. Moreover, faced with a torrent of interpretations whenever we need to make a decision, it is important to be able to find a legislative institution or a parliament that interprets collectively, since in this day and age, there is no longer room for absolutist or individual interpretations. In other words, the authority that makes the rules should not be in the hands of a single scholar or group of scholars, but in the hands of the nation's representatives, assisted by experts. There was a time when the legislative function was performed by scholars, but today it is the responsibility of elected councils and people's representatives in consultation with legal, economic and other experts in a variety of fields. We therefore cannot say that there is a contradiction between the intellect and the text, between religion and interest or between religion and democracy; freedom lies at the core of each and every meaning of modernization, and freedom is a major value. It is also not true to say, as some colleagues have said, that if we look closely at the Quran we will not find the word 'freedom' anywhere; freedom is an integral part of hundreds of *ayas* (verses) such as, 'Then whosoever wills, let him believe; and whosoever wills, let him disbelieve.'[1] In reality, the freedoms of belief and expression are at the basis of all other freedoms, and Islam did not witness religious persecution at any time in its history. There was always co-existence among different Muslim and non-Muslim sects, whether divine or not, since the freedoms of belief and conscience underlie the rules of Islamic thought, if not Islamic doctrine.

Ben Jeddou: Dr Saadeddin Ibrahim, based on the way Sheikh Rached describes it, do you believe that there are now common denominators and a consensus on all these matters, and the situation is therefore more reassuring, since he departs from the premise that there are constants in religion and also matters that give some cause for concern. However, he said at the end that there was no contradiction between Islam and democracy, and that there is neither a theocratic state nor a 'church'. Do you believe this is reassuring, especially at this point in time given what is currently happening on the ground?

Dr Saadeddin Ibrahim*: Let me first say that when we hear Sheikh Rached speak, and it is not for the first time since our relationship dates back 30 years to when we first met, in Denmark, and we were both refugees roaming the wide world – when I listen to him he makes me like Islam and the Islamic model of state and social management; though this is only when I hear him speak. When I examine the facts, however, facts that he is not responsible for since his domain is thought, theory, spreading the call and proselytizing, when I observe reality as a sociologist doing his job by following events on the ground, I find things that scare me in the countries that have adopted the Islamist model, or which claim that their governance system is Islamist, like Iran, the Taliban in Afghanistan, or Sudan, for example. This is why we need to examine closely not only thoughts and theoretical interpretations but also actual practices, and these are not reassuring. Therefore, what was said after the Islamists came to power in Algeria, or almost did, namely that, 'Yes, we do believe that every citizen has one vote, but it is for one time only, since once we come to power there will be no such thing anymore,' such a statement, God only knows, is not reassuring.

Ben Jeddou: Today, some Islamist movements have come to power through the ballot box. Let us speak about what is happening now: what is your opinion about that? This is their discourse and this is how they behave. Where do they reassure you and where do they unsettle you?

Dr Saadeddin Ibrahim: As I said before, the countries that we have been observing for years unsettle me. If we talk about Tunisia, Egypt, Libya and Yemen, i.e. the Arab Spring countries, there are unsettling and frightful practices taking place in the name of religion. On the other hand, some good things are taking place as well. I would, of course, like to speak about Egypt, an experience in which I am directly involved, since many among the Islamists were my colleagues in jail, including current president Mohammed Morsi, a 'Porsche colleague',[2] as was Khaled al-Shater, both of whom are currently high officials in the Muslim Brotherhood. I had several long, animated and

*Director, Ibn Khaldoun Centre.

convoluted discussions in jail with members of the Brotherhood and with jihadists and other Islamist groups, which shows that Islamists of all shades were with me in jail. Then, I saw them when they were released and saw the way they behaved; I saw a model of alienation and a desire to establish total control and a monopoly. We look at Tunisia from afar as a model, a Cinderella, the Cinderella of Arab democracy; yet ever since I arrived in Tunisia, over the past few days to be precise, I have begun to hear of disquieting things from my Tunisian brethren, such as the Salafist attacks against citizens whom they believe are not applying their idea of Islam, which is something we have started to see in Egypt as well. Therefore, when the Islamists came to power, some of them began taking the law into their own hands, and this is disturbing. We should be aware of such practices from the start, but I have always opposed attempts to sideline the Islamists from power.

Ben Jeddou: Dr Nassar, you have heard what has been said so far, and there are things that reassure us on the theoretical level; the man speaks also from a position of knowledge as the leader of one of the strongest movements in Tunisia, although there are some who view it negatively, even with apprehension. We want to focus on both the negative and positive aspects, to hold onto the latter and overcome the former. What do you say about that?

Nasif Nassar[*]: Although I could approach the subject from two different angles, one philosophical the other sociological, I will simply state my opinion from the philosophical–theoretical angle within which Sheikh Rached's intervention falls. We could return to the sociological angle at a later stage.

The title of the seminar these past three days has been 'The Relationship between the State and Religion in the Arab World'. The intention here is to address the religious phenomenon in general, including Islam, and statehood, in general, including the Arab states. We cannot delve directly into the subject by addressing Arab and Islamic specificities straight on. We should first view the subject from the general human perspective, for only by looking at it from the human and historical perspective will we be able, gradually, to look at it from the Islamic perspective, and all that relates to Islam and the Arab situation. In this context, I believe that the first principle we should accept is that religion is one thing and politics is another, and that the nature of religion is one thing and the nature of politics is another. If we do not accept this essential difference between the natures of religion and politics, our conversation will – in my opinion – quite simply be based on an incorrect premise. However, if we accept this fact, then we should conceive of politics at the level of human society rather than Arab society, or from an Islamic perspective. At the core, politics as a phenomenon of human society comprises three levels, and here we should carefully distinguish between these levels lest the discourse becomes confused. Firstly, there is the statehood level, i.e. the main political level; secondly, the governance system level and, thirdly, the political practice level, i.e. actual implementation.

At the statehood level, we should view the entire state as a phenomenon of human society, with roots deeply embedded in social life and its laws, regardless of religion. I believe, in short, that, in this day and age, the world has by and large accepted the premise that the nation is the social basis of the modern state, as are the national

*Professor.

society, national identity and national belonging. All these revolve around the national phenomenon at the root of the state's formation as an independent socio-political entity.

At the governance system level, the systems change but the state does not. The state is deeper and more stable than any governance system. Today, I believe that democracy is the best system of government the human political mind has conceived of, and that we are ready and eagerly trying to transition to a democratic life and a democratic system, with all that it involves. However, having said that, I should also concede that democracy is not simply a series of procedures to bring a ruler to power or to replace him. Democracy presupposes a philosophical view of man, of people, of work and the relationship between the individual and the state. Freedom is the essential principle of democracy. Equality among the citizens does not depend on their being believers, whether they are Muslim or non-Muslim; the believers are an inseparable part of the citizenry, though the citizen is a citizen regardless of his religious affiliation.

Ben Jeddou: What are your reservations about the way it is being practised today?

Nasif Nassar: They concern their behaviour, teachings and considerations.

Ben Jeddou: Where?

Nasif Nassar: In all the Arab countries, in the current revolutionary countries, in Sheikh Rached's discourse, and in the Muslim Brotherhood's discourse in Libya. The freedom we are talking about is individual freedom; therefore, when Sheikh Rached talks about the people, for example, he speaks as a Muslim believer. This is as far as the text is concerned; but if facing a population divided among several religions and sects, how would he behave? Will he go back to religious rule? This religious rule is not at the root of the legal system or the laws; at this point, the religious dimension should be pushed to the back and the citizens should behave according to their national affiliation and on the basis of total equality among them. How does one deal with a diverse sectarian society? What if you have both Sunnis and Shias? What if you have both Muslims and non-Muslims, Christians and non-Christians? What would you do when there are Muslims in countries where religion is not a basis of citizenship? What would you do then; how would you apply the law and how would you implement political rights? Political rights should be free of any religious restrictions. This is why they should be granted on the basis of total equality, including equality between men and women.

Ben Jeddou: Sheikh Jawad al-Khalesi, we are talking here about the different Muslim experiences that exist today; there are new Islamic experiences born of the Arab Spring and Arab revolutions, and others that already exist. It seems that all Islamist experiences in existence today are the object of reservations and suspicion. The ones that already existed are disturbing, and the new ones are perhaps even more so; what do you say about that as a religious scholar?

Sheikh Jawad al-Khalesi[*]: In the name of God the Merciful the Compassionate; I do not understand the reason for this extreme sensitivity because the election results

*Instructor at Madinat al-Ilm University of the Imam al-Khalesiand and President of the National Foundation Congress.

favoured one particular side; why do people have suspicions and doubts about the integrity of the process? We sometimes talk about democracy, but when some elections are held we say that they [the results] are wrong; yet, when the Muslim lists do not win, we say they are correct. These reservations indicate a lack of conviction and lack of belief in the will of the nation, or of the people, as they say. Yet, these reservations exist and some are justified, and we accept that; but others are not and are simply the result of hearsay and rumour. What we have just heard from Dr Nasif Nassar will be answered, because much of what he said has no basis in reality.

The issue is very clear; I do not want to sugar-coat the situation, but the study should be serious. We have a particular philosophy on governance in Islam and this philosophy is our reference point. Those aspects of democracy that agree with this philosophy we support, and those that do not agree with this philosophy we do not consider right or suitable for the *Ummah* (Muslim community). *Shura* is an integral part of Islam, but the rulings that contradict the religious laws are unacceptable to Islam. Some, like Nassar and others, said during the sessions that we have to abide by what the *Ummah* wants in all cases, yet we refuse to do so when the *Ummah* votes. We heard that just now, which means that there are doubts.

Ben Jeddou: He did not reject the results; he was talking theoretically about actual practices.

Sheikh Jawad al-Khalesi: They say that there is fear; fear of what? Elections were held, and a certain group came to power as a result; who said that the vote is for one time only? This is akin to the rumours spread without being authenticated, when certain parties repress the Muslims and create sedition in Algeria, amongst others. They then say: we are afraid that they will not implement democracy later on! They instantaneously do away with democracy, then fear the results.

Let me summarize the issue in a few words: we believe that the *Ummah* has an effective role to play, the entire *Ummah*, even non-Muslims who live in a Muslim society; it is in the custody of the city that the Prophet (ﷺ) has converted into reality, and it involves everyone, Christians and Jews included. When we live together in one city, the city that the Prophet (ﷺ) changed from Yathreb, what we have is a complete *Ummah* that acts to protect this society against division and dislocation – however this is based on certain rules.

Ben Jeddou: What do you mean by *Ummah*? Is it the *Ummah* within the nation rather than just the Muslim *Ummah*?

Sheikh Jawad al-Khalesi: There is only one *Ummah* in the nation, as the Prophet (ﷺ) said, in the custody of the city; he instituted equality among the people as far as the responsibility for building that *Ummah* was concerned.

Nasif Nassar: And the political rights?

Sheikh Jawad al-Khalesi: The political rights are very clear.

Nasif Nassar: Total equality for all?

Sheikh Jawad al-Khalesi: Yes ... yes, total equality for all.

Nasif Nassar: The state … can the head of state be non-Muslim?

Sheikh Jawad al-Khalesi: If the majority of Muslims or the overwhelming majority of non-Muslims elect him, then so be it. Has there been a Muslim president in the United States so far? They had one Catholic president and they killed him. Kennedy was killed because he was not a Catholic in the right sense of the term.

To conclude, I would like to focus on a few realistic matters; we are talking about unrealistic matters, and the seminar, despite its usefulness and important role in bringing together such a large number of researchers and intellectuals, and the valuable research it has put at our disposal, and I admit that I have benefited considerably from it, has had some unrealistic aspects. It addresses an issue that some see as imaginary, philosophical and utopian. In reality, we have countries that we need to protect against dismemberment and foreign domination, and allow their citizens, both Muslims and non-Muslims, to take part in building their state on the basis of equality, respect and affection.

Ben Jeddou: Mounir Shafiq, when Dr Nasif Nassar asks that a state governed by the Islamists takes into account a multi-religious and sectarian society, how could that be done?

Mounir Shafiq*: I would like to begin by clarifying three initial points; in my opinion, we should draw a clear line between the old and the modern state. First, the modern Western capitalist state has certain characteristics that should be discussed on their own merits, and this pertains until the colonial era. Second, I believe that the modern state is an autocratic state and should receive its share of criticism, rather than endowing it with a halo of divinity and placing it above everything else.

Ben Jeddou: Which state is this?

Mounir Shafiq: All states. A state is by nature above all else, but by its very nature it also tends to impose itself and its control on everyone in society. However, despite the relative differences between states, the Islamists, liberals and nationalists should, in principle, study this phenomenon diligently because I believe that everyone who leads this state will fall prey to this tendency, especially if he comes to power through a revolution and has principles. I also believe that the state needs a strong dose of antibiotics to prevent it from imposing itself and its control on society. These antibiotics should start working from within society, which is why I believe that the Islamists' relationship with the state should not be based primarily on Islamizing the modern state: this is not possible. If this state is understood in its wider comprehensive democratic context, it cannot be Islamized lest it destroys Islam; the Islamists are the ones who will be corrupted! They will learn how to be autocratic and corrupt, and this will alienate them from the public. I apply this to the socialist state, the communist state and the liberal state, including Western capitalist states. As far as the state in our countries is concerned, let us be frank, if Western secularism sought to separate the state from religion because religion or the church tried to impose itself on the state, in the Arab countries it is the state that tries to impose itself on religion and control it. I

*General Coordinator of the Nationalist Islamist Conference, Beirut, Lebanon.

am calling for the liberation of religion from the state, for ending the state's control over religion. For example, the *awqaf* (religious endowment), intended to be the main source of assistance to help society build its strength, whether through education, health services or proselytization, has been under the control of the state that destroyed it and left society bereft of its basic strength. This is why I say to the secularists, who sanctify the state and fight for it as if they have no role to play in society, that they have to accept religious institutions, or religion in Islam, just as Christianity is accepted in France and Europe. In my opinion, the secular state in our countries will not have enough courage to grant Islamic institutions the same rights and freedoms as in the West, but rather the opposite. This is why, in my opinion, the main role of Islam in the state should be to protect the general identity of the state, rather than steer its best efforts towards the inside, because it is incumbent on them to act as the external antibiotics which control the state.

Ben Jeddou: Sheikh Rached, what is required and what is not? And if the Sheikh allows us, the Islamist movement tells us directly what you just told us a while ago – that Islam is both a state and a religion.

Sheikh Rached Ghannouchi: The authoritarianism that prevailed in the region has prevented us from getting to know one another; we began to learn about each other through the media, which are themselves controlled. Even at the academic level, many academicians do not have access to all the Islamist movement's documents because the movement is pursued. My own writings, and I am just a simple man and have a limited number of publications, were hounded everywhere. For example, the Centre for Arab Unity Studies published my book *Al-Hurriat al-Aamah* (Public Freedoms), and that book was attacked everywhere and the Centre for Arab Unity Studies was expelled from Tunisia. I am surprised at an esteemed professor like Dr Nassar, who I doubt has read the book – for which I forgive him since it is not available – a book devoted to the defence of freedom and which bases Islam in its entirety on freedom, i.e. bases political Islam as a whole on the principle of freedom. I am not saying that this opinion expresses the wide variety of Islamist views; I am also not denying these writings are unusual. However, there are prominent intellectuals, including Mounir Shafiq, Salim Al-Awwa and others, who have underlined the principle of freedom in Islam and the fact that the entire system is based on the idea of freedom. The principle of equality among the citizens, for example, is a constant and the Muslim community has no caretaker. The Muslim community is the one to choose its own state, criticize it, or depose it. It is its own caretaker and has sovereignty and total control over it. This is why Dr Nassar might find the *Jama'a Islamiya*'s idea of forming an Islamic Party strange, a party in which women and non-Muslims are barred from becoming president of the republic. We took it upon ourselves to criticize this project, said that it was not binding on Islam and that the people have the unrestricted freedom to elect a Muslim or non-Muslim woman or man, because such is the freedom that Muslim society enjoys. This thought was attacked by the autocrats and titans, and the phony media took it upon themselves to make it seem as if the concept was inherently contradictory, and will lay the ground for civil wars that begin with thought, with total intellectual contradictions, and end who knows where. They say that the war starts with words, and we are therefore the victims of knowing each other too little; these seminars are very important because they give us the opportunity to get to know one another. I will say again that there is total equality among all citizens, male, female, Muslim and Christian, and that the state has no source of legitimacy other than the people, the citizens, because these citizens deserve equal rights on this earth. It is the earth on which they live, with no caretakers at all.

I say to Dr Saadeddin who said that the Islamists monopolize power: before the elections, we here in Tunisia insisted on the principle of consensus, although it is not necessarily a democratic principle. Democracy gives the majority the right to govern, and Dr Saadeddin is an expert on the subject. If an Islamist party wins a majority in free and fair elections, democracy means that there will be two parties on the scene: one in government and the other in opposition. The minority should enjoy full rights, including the right to oppose and to become the majority, based on the rotation of power principle. Elections are not held only once. I am certain that the Algerian issue was simply a propaganda ploy since no one in that country has ever said such a thing; it was simply the secular elite trying to justify itself at the time for going out in a demonstration that called on the army to stage a coup, and to justify its fears for modernity and for democracy. The other issue concerns the Salafists; in our country the Salafists are part of the social fabric and they exist in this country, just like the Sufis do, with full rights. There is no war against the Salafists and no war against the Sufis; however, those who break the law should be punished, and this is what is happening today in Tunisia.

Some people want us to conduct mass arrests and build detention centres to house tens of thousands of people; if we want the Salafists to come to power in ten or 15 years, we should do that right now, because this is what Ben Ali did to us before and here we are in power today. When the Salafists escaped and took up arms and engaged in confrontations, some of them were killed; when they assaulted and breached a foreign mission, four or five of them were killed, 70 were wounded and many were sent to jail. What else do people want? All they want is to incite people against each other until they can say: draw down each other's numbers and cancel one another out, this way we will be rid of everyone.

Ali Fayyad*: I would like to start with Dr Saadeddin Ibrahim's fear of the Islamists. Although there are perhaps certain examples in the Arab world that justify this fear, it is not right to equate the examples he mentioned; not only is it a grave injustice, it is neither realistic nor authentic. In any case, the discussion that has so far taken place is a continuation of the one that started in the seminar, as if there is an opinion which says that without total Western-style democracy, there is no chance for democracy in the Arab world. What I am trying to say is that the basis is the relationship itself, which is deeper than democracy, i.e. the relationship between the ruler and subjects which should be based on acquiescence and mutual acceptance. Although this relationship expresses itself in a variety of ways, the underlying factor remains wilful mutual acceptance and acquiescence between ruler and subjects. I believe that if a harmonious monolithic society, like Libya for example, wanted to choose a governance formula and the overwhelming majority agreed, do we have the right to reject that formula, or should we submit to the wishes of the majority in this monolithic society? This is one model. In other more complex Arab societies with dual or multiple identities, like Lebanon and Iraq for example, we should not rely, in my opinion, on the principle of majority and minority. In dual or complex societies, it is necessary to institute a system based

*Deputy in the Lebanese Parliament and Professor at the Lebanese University.

on consensus among different communities, because it is impractical to configure a model based on a majority, lest it jeopardizes the country's political and social stability and threaten the foundations of the state. In the past few days, the most important point on which there was consensus is the fact that the principles of statehood and political system were rooted in the idea of no coercion in religion. If God Almighty has given Man freedom of choice in the most sensitive issue he faces, his religious convictions, then it should be even more so in the political sphere which is open to everyone? This is why we should establish states for all citizens without exception. I do not want to use the term 'state neutrality' here because it is confusing and some could blame me for bringing it up; what we need are states in the traditional sense of the term, states capable of performing their basic duty towards society, i.e. to defend and protect and provide life's basic necessities, such as shelter, health and education. However, any ruling authority in any country could be biased; when, at any moment in time, a society chooses a given authority, a government, or a party, based on a given political programme, this government or party should perform its politically biased role according to the programme for which the people have elected it.

The final point I would like to make is that we put the Islamists in a corner and pursue them in an accusatory manner in order to distance ourselves from their beliefs. There is an alternative formula, in my opinion, since God Almighty has said in the Holy Quran: 'And it behoves not a believing man and a believing woman that they should have any choice in their matter when Allah and His Apostle have decided a matter.'[3] The *aya* talks about the believers rather than society (the believing man and believing woman); it means that the believers are the ones who should be loyal to their convictions, thoughts and rituals. However, they should propose their convictions to society, as well: if it accepts these, then all is well; if it does not and objects to them, it becomes society's own responsibility. We return here to the golden rule that neither we nor anyone else has the right to coerce society into doing anything against its will.

Arous al-Zubair[*]: The argument regarding the relationship between politics and religion is the Prophet's (ﷺ) own experience; it is a highly significant matter, as is using Islamic history as justification to show that it is a history of tolerance, maturity and justice. This is also not true. Let us go back to the Algerian experience. Sheikh Rached said that the secularists were the ones who asked that the electoral process be stopped, and some of that is true. However, there are also a number of documents showing that some of those who took part in the decision to stop the electoral process in Algeria said that members of the Islamists' moderate wing were also part of that decision, and I am against this matter. Second, the elections idea …

Ben Jeddou: Excuse me; the point you made is somewhat dangerous; has this information been confirmed?

Arous al-Zubair: Yes, I can confirm that, and I also want to speak about my position on democracy. Sheikh Rached knows Ali Belhaj's famous writings well, including the paper entitled '*Al-Damgha al-Qawiya li-Nasf 'Aqidat al-Dimocratia*' (The strong stamp to thwart the doctrine of democracy), published in *Al-Munqeth*, the official

*Professor of Higher Education, Algiers University, Mudeer Makhbar al-Din wal Mujtama' (Director of the Laboratory of Religion and Society).

newspaper of the Islamic Salvation Front, and his condemnation of the elections as a means of reaching power. Sheikh Rached also knows the position of Mohammad Said, God rest his soul, who called on the Algerian people to prepare to change their lifestyle, including the way they dress, eat, etc. Therefore the issue is not as easy as Sheikh Rached makes it sound when he speaks as a wise and logical man calling for a just state; this is Rached al-Ghannouchi. However, there are entirely different voices and practices out there, meaning that Islam, or so-called political Islam, comprises different currents, attitudes and positions, and we therefore cannot depend solely on Rached Ghannouchi's views and experience, as if they are the only model likely to be implemented in the Arab and Muslim region.

Ben Jeddou: In any case; we might have arrived here at a very important conclusion, namely the need to avoid generalizations; I believe this is one of the essential conclusions. Having done that, our approach and critique of various issues become more scientific; in other words, we cannot talk about secularism as being entirely beneficial or harmful to the Arab world, as a whole. The same goes for the Islamist experience; it is neither entirely bad nor entirely good.

Youssef Sawani[*]: I have three remarks to make: the first has to do with the differences between the Arab countries. For example, in Libya and Tunisia, and I believe in Algeria as well, the population is entirely Muslim. In Libya, 95% of the population is Sunni Muslim and follows the Maliki sect, which is why many of the questions and issues raised here do not necessary apply to Libya. The second remark is that those who fear and question the fate of democracy, the shape of the state, the political system and the place of Shari'a in the constitution, wager on an issue which, in my opinion, overlooks an important political fact, namely that the Islamist movements have come to power, or have gained power, by winning the majority vote. The third remark is that democracy is not simply a series of mechanisms but a culture that needs to be rooted and institutionalized over time, and we have not reached that stage yet. The fact remains however that we are facing a challenge involving those who question what has actually taken place, i.e. the fact that the people have voted for the Islamists. There is a need, therefore, to address the issue in an entirely different manner than the one based on fear of the transformations taking place, especially since these are entirely unprecedented. These are transformations initiated by the youth and around 65% of North Africa's or the Arab Maghreb's population are young people who have a different understanding of religion, politics, statehood and democracy. One final remark is that we should understand how Islam operates at the grassroots level. Libya provided several examples of this when the street intervened and, in a hitherto unprecedented move, confronted forces known for their extreme positions and called for the dismantling of all armed factions and for confronting extremism, and I think that you all heard about the 'Friday of Saving Benghazi', and the events that followed.

Rifaat Sayed Ahmad[†]: Thank you very much. I will repeat the question you asked Sheikh Rached Ghannouchi earlier, and which he did not answer; I wish the other speakers would answer it as well; it is the absence of Palestine from the Arab

*Acting Secretary General of the Centre of Arab Unity Studies, Beit al-Nahda Building, Al-Basra Street.

†Director of Markaz Yafalil-Dirasat (Jaffa Center for Studies).

Spring's agenda. Though the question might seem generally political, it has to do, one way or another, with the subject of this seminar. We launched these revolutions to achieve a number of objectives: life, freedom, social justice and human dignity. In my opinion, human and national dignity will not be achieved as long as Palestine is occupied. Those who launched these revolutions have forgotten Palestine, chosen to forget it or to postpone it, regardless of whatever we wish to call what is going on. This is what we see in the Ennahda Movement's annulment of Article 27 of the Tunisian Constitution regarding resisting normalization with the Zionist enemy, in response to which demonstrations by nationalist Tunisian groups took place yesterday and the day before. The same goes for Egypt, which is the more dangerous case, where the Muslim Brotherhood is insisting, unnecessarily, on its commitment to Camp David and the appointment of the Israeli Ambassador.

Ben Jeddou: Why do you think this is the case?

Rifaat Sayed Ahmad: I believe that a mistake was made in this case, and they wanted to correct it. I do not doubt the Muslim Brotherhood's patriotism and positions, although their long history of fighting the Zionist project makes us wonder all the more?! I think the Americans are putting pressure on certain Islamist movements, by making reference to these agreements in a bid to delay such moves. This is connected somehow to the loans that Egypt has asked the International Monetary Fund and World Bank for, one of which is conditional on maintaining strong and normal relations with the Zionist enemy. There is another issue that has been shrouded in silence – an issue about which we know nothing and would like to learn more in order to be reassured. In my opinion, the Palestinian issue is the issue that will determine the criteria of freedom and democracy, and the relationship between religion and the state, during the next stage. I also believe that, although it has now receded into the background, it will remain a key factor in the next stage. Light should be shed on the Islamists' position on this issue and on the confusion that surrounds it.

Ben Jeddou: My question now is: does anyone fear a new authoritarianism that speaks a different language, the language of coercion and the like?

Hassan Hanafi*: The issue of state versus religion comes to us from the West, based on the Church versus the State issue. The influence of Western culture on us, especially among the well-educated, makes us adopt an issue that was never part of our history. This does not mean, however, that we do not have a similar issue, since there is the issue of the implementation of *Shari'a* which the Islamists have raised. First, cultural self-criticism is very important, as is Arab creativity; in the final analysis, we are taking the issue out of its psycho-political context. These groups, which spent the past 30–40 years in jail, suddenly found themselves in the palace, brought to power by the ballot box, which is why their behaviour in trying to protect their newfound power and alienating the other is only temporary, until they feel that there is no victor but God. They have actually gone from 'the Porsche' to the Palace. The reform movements did not succeed well enough and secular modern ideologies did not succeed enough either. People escape to Islam rather than choose it.

*Philosophy Professor at Cairo University.

Thus, Islamic *Shari'a* is implemented. But who says that implementing Islamic *Shari'a* is tantamount to the Penal Code? The Penal Code involves responsibilities that come after rights; so give me first my rights. A system that is based on equality, the single society, has a single individual. In the end, who says that the *Ummah* should be divided according to sect or religion, majority or minority? This is stepping into sectarianism through the back door. We are fighting for the kind of citizenship that guarantees equality between Muslims and non-Muslims; a just non-Muslim cleric is more favoured by God than an unjust Muslim Imam; and the same goes for the women's issue.

One thousand years separate us from the old jurisprudence; so why don't we try harder? The Khawarej and Ibadiyah believe that women have the right to become head of state, but we no longer exercise independent interpretation. Islam has propelled women back to the Jahiliya period and to half her rights, although in the Jahiliya women did not even have the right to live: 'And when the female infant buried alive is asked /For what sin she was killed.'[4] Islam allowed her half a testimony and half an inheritance; do I, as an independent interpreter infused with the spirit of Islam have the right, one thousand years later, to push for another step forward, to interpret and complete the half that remains and that Islam has left out? Therefore, the door of independent interpretation is open and there is room for change; I cannot live in one century, yet repeat and implement a thousand-year-old jurisprudence.

Adounis al-'Akra[*]: As far as the issue of state versus religion is concerned, I would like to clarify the use of a certain term that has been used erroneously since the Nineteenth Century: 'secularism'. Sheikh Rached was kind enough to use the term 'comprehensive secularism', the kind that marginalizes religion. The fact is that secularism does not lend itself to descriptions, be they comprehensive, partial or particular, the believer's or non-believer's secularism. Secularism distinguishes between two essential matters: religion and politics. It says religion is based on an absolute truth and politics is based on a variable contract among the people. Therefore, we should not rule people based on an absolute truth, whether it is descended from heaven, like religion, or an earthly product, like ideology. If mistakes were made in the practice of secularism, it is only natural, and these should not be blamed on the nature of secularism, as happened with democracy. Even today, we have long-standing democracies that admit that although their states are democratic, they practise democracy in the wrong way; why?

Ben Jeddou: Would you apply the same principle if the Islamist movements in power are the ones who commit the mistakes? Would you refrain from generalizing and say that the problem is not particular to the ideology, but that the movement is the one that made the mistakes?

Adounis al-'Akra: Of course; if they make a mistake it does not mean that the mistake is inherent to the ideology. They should however delineate this ideology's path and nature, in order to know how to deal with it.

---

*President of the Arab Philosophy Union and University Professor.

Birgitta Holst-Alani*: Citizens usually do have the right information and try to get it. In a democracy, everyone has access to the experts' objective evaluations. The valuable research presented at this seminar and the participants' interventions have shed light on several aspects of the relationship between state and religion, and the importance of agreeing on acceptable formulas for this relationship at this important stage of the Arab world's history – a world undergoing a democratic transition. I believe therefore that this seminar should be followed by another that brings together thoughts and analyses that can help crystallize a number of tangible formulas and alternatives for this relationship. Again, I would like to thank everyone for this wonderful seminar.

Sheikh Rached Ghannouchi: I would like to underline a number of issues: first, we are a young two-year-old democracy and we should therefore not be compared to hundred-year-old democracies; we are learning and we should not be ashamed of the fact that we are learning without arrogance. Second, we operate in a state that our colleague Mounir has just described, i.e. one that is *not* all-encompassing; it is a state with limited abilities and potential and we should therefore avoid pinning all our hopes and ideals on it because it will simply collapse if we overburden it. Therefore, challenges that sometimes take the shape of an outbidding exercise are superfluous. I remember when I was a student in Damascus in 1964, and beyond, and the Baath regime was trying to out-do Abdel-Nasser to compel him to take risks; it actually succeeded in having the United Nations representatives withdrawn and disaster ensued. We should cease this kind of talk in which we use our most treasured ideals as a means of out-doing one another; there are issues that unite us, like the Palestine cause, which no one should use to outbid the other. Everyone should support this cause to the best of their abilities without trying to outbid each other. The Islamists were the first in the *Ummah* to devote their efforts to this cause; the Muslim Brotherhood shed blood for it in 1947 and 1948, and, today, Islam is still the Palestinian cause's main standard-bearer. We still live in young democracies, in limited states with weak capabilities, and should therefore tackle major issues wisely, without challenges or idealism. For example, the incorporation of different subjects into the constitution came up for discussion, in particular whether we should incorporate the *Shari'a* issue in the constitution. A long discussion ensued at the end of which some people appeared scared of the *Shari'a*, at a time when in a neighbouring country like Libya even the party described as liberal or secular had placed *Shari'a* at the top of its agenda, which shows that the cultural orientation in one country is different from that in another. However, because constitutions should be based on common denominators, we withdrew this demand of order to promote consensus. As far as Palestine was concerned, there was a proposal to include the issue in the constitution, and some said that it was not a constitutional matter and therefore should appear in the preamble. Again, because we cared about reaching a consensus, we said that geography was not a typical constitutional matter, except for the geography of the country concerned, and thus no country is mentioned in the constitution save the one for which the constitution was originally written. On the other hand, and for the first time in Tunisia, we gave the leaders of the Palestinian revolution, including Ismail Hanya and Khaled Mish'al, a hero's welcome. I also wanted to draw attention to the fact that democracy can only be built on a sound basis, i.e. the government should be in the hands of the majority. However, in order for democracy to develop and stabilize, the

*Ambassador and Director of the Swedish Institute, Alexandria.

transition should not be between groups at the opposite ends of the spectrum, but between similar ideologies; in other words, there should be common ground among the elite. If this does not happen, the transition from one party to the other would be tantamount to a coup. Furthermore, because our democracies are still young, we should insist on consensus rather than majority rule, because in our region the world of the elite is still divided and dictatorship never gave us the chance to get to know one another. This means that we need a long time to get to know one another, to familiarize ourselves with each other, to stop demonizing the other and start searching for what is different rather than what we all agree upon – and there are many such issues. These nations belong to their people in equal measure, regardless of gender, ethnicity or religion; nations belong to their citizens and rights should be accorded on that basis.

Furthermore, our nations' unity is not a bargaining matter. We should preserve our nations' unity because we should do our best to turn our *Ummah* into reality; we should start with active cooperation and bring our interests closer together because we are one nation, and should continue to forge ahead without adventurism. Freedom is one of the constants, and it is because of it that the revolution took place at all. Social justice is another constant; we should put an end to the situation whereby one small group owns all the wealth, makes all the decisions and monopolizes culture, while the rest are relegated to the sidelines. The liberation of Palestine is another constant; it is a common constant that unites the Islamist and Nationalist currents. Equality among the people is also a constant. We therefore say if, at this stage, the Islamists are the ones who were voted into power, it would be in the democratic transition's favour if they relied on the principle of consensus and involved the others in the process. Even if democracy allows them to govern single-handedly, it is not forever but only until the next round. They should give the others the chance, and should not over-exhaust them, wager on making it impossible for them, or wilfully cause them to fail. Causing them to fail means causing the failure of the entire democratic experiment in its first test, and some are betting on the failure of this young, fragile and still tender democracy. This is what will drag these countries into chaos and put pay to the hope that has raised its head after several decades. This hope is that we will have our own Arab and Islamic democracies – that we would own our states, rather than them owning us – and that these states would fear us instead of us fearing them.

Ben Jeddou: Professor Mounir Shafiq, on the point mentioned just now regarding the Palestinian issue; you are not in power and are free of any position of authority. With regard to this point in particular, do you consider it normal for the Islamists, who raised so many slogans in the past decades, to act in this manner, or do you see something wrong in their behaviour?

Mounir Shafiq: I think that the Palestine issue lies at the very heart of the *Ummah* and its consciousness; it is forever present among us. If what we are required to do is gather armies and march to Palestine, I do not think that what these revolutions are required to do is put their armies on a war footing. What they should do is rebuild these armies, develop a war strategy, and support the resistance in Palestine. I think the ball is in the Palestinians' court rather than the Arab revolutions' court. If we in Palestine do not reorient the resistance towards its political role, and if we do not ignite a third *intifada* in the West Bank to bring down the occupation, dismantle the settlements and strongly challenge the Zionist project, we would be derelict in our duty towards our cause. I do not understand how the entire nation can rise up while the West Bank remains hostage to the security agreements and the authority in Ramallah; this authority should be dissolved and the security agreements annulled. The struggle for Palestine should start in Palestine, and you will see at that point how these revolutions will behave and how the Islamist movements and their leaders, as well as the liberal and nationalist movements and the entire *Ummah*, will rally around the Palestinian *intifada* once it ignites. These revolutions have greatly contributed to laying the ground for us in Palestine to move, and the unlimited support we are receiving is greater than ever before. In my opinion, the Zionist entity is trembling in fear of what is unfolding in the region, especially if we succeed again in forging an alliance between the nationalists and Islamists, alongside the leftists and liberals, and restoring internal unity to these revolutions. I believe that the fears being voiced today are a threat to these revolutions, as is all the doubt that surrounds the Islamist issue. I can understand the criticism, and understand that there are certain expectations; however, I do not know if the Islamists actually control these countries? They are in a very precarious situation in these states. Elections are still a top-down phenomena that parachuted down on these countries and nations. No one should think that what we witnessed is a military coup and that the Brotherhood is in control of the situation, and that is that. The next elections are around the corner and the public will punish those who do not deliver on what they promised, and, in line with what Engels says, I believe that, theoretically, fears do not constitute a proof. This is meant for the leftists: We fear that you will do this and that. How so? You separate me from reality then hold me accountable for my actions? What is required now, in my opinion, is for this game to calm down from the inside, be it in Tunisia or Egypt, and for alliances, understandings and consensus-building to begin. By the way, let me tell you that Western democracy only settled down when those in control of foreign strategy and domestic affairs arrived at an agreement. In our case, and until this moment, we are stuck between the forces that launched the revolution and are now fighting among themselves over the state's foreign strategy. Will this strategy count Palestine among its priorities? Will America resist or will it create other policies? Will these revolutions turn towards Arab unity and become convinced that individual states cannot achieve development and independence?

If you want to undertake real democratic action and ensure stability, you should first forge a genuine national consensus and reach an understanding on foreign strategy and the country's internal system. We notice that in the West all political parties are of the same ilk; Ralf Nader says in this context that the difference between the Democratic and Republican Parties is like the difference between Pepsi Cola and Coca-Cola. But you are in the Arab world and the difference is not like that between Coca-Cola and Pepsi Cola; the fact that there are deep political tendencies and divisions means that democracy will remain under threat as long as there is no agreement on the major contentious issues.

Ben Jeddou: There are a number of apprehensions, and the esteemed lady spoke about certain apprehensions; the word is yours.

Amani al-Taweel*: In fact what interests me in this matter is the difference I noticed between Sheikh Rached and Sheikh Jawad al-Khalisi. What Sheikh Rached has said

*Ahram Centre for Political and Strategic Studies.

is exactly what our Islamic societies aim for: freedom and Islam's objectives. However, what Sheikh Jawad has said, namely that Islam is a government philosophy and that we do not allow any legislation that contradicts this philosophy, is his own conviction. But if society chooses certain legislation that contradicts the philosophy of Islam, what mechanism do we use? This is what interests me about society; what is the mechanism through which this disagreement can be resolved? What does *takfeer* (accusing someone of apostasy) mean? Does it mean the others have to go to jail? It is obvious that there is diversity among Islamist political movements, and between some of these movements and their counterparts in other countries. However, it is the mechanism used to resolve these issues which scares people the most because, as Dr Nasif Nassar has said, it has to do with accusing the other of apostasy, and we see the Islamist movements even fight one another under the banner of *takfeer*. I would also like to speak about Egypt, particularly about the Muslim Brotherhood's behaviour, the Islamist political movement in parliament so far. We are talking about the practices that gave rise to these fears, in the sense that the issue is not simply trying to out-do the other or sideline those who won the public vote, for a variety of reasons, among which is escaping to Islam and giving the Islamists a chance after a long period of political ostracization. Some members of the Muslim Brotherhood said in parliament that the law that allows a woman to divorce her husband, known in Egypt as the *Khula'* law, should be revoked. However, although this is a *Shari'a*-based law, we find some who say that even if this issue were enacted into law, it should be placed under the jurisdiction of a judge, as in Saudi Arabia, so that a woman could not divorce her husband directly.

Ben Jeddou: Is this coming from the Muslim Brotherhood or the Salafists?

Amani al-Taweel: Let me tell you their tactic; the Muslim Brotherhood prods the Salafists to test the waters.

Ben Jeddou: Why do you say tactic? Why don't you say that this is what the Brotherhood thinks and proposes, and this is what the Salafists think and propose – why do you see it as a tactic?

Amani al-Taweel: Because in several political situations, this is what has actually happened.

Another parliament-related issue is the heightened interest in issues that restrict women's freedom versus a total disinterest in laws that help improve social conditions, social justice laws, or even political disqualification laws. What is on the table right now is the Protection of the Revolution Law, the other facet of the Emergency Law, all of which is the Muslim Brotherhood's doing; this is what is being proposed to us in Parliament now. Morsi's presidential discourse does not take into account the fact that Egypt is a diverse country made up of Muslims and Copts.

The other issue is that we are not talking here about superficial matters, but about actual facts on the ground. A big part of President Mohammad Morsi's political discourse is religious in nature; he does not address the Egyptian people as 'dear citizens' but as 'my people', 'my tribe', etc. What we need is a citizenship discourse; our Christian brothers feel alienated and scared in their own country. In Egypt right now, something called the Christian Brotherhood is being formed – what does this mean? It means that there is a polarization based on sects and religion, which opens the door to foreign intervention. In front of us is the example of Sudan where foreigners have entered through the open door of ethnic, cultural and religious divisions. There are those in Congress who speak about the need to protect the Copts; there is the issue of dealing with minorities and women, and the Constitutional Committee's attitude is another form of alienating the other. Egyptian women generate 30% of Egypt's national product, and this includes both material and moral revenues. However, these moral revenues are nowhere to be seen, whether in the Constitutional Committee or in Parliament, since in Egypt women's representation is barely 1.8% due to the political and legal environment instituted before the elections.

Sheikh Jawad al-Khalesi: Mrs Amani mentioned that I said that we have a philosophy, and I do not think that anyone, whether Muslim, Christian or any other human being, does not have a philosophy! People by nature have a brain and this brain produces certain thoughts, philosophies or beliefs. He either believes in the single God, a tree or anything else; even those who claim not to believe in anything actually believe in their own theory or in their assumed Godlessness. However, the Professor's question is in the right place; suppose, as she said, that we do not accept anything that contradicts this belief – what is the solution in this case? The solution is simple: we go back to the *Ummah*, put our case in front of it again, say that what happened was wrong, and go into opposition. We in Iraq have had experience with the state and religion issue, given the American occupation's claim that it came to liberate a certain sect from another, and which sowed sedition in the country. However, when we fail to enact certain legislation we go back to the people rather than stage a military coup; we do not have military power. What Mrs Amani has said is very important because many of the seminar's discussions have focussed on these apprehensions based on preconceived notions. You are telling her now that this is heritage when in fact it is not; how could it be a heritage when the events happened less than one year ago? It is old accumulated heritage and everything that Sheikh Rached has said is true. We should be diligent, wise and alert to the big powers' attempts to contain us, to hijack our revolutions, to steal our blood, to make us forget the main issues and leave us at odds with each other.

Ben Jeddou: Professor Mounir Shafiq [earlier] quoted Ralf Nader as saying that there is no difference between the Democratic and Republican Parties in the United States, with one like Coca-Cola and the other like Pepsi Cola. However, we said earlier that we should not generalize about the various Islamist experiments and movements. Dr Saadeddin, do you think that the difference between different Islamist groups is like the difference between Coca-Cola and Pepsi Cola?

Dr Saadeddin Ibrahim: I do not think so; we have several actual examples from Indonesia, Malaysia and various African countries with Muslim majorities, and the difference between them is not necessarily like that between Coca-Cola and Pepsi Cola. There is a difference between the Taliban in Afghanistan, the *mullah*s in Iran and the Turkish experiment – the latter being an enlightening experiment whose standard bearer, Recep Tayyip Erdoğan, was given a hero's welcome in Egypt.

Ben Jeddou: You put the Taliban and *mullahs* in Iran on one side and Erdoğan's experience on the other?

Dr Saadeddin Ibrahim: Yes, the differences between them are enormous, and there is also a wide range of colours between them. This is why we should not generalize or simplify the issue by using the Coca-Cola and Pepsi Cola equation, because there is Coca-Cola and there is the liquorice drink which is very popular in our country. There is a difference between the Taliban liquorice drink and the Democratic carob drink, i.e. Pepsi Cola.

Ben Jeddou: There are different experiments, and the current apprehensions perhaps do not have credibility on the ground. We should differentiate between the Brotherhood and the Salafists; there are Brotherhood organizations in various countries and there are Salafist organizations in the same or in different countries.

Dr Saadeddin Ibrahim: This is necessary; it is the social scientists' job to categorize, measure and sort, and rather than generalize, we should analyse and gauge the difference. We have standards and measures for these matters, and I was among the first to say that we should give the Muslim Brotherhood, and the Islamists in general, a chance. As I said before, I was in jail with them, I know them well and I am not afraid of them. I voice certain criticisms openly and they accept them in the context of open debate, and there are things that they do not accept, and this is their right. What is important is a democratic experiment that has room for diversity and tolerance towards the other's opinion, a necessary condition in the early stages of entrenching and deepening democratic transitions in our Arab region.

Ben Jeddou: Dr Nasif, Mrs Amani spoke about the situation of the Christians in Egypt, in particular the Copts, and said that some have started talking about a Christian Brotherhood, while others talk about a law in Congress. Yes, there is a lot of talk filled with fear and suspicion among the Copts and Christians in Egypt. Do you think that these apprehensions and suspicions are exaggerated? In other words, are they based on preconceived notions and fears regarding the Islamists eventually coming to power and imposing *Shari'a* law at the expense of the Christians; or is there a certain terminology that scares you?

Nasif Nassar: Do not confine me to the Egyptian case; I am not an expert in these details and Dr Amani knows more about the subject than I do. In my opinion, these fears are not recent; they are real and their history and roots date back to a much earlier period than now. However, although they have been exacerbated by a number of current issues, we should not reduce the Copts' condition in general to the way it is today. We should understand their situation in the context of Egyptian nationhood. As far as I know, the Copts feel that they are the 'real' Egyptians and that the others have come to Egypt and, with time, have become Egyptians. As far as they are concerned, the main point of reference is Egyptian nationhood, or Egyptian nationalism for some, i.e. the long historical affiliation that succeeded in absorbing the different minorities and peoples who made their way to Egypt, people who are supposed to coexist on the basis of total equality of citizenship. The Copts have a long history of different relationships with successive Egyptian governments, including periods of persecution, tolerance and sometimes leniency, and the matter should be studied from this perspective. I am with the sociologists who believe that there are different cases and each case has its own particularities; this is correct and necessary. As I said before, we should avoid making generalizations, yet at the same time, we need to preserve some common notions lest we lose the ability to understand one another. When we speak about democracy, if each country had its own democracy, and each regime has its own democracy, and for every case and era there is a democracy – what does democracy mean then? No one will be able to describe it at that point. We therefore need a common notion, and notions are general by nature; however, particularities and specifics come after implementation. However, I would like to laud Sheikh Rached Ghannouchi's position which I believe is more advanced than others on the path towards democracy, and I believe that what the Sheikh has in mind is the Western Christian model of democracy in the secular countries. Christian democracy in Germany, Christian democracy in Italy – he has mentioned these more than once in his speeches and writings. If we take this model, what does it mean? It means that in the secular countries religion was kept as a reference in politics, but that they also kept political activism as a democratic phenomenon based on national affiliation, i.e. on German nationalism in the case of (Christian) German democracy, and on Italian nationalism in the case of Italian democracy. As far as the Islamist movements are concerned, it means that there is an acceptance of democracy and its philosophy whereby it is no longer the monopoly of the West, as Dr Ali Fayyad wants it to be, but, on the contrary, democracy is a human phenomenon as much as it is the product of the global human political mind. As far as we in this region of the world are concerned, it means that we practise politics on its own merit, i.e. on a national and nationalist basis and in the people's interests, in general, but we practise it from an Islamic moral perspective. Islamic morality is an inseparable part of Islam and can be applied to all aspects of life, especially to politics, since it is necessary to maintain – and I am speaking philosophically here – the link between politics and morality. Many philosophies seek to separate politics from morality although, based on the practice of democracy and according to certain philosophical theories, it is in fact impossible to separate politics from morality. In the final analysis, politics depends on value-based criteria; this means that Islam has a clear perspective on values, what we call reference values, such as ensuring justice, or other such criteria. Though this value-based reference protects the Islamic identity in the practice of politics, it does not actually trespass on political activities given that the latter is a genuine occupation unto itself, separate from religion.

Ben Jeddou: It is clear that Dr Nassar still insists on the need for total separation between religion and politics?

Nasif Nassar: No, no, on the contrary, I am linking them. … I built a bridge between them … a complete and wide bridge.

Ben Jeddou: Would you have no problem with a programme based on an Islamist ideology?

Nasif Nassar: Only if it is based on a moral value system; a political programme is a political programme that is held politically accountable. As for issues related to education, development, the economy, domestic and foreign relations, etc., these are political matters defined by the political human mind, according to the political will and national interest, and are held accountable on that basis. Their general direction, spirit, soul and boundaries should be inspired by a moral code.

Ben Jeddou: This means that you have no problem with a pious person who calls himself an Islamist?

Nasif Nassar: A Muslim … a Muslim … not an Islamist.

Ben Jeddou: I am saying an Islamist; would you have a problem with a person whose departure point is a project that he calls Islamist and introduces himself as an Islamist … and says I am part of an Islamist movement, I practise politics and I will come to power based on that programme?

Nasif Nassar: If he accepts the principle of total equality amongst all citizens, I will have no problem with him.

Abdessamad Belkabir*: The issue at the root of the relationship between religion and the state, or politics, is the relationship between the moral domain, i.e. responsibilities, and the domain of politics, i.e. the possible. In that particular case, the Islamist discourse seems almost identical to the modernists'.

Ben Jeddou: The Islamist?

Abdessamad Belkabir: The Islamic … the Islamist … as you wish.

Ben Jeddou: You need to specify: it is either 'Islamic' or 'Islamist'. I believe that here there are some who are Islamic, and who would prefer to be called Islamic not Islamist.

Abdessamad Belkabir: It is not a taunt, but simply a formula to show that there is religion and there is religious ideology, and that there is a difference between the two. I am a religious man and a believer, but not an Islamic I am secular. The entire Arab elite are in crisis. The Professor says 'the link'; what is linked is separate because we can only link that which is separate. Where does the dysfunction lie then? It is neither in the Algerian, Libyan, Egyptian nor Tunisian case but in the origin itself. The Brotherhood who say that this is the era of democracy are wrong because they are not proposing what is possible but what is necessary and this is a strategic objective. The freedom fighters in South Africa and Spain, for example, did not propose democracy but a transition to democracy, which is why a great man like Mandela sat down with De Clerk, whose hands were dripping with the blood of South Africans, while we are unable to sit down with our adversaries, not to say our enemies. Have we solved any problems so far? Therefore Islam is the wrong solution, democracy is the wrong solution and socialism is the wrong solution. The solution is a transition to democracy, and the democratic transition's logic is different from democracy's logic, which means alienation and elections. Since the revolution, I believe this intellectual chaos has been generated in the minds of Arab intellectuals by the West through television channels, the press, or intellectuals.

Ben Jeddou: What is religious chaos?

*Qadi Ayyad University, Faculty of Arts.

Abdessamad Belkabir: It is the *mental* chaos [not 'religious' Ben Jeddou misheard – Editor's note]; all these faulty notions being bandied about … non-historical notions that call for what people hope for rather than what is actually possible. Therefore the mistake in Tunisia was that the state thought it possible to go straight to democracy without passing through a transitional period. This problem is still there. The Brotherhood in Egypt, as in Libya and Tunisia, drafted their constitution before the elections, which meant that we had to reach a consensus. What does consensus mean? It means competing over concessions rather than trying to outbid each other. This is what is required. The Moroccan socialist, for his part, proposes a democratic transition because the historic unit, front or bloc requires this good deed.

Ben Jeddou: Why, if these Arab revolutions were not producing movements fighting to implement their programmes on the basis of democracy and freedom?

Abdessamad Belkabir: This is where the mistake lies. Let me give you an example: the Brotherhood speaks about freedom, but freedom is not the issue now, democratic freedoms are. The remaining freedoms are for a later stage, not this one; what interests me now is pluralism, political parties' rights, freedom of expression and the right to organize – the rights of homosexuals, gambling, drugs, to marry an animal etc. are not issues! This is why demands should be restricted and why elections are not an indication of democracy. Let me give you another example: they did not have free and fair elections in France until 1967 because before that decisions were based on consensus.

Al-Sayed Zahra*: In fact I don't know why the Muslim Brotherhood, or those affiliated with Islamist groups, are always angry and intolerant when people criticize them and express fear and apprehension regarding the possibility of their coming to power. I do not mean intolerance only here in this hall, but in general and in society at large. Whenever anyone voices a certain criticism or expresses a certain apprehension, they tell him that they came through the ballot box and that they have the right to be given a chance. We do not object to that, but this is not a valid justification; if we have reason to be apprehensive, then we should express it. If the elections had brought the liberals and communists to power, many would also have spoken about their fear and apprehension. It is true that Sheikh Rached's discourse is both advanced and enlightened in all matters related to state and religion, secularism, rights, etc. but we have three major problems in this respect: the first is that not all the Islamists that came, or did not come, to power espouse Sheikh Rached Ghannouchi's discourse. It is rather the contrary – many of them do not agree with it. For example, he spoke a while ago about consensus as a general principle of governance even if a majority exists; the Brotherhood in Egypt rejects this principle and does not apply it.

Ben Jeddou: How so? How can you say that the Brotherhood in Egypt does not believe in consensus? To the contrary, there are some who say, for example, that it is the allies who refused to participate. Even Hamdeen Sabbahi, your friend and ours, is the one who rejected consensus.

---

*Deputy Editor of *Akhbar al-Khaleej* newspaper.

Al-Sayed Zahra: No, we differentiate between two stages. Before the elections, the Brotherhood adopted a discourse to the Egyptian people that closely resembled Sheikh Rached's discourse. The Brotherhood said that it believed in a civil state and that governance was a participatory process – all of which is in line with the idea of consensus etc. However, no sooner had they won the elections and the presidency than we began to see a number of signs that indicated the exact opposite. We found an entirely new discourse. We found first, that the noose had become much tighter round the liberals' necks, coupled with an obvious intention to alienate them and prevent them from taking part in the process. Second, we found a clear intention on the Brotherhood's part to put its hands on all levels of the state, and third, we found a markedly unfriendly attitude towards press freedom, etc. What I want to say is that all these indications are a real cause for concern and raise several questions, and people have the right to express themselves. The other issue, which is no less important and concerns Egypt and perhaps Tunisia as well, is that what has so far reinforced these concerns is not the Brotherhood's declared discourse, or actual practices on the ground, but the fact that they have so far failed to present any practical programme aimed at achieving the demands of those who took part in the revolution – a move that could perhaps have helped dispel people's fears.

Ben Jeddou: They told you that they were barely four months old.

Al-Sayed Zahra: I am not saying that they should implement the programme in 100 days, four months or even a year. I will give you an example so that the idea is clear: until this moment, neither I nor any other Egyptian knows what Morsi's economic programme is, how he will go about instilling social justice and who will implement this plan; there is none of that.

Ben Jeddou: Was he not elected by the people?

Al-Sayed Zahra: I did not say that the people did not elect him. But the people who elected him did so for this particular purpose, and not for involving society in a struggle with the liberals etc. They elected him to propose and begin implementing a programme of social justice, and to enshrine the civil state and public freedoms.

The second and very important point is that I agree with all the professors who spoke earlier and expressed certain fears regarding the fate of religious minorities in general, be they the Christians in Egypt or others. Why do I agree? Because this seminar is discussing state and religion in the Arab world and all the papers, research and discussions have automatically assumed that 'religion' means Islam – and this is a grave mistake since we, in the Arab countries, have Christian and other minorities, as well. This is why the research and discussions lacked any perspective on the relationship between state and religion from the minorities' point of view. What I am driving at is that, given that this issue is so totally absent even among the intellectual elite, one can only imagine how things would be when those in power are a religious group with an unfriendly attitude towards minorities and other sects! We therefore, as Arab societies, need guarantees – guarantees that ensure there will be a civil state, a citizenship state that respects the constitution, abides by the rule of law, and where justice prevails.... What are these guarantees? I do not know, perhaps the first step is the constitution, which is also the main step.

Perhaps what is required is separating religion from politics rather than the state from religion, in a manner whereby religion will no longer hold sway over the governance system or the elections, etc.

What I want to say is that the rise of the Islamists to power is a step that no one objects to, but as I said at the beginning, yes, there is cause for concern, there is cause to engage in debate, and the Islamists should hear this kind of talk.

Antoine Messarra*: Today, the relationship between the state and religion in the Arab world is in chaos, not only on the ground but in our minds and among the academics, researchers and university professors, and it should therefore be organized. Most Western societies have arrived at a reasonable, and I do not say ideal, level of organization. Here, not only does the situation give cause for concern, it is fearful and tragic; violations of people's basic human rights are taking place in the name of religion. So what do we do about that? There is the threat of authoritarianism in the name of religion, a phenomenon that all human societies have experienced. Zionist Judaism converted God into a real estate agent and land investor, Christianity had its share of authoritarianism in the name of religion, and Islam could be experiencing the same thing today with the Arabism of jails and the Islamism of jails.[5] What then to do? We need to change paths, to adopt a practical and implementable one that addresses various practices on a case by case basis. Let me give you a few examples: we should guarantee political participation – but how do we do that? What mechanisms do we use? And the issue of criticism of religion – how do we control it and what are its limits and parameters? And the old case of Hamed Abu Zeid – what are its limits? And the issue regarding the *Awqaf* (Muslim religious endowment) Ministries in a number of Arab countries that behave as super-ministries without any supervision or accountability; how do we organize that? There are also the Friday sermons in the mosques . . . .

Ben Jeddou: I will come to you; speaking about the *Awqaf* Ministry; frankly speaking, all religious institutions – even the Christian Church's institutions – do they not behave, in general, as if they are empires unto themselves?

Antoine Messarra: Of course; I did not say 'Islamic' but 'religious'; Arab societies need to institute control mechanisms, especially legal controls.

Ben Jeddou: What about Friday sermons?

Antoine Messarra: Friday preachers, especially in mosques, are mostly illiterate and sometimes preach to an illiterate crowd; these leave the mosque intent on perpetrating violent actions. There were 80 such violent incidents in a single year in Egypt; how could this be addressed? Is the *Awqaf* Ministry responsible for supervising the mosques? Does the *Dar al-Ifta'* (main authority for issuing religious verdicts) coordinate such matters? We should have rules, and genuine rules are the law. Humankind has invented the law, and religious laws are a source of values for legislation, but they are not a procedural source.

---

*Member of the Constitutional Council, Lebanon, Abdelwahab al-Inglisi Street.

Darim al-Bassam*: I think that our colleague, Abdessamad, raised a very important issue, an issue that unfortunately has not been given its due attention in the debate; it is the transition to democracy that could take two or three years to accomplish. During that stage, the common denominator should be consensus not competition, and the national interest rather than narrow partisan interests. This stage is designed to lay the ground for what happens after the democratic game. During the transitional period, the security issue is resolved and the state regains its status and reclaims its rightful place in society. Also raised during this stage are the rules, regulations and laws, such as the election law and the information law, as well as institution-building, given all the destruction that has taken place during the conflict period. All these issues require consensus and we should totally forget about anything called competition; it is a phenomenon known in the relevant literature as a 'Soft Landing Transition'. The rough landing, if we may call it that, i.e. competition, comes right after change and leads to a situation known as 'post-authoritarian'.

Ben Jeddou: Any Islamist could argue with you and say: why are you talking about a democratic transition and these safety issues now that the elections have brought the Islamists to power through the ballot box? Had the people voted for secularists, leftists and socialists, i.e. non-Islamists, would the elite have used that same logic, i.e. talked about a democratic transition and such like?

Darim al-Bassam: I don't agree with you, Ghassan; if the safe transition I talked about, and I have expertise in the matter and work in this domain with the United Nations, can spare you all these conflicts and sharp differences, because this stage should be devoted to consensus-building round the democratic game – this will lead, among others, to a kind of behavioural distortion.

Ben Jeddou: How would you respond and convince an Islamist who now tells you: we have suffered from authoritarianism and dictatorship for decades, and we now have an historic opportunity, based on revolutions and transitions, and now the people have the final word. All this should be actualized on the ground through a new constitution, direct elections and a new governance system, and let the ballot box decide through the peaceful rotation of power.

Darim al-Bassam: I believe that our responsibility, as an intellectual group, is to pay special attention to this stage. Every junction of Arab history has brought a new thought; where is the thought that looks at this particular stage? It does not exist; but there are mechanisms. Although the ballot box is a mechanism, it does not organize the rules of the democratic game. I believe that it is incumbent upon us to draw the framework for this theory and notion in order to embody the responsibilities of the next stage.

Sheikh Jawad al-Khalesi: I agree with Drs. Abdessamad and Darim; the transition to a new stage should be prepared in advance via a long period that everybody agrees on – if not we will find ourselves in a situation similar to Iraq's. I personally have reservations about the term 'Arab Spring' and do not use the term 'democracy' either, this is my

*Senior advisor, United Nations Development Programme (UNDP).

personal view, and I have my own terminology. However, I agree with the result. I agree and respect the people's opinion and I do not accept that anything can be imposed on them. This preparation, or safe transition, is necessary to safeguard society or else it will be divided and dismembered.

Ben Jeddou: There is another matter, if you allow me. Two urgent points have been raised: the first is the one that Sheikh Rached Ghannouchi raised, which is causing the Islamists to fail, which is tantamount to causing the democratic experiment to fail. The second point was raised by Dr Saadeddin Ibrahim, namely that we now have two different Islamist models: the Mullahs in Iran and the Taliban in Afghanistan versus the model of Turkish President Recep Tayyip Erdoğan. We have therefore two models.

Antoine Seif*: In my opinion, it is difficult to characterize what has been happening in the Arab World at this point in time. The characterizations that have been made, call it a 'transitional period' – a political description par excellence. This implies that there is a specific political system that no longer exists, and that new ones are on the way. This is where the word 'crisis' comes into play. What does crisis mean? Crisis means that the old has died before the new has been born; this is when we are in a real crisis, and this crisis stage does not lend itself to absolutist judgements, it is a trial stage in which we enter democracy without actually practicing it, and he who does not practise democracy is not a democrat. It is not enough to say that you are a democrat; you should be tested in real situations in order to know whether democracy is genuine or not. This is something that we never practised under the deposed regimes; however, this does not mean never practised at all, and we should never say that only the Muslims or the Islamists bear the responsibility for the alienation and injustice that befell people in the past. When there is authoritarianism, everyone is touched by it, and no single group can reap the rewards by shoving the others aside and claiming that it is the only victim and that it alone has earned the right to be in power. In fact, a tyrannical regime has no equal save for the monolithic regime, and monolithic regimes do away with freedoms, democracy and citizenship, although this model has claimed equality ever since the French Revolution and the Age of Enlightenment. Equality amongst human beings is a very important factor in human history, and when we can say that all people are equal, whether they are believers or not, rich or poor, black or while, it means that we have laid the proper foundations for a complete society. I come from a society in which no one has ever proposed that the central authority be a religious one, by which I mean Lebanon; it is a diverse and pluralistic society. However, I know that many institutions in Lebanon do not feel that they are living in an unjust society, at all. One of the learned Sunni Sheikhs said before the Lebanese civil war (1975–90), 'I practise freedoms that have not been practised! As a Sheikh, I practise Muslim Islamic religious freedom like nowhere else in the Arab world, because in the other Arab countries my colleagues, the Sheikhs, are convened on Thursday night and told what to say and what not to say in their Friday sermons, whereas no one ever told me what to say or not to say.' What does this mean? It means the very important question that this seminar has asked, namely whether the state is a religious necessity, yes or no? Why do we look down on Muslims outside the Muslim world, in

*Philosophy Professor, Lebanese University.

Europe, for example? Why do we despise them? They have no ambition either to obtain or be in power. They are not second-class Muslims either; certain Arab intellectuals speculate that if Islam is witnessing new experiences, these are bound to have originated among those who live in societies that are steeped in democracy, at a time when we still aspire for a new democracy. Sheikh Rached Ghannouchi's statement does not make me fear for democracy for he spoke well – in the final analysis, history judges actions not words. This is why we fully expect this kind of response at this stage and should not do anything to thwart it. The Islamists need to be democratic and we shall see if the stuff they are made of can accommodate democracy or not; this is the point at which we will no longer be in a dormant state of civil war; now, however, each one of us is waiting for the other to trip.

Ben Jeddou: You are therefore with those who say that the Islamists' experience should not be made to fail?

Antoine Seif: Of course; because any such attempt would have undemocratic repercussions and would be disastrous for this particular stage. We should be more democratic than necessary at this point in time.

Hisham al-Awadi*: Although I am actually from Kuwait, my expertise is in the Muslim Brotherhood and the Egyptian political system. I visited Egypt last September, stayed there for ten days, met several Brotherhood leaders and came out with certain impressions that I would like to share with you. There is a book by Nathan Brown entitled *Al-Musharakah Laa al-Mughalabah* (Participation Rather than Domination)[6] in which he talks about the Islamist movements' experience, particularly the Muslim Brotherhood in Jordan, Palestine, Kuwait and Egypt. He reaches a conclusion which he summarizes in one line, 'Though Islamists are committed to democracy, practically speaking, they do not represent a true democratic movement as they were brought up under quasi-authoritarian regimes.' I remember hearing Sheikh Rached saying those same words when I was a student in Britain, and he came to attend conferences and give lectures; I will never forget his words because he repeated them so often. The same goes for Tahar Ben Achour who was the first to talk about the objectives of freedom and justice. He said, 'The Islamists, secularists and liberals have all drunk from the same breast of backwardness'; therefore, his saying that we are only in our first year of democracy is a reality based on that very notion – he is looking at a cultural situation but it comprises many ideological affiliations. I believe that we are now at the stage of the challenge that the Islamists face; they are setting a democratic precedent whereby a generation will come to power four years from now that will compare itself not to Hosni Mubarak but to Mohammad Morsi. Many Egyptians who voted for Morsi did so for fear of Shafiq. When the next generation of Egyptians goes to vote, we want it to vote for Morsi, or any other, without considering Mubarak and Shafiq because this stage is over; we want them to consider Morsi's achievements on their own merit. The challenge that faces the Islamists today is that they are only laying the foundations for the ABC of democracy, and not for the entire concept; they are setting a precedent against which the next generation can compare itself, and heighten expectations.

*Professor of History and International Relations, American University, Kuwait.

Ben Jeddou: Then this is a point in their favour?

Hisham al-Awadi: It depends on the outcome; the target in those four years is to serve me as an individual and improve Arab democracy for my sake. If you do this for four years and I never see you again after that, I will come back and thank you. This is number one regardless of the future.

I met many young people who had broken away from the Brotherhood, some of whom had gone on to form new parties, and I am not talking here only about Dr Abdel Moneim Aboul Fotouh. Some of these youths, aged 18 to 30, told me that they submitted a paper to the Guidance Bureau and the Brotherhood's leadership two years before the revolution, in which they had asked for a revolution, for action to prevent President Mubarak from running in the next elections or, at least, to take part in the demonstrations and sit-ins staged by the Mahalla and textile workers, and so on, instead of continuing this negative isolationist stance. The answer was 'No'; they had already been stung, assaulted, detained and had become fearful, and as the saying goes, 'once bitten twice shy'. These youths were the ones who led the revolutionary track in the Brotherhood.

On the other hand, although we talk a lot about a dialogue between the Islamists, secularists and nationalists, I am calling for a vertical dialogue between the Islamist movement's leadership and the young Islamists. I will end very quickly: there is a play by Mohammad Subhi entitled 'The Lesson is Over you Idiot', and I say, the lesson has just begun, you smart people. The biggest lesson of the revolution, and I am thinking aloud here with Dr Saadeddin, is that the 'one man, one vote, one time' could perhaps have served its purpose after the revolution. However, the most powerful lesson of the revolution remains that none of the Islamists, or non-Islamists, will dare to play this game because they know where the people will go. They will go to Tahrir Square, as they did against Mubarak, and Morsi knows that they are able to rally the people against him as well.

Talal Atrissi*: First, we arrived at the conclusion that we should not generalize about the Islamist movement's experience. In my opinion, this is not an achievement in itself because avoiding generalizations is supposed to be a logical choice rather than a conclusion, especially after all these years of studying and showing interest in the Islamist movements. The second point is that we should not generalize in our criticism of the Islamist movements and experiences. There is what I could call a degree of sociological arbitrariness in placing the Taliban and Iran in the same basket, then comparing their experiences with Turkey's pioneering experience. This assessment is not based on scientific criteria, given the Taliban's experience versus Iran's 33-year experience. The third point is that we have failed to notice that, in the past two decades or more, the Islamist movements have tried to take part in the democratic process, despite its limitations. They tried to infiltrate in order to participate in the elections; they have changed many of the modes of operation in various countries of the region, from Kuwait to Lebanon to Jordan and many others. They took part in the elections either directly through their own political parties, or through other parties as they did in Egypt when they were prevented from participating directly. We should take this into consideration. Moreover, many Islamist movements, or parts of them, broke

*Director of the Institute of Social Sciences, Lebanese University.

away from the Brotherhood and resorted to violence but, once in prison, reconsidered their options and chose to pursue the democratic path, to engage in legal activities and accept constitutional institutions. The above indicates a change in the way the Islamist movements and their leaders think. I am not against criticism, but all for it – as are the Islamist movements until they themselves are criticized. Many are anxious, fearful and tense regarding the Islamists' rise to power, although they did so through the very means that those who fear them the most are advocating. This is why when we criticize, we should take into account three specific and important levels: *first*, this criticism should not lead to the return of the old regime; *second*, we should ensure that this experience does not lead to internal violence and, *third*, we should not allow this experience to fall into the hands of the West. I am summarizing here since there is a lot more that could be said about these points.

Ben Jeddou: This debate's conclusion places Arab society at the next stage, seriously on the path of pluralism and consensus despite all the constants surrounding us that still endure.

Nasif Nassar: I believe that the well-established difference between the condition of Arab society before these revolutions and at the present time lies in these very issues – the issues of diversity, democracy, human rights, women's rights, etc. Today, these have taken their place at the centre of the debate and become open for discussion, whereas in the past they were taboo subjects, suppressed and shoved aside. The authoritarian stage was destructive to freedom of thought, to debate and to other rights, but now the debate is open. The main positive development is that, in certain countries, the Islamists have benefited from the changes more than anyone else, to the extent that they have been able to attain power; this is one of the many developments that this stage has made possible. The main condition that will allow us to progress towards pluralism, civil society, freedom and equality is for this debate to remain open, and for the Islamists to refrain from controlling it in an attempt to impose a new form of authoritarianism over people's minds. This is the essential condition.

Ben Jeddou: Dr Saadeddin Ibrahim – Of course, every environment has its own mechanisms and experiences, which is why you came to the conclusion that the Islamists have had certain experiences that could lead to genuine democratic experiments and to development, and you probably believe that the Turkish model is one to emulate. I refer you to two issues to help you to arrive at what you want to say. The first is that someone could argue with you and say, you placed the mullahs of Iran and the Taliban of Afghanistan in the same basket as a negative model, although in fact they agree on only one point which is their enmity towards the United States of America, or American policies, to be precise, while the Turkish model is positive and beautiful although Turkey is a member of NATO and has good relations with the American administration. The second point is that you are now giving the Islamists the best of gifts, one which they will thank you for. You are presenting the Turkish model as one to emulate, and the Islamist movements, which you now fear and criticize, could actually implement this very Turkish model.

Dr Saadeddin Ibrahim: First, I did not confine myself to the Turkish experiment or model – I mentioned Indonesia and Malaysia as well.

Ben Jeddou: But I beg your pardon, these are Muslim nations, but the Turkish experiment is based on a secular movement, even if this was not officially announced, whilst in Malaysia they are Muslims.

Dr Saadeddin Ibrahim: No sir, no, I choose my words carefully. I am talking about the democratic transition. Indonesia went through a democratic transition from Suharto's dictatorship, which lasted over 30 years, to democracy and pluralism. Therefore I choose my words and examples carefully.

Ben Jeddou: But the Islamist movements did come to power.

Dr Saadeddin Ibrahim: Isn't it obvious?! In Indonesia, after Suharto's downfall, the Islamists came to power and left it based on the results of the elections. It is therefore also an example to be emulated. No matter, I studied this experience well.

Ben Jeddou: It is not a charitable society, and therefore reached power.

Dr Saadeddin Ibrahim: This will lead you to issues without end. The apprehension that surrounds the Brotherhood's experience in Egypt comes from a variety of sources, including from the Copts, whose requests for immigrant status elsewhere have doubled since the Brotherhood's arrival in power. Indeed, Holland has opened its doors to Egypt's Copts in order to address these fears and the pressures brought to bear by different groups in Europe.

Second, some of these apprehensions are justified. It is true that apprehensions could develop into fears, and fears into terror, which already exists among many women, even Muslim women. Women see themselves as the granddaughters of Hoda Sharawi, who removed her veil in the 1919 Revolution, and now find it very difficult to go out and live like their mothers and grandmothers used to live 50 or 60 years ago. These are real fears and we are talking here about half of society. What I am trying to arrive at is that in the last elections, many villages with Coptic majorities in four different governorates of the Sa'eed were forcibly prevented from taking part in the second round of the presidential elections.

Ben Jeddou: Who prevented them?

Dr Saadeddin Ibrahim: Islamist groups and militias acting in the name of the Muslim Brotherhood and the Salafists, but the Brotherhood in particular; and I have mentioned this before. We had 7000 observers and we documented it – this is not propaganda; we said it and wrote about it, and you can read about it in the magazine we distributed to you. However, what I personally wish for, as an individual at the Ibn Khaldoun Centre, is to protect the democratic experiment despite the transgressions here and there. I want it to continue and will therefore not make too much of these transgressions, although we did document them and sent details to the United Nations in Geneva and to several other legal societies. What I would like to say regarding some of the interventions, is that the difference between the Tunisian experience, specifically the difference between the thoughts and writings of Sheikh Rached Ghannouchi and those of the Muslim Brotherhood, is 20 years of breathing fresh air in the democratic societies in which he lived. This has made his thought and vision entirely different from the thoughts and visions of those who have not breathed the fresh air of democracy.

Although, as a good Muslim, the man kept his constants intact, his thinking would not have developed thus had his experiences been confined to Syria and Tunisia! There are a lot of issues and interactions we ought to pay attention to and benefit from, whether enlightened Islamist experiences like Indonesia, Malaysia and Turkey, or negative ones, which we should avoid, like the Taliban, Afghanistan, Sudan and Iran. There are also new experiences which we ought to laud and support, but also critique them in a positive way.

Hassan Hanafi: Democracy requires that we acknowledge the other's opinion, while the political culture we live in accuses the other of apostasy and relies on the notion that truth is the monopoly of a single group which will be saved while the rest are doomed. We sometimes forget that democracy is simply a tool; in the United States, you support the invasion of Iraq whether you are a Democrat or a Republican, while in England, there was support for the invasions of Iraq and Afghanistan by members of both the Labour and Conservative Parties. This means that democracy is a tool rather than an objective in itself. We, the Arabs, perhaps need a national coalition that delineates the main challenges that surround us from all sides: the liberation of Palestine, liberation of the individual, social justice, unification of the *Ummah*, development, etc. Which specific political culture could help us achieve these objectives? Whether you are an Islamist or a secularist, the liberation of the land happens either through national movements or *jihad* (holy war); likewise, we all want social justice, whether we are Islamists, liberals or socialists. The question therefore is how can I achieve my unified national programme via political pluralism and with so many theoretical frameworks? In our old jurisprudence, truth and right are multidirectional. This, in brief, is the challenge that faces Arab creativity: theoretical frameworks that do not conflict but agree on a single national programme, and challenges that depart from reality, rather than slogans.

Rifaat Sayed Ahmad: I support and endorse all the participants' constructive criticisms of the relationship between state and religion within the context of the Islamist movements' experience. However, I would like to reiterate what I said before, namely the marked absence of the key issue of Palestine from these movements' policies and practices. I believe that this issue will be pivotal and will impose itself on the next stage, whether they want it to or not. It will also determine these movements' credibility, since it will be imposed on us in the next stage anyway. One way or another, their credibility will be linked to the economic situation – the main concern of those who started the revolution – and linked to the loans and the relationship with the IMF and the World Bank, etc.

My second remark has to do with what Dr Saadeddin has said; though experiences differ, we need more documented studies of these experiences, in particular the two that have survived the longest, i.e. the Iranian and Turkish models. Over a 30-year period, the Iranian model has seen six different presidents of the republic come and go, while some of the Gulf sheikhs have been in power for 50 years, and in a country like Egypt, the president remained in place for 30 years. We should therefore avoid prejudging anyone's experience. Critique is absolutely essential even if some experiences are not all that bad. However, generalizations and media attacks are taking place against those that support the Palestinian cause and I fear that the same will happen in the countries that witnessed revolutions if their genuine revolutionary movements actually adopt a position that displeases those who do not harbour such visions, in which case their experiences will become negative ones. I believe that it is mainly Iran's support for the Palestinian cause that gave rise to this negative image among large segments of the population. However, the rotation of power principle exists and has many examples. My final remark concerns the disagreement between the Salafists and the Muslim Brotherhood in Egypt, a disagreement which I believe is linked to the disagreement between the major players in the Gulf region. There is disagreement between two states in the Gulf, which will remain nameless, over which one of them better serves the American project in the region. They are playing a major funding and guidance role through the Salafist and Brotherhood currents in Egypt, and these two movements should shed more light on that in the future. Thank you.

Ali Fayyad: In fact, no one can expect the experiment to succeed all in one go. We are still at the beginning of the road, so let us give it a chance to take at least the first steps in building an Arab democracy. I would like to remind you of a book entitled *Al-Arab wa Mushkilat il Dawla* (The Arabs and the Issue of Statehood) by Nazih Nasif al-Ayoubi (Beirut: Dar Al Saqi, 1992), an Arab author. In the book, al-Ayoubi addresses different models of democracy-building and says that there are others besides the individualistic Western model. He analyses at length the Japanese model where democracy followed a different path from that of Western democracy. We need to build our own model of democracy. Let me also add that we cannot, under any circumstances, put the Taliban and Iranian models on the same footing: the Taliban's is a destructive, divisive and *takfiri* model that caused many problems in its own society, while the Iranian model is sovereign, independent and civilized, and based on the democracy of elites or a controlled religious democracy. We could disagree about the names, but it is one of many forms of democracy and one that the Iranian people have chosen for themselves. On the other hand, yes, we do have the Turkish model, which is a secular model under Islamist management; it has its own philosophy and mainstays, including the logic of prosperity and economic expansion. Yes, we do have these two models in front of us in the Muslim world but the Taliban are an entirely different matter.

And with this the moderator brought the discussion to a close.

Notes

1. The Holy Quran, Surat al-Kahf, aya 29.
2. An Egyptian term indicating the place where prisoners sit inside the jail. The speaker made his remarks some months prior to the ouster of Morsi from the Egyptian Presidency in July 2013.
3. The Holy Quran, Surat al-Ahzab, aya 36.
4. The Holy Quran, Surat al-Takweer, al-Itan 8, 9.
5. Editor's note: this means that prisons will be full of Arab Nationalists and members of different Islamic groups.
6. This is the translated version of his book, *When Victory Is Not an Option: Islamist Movements in Arab Politics* (Cornell University Press, 2012).

Index

Note:
Page numbers in *italic* type refer to tables
Page numbers followed by 'n' refer to notes